# Core Skills:
## Foundation Level

Communication
IT
Application of Number

Longman Group Limited

Edinburgh Gate, Burnt Mill, Harlow, Essex, CM20 2JE, England and Associated Companies throughout the World.

© Longman Group Ltd 1996

All rights reserved. No part of this publication may be reproduced, stored in a retrieval system, or transmitted in any form or by any means, electronic, mechanical, photocopying, recording, or otherwise without either the prior written permission of the Publishers or a licence permitting restricted copying, issued by the Copyright Licensing Agency Ltd, 90 Tottenham Court Road, London, W1P 9HE.

ISBN 0582 27460 5

First published 1996
Produced by Longman Singapore Publishers (Pte) Ltd.
Printed in Singapore

Acknowledgements

We are grateful to the following for permission to reproduce copyright material:

Health Education Authority for the Height/Weight chart from the *Enjoy Healthy Eating* booklet © Health Education Authority; the Controller of HMSO for extracts from *A Good Start To Assessing Placement Safety* (Department of Employment), *Health and Safety Commission Annual Report 1992–93*, and *Employment Gazette* September 1992 (Health and Safety Executive) Crown Copyright; InterCity West Coast for an extract from the London to Shrewsbury and Telford Timetable; Ministry of Defence (DAR Pubs) for an extract on *Joining the Army* from the booklet *An Introduction to the British Army* CP(A)142 of February 1994, reproduced by courtesy of the Director of Army Recruiting; Royal Mail for an extract from 'UK Letter Rates'.

We are also grateful to the following for permission to reproduced photographs and other copyright material:

Cornwall and Isles of Scilly Health Authorities and CREATE; Dennis Publishing; Land Rover; Kerrier District Council; The National Trust; Sunnyside Surgery; TVTimes; Paul Watts.

# CONTENTS

Introduction                           1

Student's guide

    Introduction                       5

    What are core skills?              6

    The resource sheets                7

    Projects and assignments          10

    Topics
        Application of number         12
        Communication                 23
        Information Technology        33

    Index                             43

Application of Number
    Element 1                         49
    Element 2                         75
    Element 3                        109

Communication
    Element 1                        137
    Element 2                        153
    Element 3                        177
    Element 4                        203

IT
    Element 1                        233
    Element 2                        257
    Element 3                        285
    Element 4                        301

# GNVQ Core Skills

## Foundation Level

Note to the student

This book is divided into two parts:

- guidance on how to use the resource sheets; *this is from pages 3–45*

- a collection of resource sheets which will help you develop Core Skills for your Foundation level programme; *these are on pages 47–346*

The book covers the three mandatory Core Skills of Application of Number, Communication, and Information Technology.

The resource sheets printed in this book are drawn from three photocopiable resource files published by Longman. All the Foundation level resource sheets are provided for you here.

You will notice that each sheet is labelled on the top-right hand corner – for instance, **IT 22**. This states the Core Skill – Information Technology – and the number of the sheet. (The 'missing' sheet numbers apply to resource sheets for Intermediate and Advanced levels only.)

If you want more information about the topic, you can use pages 12–43 of this book to help you find sheets from the Intermediate and Advanced levels. You can then work from these from the resource files. (Ask your teacher about how to locate the resource files.)

The first part of the book tells you about Core Skills and explains how to use the resource sheets. It lists and describes all the sheets in the resource files – at Foundation, Intermediate and Advanced levels. The second part of the book has the resource sheets for the Foundation level.

# GNVQ Core Skills: Student's guide

# Introduction

As part of your work towards your GNVQ you will be expected to develop core skills in three important areas:

- Communication
- Application of number
- Information technology.

Core skills are the basic skills that everybody needs, no matter what type of work they are interested in doing. They are the same for all GNVQ subject areas, but you must be able to apply your core skills in the context of your studies in your own vocational area. You will need to demonstrate these skills in the portfolio of work you present for assessment.

You may be expected to develop these skills in the course of your work in your chosen subject area, while you are doing your projects or assignments. Alternatively, your college or school may teach core skills separately. Either way, these materials can help you.

Read the next few pages to find out how to use the core skills resource sheets.

# What are core skills?

Whatever kind of job you do, there are certain skills that you need to have. For example, you need to be able to communicate with other people so that you can share information. You need to understand something about using numbers in everyday life. And, at some point in your working life, you will almost certainly have to use computers.

The core skills have been set down on paper by a government organisation called the National Council for Vocational Qualifications. This is the same organisation that decided the specifications you are working towards in your vocational GNVQ. You may be taking your GNVQ through BTEC, City and Guilds or RSA - but the specifications are the same for everyone, no matter who assesses your work and awards you your qualification.

The core skills specifications are arranged in different levels of difficulty, like the GNVQ subjects. You will be taking your core skills at Foundation, Intermediate or Advanced level.

Each core skill is made up of separate elements which cover different aspects of the work. You must study all the elements.

## Application of number
Element 1   Collect and record data
Element 2   Tackle problems
Element 3   Interpret and present data

## Communication
Element 1   Take part in discussions
Element 2   Produce written materials
Element 3   Use images
Element 4   Read and respond to written materials

## Information technology
Element 1   Prepare information
Element 2   Process information
Element 3   Present information
Element 4   Evaluate the use of information technology

The specifications describe what you are expected to do for each of these elements at each level. They set out certain **performance criteria**, which explain what you need to be able to do. For example, you have to show that you can 'make contributions which are relevant to the subject and purpose' of a discussion, 'use mathematical terms correctly' and, when you are working on a computer, 'save work at appropriate intervals'.

The specifications describe the **range** of situations in which you will be expected to demonstrate these skills. They also explain ways of proving what you can do in **evidence indicators**. Sometimes it will be enough for an assessor to observe you at work – sometimes you will need to produce a written piece of work or another kind of evidence altogether. Your tutor will tell you more about the core skills specifications and how you can show that you have covered them.

You will probably find your work on core skills a very enjoyable part of your course. They are quite different from the work you did at school when you were younger because they are based on how things are done in the adult world of work. These are real skills that have a practical point to them.

# The resource sheets

These materials are presented on a series of resource sheets. You don't have to work through all the sheets but can pick out the ones you need. This allows you to concentrate on the areas where you need to develop your skills.

The resource sheets are designed so that you can work on them on your own – either in class or at home. They are self-contained and you don't usually need any other resources to complete the activities.

The resource sheets also suggest practical ways in which you can demonstrate your skills in your vocational area. Some of these suggestions will take a little longer to complete. They are intended to improve the quality of your on-going work.

This is what a resource sheet looks like. We've labelled the features that you'll find on every sheet.

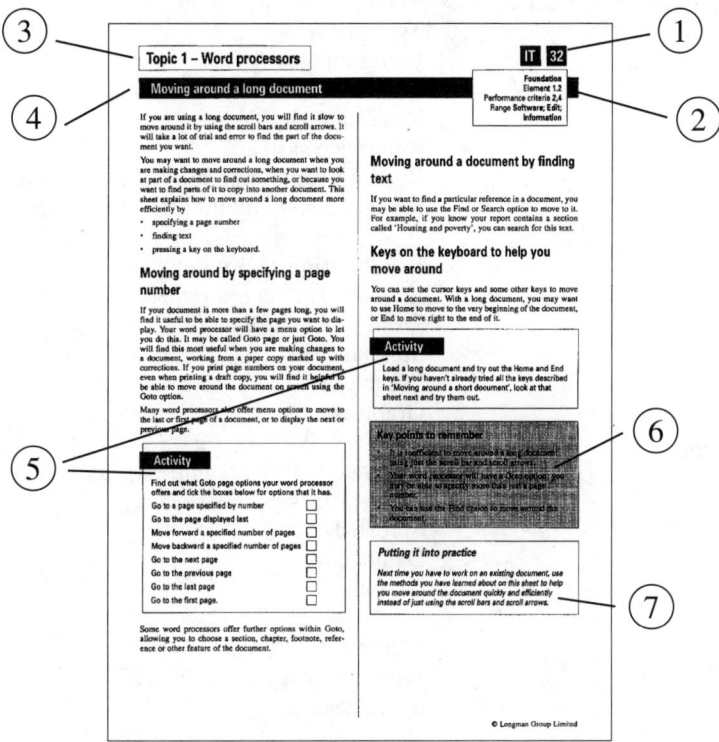

(1) This tells you which core skill the sheet is about [**C/AN/IT**]

(2) The information in the box tells you:
- the **level** (this sheet can be used at all three levels)
- the **element** that the sheet belongs to
- which **performance criteria** are covered
- which parts of the **range** are covered.

(3) This tells you which **topic** (group of sheets) it belongs to – you'll find out more about topics on page 8 of this booklet.

(4) The title of the resource sheet

(5) Activities are provided to help you to develop your skills.

(6) A useful summary of the resource sheet – you may want to refer to it again later.

(7) Something you can do to provide evidence that you have developed a new skill.

## How the resource sheets are arranged

The resource sheets are arranged in the same way as the core skills specifications. They are divided into Application of number, Communication and Information technology.

Within each core skill, the sheets are divided into different elements.

## Topics

Within each element, the sheets are grouped into various **topics**. You won't find these topics mentioned in the specifications – they are unique to this set of materials. All the resource sheets in a topic are on a similar subject. Sometimes you will want to look at several resource sheets in a topic and sometimes you may only need to pick out one or two. A topic contains resource sheets at Foundation, Intermediate and Advanced levels.

---

This chart shows all the topics covered by the resource sheets.

**Application of number**
*Element 1: Collect and record data*
Measuring
Estimating and checking
Surveys and other sources of data
Levels of accuracy

*Element 2: Tackle problems*
Measuring shapes and solids
Useful techniques
Number problems
Solving problems

*Element 3: Interpret and present data*
Diagrams, maps and plans
Representing and displaying data
Interpreting graphs and tables
Chance

**Communication**
*Element 1: Take part in discussions*
Discussion basics
Types of discussion
Skills for successful discussions

*Element 2: Produce written material*
Grammar and punctuation
Improving your writing skills
Formats for writing

*Element 3: Use images*
Making and finding images
Types of image
Using images

*Element 4: Read and respond to written materials*
Reading techniques
Reference skills
Reading containing images and graphics
Read and respond to different formats

**Information technology**
*Element 1: Prepare information*
Word processors
Spreadsheets
Databases
Graphics

*Element 2: Process information*
Word processors
Spreadsheets
Databases
Graphics

*Element 3: Present information*
Word processors
Spreadsheets
Databases
Graphics

*Element 4: Evaluate the use of information technology*
Understanding the computer
Solving problems
Health and safety

---

The topics – and all the resource sheets they contain – are described on pages 12–41 of this book.

## How to find the resource sheet you need

There are many ways of finding your way around the resource sheets.

You can simply look through the resource sheets themselves and find sheets that are relevant to your needs.

If you want to find sheets that are relevant to a particular element in the specifications, look at the chart on page 8. This lists the topics in each element. You can read the descriptions of the sheets in each topic on pages 12–41 of this booklet.

If you want to know about a particular thing – such as drawing pie charts or attending a meeting – you can look it up in the index. The reference will tell you which pages of this booklet to look at to find descriptions of the resource sheets which can help.

If you don't know what skills you need, you can look at the charts on pages 10 and 11. These list various types of project or assignment that you may have to do and suggests the topics which can help.

# Projects and assignments

These charts list some types of project or assignment that you are likely to be involved in as part of your work towards your vocational GNVQ, and the topics that may be relevant. It cannot be a complete list – because every college and school organises their project or assigment work in slightly different ways. As you begin to work with them, you will probably begin to see lots of other useful connections between the resource sheets.

The charts show how you can use resource sheets from the three core skills of Application of number, Communication and Information technology to help in these projects or assignments. If you want to know more about a topic, turn to the relevant topic page in this book and find out which particular resource sheets you need to use.

## Conducting a survey

| Core skill | Element | page ref. | Topic | How it can help |
|---|---|---|---|---|
| Application of number | Element 1 | 14 | Surveys and other sources of data | helps you to design your survey |
| Application of number | Element 2 | 16 | Useful techniques | how to work out averages |
| Application of number | Element 3 | 20 | Representing and displaying data | how to set out your results in graphs and tables |
| Communication | Element 1 | 24 | Skills for successful discussions | useful advice if you are interviewing people |
| Information technology | Element 1 | 34 | Databases | if you want to record your data on a computer database |

## Investigating a type of work

| Core skill | Element | page ref. | Topic | How it can help |
|---|---|---|---|---|
| Application of number | 3 | 21 | Interpreting graphs and tables | how to read statistical information |
| Communication | 1 | 24 | Skills for successful discussion | how to talk to people in the workplace |
| Communication | 2 | 25 | Grammar and punctuation | writing letters that will impress employers in your vocational area |
| Communication | 4 | 29 | Reading techniques | if you are doing research in books and magazines |
| Information technology | 3 | 37, 38 | Word processors, Databases, Graphics | presenting your information effectively |
| Information technology | 4 | 39 | Understanding the computer | looking at the role of IT in the workplace |

## Organising an event or exhibition

| Core skill | Element | page ref. | Topic | How it can help |
|---|---|---|---|---|
| Application of number | 1 | 12 | Measuring | measuring the space available |
| Application of number | 2 | 15 | Measuring shapes and solids | planning your use of space |
| Application of number | 3 | 19 | Diagrams, maps and plans | drawing up plans |
| Communication | 3 | 27 | Making and finding images | using images for impact |
| Communication | 3 | 28 | Using images | making posters, leaflets, etc., planning your preparations with a group |
| Information technology | 3 | 34 | Graphics | displaying images on computer screens |

## Writing a report

| Core skill | Element | page ref. | Topic | How it can help |
|---|---|---|---|---|
| Application of number | 3 | 20 | Representing and displaying data | adding graphs and tables |
| Communication | 2 | 25 | Improving your writing skills | how to plan and draft your work |
| Communication | 2 | 26 | Formats for writing | how to set out a report |
| Communication | 3 | 28 | Using images | improving the appearance of your report |
| Information technology | 2 | 35, 36 | Word processors, Spreadsheets, Databases | working on your research data |
| Information technology | 3 | 37, 38 | Word processors, Spreadsheets, Databases | presenting your work effectively |

## Designing something

| Core skill | Element | page ref. | Topic | How it can help |
|---|---|---|---|---|
| Application of number | 1 | 12 | Measuring | planning your design |
| Application of number | 1 | 14 | Levels of accuracy | working out errors and tolerances |
| Application of number | 2 | 15 | Measuring shapes and solids | working out the details of your design |
| Communication | 1 | 24 | Skills for successful discussions | discussing your plans with your tea |
| Communication | 3 | 27 | Making and finding images | designing for the tastes of your audience |
| Information technology | 2 | 36 | Graphics | using a computer to develop your design ideas |

## Presenting your ideas to an audience

| Core skill | Element | page ref. | Topic | How it can help |
|---|---|---|---|---|
| Application of number | 3 | 20 | Representing and displaying data | using graphs and charts |
| Communication | 1 | 23 | Discussion basics | thinking about your audience |
| Communication | 3 | 28 | Types of image | producing OHPs |
| Information technology | 3 | 37, 38 | Word processors, Graphics | designing handouts |
| Information technology | 3 | 37, 38 | Word processors, Databases, Graphics | presenting your information effectively |

# Topics

## Application of number

### Measuring

**Application of number**
Element 1: Collect and record data

When you are measuring, you must be able to read scales correctly, and must also know how accurate you need to be. You need to be familiar with different types of unit so that you can record your measurements in the most appropriate form.

These resource sheets will help you when you have to measure things and record what you have found out. They give practical tips on using different kinds of measuring scales and dealing with very large (and small) numbers.

| Resource sheet | Reference | How it can help | Foundation | Intermediate | Advanced |
|---|---|---|---|---|---|
| Reading decimal scales | 1 | an introduction to using scales that are marked in tens | | | |
| Large and small numbers | 2 | some tips on reading numbers which contain lots of digits | | | |
| Reading fraction scales | 3 | how to read scales that are marked in halves, quarters and other fractions | | | |
| Estimating on scales | 4 | what to do when you can't measure exactly | | | |
| Varied scales | 5 | getting used to different kinds of scale | | | |
| Measuring changes | 6 | using scales to measure how readings have changed | | | |
| Calculator readings | 7 | dealing with large numbers on a calculator | | | |
| Money and metric measurements | 8 | some reminders about working with metric measurements and money | | | |
| Time and temperature | 9 | what you need to remember when measuring time and temperature | | | |
| Measurement with imperial units | 10 | working with feet and inches and other imperial measurements | | | |
| Capacity and volume | 11 | measuring the size of containers or spaces | | | |
| Rates and other compound units | 12 | understanding measurements written as 'money per hour' or 'cost per unit' | | | |

**These resource sheets will help you when:**
- you measure the size, weight or cost of something
- you read measurements from any type of scale.

## Estimating and checking

**Application of number**
Element 1: Collect and record data

When you are collecting data, you don't always have to work in exact numbers. It's very useful to be able to have a rough idea of what the figures should come to. This will help you to check whether you are right and also help you to make forecasts about the future. This group of resource sheets also contains other suggestions for checking your data.

| Resource sheet | Reference | How it can help | Foundation | Intermediate | Advanced |
|---|---|---|---|---|---|
| Estimating | 13 | how to get an approximate answer by only measuring or counting part of something | ■ | ■ | ■ |
| Checking | 14 | using estimating to check your answer | ■ | ■ | ■ |
| Cross-checking | 15 | how to double check your answers | | ■ | ■ |
| Rough estimates | 16 | how to round off numbers to work out approximate answers first | | ■ | ■ |
| In proportion | 17 | dealing with measurements that are in proportion to each other | | ■ | ■ |
| Working with proportion | 18 | scaling up number to make estimates | | ■ | ■ |
| What would happen if...? | 19 | some points to watch out for when you are scaling up numbers | | ■ | ■ |

**These resource sheets will help you when:**
- you are collecting large amounts of data
- you want to check that you've recorded data correctly
- you want to get a rough idea of what your data mean.

## Surveys and other sources of data

**Application of number**
Element 1: Collect and record data

You will almost certainly be asked to conduct a survey at some stage. This group of sheets will help you to decide how to go about it. It also describes some other sources from which you can collect data.

| Resource sheet | Reference | How it can help | Foundation | Intermediate | Advanced |
|---|---|---|---|---|---|
| Talking to people | 20 | some advice about gathering data by asking people questions | | | |
| Variety of sources | 21 | other useful sources of data | | | |
| Experiments and competition | 22 | finding things out by doing experiments and looking at what the competition is doing | | | |
| Introducing surveys | 23 | basic information about surveys | | | |
| Planning a survey | 24 | whom, what, when and how to ask - to get the data you need | | | |
| Samples and populations | 25 | tips on picking the right people to ask | | | |
| Sample sizes | 26 | deciding how many people to ask | | | |
| Asking clear questions 1 | 27 | the importance of asking clear questions | | | |
| Asking clear questions 2 | 28 | how to ask clear questions | | | |
| Survey types | 29 | deciding on the best way to collect the data you need | | | |
| Tally tables | 30 | a simple way of recording data from a survey | | | |
| Recording sheets | 31 | using tables to record data from a survey | | | |
| Continuous data | 32 | how to group figures so that you can see what they mean | | | |
| Two-way tables | 33 | how to compare two kinds of data from a survey | | | |

**These resource sheets will help you when:**
- you are conducting a survey
- you need to collect data in other ways.

## Levels of accuracy

**Application of number**
Element 1: Collect and record data

When you gather data, you must know how accurate the information is. Sometimes you may have to decide on the level of accuracy yourself. This group of sheets tells you how to round off numbers and record the level of accuracy you are using.

| Resource sheet | Reference | How it can help | Foundation | Intermediate | Advanced |
|---|---|---|---|---|---|
| Rounding | 34 | how to round off numbers | | | |
| How accurate? | 35 | deciding how accurate you need to be | | | |
| Describing accuracy | 36 | rounding figures to decimal places and significant figures | | | |
| Tolerances and errors | 37 | what happens when you work with approximate measurements | | | |
| Units and conversion | 38 | some tips on the accuracy of figures that have been converted from other measurements | | | |

**These resource sheets will help you when:**
- you are recording measurements and need to record the level of accuracy
- you are deciding how accurate to be
- you are working with measurements that have already been rounded off.

# Measuring shapes and solids

**Application of number**
Element 2: Tackle problems

There are many situations in which you need to work out how much space things take up. This group of resource sheets deals with perimeter, area and volume.

| Resource sheet | Reference | How it can help | Foundation | Intermediate | Advanced |
|---|---|---|---|---|---|
| Perimeter | 39 | how to work out the distance around something | | | |
| Area by counting squares | 40 | one method of working out how much space something takes up | | | |
| Working with area | 41 | how to estimate the area of something | | | |
| Working with small and large areas | 42 | working out areas by multiplying the length by the width | | | |
| Finding areas | 43 | more situations where you need to work out areas | | | |
| More about areas | 44 | areas of triangles and other shapes | | | |
| Circumference of a circle | 45 | how to work out the distance around a circle | | | |
| Area of a circle | 46 | how to work out the space inside a circle | | | |
| Working with shapes | 47 | working out the area of complicated shapes | | | |
| Volume of cubes and cuboids | 48 | working out the space inside box-shaped things | | | |
| Volumes of simple shapes | 49 | the volume of things that are made up of several box-shapes put together | | | |
| Volumes of cylinders | 50 | working out the volume of tube-shaped things | | | |
| Volume of a triangular prism | 51 | how to work out the volume of a triangular tube | | | |
| Enlargement and area | 52 | working out the area of something that is shown on a map | | | |
| Enlargement and volume | 53 | how the volume of something changes when you scale up the measurements | | | |

**These resource sheets will help you when:**
- you need to work out the distance round something
- you need to know how much space something takes up
- you are planning how to use space in a room layout or exhibition
- you are designing packaging.

# Useful techniques

**Application of number**
Element 2: Tackle problems

This group of resource sheets brings together some mathematical techniques that should save you time. They show you how you can write a formula instead of working out a similar sum several times using different sets of numbers. They also describe different ways of converting from one set of units to another. There are also three sheets dealing with different types of average.

| Resource sheet | Reference | How it can help | Foundation | Intermediate | Advanced |
| --- | --- | --- | --- | --- | --- |
| Using simple formulae | 54 | a time-saving way of working out similar calculations using different numbers | ■ | | |
| Conversion with equations | 55 | using equations to convert from one type of unit to another | | ■ | ■ |
| Writing equations | 56 | more situations in which simple equations can save you time | | ■ | ■ |
| 'Less than' and 'greater than' | 57 | how to describe numbers that are less than or greater than each other | | ■ | ■ |
| Coordinates | 58 | how to describe where something is on a map or a grid | | ■ | ■ |
| Using graphs to predict | 59 | how graphs can (and cannot) be used to predict what will happen in the future | | ■ | ■ |
| Conversion rules | 60 | how to get a rough answer when you are converting from one unit to another | ■ | | |
| Scales and conversion factors | 61 | how to get a more accurate answer when you are converting from one unit to another | ■ | | |
| Conversion tables and graphs | 62 | using tables and graphs to convert from one unit to another | | ■ | ■ |
| Conversion graphs | 63 | more about using graphs to convert from one unit to another | | ■ | ■ |
| Graphs and equations | 64 | using graphs to work out the answers to problems | | ■ | ■ |
| Using a mean of a set of data | 65 | an introduction to the most commonly used type of average | ■ | ■ | ■ |
| Finding the mode | 66 | how to find the figure which occurs most often in a set of results | ■ | ■ | ■ |
| Finding the median | 67 | how to find the 'middling' value in a set of results | ■ | ■ | ■ |

**These resource sheets will help you when:**
- you need to repeat the same calculation using different numbers
- you are converting money or measurements
- you need to find the average from a group of numbers.

## Number problems

**Application of number**
Element 2: Tackle problems

This group of sheets is all about adding and subtracting numbers. It provides you with some basic reminders about what to do – and some hints about special situations that you may come across.

| Resource sheet | Reference | How it can help | Foundation | Intermediate | Advanced |
|---|---|---|---|---|---|
| Addition 1 | 68 | how to add up figures | ■ | | |
| Addition 2 | 69 | more practice in adding things up | ■ | | |
| Large numbers | 70 | practice in working with large numbers | | ■ | ■ |
| Negative numbers | 71 | working with numbers that are less than zero | | ■ | ■ |
| Subtraction | 72 | practice in taking numbers away | ■ | | |
| Working with subtraction | 73 | what to remember when you are subtracting hours and minutes and other times | | ■ | ■ |
| Addition subtraction and multiplication | 74 | working with measurements and money | ■ | | |
| Time – addition and subtraction | 75 | more practice in working with hours and minutes | | ■ | ■ |
| Working with addition and subtraction | 76 | using charts when you are adding and subtracting | | ■ | ■ |

**These resource sheets will help you when:**
- you are adding up several items on a list
- you are calculating the cost of something
- you are working with schedules and time sheets.

# Solving problems

**Application of number**
Element 2: Tackle problems

In this group of resource sheets you will find information on fractions, decimals and percentages. There is also some practice in multiplying and dividing numbers in the kind of situation you may come across at work or in your project or assignment work.

| Resource sheet | Reference | How it can help | Foundation | Intermediate | Advanced |
|---|---|---|---|---|---|
| Use of a calculator | 77 | hints for using a calculator | ■ | | |
| Multiplication and division 1 | 78 | when it is quicker to multiply things than add them up | ■ | | |
| Multiplication and division 2 | 79 | practice in multiplying and dividing | ■ | | |
| Working with multiplication and division | 80 | multiplying and dividing in your head – and using a calculator | | ■ | ■ |
| Fractions | 81 | an introduction to fractions | ■ | | |
| The calculator fraction button | 82 | working with fractions on your calculator | ■ | | |
| Use of fractions to describe | 83 | working out fractions of things | | ■ | ■ |
| Fractions and decimals | 84 | working with fractions and decimals | ■ | | |
| Use decimals to describe | 85 | working with decimals | ■ | | |
| Using decimals | 86 | practice in working with decimal numbers and decimal measurements | | ■ | |
| Use fractions to solve problems 1 | 87 | some everyday situations where it is useful to use fractions | | ■ | |
| Use fractions to solve problems 2 | 88 | more everyday situations where fractions are useful | | ■ | ■ |
| Use decimals to solve problems 1 | 89 | making rough estimates and using your calculator | | ■ | |
| Use decimals to solve problems 2 | 90 | more practice with decimals | | ■ | ■ |
| Use percentages 1 | 91 | working with percentages | | ■ | |
| Use percentages 2 | 92 | percentages, decimals and fractions | | ■ | |
| Use percentages 3 | 93 | working out what one number is as a percentage of another | | ■ | ■ |
| Use ratios 1 | 94 | working with ratios on maps and in other situations | | ■ | ■ |
| Use ratios 2 | 95 | using ratios to share costs and profits | | ■ | ■ |

**These resource sheets will help you when:**
- you need to compare numbers with each other
- you are working out costs and timings
- you are writing up the results of a survey.

# Diagrams, maps and plans

**Application of number**
Element **3**: Interpret and present data

It is often useful to draw diagrams of various kinds to illustrate your work. You will probably also have to interpret diagrams and maps that other people have drawn up. This group of resource sheets also contains reminders of the common mathematical shapes that we see in everyday life.

| Resource sheet | Reference | How it can help | Foundation | Intermediate | Advanced |
|---|---|---|---|---|---|
| Describing two-dimensional shapes | 96 | the mathematical names we use for various 2D shapes | ▓ | ▓ | ▓ |
| Describing three-dimensional shapes | 97 | the mathematical names we use for common 3-D objects | ▓ | ▓ | ▓ |
| Using flow charts to convert measurements | 98 | a method of using a flow chart to help you to do a calculation | ▓ | | |
| Use simple maps | 99 | how to draw a simple map | ▓ | | |
| Use diagrams | 100 | how diagrams can be used to explain a process | | ▓ | ▓ |
| Looking down on things | 101 | using plans to work out the layout of rooms | | ▓ | ▓ |
| Side views and front views | 102 | reading and drawing elevations | | ▓ | ▓ |
| Planning your time | 103 | using network diagrams to plan how you will organise your time | | ▓ | ▓ |

**These resource sheets will help you when:**
- you need to describe shapes using the correct mathematical terms
- you are using maps and plans
- you want to explain how to do something by drawing a diagram.

# Representing and displaying data

**Application of number**
Element 3: Interpret and present data

This group of sheets shows you how to present the data you gather in tables and graphs. It introduces some simple statistical ideas, such as the 'range' and helps you to choose the right kind of graph for your data.

| *Resource sheet* | *Reference* | *How it can help* | *Foundation* | *Intermediate* | *Advanced* |
|---|---|---|---|---|---|
| Counting your results | 104 | using a table to present your results | ■ | | |
| Tables for continuous data | 105 | using a table to show results you have measured | | ■ | ■ |
| Finding the mean (discrete data) | 106 | how to work out the average from a set of figures | | ■ | ■ |
| Finding the mean (grouped data) | 107 | how to work out the average from a set of measurements | | ■ | ■ |
| Using a calculator to find the mean | 108 | how a scientific calculator can make it easy to work out the mean | | ■ | ■ |
| Choosing the right average | 109 | the mean, the median and the mode – which type of average to use in any situation | | ■ | ■ |
| Bar charts | 110 | how to draw a bar chart | ■ | ■ | ■ |
| Pie charts | 111 | how to draw a pie chart | | ■ | ■ |
| Histograms (equal intervals) | 112 | how to draw a histogram | | ■ | ■ |
| The range | 113 | looking at the variation in your results | ■ | ■ | ■ |
| Inerquartile range – the middle 50% | 114 | looking at the middle of your sample of results | | ■ | ■ |
| Line graphs | 115 | how to draw line graphs | ■ | ■ | ■ |
| Scatter diagrams | 116 | how to draw scatter graphs | | ■ | ■ |
| Best-fit lines – making predictions | 117 | using scatter graphs to predict what is going to happen | | ■ | ■ |
| Choosing the right diagrams | 118 | choosing the most appropriate type of graph in any situation | ■ | ■ | ■ |
| Two-way tables | 119 | using tables to show how facts are related | | ■ | ■ |

**These resource sheets will help you when:**
- you are presenting the results of a survey
- you are presenting any sets of figures to other people.

Topics 21

## Interpreting graphs and tables

**Application of number**
Element 3: Interpret and present data

You will often have to make sense of information in books and newspapers that is presented in graphs and tables. This group of resource sheets explains how to read the various different types of graph and table that you are likely to come across. The last two sheets point out some ways in which graphs can sometimes be very misleading in the way they are drawn.

| Resource sheet | Reference | How it can help | Foundation | Intermediate | Advanced |
|---|---|---|---|---|---|
| Reading tables | 120 | how to understand data that is presented in tables | ■ | ■ | ■ |
| Reading bar charts | 121 | how to interpret bar charts | ■ | ■ | ■ |
| Reading pie charts | 122 | how to interpret pie charts | ■ | ■ | ■ |
| Reading histograms | 123 | how to interpret histograms | | ■ | ■ |
| Reading line graphs | 124 | how to interpret line graphs | | ■ | ■ |
| Reading scatter diagrams | 125 | how to interpret scatter diagrams | | ■ | ■ |
| Misrepresenting data 1 | 126 | some points to be careful about when you are looking at other people's graphs | | ■ | ■ |
| Misrepresenting data 2 | 127 | more ways in which graphs can give the wrong impression | | ■ | ■ |

**These resource sheets will help you when:**
- you are interpreting graphs and tables you find in published materials
- you are describing your own graphs and tables to other people.

## Chance

**Application of number**
Element 3: Interpret and present data

People at work sometimes need to consider how likely something is to happen, so that they can make advance plans of what to do. These resource sheets show you how to work out probabilities.

| Resource sheet | Reference | How it can help | Foundation | Intermediate | Advanced |
|---|---|---|---|---|---|
| Probability and chance | 128 | how to work out the chances of something happening | ■ | ■ | ■ |
| Estimating probabilities in real life | 129 | how probability is used in work situations | ■ | ■ | ■ |
| Probabilities for alternative outcomes | 130 | more complicated situations where probability has to be calculated | | ■ | ■ |
| Two things happening together – tree diagrams:1 | 131 | when you need to work out the chances of two events happening together | | ■ | ■ |
| Two things happening together – tree diagrams:2 | 132 | real life situations when you need to work out the chances of two events happening together | | ■ | ■ |
| Independent and non-independent events | 133 | working out probability when one event affects another | | ■ | ■ |

**These resource sheets will help you when:**
- you are planning an event or an important piece of work
- you are in any situation where it could be dangerous or expensive if something went wrong.

# Communication

## Discussion basics

**Communication**
Element 1: Take part in discussions

Before you talk to people, it is worth giving some thought to who they are and what you want to say. This is especially important at work, where you may need to be more careful in what you say.

| Resource sheet | Reference | How it can help | Foundation | Intermediate | Advanced |
|---|---|---|---|---|---|
| Know your audience | 1 | deciding how to talk to people | ■ | | |
| Know your purpose | 2 | the importance of knowing what you are trying to say before you start talking | ■ | | |
| Your audience | 3 | choosing the best way of talking to people in different situations | | ■ | ■ |
| Your purpose | 4 | the importance of being clear about what you want to say | | ■ | ■ |
| Dealing with customers, clients and visitors | 5 | making a good impression on people | | ■ | ■ |

**These resource sheets will help you when:**
- go on work placement or get a job
- are involved in discussions at college
- interview people in the workplace.

## Types of discussion

**Communication**
Element 1: Take part in discussions

There are various situations in which you need to talk to people – from simple conversations about everyday matters to formal meetings. This group of resource sheets looks at the special skills you can use in different circumstances.

| Resource sheet | Reference | How it can help | Foundation | Intermediate | Advanced |
|---|---|---|---|---|---|
| Face-to-face discussions | 6 | hints on talking to people | ■ | | |
| Meetings | 7 | how to take part in meetings | ■ | | |
| One-to-one discussions | 8 | skills you can use when talking to people face-to-face | | ■ | |
| Attending meetings | 9 | how meetings are organised – and how to play your part | | ■ | |
| Straightforward or routine matters | 10 | talking about everyday things at work | | ■ | |
| Discussions on complex or non-routine matters | 11 | more difficult discussions | | | ■ |
| Discussions on straightforward or routine matters | 12 | talking about everyday things at work | ■ | | |
| Using the phone | 13 | hints for using the phone | ■ | | |
| Making phone calls | 14 | getting the most out of the phone calls you make | | ■ | ■ |
| Taking phone calls | 15 | how to answer the phone effectively | | ■ | ■ |

**These resource sheets will help you when:**
- you are involved in discussions at college
- you attend meetings at work
- you talk to people at work
- you make or receive phone calls.

# Skills for successful discussions

**Communication**
Element 1: Take part in discussions

You can get a lot more out of your discussions with people if you learn how to listen and how to ask questions effectively. These resource sheets also ask you to think about how you use your voice – and what your body language tells people. There are also some hints about ending discussions and making your views clear without causing offence.

| Resource sheet | Reference | How it can help | Foundation | Intermediate | Advanced |
|---|---|---|---|---|---|
| Good listening | 16 | the importance of listening to people | ▓ | | |
| Checking understanding | 17 | how to check you have understood what you hear | ▓ | | |
| Active listening | 18 | the skills of effective listening | | ▓ | ▓ |
| Conversational techniques | 19 | how you can get the most out of a conversation | | ▓ | ▓ |
| Raising questions | 20 | the skill of using questions to get the information you need | | ▓ | ▓ |
| Asking questions | 21 | how to get information out of people | ▓ | | |
| Giving and receiving feedback | 22 | letting other people know what you think | ▓ | | |
| Feedback | 23 | how to let other people know your reactions | | ▓ | ▓ |
| Using body language | 24 | what your expression and posture say | ▓ | | |
| Your voice | 25 | how to use your voice to get your message across | | ▓ | ▓ |
| Body language | 26 | how to communicate without using words | | ▓ | ▓ |
| Leading and directing discussions | 27 | how to take control of a discussion | | ▓ | ▓ |
| Assertiveness | 28 | how to make your position clear without offending people | | ▓ | ▓ |
| Using your voice | 29 | different ways of using your voice | ▓ | | |
| Ending discussions | 30 | what you need to do at the end of a discussion | ▓ | | |
| Concluding discussions | 31 | ways of ending formal and informal discussions | | ▓ | ▓ |

**These resource sheets will help you when:**
- you are involved in any type of discussion or formal meeting
- you are interviewing people
- you are trying to get information from people
- you want to make your views clear to people you are talking to.

## Grammar and punctuation

**Communication**
Element 2: Produce written material

If you can use conventional grammar and punctuation, your writing will be much easier for other people to understand. It is also often very important at work to write correctly. These resource sheets will help you to identify any areas where you need to work on your grammar and punctuation.

| Resource sheet | Reference | How it can help | Foundation | Intermediate | Advanced |
|---|---|---|---|---|---|
| Full stops and commas | 32 | how simple punctuation can make your meaning clearer | ▓ | | |
| Using full stops and commas | 33 | how to use simple punctuation to make your meaning clear and create a good impression | | ▓ | ▓ |
| Capital letters | 34 | when to use capital letters – and when not to use them | ▓ | | |
| Using capital letters | 35 | the rules on using capitals letters in writing | | ▓ | ▓ |
| Sentences | 36 | writing complete sentences | ▓ | | |
| Checking spelling | 37 | how to check words you don't know how to spell | ▓ | | |
| Writing sentences and paragraphs | 38 | using complete sentences and paragraphs in your writing | | ▓ | ▓ |
| Spelling rules and tips | 39 | the importance of spelling correctly – and some tips to help you do it | | ▓ | ▓ |
| Apostrophes, colons and semi-colons | 40 | using more complicated punctuation in your writing | | ▓ | ▓ |

**These resource sheets will help you when:**
- you are writing anything that will be seen by other people.

## Improving your writing skills

**Communication**
Element 2: Produce written material

If you are writing something important, it is well worth planning out your ideas first and then writing a rough draft. Then, when you come to write your final draft, you can make sure that it is as good as it possibly can be. This group of resource sheets also contains some suggestions on making notes.

| Resource sheet | Reference | How it can help | Foundation | Intermediate | Advanced |
|---|---|---|---|---|---|
| Deciding what to write | 41 | planning what you write before you start | ▓ | | |
| Writing a rough draft | 42 | how to write a first draft | ▓ | | |
| Taking notes | 43 | how to take accurate notes | ▓ | | |
| Organising your ideas | 44 | getting your ideas into shape before you start writing | | ▓ | ▓ |
| Making notes | 45 | hints that will help you when you need to take notes | | ▓ | ▓ |
| Drafting | 46 | a step-by-step approach to writing a first draft | | ▓ | ▓ |
| Your final draft | 47 | tips on writing and checking your final draft | ▓ | | |
| Writing a final draft | 48 | how to write, check and present your final draft | | ▓ | ▓ |

**These resource sheets will help you when:**
- you are writing an essay
- you are writing up a project or assignment
- you are writing a report or any important document at work
- you are taking notes.

# Formats for writing

**Communication**
Element 2: Produce written material

This group of resource sheets looks at various different kinds of writing that you may have to do when you are at work or are looking for a job. For each of the formats described here, there is a conventional way of doing things which you need to be aware of.

| Resource sheet | Reference | How it can help | Foundation | Intermediate | Advanced |
|---|---|---|---|---|---|
| Introduction to filling in forms | 49 | how to fill in forms | ■ | | |
| Filling in complex forms | 50 | how to fill in more complicated forms | | ■ | ■ |
| Introduction to writing memos | 51 | how to write simple memos at work | ■ | | |
| Writing memos | 52 | when to use memos at work – and how to write a good memo | | ■ | ■ |
| Writing standard letters | 53 | an introduction to letter writing | ■ | | |
| Writing a letter | 54 | simple and more complicated letters | | ■ | |
| Writing a CV | 55 | how to arrange and write your CV | ■ | | |
| Writing a report | 56 | the conventions of writing a report | | ■ | ■ |
| Writing leaflets and brochures | 57 | how to write publicity material | | ■ | |
| Writing references | 58 | how to describe where you obtained your information | | ■ | ■ |

**These resource sheets will help you when:**
- you are applying for a job
- you are writing letters or memos at work
- you are writing to people as part of your assignment or project work
- you are writing up the results of an assignment or project in a report.

# Making and finding images

**Communication**
Element **3**: Use images

Pictures, diagrams and other types of image can make your work come to life. This group of resource sheets helps you to choose the right image, whether you are using an image that you have found or designing a new one yourself. There is also information here on copying images and making your work look as effective as possible.

| Resource sheet | Reference | How it can help | Foundation | Intermediate | Advanced |
|---|---|---|---|---|---|
| What can images do? | 59 | the many ways in which you can use images in your work | ■ | ■ | ■ |
| Choosing images | 60 | what to look out for when you are choosing an image | ■ | | |
| Finding images | 61 | useful sources of images | ■ | | |
| Copying images | 62 | what you can photocopy – and the rules about what you are allowed to copy | ■ | | |
| Thinking about your audience | 63 | choosing your images to suit your audience | ■ | | |
| Using and making images | 64 | when to use a ready-made image and when to make a new one | ■ | | |
| Photocopying | 65 | tips on using the photocopier – and when to use it | | ■ | ■ |
| Introducing design | 66 | how to give your work the right impact | | ■ | ■ |
| Introducing typography | 67 | how the appearance of your text can make your meaning clearer | | ■ | ■ |
| Using colour | 68 | the language of colour – and how to use it | | ■ | ■ |
| Printing and binding | 69 | some suggestions for presenting your documents | | ■ | ■ |
| Copyright | 70 | what to do if you want to use other people's images in your work | | ■ | ■ |

**These resource sheets will help you when:**
- you are planning any piece of written work
- you need to find illustrations to show what you mean
- you are using illustrated materials at work.

## Types of image

**Communication**
Element **3**: Use images

Different types of image are useful in different circumstances. This group of resource sheets gives practical advice about using a variety of different kinds of image – from photographs to cartoons.

| Resource sheet | Reference | How it can help | Foundation | Intermediate | Advanced |
|---|---|---|---|---|---|
| Symbols | 71 | when symbols can help you to get your message across | ✓ | ✓ | ✓ |
| Diagrams | 72 | using diagrams to explain your ideas | ✓ | | |
| Graphs and tables | 73 | how graphs and tables can help people to understand figures | ✓ | | |
| Photographs | 74 | some hints on choosing and taking photographs | ✓ | ✓ | ✓ |
| Drawings and cartoons | 75 | what drawings and cartoons can add to your work | ✓ | ✓ | ✓ |
| Tables and charts | 76 | how to design tables and charts | | ✓ | ✓ |
| Diagrams and flow charts | 77 | several ways of using diagrams | | ✓ | ✓ |
| Maps and plans | 78 | how to draw a map which contains the information people need | ✓ | ✓ | ✓ |
| Graphs | 79 | some tips on preparing graphs | | ✓ | ✓ |
| OHPs | 80 | how to prepare overhead projector transparencies | | | ✓ |
| Video | 81 | an introduction to using video | | ✓ | ✓ |

**These resource sheets will help you when:**
- you want to illustrate any type of written work
- you want to make a record of your work
- you need to explain things to other people using images
- you are organising a presentation.

## Using images

**Communication**
Element **3**: Use images

This group of resource sheets looks at some specific situations in which you can exploit your skill in using images. The first sheet shows how you can use diagrams to help to plan your work – either on your own or with a group of other students. The other sheets all cover situations where you are trying to make an impression on other people.

| Resource sheet | Reference | How it can help | Foundation | Intermediate | Advanced |
|---|---|---|---|---|---|
| Planning your work | 82 | using mind maps and flow charts to plan your work | ✓ | ✓ | ✓ |
| Posters | 83 | issues to think about when you are designing a poster | ✓ | ✓ | ✓ |
| Leaflets | 84 | how to design a leaflet | | ✓ | ✓ |
| Reports | 85 | how to make a report look effective | | ✓ | ✓ |
| Exhibitions | 86 | issues to think about when you are setting up an exhibition | | ✓ | ✓ |
| Presentations | 87 | how to give a presentation | | ✓ | ✓ |

**These resource sheets will help you when:**
- you are planning a project
- you want to publicise an event
- you want to show your ideas to a large number of people.

# Reading techniques

**Communication**
Element **4**: Read and respond to written materials

When we first learn to read, we look at every word carefully. As an adult, you need to develop more sophisticated reading skills. You need to scan through directories and lists to find the information you need – and dip into books and articles to decide whether they are relevant to your work. Sometimes, you also have to be prepared to take time to read important or difficult text very carefully. This group of resource sheets explores some reading techniques you will find useful in your studies and at work.

| Resource sheet | Reference | How it can help | Foundation | Intermediate | Advanced |
|---|---|---|---|---|---|
| Why read? | 88 | deciding what you need to read | ■ | | |
| The purpose of reading | 89 | choosing what you need to read and what you can ignore | | ■ | ■ |
| Selecting a reading strategy | 90 | deciding whether you need to read something carefully | ■ | ■ | ■ |
| Scanning | 91 | picking out the information you need | ■ | ■ | |
| Scanning a text | 92 | the skill of finding the information you need quickly | | ■ | ■ |
| Skim reading | 93 | how to get the main idea of what a piece of writing is about | ■ | | |
| Skimming | 94 | the skill of sampling text to decide whether it is relevant | | ■ | ■ |
| Careful reading | 95 | hints on reading text carefully | ■ | | |
| Reading carefully | 96 | some hints on reading difficult information | | ■ | ■ |

**These resource sheets will help you when:**
- you are doing research for a project or assignment
- you are using directories or lists
- you need to decide whether it's worth reading something carefully
- you are trying to understand difficult or important text.

## Reference skills

**Communication**
Element 4: Read and respond to written materials

Sooner or later, everyone has to look something up. This group of resource sheets shows how various kinds of reference sources can help you to find the information you need quickly. It also describes how to use indexes and contents lists to find your way around publications.

| Resource sheet | Reference | How it can help | Foundation | Intermediate | Advanced |
|---|---|---|---|---|---|
| How to use a dictionary | 97 | hints on using dictionaries | ■ | | |
| Using a dictionary at work | 98 | some ways in which a dictionary can help you at work | ■ | | |
| Using a dictionary | 99 | checking meanings and spellings | | ■ | ■ |
| Using an index to find information | 100 | how to use an index | ■ | | |
| Using an index | 101 | how an index can help you to find the information you need | | ■ | ■ |
| Using a contents list | 102 | how contents lists can speed up your research | | ■ | ■ |
| Using a contents list to find information | 103 | using a contents list to find your way around a publication | ■ | | |
| Choosing the right reference source | 104 | where to get different types of information | ■ | | |
| Using reference sources to find information | 105 | knowing where to go to find the information you need | ■ | | |
| Using various reference sources | 106 | information sources you can use in your research | | ■ | ■ |

**These resource sheets will help you when:**
- you don't know how to spell a word
- you don't understand what something means
- you need to find any type of information quickly
- you need to know whether a book contains information you want.

## Reading containing images and graphical illustrations

**Communication**
Element 4: Read and respond to written materials

Text is often illustrated with graphs, charts and other illustrations. These are included to help to get the meaning across and it is important that you are as comfortable about extracting information from them as you are in reading the text itself. This group of resource sheets provides lots of practice in interpreting graphical illustrations.

| Resource sheet | Reference | How it can help | Foundation | Intermediate | Advanced |
| --- | --- | --- | --- | --- | --- |
| The use of graphical illustrations in reading | 107 | how illustrations are used | ▓ | ▓ | ▓ |
| Getting the main idea from graphical information | 108 | using the illustrations to help you to understand what you are reading | ▓ | | |
| Getting the main idea from graphs and charts | 109 | reading graphs and charts | ▓ | ▓ | |
| Grasping graphics | 110 | interpreting graphical illustrations | | ▓ | ▓ |
| Understanding graphs and charts | 111 | getting useful information from graphs and charts | | ▓ | ▓ |
| Reading text containing graphical material | 112 | more practice in interpreting graphs | ▓ | | |
| Reading text containing images and graphics | 113 | looking at text and graphics together | | ▓ | ▓ |

**These resource sheets will help you when:**
- you are doing research for a project or assignment
- you are reading any illustrated material
- you need to extract information from graphs, charts and other illustrations.

## Read and respond to different formats

**Communication**
Element 4: Read and respond to written materials

Many people find forms, timetables and other specialised formats quite daunting to read. This group of resource sheets explains why some documents are arranged in particular ways and helps you to practise extracting the information you need.

| Resource sheet | Reference | How it can help | Foundation | Intermediate | Advanced |
| --- | --- | --- | --- | --- | --- |
| Reading different formats | 114 | getting used to reading forms | ▓ | | |
| Reading timetables and price lists | 115 | practice in reading timetables and price lists | ▓ | | |
| Standard formats | 116 | reading forms, record cards and other documents that follow a set format | | ▓ | ▓ |
| Outline formats | 117 | extracting information from documents that follow a simple framework | | ▓ | ▓ |
| Other types of reading | 118 | a reminder about some of the different types of formats you may come across | | ▓ | ▓ |

**These resource sheets will help you when:**
- you have to extract information from forms, timetables and price lists
- you are working out costs or planning a journey
- you are faced with documents which use a format you are not familiar with.

# Information technology

## Word processors

**Information technology**
Element 1: Prepare information

| Resource sheet | Reference | How it can help | Foundation | Intermediate | Advanced |
|---|---|---|---|---|---|
| Typing text | 1 | getting to know the keyboard | ✓ | ✓ | ✓ |
| Choosing a format | 2 | using set formats for your work | ✓ | ✓ | ✓ |
| Saving your work | 3 | how to save your work | ✓ | | |
| Typing special characters | 4 | how to use symbols and characters which are not on the keyboard | | ✓ | ✓ |
| Styling your text 1 | 5 | fonts, typesizes, bold, italic and underlining | | ✓ | ✓ |
| Styling your text 2 | 6 | more ways of setting the style of your document | | ✓ | ✓ |
| Keeping your work safe | 7 | saving your work automatically – and other safety precautions | | ✓ | ✓ |

This group of resource sheets gives you the basic information you need to start typing information into a word processing program.

**These resource sheets will help you when:**
- you begin using a word processor
- you are writing a letter, a memo or any document that follows a set format
- you want to save your work.

## Spreadsheets

**Information technology**
Element 1: Prepare information

Spreadsheets are computer-based charts that allow you to perform calculations. These resource sheets

| Resource sheet | Reference | How it can help | Foundation | Intermediate | Advanced |
|---|---|---|---|---|---|
| Introducing spreadsheets | 8 | what spreadsheets can do | ✓ | ✓ | ✓ |
| Getting to know spreadsheets | 9 | how information is arranged in a spreadsheet | ✓ | ✓ | ✓ |
| Exploring how spreadsheets works | 10 | finding out more about the spreadsheet you use | | ✓ | ✓ |
| Entering data in an existing spreadsheet | 11 | how to start using a spreadsheet | | ✓ | ✓ |
| Setting up new spreadsheets | 12 | how to set up a new spreadsheet | | ✓ | ✓ |
| Making a master spreadsheet | 13 | designing a master spreadsheet | | ✓ | ✓ |

explain some of the jobs that spreadsheets are good at – and show you how to start using them.

**These resource sheets will help you when:**
- you start to use spreadsheets
- you have to do the same calculation for a lot of figures
- you need to enter data into a spreadsheet
- you need to set up a new spreadsheet.

## Databases

**Information technology**
Element 1: Prepare information

A database is like an enormous computer-based filing cabinet – with the benefit that you can find the information you need very quickly. These resource sheets provide an introduction to databases and show how you can start using them.

| Resource sheet | Reference | How it can help | Foundation | Intermediate | Advanced |
|---|---|---|---|---|---|
| Introducing databases | 14 | what databases can do | | | |
| Getting to know databases | 15 | files, records and fields – database terminology | | | |
| Entering data into an existing database | 16 | how to add data to an existing database | | | |
| Making a new database | 17 | setting up a new database | | | |
| Introducing data types | 18 | the various kinds of information you can put into a database | | | |
| Designing a screen for entering data | 19 | making it easier to enter data into a database | | | |

**These resource sheets will help you when:**
- you start using a database
- you want to store a lot of information that is presented in the same format
- you need to enter information into a database.

## Graphics

**Information technology**
Element 1: Prepare information

These resource sheets will help you to get started with a simple graphics program.

| Resource sheet | Reference | How it can help | Foundation | Intermediate | Advanced |
|---|---|---|---|---|---|
| What type of picture do you want? | 20 | deciding whether you need to do a painting or a drawing | | | |
| Starting a drawing | 21 | first steps with a drawing program | | | |
| Starting a painting | 22 | first steps with a painting program | | | |
| Lines and line styles | 23 | some things you can do with lines | | | |
| Diagrams and plans | 24 | making simple diagrams in a drawing program | | | |
| Using clip art | 25 | using ready-made pictures | | | |
| Taking images from printed materials and video | 26 | some tips on using images from other sources | | | |

**These resource sheets will help you when:**
- you start to use a graphics program
- you want to produce images on the computer.

## Word processors

**Information technology**
Element 2: Process information

Word processors make it easy to edit what you have written. These sheets help you to explore some of the things you can do, such as moving text around or checking particular words wherever they appear in a document.

| Resource sheet | Reference | How it can help | Foundation | Intermediate | Advanced |
|---|---|---|---|---|---|
| Making simple changes to text | 27 | how to edit your work | | | |
| Checking your text | 28 | checking with your source material | | | |
| Cutting, copying and moving text | 29 | working with blocks of text | | | |
| Moving and copying text between documents | 30 | how to save time by copying text from one document to another | | | |
| Moving around a short document | 31 | some tips on moving around inside a document | | | |
| Moving around a long document | 32 | using go to options and other ways of moving around a long document | | | |
| Arranging blocks and tables | 33 | indenting, columns and tables | | | |
| Finding and replacing text | 34 | a simple way to find and change particular words in your document | | | |
| More about finding and replacing text | 35 | other tips on finding and replacing text | | | |
| Working with complex documents | 36 | chapters, cross-references, footnotes, contents lists and indexes | | | |
| Transferring text between different applications | 37 | preparing text to be read in different systems | | | |

**These resource sheets will help you when:**
- you need to edit what you have written
- you need to move blocks of text around
- you need to check your work
- you need to move around a document.

## Spreadsheets

**Information technology**
Element 2: Process information

This group of resource sheets describes some of the ways you can change a spreadsheet. You can alter information in particular cells, or add or delete whole columns and rows.

| Resource sheet | Reference | How it can help | Foundation | Intermediate | Advanced |
|---|---|---|---|---|---|
| Changing cell contents | 38 | changing the data in a spreadsheet | | | |
| Adding and deleting rows and columns | 39 | making space for new data and deleting data you no longer need | | | |
| Building multiple spreadsheets | 40 | working with groups of connected spreadsheets | | | |
| Sorting a spreadsheet | 41 | arranging your spreadsheet alphabetically or numerically | | | |

**These resource sheets will help you when:**
- you are updating a spreadsheet
- you are adding to a spreadsheet
- you want to get rid of data you no longer need.

## Databases

**Information technology**
Element **2**: Process information

These sheets explain how to change the data in your database and how to rearrange data so that the information is easier to understand if you need to print it out.

| Resource sheet | Reference | How it can help | Foundation | Intermediate | Advanced |
|---|---|---|---|---|---|
| Making changes | 42 | how to update your data | ░ | ░ | ░ |
| Finding a record | 43 | how to find a record so that you can change it | ░ | ░ | ░ |
| Sorting the database | 44 | how to arrange information so that it is easier to find in a printout | ░ | ░ | ░ |
| Changing the database structure | 45 | improving the structure of a database | | ░ | ░ |
| Using search and replace to make alterations | 46 | a quick way of making changes | | ░ | ░ |
| Copying records | 47 | moving records into a new file | | ░ | ░ |

**These resource sheets will help you when:**
- you are updating the information in a database
- you need to find a particular record
- you are going to print from a database.

## Graphics

**Information technology**
Element **2**: Process information

These resource sheets describe how you can improve your pictures by adding more details and making other changes.

| Resource sheet | Reference | How it can help | Foundation | Intermediate | Advanced |
|---|---|---|---|---|---|
| Making simple changes to a drawing | 48 | how to edit a drawing | ░ | ░ | ░ |
| Making simple changes to a painting | 49 | how to edit a painting | ░ | ░ | ░ |
| Moving graphics between pictures | 50 | how to save time by using part of a picture again | | ░ | ░ |
| Checking and correcting your work | 51 | the importance of consistency, accuracy and good design | | ░ | ░ |
| Using colour and pattern | 52 | ways of making your picture more interesting | ░ | ░ | ░ |
| Working accurately | 53 | using a grid to make your work more accurate | | ░ | ░ |
| Scale and rotation in drawings | 54 | altering the size, shape and angle of objects in your drawing | | ░ | ░ |

**These resource sheets will help you when:**
- you have a picture that you want to work on further
- you are producing graphics for leaflets, posters or reports.

# Word processors

**Information technology**
Element **3**: Present information

When you've finished writing something on a word processor, it's very tempting to print it out immediately. However, there are various things you should check first and your word processor program will contain tools to help you do this. These resource sheets describe some ways in which you can make sure that your document looks as professional as possible.

| Resource sheet | Reference | How it can help | Foundation | Intermediate | Advanced |
|---|---|---|---|---|---|
| Designing your page | 55 | how good design improves your work | | ✓ | ✓ |
| Checking your spelling and grammar | 56 | using the tools in your word processor to check your work | | ✓ | ✓ |
| Arranging your text on the page | 57 | more ideas about layout | | ✓ | ✓ |
| Checking the layout of a document before printing | 58 | things to check before you print | | ✓ | ✓ |
| Printing a text document | 59 | using the print settings on your word processor | | ✓ | ✓ |
| Combining text, graphics and calculations in documents | 60 | using different applications together | | ✓ | ✓ |

**These resource sheets will help you when:**
- you have finished writing something
- you are ready to print out
- you want a document to make a good impression on your readers.

# Spreadsheets

**Information technology**
Element **3**: Present information

You may need to print out a spreadsheet so that you can include it in a report or give it to people who do not have access to the computer screen. These sheets describe how to print out all, or part of, a spreadsheet.

| Resource sheet | Reference | How it can help | Foundation | Intermediate | Advanced |
|---|---|---|---|---|---|
| Printing a spreadsheet | 61 | when and how to print out a spreadsheet | ✓ | ✓ | ✓ |
| Printing selected parts of a spreadsheet | 62 | issues to consider when you are printing only part of a spreadsheet | ✓ | ✓ | ✓ |
| Improving the look of a spreadsheet | 63 | how to make your spreadsheets easy to follow | | ✓ | ✓ |
| Displaying numbers | 64 | different ways of displaying numbers in a spreadsheet | | ✓ | ✓ |
| Importing and exporting | 65 | moving data in and out of spreadsheets | | ✓ | ✓ |

**These resource sheets will help you when:**
- you need to present a spreadsheet to other people.

## Databases

**Information technology**
Element **3**: Present information

When you are working with a database, you may need to print out lists of information for other people to use. These resource sheets describe how you can select the records you need and present them effectively.

| Resource sheet | Reference | How it can help | Foundation | Intermediate | Advanced |
|---|---|---|---|---|---|
| Introducing reports | 66 | how to print out information from a database | | | |
| Filters and queries | 67 | how to display selected information in a database | | | |
| Printing selected records | 68 | how to print out selected information | | | |
| Designing a report | 69 | how to make your printout clear and easy to use | | | |
| Complex record selection | 70 | some more ways of selecting information | | | |

**These resource sheets will help you when:**
- you are extracting information from a database
- you want to analyse the information you have on a database
- you need to provide printed lists of information from your database.

## Graphics

**Information technology**
Element **3**: Present information

These resource sheets describe the final stages of preparing a picture for printing or display on the screen.

| Resource sheet | Reference | How it can help | Foundation | Intermediate | Advanced |
|---|---|---|---|---|---|
| Checking a picture before printing | 71 | last checks to make before you print | | | |
| Texture and media in paintings | 72 | some sophisticated final touches | | | |
| Printing a picture | 73 | using the options in your program when you print out your picture | | | |
| Displaying pictures on screen | 74 | issues to think about when you are presenting your pictures as an on-screen display | | | |
| Labelling drawings | 75 | effective ways of labelling your drawings | | | |
| Layered drawings | 76 | building up a drawing in layers | | | |
| Designing a picture | 77 | thinking about the situation in which your pictures will be seen | | | |
| Special tasks with graphics | 78 | some advanced techniques | | | |

**These resource sheets will help you when:**
- you want to print a picture
- you want to display a picture on screen.

## Understanding the computer

**Information technology**
Element 4: Evaluate the use of information technology

This group of resource sheets provides an introduction to working on the computer. If you already have some computer experience, they may show you how to work more professionally. The sheets will help you to get to know what the various parts of the system do and the ways in which particular types of program can help. They also emphasise essential precautions you should take to protect and organise your work.

| Resource sheet | Reference | How it can help | Foundation | Intermediate | Advanced |
|---|---|---|---|---|---|
| Naming the parts | 79 | getting to know the computer you are going to use | | | |
| Computer equipment and computer programs | 80 | understanding the difference between hardware and software | | | |
| Starting to use the computer | 81 | first steps on the computer | | | |
| How the computer can help you to work accurately | 82 | features you can use to check your work | | | |
| Why you need to work accurately with the computer | 83 | the importance of working accurately | | | |
| Avoiding mistakes | 84 | some tips on working accurately | | | |
| Naming and organising your document | 85 | how to keep your documents in good order | | | |
| Save money by using the computer | 86 | avoiding unnecessary printing | | | |
| What can a computer do? | 87 | the kind of jobs that a computer can – and cannot – do for you | | | |
| Organising your work | 88 | how to file your work effectively | | | |
| Using your time on the computer efficiently | 89 | how to make the most of your time on the computer by preparing properly first | | | |
| Working with a network | 90 | introducing networks | | | |
| Do you need to use the computer? | 91 | deciding when you need to use a particlar type of program | | | |
| Finding out about applications | 92 | assessing what programs can do | | | |
| Creating batches of similar letters | 93 | using mail-merge | | | |
| Desktop publishing | 94 | introducing DTP programs | | | |
| Computers and special neeeds | 95 | adapting computer equipment to meet the requirements of people with special needs | | | |
| Protecting your work during your session | 96 | safety procedures to use while you are working at the computer | | | |
| Protecting your work on a network | 97 | how to prevent other people getting access to your work through the network | | | |
| Keeping copies of your work – back-ups | 98 | safety routines to protect your work | | | |

**These resource sheets will help you when:**
- you first start working on a computer
- you are using a computer in a work setting for the first time
- you are deciding which program to use
- you need to organise your work.

## Solving problems

**Information technology**
Element 4: Evaluate the use of information technology

These resource sheets provide a trouble-shooting guide when something goes wrong. There are some problems that you can sort out quite easily yourself - but for others you will need expert assistance. These sheets should help you to tell the difference between them and to stop you making the situation worse by taking inappropriate action. You will also find advice here on how to protect yourself against certain problems.

| Resource sheet | Reference | How it can help | Foundation | Intermediate | Advanced |
|---|---|---|---|---|---|
| Printers: simple problems | 99 | what to do if you can't get a printer to work | | | |
| Printers: harder problems | 100 | some more things that can go wrong with printers | | | |
| Switching the computer on: hardware failure | 101 | what to do if your computer doesn't work when you switch it on | | | |
| Floppy disks | 102 | problems with disks | | | |
| Hard disks | 103 | how to avoid problems with your hard disk | | | |
| Mouse problems | 104 | what to do when your mouse won't work | | | |
| Switching the computer on: software failure | 105 | how to avoid damaging the software that makes your computer work | | | |
| Keyboards | 106 | some problems with keyboards | | | |
| Software crashes and general protection faults | 107 | what happens when a program crashes | | | |
| Opening files | 108 | things that can go wrong when you try to open a file | | | |
| Running programs | 109 | reasons why some programs won't run on your computer | | | |
| Undoing mistakes | 110 | some ways of putting your mistakes right | | | |
| Retrieving deleted files | 111 | how to retrieve work you have deleted by mistake | | | |
| Viruses | 112 | how to protect yourself against computer viruses | | | |
| Finding files | 113 | how to recover files when you can't remember where they are | | | |

**These resource sheets will help you when:**
- something goes wrong with your computer equipment
- you want to protect your work
- a computer program doesn't work.

## Health and safety

**Information technology**
Element 4: Evaluate the use of information technology

Everyone who spends any time working with computers should be aware of health and safety issues. You can be caused permanent physical damage if you ignore danger signs. Computers and printers should be treated with the same respect as other electrical equipment. These resource sheets explain how you can protect yourself and help to avoid accidents.

| Resource sheet | Reference | How it can help | Foundation | Intermediate | Advanced |
|---|---|---|---|---|---|
| Repetitive strain injury | 114 | how to avoid damaging your wrists | ■ | ■ | ■ |
| Back pain | 115 | the importance of sitting in the correct position at the computer | ■ | ■ | ■ |
| Eye strain | 116 | how to protect your eyes | ■ | ■ | ■ |
| Monitor radiation | 117 | the possible dangers of radiation from your monitor and how to protect yourself | ■ | ■ | ■ |
| Cables | 118 | the dangers computer cables can pose | | ■ | ■ |
| Electrical equipment | 119 | how to avoid fires and electric shocks | ■ | ■ | ■ |
| Protecting equipment | 120 | safety suggestions to protect your equipment from accidental damage | ■ | ■ | ■ |

**These resource sheets will help you when:**
- you spend any time working on a computer
- you are working on a computer in an unfamilar environment.

# Index

## A
Accidents with computers . . . . . . . . . . . . . . 41
Accuracy of measurements . . . . . . . . . . . . . 12
Active listening . . . . . . . . . . . . . . . . . . . . . . 24
Addition . . . . . . . . . . . . . . . . . . . . . . . . . . . . 17
Apostrophes . . . . . . . . . . . . . . . . . . . . . . . . . 25
Applications on the computer . . . . . . . . . . . 39
Area . . . . . . . . . . . . . . . . . . . . . . . . . . . . . . . 12
Assertiveness . . . . . . . . . . . . . . . . . . . . . . . . 24
Audience for images . . . . . . . . . . . . . . . . . . 27
Audience, when you are talking . . . . . . . . . 23
Averages . . . . . . . . . . . . . . . . . . . . . . . . . . . 16

## B
Back pain . . . . . . . . . . . . . . . . . . . . . . . . . . . 41
Back-ups of computer files . . . . . . . . . . . . . 39
Bar charts . . . . . . . . . . . . . . . . . . . . . . . . . . 20
Best-fit lines . . . . . . . . . . . . . . . . . . . . . . . . . 20
Body language . . . . . . . . . . . . . . . . . . . . . . 24

## C
Cables . . . . . . . . . . . . . . . . . . . . . . . . . . . . . 41
Calculators . . . . . . . . . . . . . . . . . . . 12, 18, 20
Capacity . . . . . . . . . . . . . . . . . . . . . . . . . . . 12
Capital letters . . . . . . . . . . . . . . . . . . . . . . . 25
Cartoons . . . . . . . . . . . . . . . . . . . . . . . . . . . 28
Chance . . . . . . . . . . . . . . . . . . . . . . . . . . . . 21
Charts . . . . . . . . . . . . . . . . . . . . . . . . . . 28, 31
Checking your measurements . . . . . . . . . . . 13
Circumference of a circle . . . . . . . . . . . . . . . 15
Clip art . . . . . . . . . . . . . . . . . . . . . . . . . . . . . 34
Colons . . . . . . . . . . . . . . . . . . . . . . . . . . . . . 25
Colour . . . . . . . . . . . . . . . . . . . . . . . . . . . . . 27
Commas . . . . . . . . . . . . . . . . . . . . . . . . . . . 25
Computer equipment . . . . . . . . . . . . . . . . . 39
Contents lists . . . . . . . . . . . . . . . . . . . . . . . . 30
Continuous data . . . . . . . . . . . . . . . . . . . . . 14
Conversation . . . . . . . . . . . . . . . . . . . . . . . . 24
Conversion . . . . . . . . . . . . . . . . . . . 14, 16, 19
Conversion tables . . . . . . . . . . . . . . . . . . . . 16
Coordinates . . . . . . . . . . . . . . . . . . . . . . . . 16
Copying records on a database . . . . . . . . . 36
Copying text . . . . . . . . . . . . . . . . . . . . . . . . 35
Copyright . . . . . . . . . . . . . . . . . . . . . . . . . . 27
Cross-checking . . . . . . . . . . . . . . . . . . . . . . 13
Cross-references . . . . . . . . . . . . . . . . . . . . . 35
Cubes and cuboids . . . . . . . . . . . . . . . . . . . 15
CVs . . . . . . . . . . . . . . . . . . . . . . . . . . . . . . . 26
Cylinders . . . . . . . . . . . . . . . . . . . . . . . . . . . 15

## D
Database terminology . . . . . . . . . . . . . . . . . 34
Databases . . . . . . . . . . . . . . . . . . . . 34, 36, 38
Decimals . . . . . . . . . . . . . . . . . . . . . . . . . . . 18
Deleted files . . . . . . . . . . . . . . . . . . . . . . . . . 40
Design . . . . . . . . . . . . . . . . . . . . . . . . . . . . . 27
Designing your text . . . . . . . . . . . . . . . . . . . 37
Desktop publishing . . . . . . . . . . . . . . . . . . . 39
Diagrams . . . . . . . . . . . . . . . . . . . . . 19, 31, 38
Dictionary . . . . . . . . . . . . . . . . . . . . . . . . . . 30
Discrete data . . . . . . . . . . . . . . . . . . . . . . . . 20
Discussions . . . . . . . . . . . . . . . . . . . . . . . . . 23
Division . . . . . . . . . . . . . . . . . . . . . . . . . . . . 18
Documents . . . . . . . . . . . . . . . . . . . . . . 35, 39
Drawing pictures . . . . . . . . . . . . . . . . . . . . . 28
Drawing programs . . . . . . . . . . . . . . . . . . . 34

## E
Editing drawings . . . . . . . . . . . . . . . . . . . . . 36
Editing paintings . . . . . . . . . . . . . . . . . . . . . 36
Editing text . . . . . . . . . . . . . . . . . . . . . . . . . 35
Electrical equipment . . . . . . . . . . . . . . . . . . 41
Elevations . . . . . . . . . . . . . . . . . . . . . . . . . . 19
Enlargement . . . . . . . . . . . . . . . . . . . . . . . . 15
Equations . . . . . . . . . . . . . . . . . . . . . . . . . . 16
Estimating when measuring . . . . . . . . . . . . 13
Exhibitions . . . . . . . . . . . . . . . . . . . . . . . . . . 28
Experiments . . . . . . . . . . . . . . . . . . . . . . . . 14

## F
Face-to-face discussions . . . . . . . . . . . . . . . 23
Feedback . . . . . . . . . . . . . . . . . . . . . . . . . . . 24
Feet and inches . . . . . . . . . . . . . . . . . . . . . . 12
Filters and queries . . . . . . . . . . . . . . . . . . . . 38
Final drafts . . . . . . . . . . . . . . . . . . . . . . . . . . 25
Finding and replacing . . . . . . . . . . . . . . . . . 35
Finding files . . . . . . . . . . . . . . . . . . . . . . . . . 40
Floppy disk problems . . . . . . . . . . . . . . . . . 40
Flowcharts . . . . . . . . . . . . . . . . . . . . . . . 19, 28
Fonts . . . . . . . . . . . . . . . . . . . . . . . . . . . . . . 33
Footnotes . . . . . . . . . . . . . . . . . . . . . . . . . . 35
Forms . . . . . . . . . . . . . . . . . . . . . . . . . . . 26, 31
Formulae . . . . . . . . . . . . . . . . . . . . . . . . . . . 16
Fraction scales . . . . . . . . . . . . . . . . . . . . . . . 12
Fractions . . . . . . . . . . . . . . . . . . . . . . . . . . . 18
Full stops . . . . . . . . . . . . . . . . . . . . . . . . . . . 25

## G
General protection faults . . . . . . . . . . . . . . 40
Grammar . . . . . . . . . . . . . . . . . . . . . . . . 25, 37
Graphics . . . . . . . . . . . . . . . . . . . . . 34, 36, 38
Graphs . . . . . . . . . . . . . . . . . . . . . . . 16, 28, 31
Grouped data . . . . . . . . . . . . . . . . . . . . . . . 20

## H
Hard disk problems . . . . . . . . . . . . . . . . . . . 40
Hardware . . . . . . . . . . . . . . . . . . . . . . . . . . . 39
Health and safety . . . . . . . . . . . . . . . . . . . . 41
Histograms . . . . . . . . . . . . . . . . . . . . . . . 20, 21

## I
Illustrations . . . . . . . . . . . . . . . . . . . . . . . . . 27
Images . . . . . . . . . . . . . . . . . . . . . . . . . . . . . 27

Imperial units . . . . . . . . . . . . . . . . . . . . . . . . 12
Indexes. . . . . . . . . . . . . . . . . . . . . . . . . . 30, 35
Interquartile range . . . . . . . . . . . . . . . . . . . 20
Interviewing. . . . . . . . . . . . . . . . . . . . . . . . 24

## K
Keyboard problems . . . . . . . . . . . . . . . . . . 40

## L
Labelling drawings. . . . . . . . . . . . . . . . . . . 38
Large and small numbers . . . . . . . . . . . 12, 17
Layout . . . . . . . . . . . . . . . . . . . . . . . . . . . . 37
Leaflets . . . . . . . . . . . . . . . . . . . . . . . . 26, 28
Letters . . . . . . . . . . . . . . . . . . . . . . . . . . . 26
Levels of accuracy . . . . . . . . . . . . . . . . . . 14
Line graphs . . . . . . . . . . . . . . . . . . . . 20, 21
Listening . . . . . . . . . . . . . . . . . . . . . . . . . 24

## M
Maps . . . . . . . . . . . . . . . . . . . . . . . . . 19, 28
Mean . . . . . . . . . . . . . . . . . . . . . . . . . 16, 20
Measurement . . . . . . . . . . . . . . . . . . . . . . 12
Median. . . . . . . . . . . . . . . . . . . . . . . . . . . 16
Meetings . . . . . . . . . . . . . . . . . . . . . . . . . 23
Memos. . . . . . . . . . . . . . . . . . . . . . . . . . . 26
Metric measurements . . . . . . . . . . . . . . . . 12
Mind maps. . . . . . . . . . . . . . . . . . . . . . . . 28
Misrepresenting data . . . . . . . . . . . . . . . . 21
Mode . . . . . . . . . . . . . . . . . . . . . . . . . . . . 16
Money . . . . . . . . . . . . . . . . . . . . . . . . . . . 12
Monitor radiation . . . . . . . . . . . . . . . . . . . 41
Multiplication. . . . . . . . . . . . . . . . . . . 17, 18

## N
Negative numbers . . . . . . . . . . . . . . . . . . 17
Network diagrams . . . . . . . . . . . . . . . . . . 19
Networks . . . . . . . . . . . . . . . . . . . . . . . . . 39
Notes . . . . . . . . . . . . . . . . . . . . . . . . . . . . 25

## P
Painting programs . . . . . . . . . . . . . . . . . . 34
Paragraphs . . . . . . . . . . . . . . . . . . . . . . . . 25
Percentages . . . . . . . . . . . . . . . . . . . . . . . 18
Perimeter . . . . . . . . . . . . . . . . . . . . . . . . . 15
Photocopying. . . . . . . . . . . . . . . . . . . . . . 27
Photographs . . . . . . . . . . . . . . . . . . . . . . . 28
Pie charts . . . . . . . . . . . . . . . . . . . . . . 20, 21
Plans . . . . . . . . . . . . . . . . . . . . . . 19, 28, 34
Populations . . . . . . . . . . . . . . . . . . . . . . . 14
Posters . . . . . . . . . . . . . . . . . . . . . . . . . . . 28
Predictions . . . . . . . . . . . . . . . . . . . . . . . . 20
Presentations . . . . . . . . . . . . . . . . . . . . . . 28
Price lists . . . . . . . . . . . . . . . . . . . . . . . . . 31
Printer problems. . . . . . . . . . . . . . . . . . . . 40
Printing a spreadsheet . . . . . . . . . . . . . . . 37
Printing a text document . . . . . . . . . . . . . 37
Printing and binding. . . . . . . . . . . . . . . . . 27

Printing from a database. . . . . . . . . . . . . . 38
Printing graphics . . . . . . . . . . . . . . . . . . . 38
Probability . . . . . . . . . . . . . . . . . . . . . . . . 21
Problems on the computer . . . . . . . . . . . . 40
Proportion . . . . . . . . . . . . . . . . . . . . . . . . 13
Protecting your work on the computer . . . . . . 39
Publicity material. . . . . . . . . . . . . . . . . . . 26
Punctuation . . . . . . . . . . . . . . . . . . . . . . . 25
Purpose, when you are talking . . . . . . . . . 23

## Q
Questions . . . . . . . . . . . . . . . . . . . . . . 14, 24

## R
Rates . . . . . . . . . . . . . . . . . . . . . . . . . . . . 12
Ratios. . . . . . . . . . . . . . . . . . . . . . . . . . . . 18
Reading . . . . . . . . . . . . . . . . . . . . . . . . . . 29
Recording sheets . . . . . . . . . . . . . . . . . . . 14
Reference sources . . . . . . . . . . . . . . . . . . 30
References . . . . . . . . . . . . . . . . . . . . . . . . 26
Repetitive strain injury. . . . . . . . . . . . . . . 41
Reports. . . . . . . . . . . . . . . . . . . . . . . . 26, 28
Research . . . . . . . . . . . . . . . . . . . . . . . . . 30
Rough drafts . . . . . . . . . . . . . . . . . . . . . . 25
Rough estimates. . . . . . . . . . . . . . . . . . . . 13
Rounding. . . . . . . . . . . . . . . . . . . . . . . . . 14
RSI . . . . . . . . . . . . . . . . . . . . . . . . . . . . . 41

## S
Safety routines on the computer . . . . . . . . . . 39
Samples . . . . . . . . . . . . . . . . . . . . . . . . . . 14
Saving . . . . . . . . . . . . . . . . . . . . . . . . . . . 33
Scale and rotation in drawings . . . . . . . . . . . 36
Scales. . . . . . . . . . . . . . . . . . . . . . . . . . . . 12
Scanning . . . . . . . . . . . . . . . . . . . . . . . . . 29
Scatter diagrams. . . . . . . . . . . . . . . . . 20, 21
Scientific calculators . . . . . . . . . . . . . . . . 20
Semi-colons. . . . . . . . . . . . . . . . . . . . . . . 25
Sentences. . . . . . . . . . . . . . . . . . . . . . . . . 25
Skim reading . . . . . . . . . . . . . . . . . . . . . . 29
Software. . . . . . . . . . . . . . . . . . . . . . . . . . 39
Software crashes . . . . . . . . . . . . . . . . . . . 40
Sources of data. . . . . . . . . . . . . . . . . . . . . 14
Special characters. . . . . . . . . . . . . . . . . . . 33
Special neeeds and computers . . . . . . . . . . . 39
Spelling . . . . . . . . . . . . . . . . . . . . . . . 25, 37
Spreadsheets. . . . . . . . . . . . . . . . . . 33, 35, 37
Styling. . . . . . . . . . . . . . . . . . . . . . . . . . . 33
Subtraction. . . . . . . . . . . . . . . . . . . . . . . . 17
Surveys . . . . . . . . . . . . . . . . . . . . . . . . . . 14
Symbols. . . . . . . . . . . . . . . . . . . . . . . . . . 28

## T
Tables. . . . . . . . . . . . . . . . . . . . . . . . . 21, 28
Talking. . . . . . . . . . . . . . . . . . . . . . . . . . . 24
Talking to people . . . . . . . . . . . . . . . . . . . 23
Tally tables. . . . . . . . . . . . . . . . . . . . . . . . 14

Telephones ................................ 23
Temperature .............................. 12
Texture and media in painting programs ..... 38
Three-dimensional shapes ................ 19
Time ................................. 12, 17
Timetables ............................... 31
Tolerances ............................... 14
Triangular prisms ........................ 15
Two-dimensional shapes ................. 19
Two-way tables ....................... 14, 20
Typesizes ............................ 27, 33
Typing ................................... 33
Typography .............................. 27

## V
Video .................................... 28
Voice .................................... 24
Volume .............................. 12, 15

## W
Word processors .................. 33, 35, 37
Working accurately on the computer ....... 39
Writing skills ............................ 25

# GNVQ Core Skills:
# AN

John Gillespie
Hilary Rimmer and Marilyn Cook
Mary Rouncefield

## AN – Collect and record data

**Element 1**

### Topic 1 – Measuring

- AN1 Reading decimal scales
- AN2 Large and small numbers
- AN3 Reading fraction scales
- AN4 Estimating on scales
- AN8 Money and metric measurements
- AN9 Time and temperature
- AN10 Measurement with imperial units

### Topic 2 – Estimating and checking

- AN13 Allowing for waste
- AN14 Checking
- AN16 Rough estimates

### Topic 3 – Data sources

- AN20 Talking to people
- AN21 Variety of sources
- AN22 Experiments and competition

### Topic 4 – Surveys

- AN23 Introducing surveys
- AN25 Planning a survey
- AN26 Sample sizes
- AN27 Asking clear questions 1
- AN28 Asking clear questions 2
- AN29 Survey types
- AN30 Tally tables
- AN31 Recording sheets

### Topic 5 – Levels of accuracy

- AN34 Rounding
- AN35 How accurate?

# Topic 1 – Measuring

## Reading decimal scales

**AN 1**

Foundation/Intermediate/Advanced
Element **1.1,2.1,3.1**
Performance criteria **1,2,3,4,5**
Range **Techniques** (Shape; space and measures); **Units**

The diagram shows a piece of wood and part of a ruler.

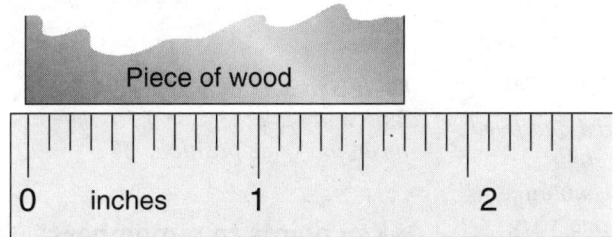

The wood measures 1⁷⁄₁₀ inches, or 1.7 inches.

- See how you measure from 0, not from the end of the ruler.
- Count the marks from 1 to 2. Make sure you count 10 marks, so there is 0.1 inch (or a tenth of an inch) between each mark.
- This is a decimal scale, because it is marked in tenths.

### Activity

The diagram shows another part of the same ruler. Arrow 'a' is pointing at 7.2.

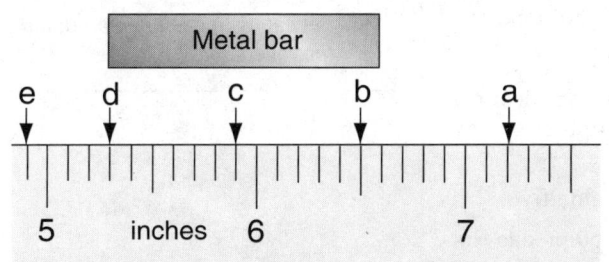

1. What measurements are the other arrows pointing at?
2. What is the length of the metal bar (from 'd' to 'b')?
3. Another bar measures from 'e' to 'a'. What is its length?

■

1. 'b' is at 6.5 inches, 'c' is at 5.9 inches, 'd' is at 5.3 inches and 'e' is at 4.9 inches.
2. From 5.3 to 6.5 is 1.2 inches.
3. From 4.9 to 7.2 is 2.3 inches. ■

### Activity

The scale below shows part of a weighing scale measuring in grams. The arrows show different readings on the scale.

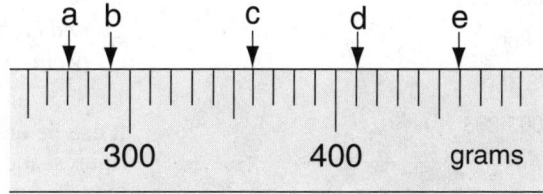

1. Read the five weights from the scale.
2. How much heavier is 'd' than 'b'?
3. How much less does 'a' weigh than 'e'?

■

1. 270 grams, 290 grams, 360 grams, 410 grams, 460 grams.
2. 120 grams (10 + 100 + 10)
3. 190 grams (60 + 100 + 30). ■

On this scale there are only five marks from 300 to 400 so the marks go up in 20s (320, 340, 360, 380 400). You have to imagine the missing marks to read the scale.

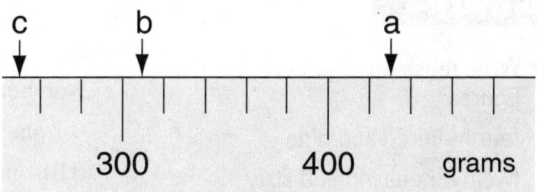

### Activity

What weights do the arrows 'a', 'b' and 'c' point at?

■ 430 grams, 310 grams, 250 grams. ■

### Key points to remember

When reading scales, make sure that the readings make sense with the numbers marked on the scales on either side of the points where you are taking the readings.

### *Putting it into practice*

*Practise measuring and using other scales at work, at home, in your local supermarket. Ask a partner to read the same scales. If you disagree, check who is correct.*

# Topic 1 – Measuring

## Large and small numbers

**AN 2**

Foundation/Intermediate/Advanced
Element **1.1, 2.1, 3.1**
Performance criteria **1, 2, 3, 4**
Range **Techniques**
(Number); **Units**

You may have to read large numbers from a scale for someone else to copy down or have to write down figures that someone else is reading out to you.

### Activity

Try reading these large numbers aloud.

345

1068

24 600

678 450

2 003 883

▮▮ *You should have said: three hundred and forty-five; one thousand and sixty-eight; twenty-four thousand six hundred; six hundred and seventy-eight thousand four hundred and fifty; two million three thousand eight hundred and eighty-three.* ▮▮

The figures in large numbers are often spaced in threes.

Sometimes they are written with a , (comma) instead of a space, like this:

24,600   678,450   2,003,883

### Activity

1  Write these numbers in figures:

four hundred and nine

twenty thousand and sixty

fifty-three thousand

four million.

2  Write these numbers in words:

88

605

71,890

29,660

70,788

625,000

▮▮

1  409, 20 060, 53 000, 4 000 000

2  eighty-eight, six hundred and five, seventy-one thousand eight hundred and ninety, twenty-nine thousand six hundred and sixty, seventy thousand seven hundred and eighty-eight, six hundred and twenty-five thousand. ▮▮

It can be quite hard to change between figures and words. If you think you may be misunderstood – or likely to make a mistake – you can say the figures one by one, like this:

409 four zero nine

20060 two zero zero six zero.

Numbers to remember

1000 one thousand

10 000 ten thousand

100 000 one hundred thousand

1 000 000 one million

For the parts of numbers after decimal points, you only say the figures one by one:

24.95 twenty-four point nine five

300.167 three hundred point one six seven.

Numbers to remember

0.1 one tenth

0.01 one hundredth

### Activity

The scale below shows amounts of liquid in litres. The amounts are all between 3 litres and 4 litres.

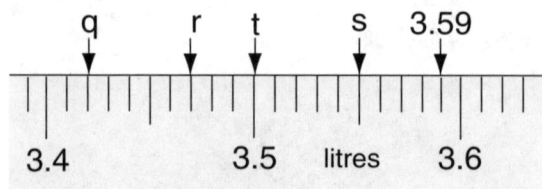

The amounts show whole litres (the '3s'), tenths of litres (the '.4', '.5' and '.6') and hundredths of litres as well.

Look at the position of 3.59, then write down the positions of 'q', 'r', 's' and 't'.

▮▮ *q is at 3.42, r is at 3.47, s is at 3.55 and t is at 3.5 or 3.50  they both mean the same position.* ▮▮

### Key points to remember

Be careful to say numbers correctly and to write them correctly – it is easy to make mistakes with large and small numbers.

### *Putting it into practice*

- *Work with a partner – one person says a number and writes it down in words  the other person writes it down in figures.*
- *Compare the two versions and make sure they both mean the same number.*
- *Repeat, with each person doing the reverse.*

# Topic 1 – Measuring

## Reading fraction scales

**AN 3**

Foundation/Intermediate/Advanced
Element **1.1,2.1,3.1**
Performance criteria **1,2,3,4,5**
Range **Techniques** (Number; Shape, space and measures); **Units**

You will often find scales marked in halves and quarters. The disc in the diagram is 1¾ inches across.

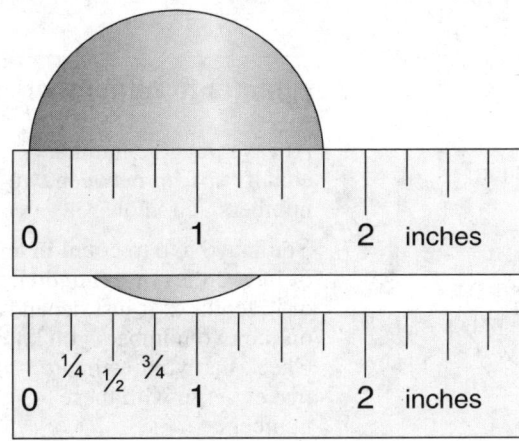

On a scale marked in quarters, some of the measurements could be read in two ways. For instance,

½ is the same as 2/4 (2 quarters).

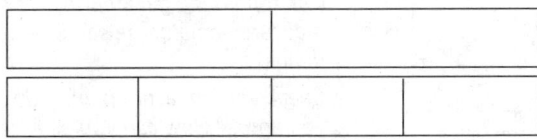

You could use 2/4 or ½, but ½ is normally used. It is a simpler fraction with smaller numbers in it.

The scale below is marked in ⅛ ths.

Arrow 'a' is at ¼ or 2/8 they are both the same, but normally you use ¼ as it is simpler.

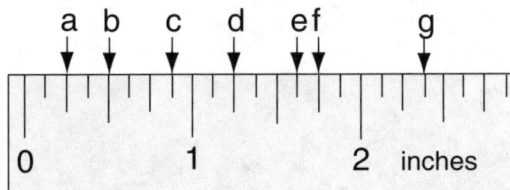

### Activity

1. Look at the scale marked in eighths. Write down the measurements for each of the arrows. For instance, 'c' is at ⅞ inches.

2. ¾ inch is midway between ⅝ inch and ⅞ inch, because ¾ inch is the same as 6/8 inch. Look at the scale above to make sure you see how this works. What measurement is midway 1⅜ inches and 1⅝ inches? Now do the same for 7⅛ and 7⅜.

■ **1** *a* is at ¼ (or 2/8) inch, *b* at ½ inch, *c* at ⅞ inch, *d* at 1¼ inches, *e* at 1⅝ inches, *f* at 1¾ inches, *g* at 2⅜ inches.

**2** 1½ inches, 7¼ inches. ■

You find the same system works for other fractions. For instance, some rules and scales are marked in ¹⁄₁₆ ths.

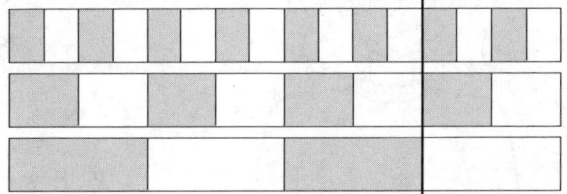

The line shows how ¹²⁄₁₆ is the same as 6/8 which is the same as ¾.

### Activity

Look at these measurements and find any which you can replace with simpler fractions.

¹⁄₁₆, ²⁄₁₆, ⁷⁄₁₆, ¹⁰⁄₁₆, ¹²⁄₁₆, ⁵⁶⁄₁₆.

■ ²⁄₁₆ is the same as ⅛, ¹⁰⁄₁₆ is the same as ⅝, ¹²⁄₁₆ is the same as 6/8, or ¾, ⁵⁶⁄₁₆ is the same as 5³⁄₈. ■

### Key points to remember

Fraction measurements can be based on halving – halves, quarters, eighths, sixteenths as well as on tenths.

### *Putting it into practice*

- Look out for scales measuring in fractions like ½s, ¼s and ⅛s and practise measuring with them.
- Possible examples: pounds (lbs) and ounces (oz), inches.

| Topic 1 – Measuring | AN 4 |

## Estimating on scales

Foundation/Intermediate/Advanced
Element **1.1,2.1,3.1**
Performance criteria **1,2,3,4,5**
Range **Techniques** (Number; Shape, space and measures); **Units; Levels of accuracy**

You may have to estimate measurements, rather than read them exactly.

This means reading the measurement as well as you can – it may not be possible to be 'dead right'.

Sometimes, each time you measure, you get a slightly different result. For instance, it is very hard to measure someone's height accurately.

Is Karen closer to 1 m 641 mm or 1 m 642 mm high?

You just can't measure that accurately. This is because the scale is not divided into 1 mm divisions – and also because Karen may move slightly and give different readings.

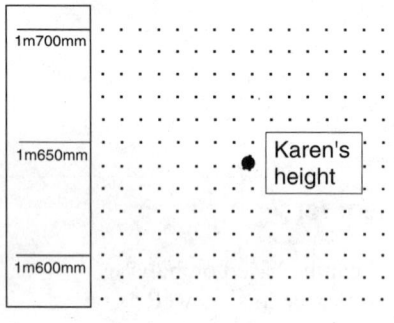

You could say that Karen is:
- just below 1 m 650 mm
- over 1 m 600 mm
- maybe 1 m 640 mm

You have to imagine the positions of the numbers between 600 and 650 (610, 620, 630, 640).

### Activity

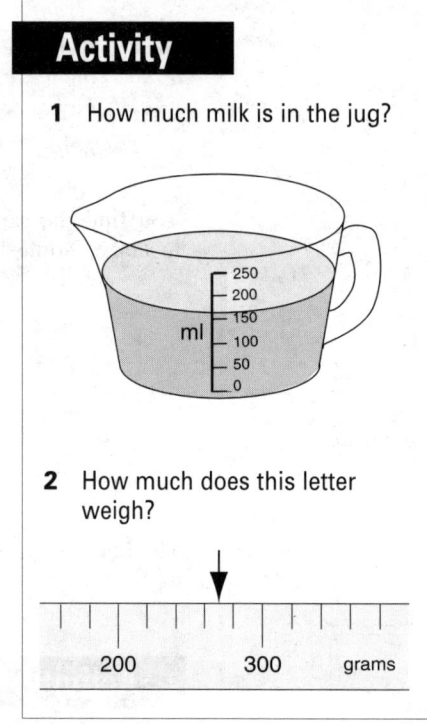

1 How much milk is in the jug?

2 How much does this letter weigh?

▌▌

*1 Imagine numbers from 150 to 200 equally spaced up the jug. 160 ml of milk is a good estimate.*

*2 The marks can't be every 10 grams ... they have to be every 20 to count from 200 and 300.*

*So the arrow points midway between 260 and 280 ... the letter is about 270 grams.* ▌▌

### Key points to remember

- Always imagine numbers equally spaced between two numbers you know.
- You may have to count in tens or in twenties or in hundreds or in tenths ... it just depends on the two numbers you know. Check that your estimate makes sense with these numbers.

### Putting it into practice

- *Practise measuring anything you can. If possible get a partner to measure some of the same things.*
- *Check your measurements – do you agree? How can you be sure?*

## Topic 1 – Measuring

### Money and metric measurements

**AN 8**

Foundation/Intermediate/
Advanced
Element **1.2, 2.1, 3.1**
Performance criteria **1, 2, 3, 4, 5**
Range **Techniques** (Number; Shape, space and measures);
**Units**

## Money

### Activity

How do you write 4 pounds and 5 pence in figures?
Is it £4.5? or £4.50? or £4.05?

■■ £4.05 is correct. Counting on in 5p units gives 4.10, 4.15, 4.20. If you see 4.5 on your calculator, though, it will mean £4.50. (Remember that a calculator does not show 0s on the right.) ■■

## Metric measurements

In this country there are two sorts of units for most measuring, metric (metres, centimetres, kilograms and litres) and imperial (inches, ounces, stones, miles and pints).

Metric units are being used more and more, but imperial units will still be in use for years to come. Metric units are based on the metre (for lengths), litre (for volumes) and gram (for mass or weights).

'Kilo-' means '1000 times as big', so

  1 kilometre (km) = 1000 metres (m)

  1 kilogram (kg) = 1000 grams (g)

'Centi-' means '1/100 as big', so

  1 centimetre (cm) = 1/100 m or 0.01 m

  1 centilitre (cl) = 1/100 l or 0.01 l

'Milli-' means '1/1000 as big', so

  1 millimetre (mm) = 1/1000 m or 0.001 m

  1 millilitre (ml) = 1/1000 l or 0.001 l

  1 milligram (mg) = 1/1000 g or 0.001 g

  10 mm = 1 cm and 100 cm (or 1000 mm) = 1 m

  10 ml = 1 cl and 100 cl (or 1000 ml) = 1 l

If money was really metric, then

  1 penny would be a 'centipound',

  1 'grand' would be a 'kilopound'!

Sometimes people talk about large amounts of money in 'k' e.g., £24 k is short for £24 000.

### Metric units and you

Most people are between 1.4 m and 1.8 m tall – that's the same as 140 cm and 180 cm.

### Activity

How tall are you?

Are you greater or less than 160 cm (that's the same as 5 feet 3 inches)?

For every inch above or below, add or subtract 2.5 cm, e.g.,

5 feet 6 inches = 160+7.5 = 167.5 cm (1.675 m)

4 feet 11 inches = 160−10 = 150 cm (1.50 m)

160 cm is the same as 1600 mm, or 1.6 m.

Write down your height in three ways – in metres, in centimetres and in millimetres. Check it by asking someone to measure you – then you practise by measuring them.

### Activity

How many litres of liquid do you drink in a day?

A cup holds about 150 ml (or 15 cl), a large mug holds about 250 ml (or 25 cl or 1/4 litre), and a pint is just under 600 ml – a little over a half a litre.

Measure the amounts your cups or mugs can hold – use a measuring jug marked in ml.

### Key point to remember

Families of metric measurements are based on multiplying or dividing by 10, 100, 1000, etc. There are common prefixes in each family, such as centi- meaning one hundredth, milli- meaning one thousandth, and kilo- meaning a thousand.

### *Putting it into practice*

- *Practise measuring objects or amounts with as many different scales as you can.*
- *Then ask someone else to make the same measurements; make sure you sort out any disagreements!*

# Topic 1 – Measuring

## Time and temperature

**AN 9**

Foundation/Intermediate/Advanced
Element **1.1, 2.1, 3.1**
Performance criteria **1, 2, 3, 4, 5, 6**
Range **Techniques** (Number; Shape, space and measures);
**Levels of accuracy**

## Time

Here are some reminders about hours, minutes and seconds.

Most times are written in figures only – like these:

10:45 a.m. (a.m. means 'before 12 midday')

3:30 p.m. (p.m. means 'after midday')

In the '24-hour clock', 1 p.m. becomes 1300, 2 p.m. becomes 1400, and so on to 12 midnight, which becomes 2400.

So 1527 means '15 hours and 27 minutes after midnight' using the 24-hour clock. This is the same as 3:27 p.m.

0850 is the same as 8:50 a.m.

Times can look just like ordinary numbers. So be careful – especially when you are using a calculator!

The hours and minutes can have a colon : between them, or a dot . or a space.

With the 24-hour clock, the hours and minutes may have nothing to separate them – you use 0s to fill up empty spaces, for instance,

0504 means 4 minutes past 5 a.m.

0540 means 40 minutes past 5 a.m.

Remember that there are 60 minutes in an hour, not 100, so

4:30 (4 h 30 min) becomes 4.5 h on your calculator because 30 min is 0.5 hours.

5:15 (5 h 15 min) becomes 5.25 h on your calculator, because 15 min = 0.25 or 1/4 hour.

4:25 (4 h 25 min) becomes 4.41666 or 4.42 hours – you divide the 25 by 60 to change from minutes to hours.

4.3 hours on your calculator means 4 hours 18 minutes – you multiply the 0.3 by 60 to change from hours to minutes.

You often need to use times in hours only for working out pay for a day's work.

### Activity

1 For your new job, you have to walk to the bus stop from home (15 minutes), wait for the bus (you are not sure of the times, but they come every 12 minutes), travel for about 40 minutes on the bus, then have another walk of 5 minutes.

You have to be at work by 8:45 a.m. When should you leave home by?

2 Record these work times in hours only:

- 8.45 to 12.45 p.m. and 1.30 p.m. to 5.15 p.m.
- 0800 to 1600 with ¾ hour lunch break
- 9.15 a.m. to 12.15 p.m. and 12.45 p.m. to 4.35 p.m.

∎∎

1 You need to allow

15 + 12 + 40 + 5 = 72 min = 1 h 12 min, so you need to leave home no later than 7:33 a.m.

2
- 4 + 3¾ = 7¾ h, = 7.75 h;
- 7.25 h;
- 6 h 50 min = 6.83 h
  (50 ÷ 60 = 0.833) ∎∎

## Temperature

Most temperatures nowadays are in 'degrees Celsius' (°C).

Room temperature is about 20 °C,

Freezing (water) is at 0 °C.

Body temperature is normally 36.9 °C, just below 37 °C, and is very rarely more than 2 °C above or below this.

Sometimes temperatures are given in 'degrees Fahrenheit' (°F).

68 °F = 20 °C

32 °F = 0 °C

98.4 °F = 36.9 °F

### Activity

1 These are all supposed to be spring or summer temperatures in this county. Which look wrongly recorded?

23 °C, 75 °F, 79 °C, 16 °C, 32 °C, 8 °C, 85 °F.

2 These are the temperatures of an elderly patient in hospital, noted each morning for a week. Which temperatures look wrongly recorded? All temperatures are in °C.

Mo. 36.9 °, Tu. 37.2 °,
We. 36.7 °, Th. 37.1 °,
Fr. 37.8 °, Sa. 38.6 °,
Su. 39.6 °.

∎∎

1 79 °C
2 Su. 39.6°. ∎∎

### Key point to remember

Remember when working with time that there are 60 minutes in an hour, not 100 so 4.50 p.m. means nearly 5 o'clock not half past four.

### Putting it into practice

*Practise working out how long different activities take by subtracting the start times from the finish times and checking that this gives the correct times for the activities.*

# Topic 1 – Measuring

## Measurement with imperial units

**AN 10**

Foundation/Intermediate/Advanced
Element **1.1, 2.1, 3.1**
Performance criteria **1, 2, 3, 4, 5, 6**
Range **Techniques** (Number; Shape, space and measures); **Units; Levels of accuracy**

### Length

12 inches (in.) = 1 foot (ft.)

3 ft. or 36 in. = 1 yard (yd.)

5280 ft. or 1760 yds. = 1 mile.

So 4¾ ft. = 4 ft. 9 in., because ¾ of 12 is 9

¼ mile = 440 yds., because ¼ of 1760 is 440.

Often the same distance can be written in different ways.

#### Activity

1. 18 inches is the same as 1½ ft. or 1 ft. 6 in.
   Change these inch measurements into feet only, and feet and inches.
   24 in., 54 in., 75 in.
2. Change these into inches only.
   2 ft. 6 in., 3 ft. 3 in., 7 ft. 6 in., 5½ ft.

■

1. 2 ft., 4 ft. 6 in. or 4½ ft., 6 ft. 3 in. or 6¼ ft.
2. 30 in., 39 in., 90 in., 66 in. ■

As you collect and record data, it's also useful to be able to change between imperial and metric systems.

Rough conversions are often enough. You can use the ≈ sign, which means 'roughly equal to'. Here are some examples.

    1 in. ≈ 25 mm or 2.5 cm or 2½ cm
    1 ft. ≈ 30 cm
    1 mile ≈ 1600 m.

In the other direction,

    10 cm ≈ 4 in.
    1 m ≈ 3 ft. 3 in. or 39 in.
    1 km ≈ 1100 yds. or ⅝ mile.

#### Activity

1. You need timber strips 1.5 in. by 3 in.

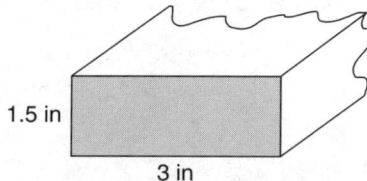

The shop sells strips with these measurements: 25 by 50 mm, 38 by 60 mm, 38 by 75 mm and 50 by 75 mm.
Which size is best for you?

Two doors measure 2 m by 750 mm.

Roughly what are these measurements in feet and inches?

■

1. ½ in. is about 12.5 mm (½ of 25 mm), so the best size for you is 38 by 75 mm.
2. 6½ ft. (or 6 ft. 6 in.) by 2½ ft. (or 2 ft. 6 in.) ■

### Volume or capacity

20 fluid ounces (fl. oz.) = 1 pint (pt.)

8 pt. = 1 gallon (gal.)

### Weight

16 ounces (oz.) = 1 pound (lb.)

14 lb. = 1 stone

Nearly all measurements of weight or capacity are in metric units, but you may come across imperial units in cooking and when working with older people.

Again rough conversions can be useful.

    1 pt. ≈ 600 ml     1 oz. ≈ 30 g     1 lb. ≈ 450 g

in the other direction

    1 l ≈ 1¾ pt.       500 g is a little more than 1 lb.
    1 kg ≈ 2.2 lb.     10 l ≈ 2.2 gal.

#### Key point to remember

Remember that imperial measurements often use scales marked in halves, quarters and eighths rather than in tenths.

#### *Putting it into practice*

- *Practise reading scales and making measurements in a variety of situations.*
- *Always check any measurements. Do they make sense? Have you written them down correctly?*

# Topic 2 – Estimating and checking

## Allowing for waste

**AN 13**

Foundation/Intermediate/Advanced
Element **1.1, 2.1, 3.1**
Performance criteria **1, 2, 3, 4**
Range **Techniques** (Number); **Levels of accuracy**

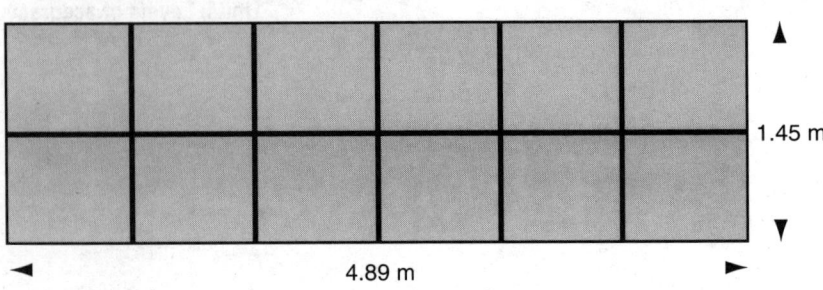

1.45 m

4.89 m

### Activity

The thick lines show ribbons dividing the space on a display board.

Without any detailed calculations, say which of these reels of ribbon would be the best to buy.

- 15 m costing £1.89
- 30 m costing £3.20
- 50 m costing £4.80
- 100 m costing £9.00

■■ The length is a little less than 5 m and the height than 1.5 m so you need about 15 m (3 lengths) + 10.5 m (7 heights) so the 30 m size would be the best. It allows for a little wastage and is cheaper than two 15 m reels. ■■

In this activity, you were rounding in your head to make the estimate. Calculating more accurately would have been a waste of time. The important thing is to have enough ribbon to do the job – and that includes making an allowance for some wastage. So you just have to be 'a bit over' on all measurements.

### Activity

1. Estimate the time it will take to get home this evening.
2. Give estimated longest and shortest times for the journey, that is, times at which you would be very surprised if your journey time fell outside them.

■■
1. Your estimate was based on past experience but was it based on the hope of getting home quickly, rather than your actual experience?
2. This may be a better way of making estimates giving upper and lower limits. For instance, my journey time is never less than 30 minutes, but it can be as much as 55 minutes, leading to a realistic estimate of between 40 and 45 minutes. ■■

### Activity

1. Your friend is planning a two-week holiday. She plans to pay for transport, bed and breakfast in advance, but still has to work out how much extra money she will need.

   How should she go about this?

2. Try it yourself for a package holiday of your choice.

■■
1. One way is to list what she thinks she might spend per day – lunch, evening meal, drinks, extras, then multiply by 14 to estimate what she needs for two weeks. Again, it may be a good idea to make two estimates for a day's expenses – a low one and a high one, and budget for something in between.
■■

In this case you are scaling up a day's expenses to give an estimated total for two weeks.

### Key point to remember

Rounding and scaling up are useful techniques when making estimates.

### Putting it into practice

You can use scaling up in many situations. Here are three:

- working out estimated profits for a month, starting from a week's figures
- estimating how many weeks' supply of coal you have for an open fire
- estimating likely savings on changes in lifestyle (e.g., reducing smoking and drinking each day). It is surprising how much you can save over a year.
- Find some ways in which you can make daily savings, then work out how much you might save over a year.

# Topic 2 – Estimating and checking

**AN 14**

Foundation/Intermediate/Advanced
Element **1.1,2.1,3.1**
Performance criteria **1,2,3,4,5,6,7**
Range **Techniques** (Number);
**Levels of accuracy**

## Checking

You can use estimating methods to help with checking.

You can also use them when you are gathering and recording data.

### Activity

The figures show the number of people entering a leisure centre each day, and the number of people paying at the till in the leisure centre snack bar.

| No. entering centre | No. paying at snack bar |
|---|---|
| 756 | 506 |
| 833 | 590 |
| 603 | 471 |
| 353 | 389 |
| 759 | 458 |
| 850 | 583 |
| 723 | 509 |

You also know that the weekly total of people entering is about 5000.

Look at the figures. Which do you think might have been recorded wrongly?

■ *Adding the entry figures gives 4877 – a bit below 5000 so it looks as though some of the entry figures should be higher.*

*Comparing the till and entry figures, shows that mostly the till figures are about 60 – 80% of the entry figures.*

$506 \div 756 = 0.67$     $590 \div 833 = 0.71$
$471 \div 603 = 0.78$     $389 \div 353 = 1.10*$
$458 \div 759 = 0.6$      $583 \div 850 = 0.69$
$509 \div 723 = 0.70$

*The result marked * looks odd.*

*If the 353 had been wrongly recorded and should be 533, then the total number of visitors would be 5057 and the till ÷ entry figure would be 0.73 – much more likely.*

*Of course there may not have been a mistake but that seems a likely error.* ■

When you are recording measurements or other data, it is a good idea to estimate what each reading will be before you record it.

As you record a reading, watch out for the obvious mistakes:

- figures in the wrong order:
  e.g., 4798 instead of 4978
- decimal points wrong:
  e.g., 48.84 m instead of 4.884 m
- mistakes in recording non-decimal numbers:
  e.g., 5 hours shared equally among four groups gives
  $5 \div 4 = 1.25$ hours
  
  misread as 1 hour 25 minutes instead of 1 hour 15 minutes (60 min $\times$ 0.25 = 15)
- figures in the wrong column or row
- figures with the wrong units:
  e.g., 1/2 litre of milk instead of 1/2 pint of milk

And do not rely on your memory!

**Always write it down!**

### Key points to remember

It is always worth checking readings.
- Do they look right?
- Do they fit with your estimates?

### Putting it into practice

*Get into the habit of making estimates for results of calculations whenever you can and watching out for mistakes when other people carry out calculations.*

# Topic 2 – Estimating and checking

**AN 16**

Foundation/Intermediate/Advanced
Element **1.1, 2.1, 3.1**
Performance criteria **2, 3, 4, 5, 6, 7**
Range **Techniques** (Number);
**Levels of accuracy; Units**

## Rough estimates

Rough estimates often give you enough data to start a task. Even very rough estimates – quick and easy to do in your head can be very useful.

Here are some examples.

- You are nearing the supermarket checkout and want to check how much your trolley load will cost.

  The items and their prices are:

  | Washing powder | 1.73 |
  |---|---|
  | Meat | 3.31 |
  | Sprouts | 0.68 |
  | Eggs | 0.78 |
  | Milk | 0.92 |
  | Cereal | 1.23 |
  | Coffee | 1.92 |
  | Tea | 0.46 |
  | Bread | 0.48 |
  | Low-fat spread | 0.64 |

You could add up all the exact costs as you near the queue. In fact it is £12.15.

But some people do not carry calculators with them or like to be seen adding up in public!

Try rounding each amount to the nearest pound – then it is easy and quick to add up the whole pounds in your head:

£2 + 3 + 1 + 1 + 1 + 1 + 2 + 0 + 0 + 1 = £12

It is surprising how close you are to the exact figure.

It comes to £12.00 again. Working to the nearest 50p will often be more accurate, but you have to decide whether it is worth the complication.

You can use the same rounding for estimating with multiplying of other items.

### Activity

1. Try rounding to whole pounds on the next few checkout till receipts you have. Get a feel for how close your estimates are to the exact amounts on the receipt.

2. You could have rounded to the nearest 50p, so £1.73 ≈ 1.50, £3.31 ≈ 3.50 etc. Use this method to estimate the total cost of the items above.

### Activity

You are checking the estimates for wood rafters for re-roofing a garage.

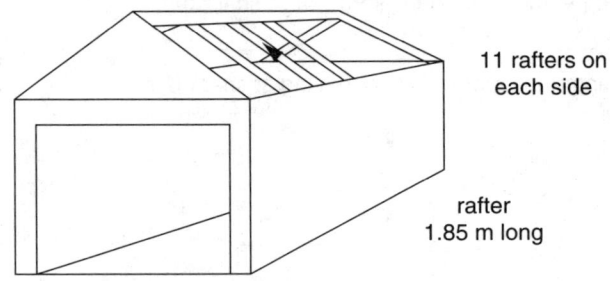

11 rafters on each side

rafter 1.85 m long

One builder says 60 metres of timber is needed for the rafters. Check if this is reasonable.

■■ *Length of timber needed for rafters*

$\approx 2\,m \times 11 \times 2 = 44\,m$

*There is no need to be more exact. You know the builder's estimate is too high.* ■■

### Activity

Each of the cases in a stack of 27 cases holds 48 cans of beans. You have been told that there are enough cans in the stack to last for 3 months (13 weeks) at the present rate of sales of 250 cans a week.

Check to see if this is reasonable.

■■ *48 is about 50, so the 27 cases hold approximately $27 \times 100 \div 2 = 1350$ cans.*

*That is enough for 5 and a bit weeks ($5 \times 250 = 1250$) so the 3 months is obviously wrong.* ■■

### Key point to remember

Rough estimates involve rounding to simpler numbers. Use them to help you spot obvious errors.

### Putting it into practice

*Take any chance you can to practise making estimates, especially those where you can check how close you are to the exact amounts.*

# Topic 3 – Data sources

## Talking to people

**AN 20**

Foundation/Intermediate/
Advanced
Element **1.1,2.1,3.1**
Performance criteria **1,2**
Range **Techniques**
(Handling data)

## What is data?

Data is another word for pieces of information – measurements, results from surveys, any number and other facts which you need to start a task.

Data helps people decide what to do, what way to cook, what car to buy, what holiday to go on.

## Sources of data

There are many sources of data. Think to yourself of the many different ways in which you collect data for your day-to-day life.

## Talking to people

People provide data directly, by observing and talking to each other and sharing information.

For example, in a health centre for the elderly, a support group wants to raise money for some new equipment. They need to find out what equipment would be best to buy.

### Activity

If you were one of the support group whom would you talk to about this problem? What information would be worth having?

■■ *The people you talk to could include*

- *the nursing and medical staff (what would help them provide better care?)*
- *some of the patients (what would make life in hospital better for them?)*
- *those involved with raising the money (what items would appeal to the public?).* ■■

### Points to watch for

- Take care that the people you talk to represent fairly all those concerned with the problem. It is easy to talk just to people you think will agree with you, then you can get a distorted or biased view of what people as a whole think.

  For instance, in the activity, suppose you talked to a group of the fund-raisers only and they said

  'We would like to buy TV sets for all the patients.'

  The patients might well think differently; there might not even be room for the sets.

- Talk to enough people to get a clear picture of people's views. Talking to a selection of people will often be enough, but generally the more people you can talk to, the better your picture will be.

- Try to ask questions which do not lead people to give you the answer you want to hear (these are called 'leading questions').

Sometimes, a person dealing with a problem is sure of having found the best solution. Questions are asked which serve only to support that solution; other, possibly better, solutions are ignored.

For instance, in the activity, suppose you had asked people

'Do you think it would be good to collect money for a new snack bar?'

Everyone might say 'yes', but that does not mean that improving the snack bar is the best use of the money. It is just that you did not give people

### Key points to remember

- Talking to people is a good source of data to support decisions about a future project.
- Take care to avoid bias by
  - asking people who fairly represent all the people who could be concerned with the project;
  - making sure you ask enough people;
  - asking questions which give people the chance to say what they think.

### *Putting it into practice*

*Make up questions to ask about a subject in two ways, one that is biased and one that is not.*

# Topic 3 – Data sources

**AN 21**

Foundation/Intermediate/
Advanced
Element **1.1, 2.1, 3.1**
Performance criteria **1, 2**
Range **Techniques**
(Handling data)

## Variety of sources

### Data from measurements

Measurements are data. Many practical tasks start with taking measurements and recording them.

You will find more about this on other resource sheets.

You may not need to take exact measurements. Often estimates will be good enough. Again there is more about estimates on other resource sheets.

### Data from records

You may need data for a task. But often the data is already recorded; your first job is to extract the data you require from those records.

For example, you need sales records for different lines in a shop to decide how much of each line to re-order. The same records could help you decide what new lines to try out.

### Computer-based records

Nowadays you can obtain much data directly from computers – bank account details from cash machines, reference book information on library book databases are just two examples.

> **Activity**
>
> Give two other examples of data that you can obtain directly from a computer.

### Data from printed material

Books, newspapers and magazines provide plenty of data – recipes, second-hand car prices, holiday offers. The data can be in lists, tables, charts or just in sentences of text.

> Be careful! Just because information is printed, it doesn't mean that it is accurate.

> **Activity**
>
> Give two examples of printed data which could well be inaccurate or false.

■■ *Advertisements are one source. Others include newspaper reports and sales leaflets.* ■■

### Data from rules or formulas

Here are some examples of rules which provide data.

- Rafters to be spaced at a maximum of 350 mm centres.
- A minimum of three care assistants is required for the project, and also there should be no more than six patients for each care assistant.

> **Activity**
>
> 1. Use the rule above to work out how many care assistants would be required for twenty patients.
> 2. How many care assistants would be required for eight patients?

■■ *1  Four assistants.   2  Three assistants.* ■■

Rules can sometimes be written as word formulas like this. Here is one to do with catering.

Total cost in pounds = fixed costs + (cost of food per person × number of people)

which can be shortened to

$$T = F + (c \times n)$$

For instance, if the fixed costs are £300, and food costing £3.50 is served to 700 people, then

Total cost in pounds = 300 + (3.50 × 700)
= 300 + 2450
= 2750

> **Activity**
>
> Find the total cost if only 400 people are served.

■■ *Cost = 300 + 1400 = £1700* ■■

> **Key points to remember**
>
> You can obtain data from:
> - measurements
> - computer-based (and other) records
> - printed materials
> - rules or formulae

> **Putting it into practice**
>
> Write down some activities in your vocational area. What would be good sources of data for each of them?

# Topic 3 – Data sources

## Experiments and competition

**AN 22**

Foundation/Intermediate/
Advanced
Element **1.1,2.1,3.1**
Performance criteria **1,2**
Range **Techniques**
(Handling data)

## Experiments

In some situations experiments can give you enough data to help you decide what to do.

For example, suppose you are thinking of selling a new flavour of ice cream, or providing a new service to people. Your best course of action may be to experiment – try out your idea and see how it goes.

Then, as the new service continues you can change it to fit with what people want.

## Problems with experiments

Problems come when it is not practical to carry out experiments. The experiments may be too big and expensive.

Or they may be self-defeating. For instance, you decide to improve the service you provide through your business by buying new equipment.

To do this you need to borrow money.

To repay the loan, you have to put up your charges.

But many of your customers are not prepared to pay the increased charges. You then find out that they would rather have paid less and would have been happy with the old service.

By now it is too late. You still have to repay the loan and you have fewer customers as well. You are in a much worse position than you were originally.

Looking back, you realise that you should have tried to find out more about people's views before borrowing the money.

This is where other sources of data, such as simply talking to people or carrying out surveys, can help.

## Competition

Find out what other businesses or services are provided in your neighbourhood.

Your own enterprise stands a much better chance of success if it provides

- cheaper or better service than others
- services not already available
- services more in tune with what is wanted in the area.

So a first step is to find out what you can about these other businesses or services – your competitors.

### Activity

Suppose you are one of a group planning to extend a leisure centre.

**1** What usefully could your group find out from other leisure centres in the area?

**2** You are thinking of doing some gardening as a part-time job. What should you find out about the people you may be competing against for work?

**1** Find out what is popular elsewhere – in particular what popular facilities other centres provide which you might copy or improve on.

Find out what the charges are and how well booked the facilities are.

Find out how far people are travelling from for these facilities. From what distance could your centre attract people?

Some of this data you can find just by visiting the other centres – some may require some sort of survey. More details are on the next resource sheet.

**2** Find out how much other gardeners charge by looking in local papers or small ads in shops in the area.

Is there a service you can provide which others do not? Which fits more closely with what they may need?

Again, some of this data may require some sort of survey.

### Key points to remember

Experiments and looking at the competition can each provide very useful data.

### *Putting it into practice*

*Think of a new business enterprise you could start. How could experiments or looking at what others are doing help you in improving your business?*

# Topic 4 – Surveys

## Introducing surveys

**Foundation/Intermediate/Advanced**
Element **1.1, 2.1, 3.1**
Performance criteria **1, 2**
Range **Techniques**
(Handling data)

## The place of surveys

The main purpose of carrying out surveys is to provide information – information that will help you or others decide what to do, or avoid making expensive mistakes.

Here are three examples of situations where surveys could help you make better decisions:

- extending a leisure centre
- opening a shop
- planning a new restaurant or sandwich bar.

Often you can't be sure how successful new ventures like these will turn out to be.

For all these, the more data you have on

- what will be popular
- what people are prepared to pay
- how they would prefer the service to operate
- what the competition is, and so on,

the more likely your venture will be successful.

Surveys can assist by helping you predict answers to questions like these, estimate what is likely to happen or how people are likely to react.

## What happens in a survey

Stage 1 – Decide the general questions you want answered. It is very important to have these clear.

Stage 2 – Plan how you will carry out the survey. This can include

- deciding how you will select people to question
- deciding how you will question them
- deciding how you will keep a record of what they say.

Stage 3 – Work out exactly what questions you will ask. Again, this needs a lot of care, including trying out the questions beforehand.

Stage 4 – Carry out your survey.

Stage 5 – Note the results of the survey.

Stage 6 – Analyse the results and draw conclusions.

Stage 7 – Present the results and decide what action to take.

## Some types of survey

### Observation surveys

After planning your survey, you observe and note down what happens at a particular place or in a particular situation.

You don't always need to talk to people.

For instance, you may count the number of times something happens in a 5-minute interval.

### Face-to-face questionnaires

Devise a set of questions. You then put the questions to selected people and note down their replies.

Devise the questions so their meaning is clear to the people you ask and so that people will be happy to answer them truthfully. This is likely to need a lot of attempts and improvements.

### Postal questionnaires

As for the face-to-face questionnaire, except that the 'respondents' read your questions and then fill in their answers on the questionnaire sheet.

Again, devising the questions is likely to need a lot of attempts and improvements.

### Activity

Think of what you need to find out.

Would a survey be a good way to find it out?

If so, what sort of survey would be good to use?

These are big questions – not to be rushed.

Begin to think of how you might go about it.

### Key point to remember

Surveys can provide very useful data, but they need careful planning.

### *Putting it into practice*

- *What information could you obtain only by carrying out a survey?*
- *What surveys which others have done could help you in your work?*

# Topic 4 – Surveys

## Planning a survey

**AN 25**

Foundation/Intermediate/Advanced
Element 1.1, 2.1, 3.1
Performance criteria 1, 2
Range **Techniques**
(Handling data)

It may help to work in a group for this resource sheet.

This sheet shows the start of a survey.

As you go through the sheet, think how you could use the ideas to answer questions in your vocational area.

## What do you want to find out?

There is little point in carrying out a survey just for the sake of it.

Most people carry out surveys to help them find out something, in order to

- make better decisions
- estimate better what may happen in the future.

So you should start with a list of things you want to find out.

Ask yourself

- How best can I find out the things I need to know?
- Could I find them out just as well
  - by talking to a few people
  - by seeing what other people are already doing and copying them?

Often, combining two or three methods gives you the best information – together they give you a fuller picture than one method on its own.

### Activity

1. Make a list of the pieces of information you want to find out for a project in your vocational area.
2. Sort the pieces on your list according to the best methods you could use to find them out: asking a few people, looking at the competition, carrying out a survey, etc.
3. Look at the 'survey' pieces – put the other groups on one side for now.

## Vegetarian snacks

Here is what one group of students did.

They have noticed that quite a few people are vegetarians at their college, but there is not much vegetarian snack food available. They are thinking of making vegetarian snacks to sell at lunchtime.

Before going further, they need to find out

a what the possible demand is for vegetarian food;

b what sort of food would be best to sell;

c what people would be prepared to pay for it;

d what level of profit they could make;

e if they would be allowed to sell their snacks in the college.

### Activity

1. What would be good ways of finding out each of the items **a** to **e** above?

■ *Here are some reasonable answers – yours may be different depending on your own circumstances.*

- *asking a few people – if the college principal says no then that may be the end of the project*
- *looking at the competition – what does the college canteen sell already?*
- *carrying out a survey.* ■

### Whom to ask

They started by asking some of their friends about vegetarian food. Then they realised that many of their friends were vegetarians anyway, but they weren't sure about other people.

### Activity

Whom do you think the students should have asked?

The students' friends may not have been representative of everyone in the college. They needed to ask more people. The resource sheets on 'Samples and populations' and 'Sample sizes' give more detail about this.

### What to ask

The first question they asked their friends was 'Would you buy vegetarian food at a snack bar in college?'

They thought they would get 'yes' or 'no' as answers.

But they got lots of different replies. Here are some of them.

- It all depends on what food is for sale.
- It would have to be good value.
- I don't know – what is vegetarian food?

This showed them that they had not made their questions clear enough.

(There are two resource sheets about 'Asking clear questions'.)

### When to ask

Most of their friends stayed in college at lunchtime so they thought they would ask people they saw at lunchtime.

But then they thought, maybe there are people who go out of college at lunchtime but who might stay if vegetarian food was available.

# Topic 4 – Surveys

## Planning a survey (continued)

### How to ask

Some of their friends said 'I haven't time to wait around and answer all your questions.'

It took the group a whole lunchtime to ask ten people. The group saw that their survey could take weeks to complete.

Then they thought maybe there were other ways of finding out what they wanted to know.

#### Activity

Can you think of any other ways the group could have got the information they needed?

▮▮ *They could have prepared a written questionnaire - or perhaps observed what type of food people chose from the main canteen. You will find more details on the resource sheet 'Survey types'.* ▮▮

#### Key points to remember

Surveys are carried out to find something out, so before undertaking a survey

- be sure you know what you want to find out
- check that a survey is the best way of finding it out.

Remember the essential question

- What am I trying to find out?

Then the four other questions

- Whom shall I ask?
- What shall I ask?
- When shall I ask?
- How shall I ask?

#### *Putting it into practice*

*Think of your own work. What would be best found out by using a survey?*

*When planning your survey, allow time for a trial run with some of your friends or colleagues to correct any mistakes or bad design features.*

# Topic 4 – Surveys

## Sample sizes

**AN 26**

Foundation/Intermediate/Advanced
Element **2.1,3.1**
Performance criteria **1,2,6,7**
Range **Techniques** (Handling data); **Levels of accuracy**

For some simple surveys and when the results are very clear, a sample size as small as 10 people may be enough.

For instance, if you wanted to test if people could tell the difference between Original Coke and Diet Coke, and you found that 9 out of the 10 people could tell the difference, you could be pretty sure that the majority of people in the population could also tell the difference.

The result is so clear, that even a small sample is enough.

But suppose you found that only 7 out of the 10 could tell the difference. Does this still mean that most people in the population could tell the difference?

It is quite possible that you picked a sample with 7 successful tasters out of 10 from a population where in fact most people could not tell the difference. This could happen as often as about 1 out of every 6 times you pick a sample.

This shows that your sample is too small. It does not fairly represent the population.

But suppose you chose a sample size of 50 people.

In fact, it would be extremely unlikely that you could pick a sample with 35 people out of the 50 (= 7 out of 10) who could tell the difference from the same population as before. This could only happen about 1 out of every 500 times you pick a sample.

So the sample size of 50 is much safer.

The following activity shows how you can check on these results.

### Key points to remember

- Choose the largest sample size you have time to deal with. Fifty is much better than 10, but 200 is better than 50.
- The more questions you ask the longer it will take to analyse the results, so do not be too ambitious!

### *Putting it into practice*

*Plan how you would select a representative sample of 100 of the people who use a local health centre. Explain how you would try to make the sample truly representative of the users of the centre.*

### Activity

1. Find ten small buttons the same as each other. Colour five of them with a felt tip. Put them in a matchbox and shake it.

   Take out a button and write C if it is coloured, N if it is not. Repeat ten times altogether. This 'simulates' the sample of 10.

2. Repeat for another ten times. Repeat again. It will not be long before you have a sample with at least 7 Cs out of 10.

## Levels of accuracy

In general, the larger the sample size, the more closely you can depend on it mirroring the population.

But the larger the sample size, the longer the survey will take to conduct, and the longer it will take you to analyse the results.

# Topic 4 – Surveys

## Asking clear questions 1

**AN 27**

Foundation/Intermediate/
Advanced
Element **1.1, 2.1, 3.1**
Performance criteria **1, 2, 6**
Range **Techniques** (Handling data); **Levels of accuracy**

This sheet is about a group of students who are planning a survey to do with setting up a vegetarian snack bar in college.

You will find more details of the group's idea on the resource sheet 'Planning a Survey'.

The students originally thought of giving everyone in the college a questionnaire form to fill in but decided against it. Instead they decided to work with a sample size of 100 and to carry out a face-to-face questionnaire.

### Activity

Give some reasons against their original idea.

▌▌ *Here are three reasons (you may have thought of others as well).*

- *The forms would have to be very short or take a very long time to analyse.*
- *People might not fill them in sensibly.*
- *Some people might fill in more than one form.* ▌▌

### Clear questions

There are some important points to remember when you are designing questions for your survey.

### Good questions

- will be clear to the person you are asking
- will have the same meaning for the person you are asking as for you
- will help you to reach decisions
- will lead to replies that are easy to analyse.

For example,

*'When did you last have some vegetarian food?'*

This may look clear and if people answered as you hoped it might give you an idea of how often people eat vegetarian food.

But just think of what could happen ...

- everyone has their own idea of what vegetarian food is; their ideas may not be what you have in mind
- people will concentrate on how long ago (last weekend last March ...)

You can probably think of other snags with this question.

Alternatively, you could ask,

*'Would you buy vegetarian samozas or low-fat flapjacks?'*

But people might give different answers such as

- Yes, if I was on holiday in Greece.
- Quite often.
- I would prefer the flapjacks.
- It depends on the prices.
- Both, if I was really hungry.

Compare these answers with the conditions for clear questions above and you can see the problems!

### Key point to remember

Clear questions which give you the information you need are not easy to devise, but they are essential if your survey is not going to be a waste of time and effort.

### Putting it into practice

*Take time to make sure your questions are clear. This may mean several rewrites of the questions to get them right.*

*Try out your questions on a small sample of people to help in the rewriting.*

# Topic 4 – Surveys

## Asking clear questions 2

**AN 28**

Foundation/Intermediate/Advanced
Element **2.1,3.1**
Performance criteria **1,2,6**
Range **Techniques** (Handling data); **Levels of accuracy**

This sheet continues from 'Asking clear questions 1'.
Think again of the information the students wanted:
- what the possible demand is for vegetarian food
- what sort of food would be best to sell
- what people would be prepared to pay for it
- what level of profit they could expect to make.

Another approach would be to start with the food that could be provided with possible prices.

> Say which of these food snacks you would buy if it was available.
> - Vegetarian samoza 65p
> - Flapjack 40p

But there are problems here too. It is not clear whether someone has to choose between them, or if they are choosing them because they like the food and think it is good value as well.

And why put in the 'if it was available'. You would not be asking if it was not available!

You have several questions all mixed together here, so the answers will be mixed as well.

### Activity

Here is another version of the question.
> Here is a list of possible food snacks.
> Tick any of the items in the list that you would buy.
> Circle a reasonable price for each item you ticked
> Vegetarian samoza    30p   40p   50p   60p
> Low-fat flapjack     30p   40p   50p   60p
> How could this question be improved?

▌▌ *It is difficult to say how you could improve the question without trying it out.*

*The clear choices of price will give you replies that are easy to analyse but it might be better to ask for the question answerer, the 'respondent', to give a reasonable price rather than pick one.*

*It depends on how people understand the word 'reasonable'. Reasonable for whom? Maybe you could say instead: For each item say what a fair price would be.* ▌▌

By now it is becoming clear that question writing is not easy!

## A check-list for question writing

Here are some points to have in mind
- Make sure people understand what the subject of the survey is.
- It is usually better to give people options to choose between, rather than questions they are free to answer as they wish.
- Avoid questions that have 'or nots' in them.

For instance, *'Would you like vegetarian food only, or not?'*
Would 'yes' mean yes to both parts?

- If you give people multiple choices (such as the prices above), make sure that you allow for all possible answers.
- If you are reading the questions to respondents, write out the longer questions on a card for them to read, so they don't have too much to keep in their memories.
- Use as few words as possible.
- Test your questions out on a sample of people; if they don't answer them as you expect, it is the questions' fault!
- Beware of biased or leading questions.

For instance, the question *'Do you think it would be a good idea to have a vegetarian snack bar?'*

This couples 'good' with 'vegetarian'. It may lead some people to want to agree that 'vegetarian' ought to be 'good'.

### Key point to remember

Clear questions are vital!

### Putting it into practice

*Write some questions for your survey, try them out and keep revising them till they work.*

# Topic 4 – Surveys

## Survey types

**AN 29**

Foundation/Intermediate/
Advanced
Element **1.1,2.1,3.1**
Performance criteria **1,2**
Range **Techniques**
(Handling data)

Use this sheet to help you decide the best way to collect the data you need. You need to keep in mind how many people can help with your survey, how much time you have, how large your sample will be, what sort of information you need.

Then choose the easiest, simplest option.

## Observation surveys

In an observation survey you repeatedly observe what happens at a location, and keep a regular record. For example, you keep a note of the length of time individuals have to wait for treatment in a health centre or the type of enquiry being made at an information point.

### Point to watch

- Make sure you carry out exactly the same observation each time you make it, so that you can compare results easily.

*Advantages include*

- no need to talk to people
- can be done without disturbing people
- gives data from many people.

*Disadvantages include*

- not possible to find people's opinions, reasons or preferences.

## Face-to-face questionnaires

In a face-to-face survey, you devise a set of questions and read these to individuals in a sample. You make a note of the answers from each person.

### Points to watch

- Questions can be read to individuals with as little extra explanation as possible, to avoid interviewers altering questions.
- Avoid questions which could embarrass, offend, or imply your own views – people may not tell the truth or may just tell you what they think you want to hear.

*Advantages include*

- People's opinions, reasons or preferences can be found out.

*Disadvantages include*

- People may rather answer questions anonymously without the interviewer knowing what they say.
- This can be very time consuming.

## Written questionnaires

As for face-to-face surveys, except that a list of written questions is given to each person in the sample, and they answer the questions on their own.

### Point to watch

- Questions have to be completely clear.

*Advantages include*

- samples can be large
- people can be anonymous.

*Disadvantages include*

- misunderstandings or frivolous (untrue) replies can occur.

## Experiments

As above, except that you change what normally happens, and observe the effects of the change. For example, you change the charges for a sports facility for an experimental period and note the changes in numbers of users, or you try selling a new product for an experimental period and note what happens.

*Advantage*

- You can observe the effects of changing one factor at a time.

### Activity

What type of survey would be suitable in these situations?

1. To find out what a mail order company's customers thought of its services.
2. To find out how long people spent queuing in a post office.
3. To find out what people thought about a change in the law.
4. To find out whether children would buy a new brand of cola.

■ *It would be best to do the first survey in a written questionnaire that could be posted to customers. The queue at the post office could be investigated in an observation. People's views about a change in the law could be surveyd in face-to-face interviews or a written questionnaire. Children's reactions to the cola could be judged in an experiment.* ■

### Key point to remember

Plan your data collecting very carefully, then test your idea with a small sample, before you start on the survey itself.

### *Putting it into practice*

Try different methods of collecting data for a project, to help decide on the best method.

# Topic 4 – Surveys

## Tally tables

**AN 30**

Foundation/Intermediate/
Advanced
Element **1.1,2.1,3.1**
Performance criteria **2,3,4**
Range **Techniques** (Handling data); **Levels of accuracy**

This sheet shows an example of recording data on a recording sheet.

## Lunch orders

In a day centre for the elderly, people fill in cards with their choices for the lunch menu, so that the correct meals can be ordered.

Here is one of the cards.

| | |
|---|---|
| Soup | – |
| Fruit cocktail | ✓ |
| | |
| Ham Salad | – |
| Shepherd's pie | ✓ |
| Roast beef | – |
| Vegetarian Pizza | – |
| | |
| Ice cream | – |
| Fruit salad | – |
| Rhubarb tart | ✓ |

There are 20 people wanting lunch.

Going through the 20 cards gives these requests:

First course
F F S S F S S S F F S F S F S S

Main course
S S R V S H H V R R S R H V H V R

Sweet
R F R R I I R F F R I R R F F

You can record these more clearly on a tally table, like this.

*First course*

| Soup | ⊢⊢⊢⊢ \| \| \| \| | 9 |
|---|---|---|
| Fruit cocktail | ⊢⊢⊢⊢ \| \| | 7 |
| | Total | 16 |

The marks | | are called tally marks.

Note how you block the tally marks in 5s – the line counts for the fifth result.

### Activity

Make tally tables for the other courses.

*Main Course*

| Ham salad | \| \| \| \| | 4 |
|---|---|---|
| Shepherd's pie | \| \| \| \| | 4 |
| Roast Beef | ⊢⊢⊢⊢ | 5 |
| Veg. pizza | \| \| \| \| | 4 |
| | Total | 17 |

*Sweet*

| Ice cream | \| \| \| | 3 |
|---|---|---|
| Fruit salad | ⊢⊢⊢⊢ | 5 |
| Rhubarb tart | ⊢⊢⊢⊢ \| \| | 7 |
| | Total | 15 |

### Key points to remember

- Make sure you know what tally means and how to block in 5s.
- Record data carefully.
- Make sure you fill in the recording sheet in the correct way.
- Check whenever you can.

### Putting it into practice

- *Plan and carry out an observation survey which provides data for a tally table.*
- *Devise some questions for the vegetarian food survey on the previous sheets. Carry out the survey among your colleagues and record the data on tally tables.*
- *Design a sheet to record data from a survey for use in your vocational area.*

## Topic 4 – Surveys

### Recording sheets

**AN 31**

Foundation/Intermediate/Advanced
Element **1.1, 2.1, 3.1**
Performance criteria **2, 3, 4**
Range **Techniques** (Handling data); **Levels of accuracy**

## Using tables

A student was investigating people's choices at a leisure centre. She wanted to find what new sport could be provided at the leisure centre.

The first version of her question number 4 was

Question 4

What is your favourite sport?

She thought this was a good clear question, but people gave all sorts of answers, and she had to write down

- sitting in front of the telly
- what do you mean watching or playing?
- winding people up ...

She realised that the question was too 'open', so she changed it like this

4. Which one of these sports would you most like available for you at the leisure centre:

volleyball, short mat bowls, petanque, netball.

As each person answered she wrote down what they said

volleyball, bowls, volleyball, volleyball.

### Activity

How could you improve her way of recording the data?

■ She could record it just using single letters: v, b, v, v, ...

Or she could make up a tally table and record the data straight into it.

| | | |
|---|---|---|
| volleyball | \|\|\|\| | 4 |
| s. m bowls | \|\|\| | 3 |
| petanque | ⊬⊬⊬ \|\| | 7 |
| netball | \|\| | 2 |
| Total | | 16 ■ |

The table is better because she has a clear picture of the data straight away and it cuts out a stage in recording, so she saves time and avoids mistakes when copying data from one place to another.

Tables also allow you to check totals. Here she can see she recorded 16 replies, for instance.

You can use a two-way table for more complicated data – you just need to allow spaces (or 'cells') for all possible replies.

Question 7   How much would you pay for these snacks?

| | 30p | 40p | 50p | 60p | Not buy | Total |
|---|---|---|---|---|---|---|
| Vegetarian samosa | \|\| | ⊬⊬⊬ | \|\|\|\| | \| | | 12 |
| Low-fat flapjack | ⊬⊬⊬ | \|\|\|\| | \|\|\| | | | 12 |
| Fruit and nut yoghurt | ⊬⊬⊬ | \|\| | \|\| | \| | \|\| | 12 |

See how the 'Not buy' and 'Total' columns in this table allow you to check that you have not missed any results, and that people can say they do not like any of the foods.

It is always a good idea to make the table cells large enough so there is plenty of room to record results – so think ahead as to the space you will need. It may be better to have several copies of the recording tables and fill in, say, 10 results on each table.

You also need enough space so that if you make a mistake you can cross it out clearly or rub it out without risking rubbing out other entries at the same time. 'Liquid paper' is probably best avoided.

### Key points to remember

- Record results clearly and in an organised way.
- Tables can help in reducing space, time and error.
- Make the tables large enough to use comfortably.
- Make sure each table is labelled clearly, so you know the question it refers to.

### Putting it into practice

- *Experiment with different layouts for tables on recording sheets – test them by using them in small surveys and improving them.*
- *See how clear tables can also help you improve the questions in your survey.*

# Topic 5 – Levels of accuracy

## Rounding

**AN 34**
Foundation/Intermediate/Advanced
Element **1.1,2.1,3.1**
Performance criteria **2,3,4,6**
Range **Levels of accuracy**

When you gather and record data, you may be given instructions like

- 'round to the nearest 10'
- 'measure to the nearest centimetre'.

This sheet explains instructions like these.

### Nearest whole number

Rounding 'to the nearest whole number' means finding 'the closest whole number'.

Here are some examples.

- 72.8 is between 72 and 73, but closer to 73, so
- 72.8 ≈ 73 (to the nearest whole number)
  (≈ means 'approximately equals')
- 4.09 is between 4 and 5, but closer to 4, so
  4.09 ≈ 4 (to the nearest whole number)
- 4.90 is between 4 and 5 but closer to 5, so
  4.90 ≈ 5 (to the nearest whole number)

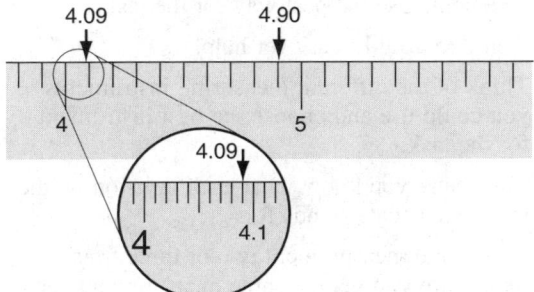

- 23.5 is exactly halfway between 23 and 24
  If in doubt, round upwards, so
  23.5 ≈ 24 (to the nearest whole number).

### Nearest 10, 25 . . .

Rounding to the nearest 10 means finding the closest whole number in steps of 10. So

- 23 ≈ 20 (closer to 20 than to 30)
- 48 ≈ 50 (closer to 50 than to 40)
- 1056 ≈ 1060
- 65 ≈ 70 (if in doubt, round up)
- 115.67 ≈ 120

Rounding to the nearest 25 means

- 23 ≈ 25 (closer to 25 than to 0)
- 48 ≈ 50 (closer to 50 than to 25)
- 1056 ≈ 1050 (closer to 1050 than to 1075)

### Putting it into practice

When making a measurement always ask yourself
- 'How accurate can I be?'
- 'How accurate do I need to be?'

65 ≈ 75
115.67 ≈ 125

### Nearest 0.1

Rounding to the nearest 0.1 means finding the nearest tenth. So

115.67 ≈ 115.7

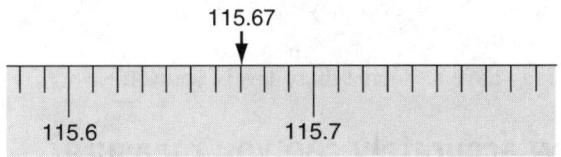

and 6.33333 ≈ 6.3
6.66666 ≈ 6.7
34.53333 ≈ 34.5

### Activity

Round the following numbers as required
- 234 to nearest 10
- 46.38 to nearest 10
- 46.38 to nearest 0.1
- 1235 to nearest 25
- £23.6666 to nearest penny
- 1.564 m to nearest cm
- 285 g to nearest 25 g

■ *234 ≈ 230 (to nearest 10)*
*46.38 ≈ 50 (to nearest 10)*
*46.38 ≈ 46.4 (to nearest 0.1)*
*1235 ≈ 1225 (to nearest 25)*
*£23.6666 ≈ £23.67 (to nearest penny)*
*1.564 m ≈ 1.56 m (to nearest cm)*
*285 g ≈ 275 g (to nearest 25 g).* ■

### Key points to remember

- Levels of accuracy can be described in a variety of ways – to the nearest whole number, to the nearest 25, etc.
- All measurement is approximate, so you always measure to a level of accuracy which you can be sure of.

# Topic 5 – Levels of accuracy

## How accurate?

**AN 35**

Foundation/Intermediate/Advanced
Element **1.1,2.1,3.1**
Performance criteria **2,3,4,5**
Range **Techniques** (Shape, space and measures); **Units; Levels of accuracy**

## How accurate do you need to be?

The measuring you do will be because you need those measurements for your task, not just for the sake of practising.

For example, if you are weighing out flour for making cakes, it will be good enough to weigh to the nearest 10 g or even to the nearest 25 g.

It would be a waste of time to weigh any more accurately. Whether you have 146 g or 148 g does not matter but it is important that you have about 150 g rather than 100 g.

If you are finding someone's temperature, you will probably want to measure to the nearest 0.1 °C – like 36.9° or 37.1°.

So the levels of accuracy depend on the task you are involved in.

You may have to decide these levels yourself.

## How accurately can you measure?

This depends on the instrument you are using to measure with.

For example, most people would find it hard to use a ruler to measure more accurately than to the nearest millimetre.

Even that may be harder that you think.

### Activity

Use a ruler to measure the maximum width of this circle – its diameter – in millimetres.

■■ *Its maximum width, its diameter, is 55 mm.* ■■

Try placing your ruler over the circle with the '0' mark on the edge.

Move your head to the right while still looking at the '0' mark.

See how the circle edge now lines up with the 1 mm mark on the ruler. So, just by moving your head, measurements can appear to change.

This shows how easy it is to measure less accurately than you think.

### Some hints

- Decide how accurately you have to measure.
- Think of different ways of making the measurement. Use the best way for the task.
- Don't be afraid to ask for help.
- Think of the different measuring instruments you could use and choose the best instrument for the task.
- Make sure you know what each division on the measuring scale stands for.
- Repeat the measurement two or three times; make sure you get the same measurement each time.
- Make sure you are measuring from 0, or that the mark on the scale goes back to 0 when you finish measuring.

### Key point to remember

Before you measure anything, decide how accurate you need to be. Use the hints on this sheet when you take your measurements.

### *Putting it into practice*

*When you are taking measurements as part of your project work, make a note of your decisions about accuracy – and how you went about taking your measurements.*

# AN – Tackle problems        Element 2

## Topic 1 – Using measurements

| | |
|---|---|
| AN39 | Perimeter |
| AN40 | Areas |
| AN41 | Working with area |
| AN42 | Working with small and large areas |
| AN43 | Finding areas |
| AN47 | Working with shapes |
| AN48 | Volumes of simple shapes |

## Topic 2 – Useful techniques

| | |
|---|---|
| AN54 | Using simple formulae |
| AN56 | Writing equations |
| AN57 | 'Less than' and 'greater than' |
| AN60 | Conversion rules |
| AN65 | Use a mean of a set of data |
| AN66 | Finding the mode |
| AN67 | Finding the median |

## Topic 3 – Number problems

| | |
|---|---|
| AN68 | Addition 1 |
| AN69 | Addition 2 |
| AN70 | Large numbers |
| AN71 | Negative numbers |
| AN72 | Subtraction |
| AN73 | Working with subtraction |
| AN74 | Addition, subtraction and multiplication |
| AN75 | Time – addition and subtraction |
| AN76 | Working with addition and subtraction |

## Topic 4 – Solving problems

| | |
|---|---|
| AN77 | Use of a calculator |
| AN78 | Multiplication and division 1 |
| AN79 | Multiplication and division 2 |
| AN81 | Fractions |
| AN82 | The calculator fraction button |
| AN84 | Fractions and decimals |
| AN85 | Use of decimals to describe |
| AN86 | Use decimals |
| AN91 | Percentages |

# Topic 1 – Using measurements

## Perimeter

**AN 39**

Foundation/Intermediate/Advanced
Element **1.2,2.2,3.2**
Performance criteria **1,2,4,5**
Range **Techniques**
(Number; Shape, space and measures)

The perimeter of a flat shape is the total distance round its outside.

The diagram shows a carpet 5 m by 3 m.

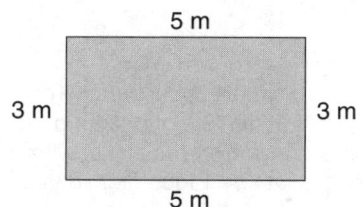

So the perimeter of the carpet is 16 m, because 5 m + 3 m + 5 m + 3 m = 16 m.

### Activity

1. What is the perimeter of this shape?

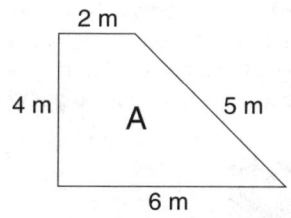

2. What is the perimeter of this shape?

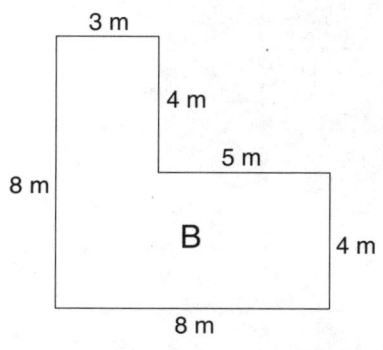

▌

*1  Perimeter of shape A is 2 m + 5 m + 6 m + 4 m = 17 m*

*2  Perimeter of shape B is 32 m* ▌

### Activity

1. The diagram below shows a display made from 3 rectangular panels.

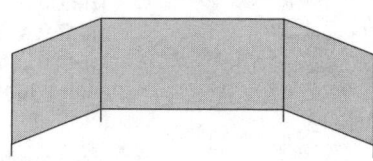

Each of the side panels is 1 m wide and 2 m high.

The centre panel is 3 m wide and 2 m high.

The display needs a border round the outside of the 3 panels as shown.

What is the total length of the border?

2. 

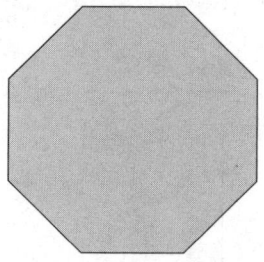

A children's play area has a perimeter of 24 m, and 8 equal sides.

How long is each side?

▌

*1  The total length of the border is 14 m.*

*2  Each side is 3 m long.* ▌

### Key point to remember

The perimeter of a flat shape is the total distance round its outside.

### Putting it into practice

*Make a floor plan of your classroom and use it to find the perimeter of the floor to the nearest whole metre.*

*Check to make sure you are correct.*

*Find the measurements of a dining table which is just large enough for 10 adults to sit round it for a meal.*

# Topic 1 – Using measurements

## Areas

**AN 40**

Foundation
Element **1.2, 2.2, 3.2**
Performance criteria **1, 2, 4, 5**
Range **Techniques**
(Number; Shape, space and measures)

### Area by counting squares

Area is the space on a flat surface.

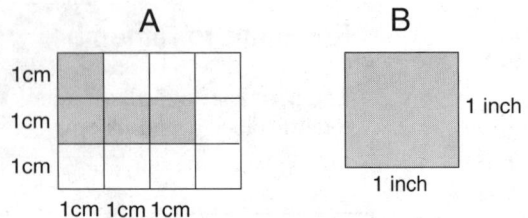

Shape A has a shaded area of 4 square centimetres (or 4 cm² for short).

Shape B has an area of 1 square inch (or 1 in² for short).

### Activity

A company logo in the shape of an L is shown below Each square on the grid is 1 cm². It is to be painted in gold paint. A tin of paint covers 15 square centimetres.

Find the area of the shape in square centimetres.

How many tins of paint are required?

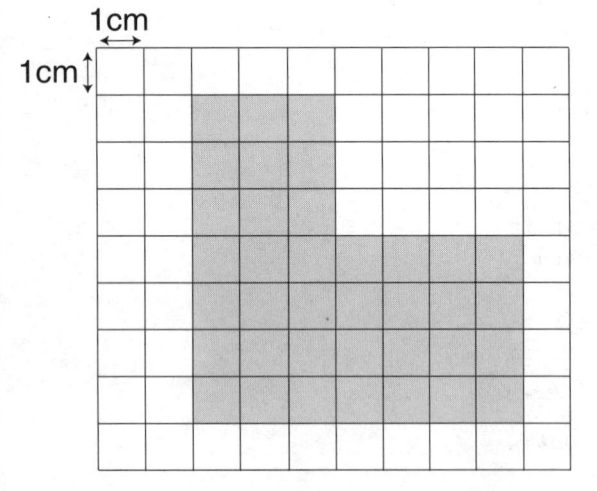

■■ The logo is 37 square centimetres in area, or 37 cm².

37 cm² ÷ 15 cm² = 2.466667, so 3 tins of paint are needed, 2 would not be enough. ■■

### Area of unusual shapes

It was simple to count the squares of the logo, because they were all complete squares. This is not always the case.

### Activity

The diagram below shows a simple apple mural. The paint we wish to use covers at the rate of one tin per four square feet. A grid is drawn over the apple, with each square representing 1 foot by 1 foot, or 1 square foot.

1 square foot, or 1 ft².

If an area covers incomplete squares then an estimate must be made such as

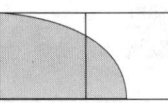

This shaded area is about one and a quarter squares.

Count how many complete squares cover the apple first, then try to pair up bits that are left to make whole squares and estimate the rest. Finally, work out how many tins of paint are required, if the apple is painted all in the same colour.

■■ 
| | |
|---|---|
| Complete squares | 59 square feet |
| Rest (estimate) | 12 square feet |
| Total | 71 square feet |

Each tin covers 4 square feet, so, 71 ÷ 4 = 17.75 and we need to buy 18 tins. ■■

### Key points to remember

Area is measured in square units. It is the space taken up by a flat surface.

### *Putting it into practice*

*What is the floor area of your classroom in m² (square metres)?*

*How much would it cost to cover it in heavy duty carpet costing £7 per square metre?*

# Topic 1 – Using measurements

## Working with area

**AN 41**

Foundation/Intermediate/Advanced
Element **1.2, 2.2, 3.2**
Performance criteria
**1, 2, 3, 4, 5, 6**
Range **Techniques** (Number; Shape, space and measures);
**Checking procedures**

Many practical activities involve working with areas and area measurement:

- planning the location of furniture and other equipment in a shop, office or other room
- working with plans and layouts for leisure, tourist and other sites and locations
- layout of printed text in leaflets and posters.

Nowadays, nearly all large areas are measured in square metres (sq. m or m²).

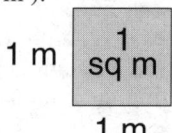

This is a side view of a small room.

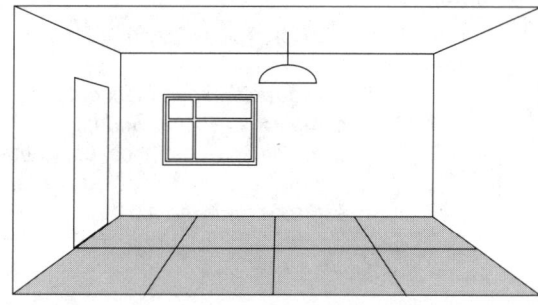

This is a 'plan view' of the floor. Each square has an area of 1 m².

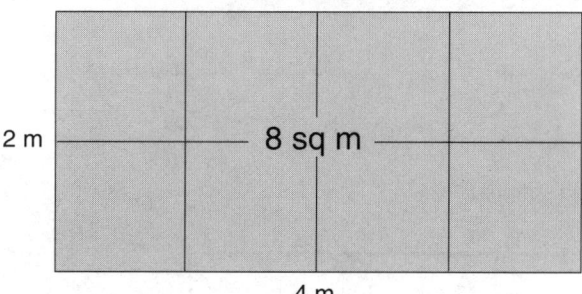

### Activity

The room above is about 2.5 m high. Roughly what is the area of the wall on the right?

▌▌ *About 5 m² – see the diagram below:* ▌▌

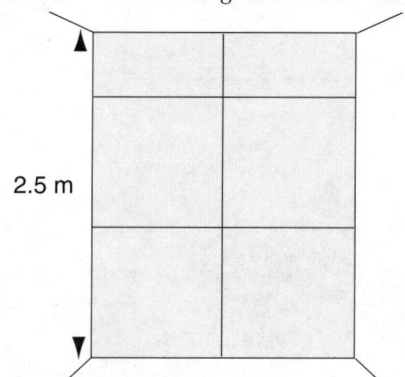

Most rooms have less convenient measurements, however.

The floor area in this room must be less than 16 m². (Look at the 'left over' bits around the edge.)

The area is about 13 m² when you take off all these bits.

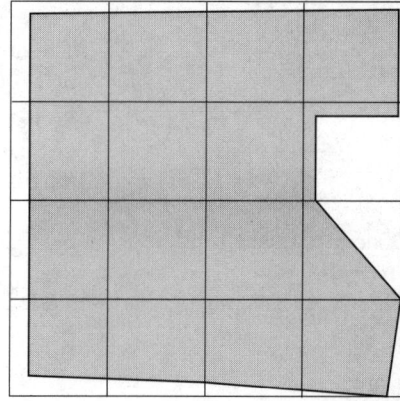

But you would need to buy 16 m² of carpet to cover the floor, and cut off the waste round the edges when the carpet was laid.

### Key points to remember

Area measurements give the amount of space on a surface. You use units such as square feet or square metres (m²).

### Putting it into practice

- *Find the floor area of the room you are in now.*
- *With this data, find the costs of carpeting it in different carpet types.*
- *Compare your results with others from other people in your working group, if you can. How closely do you agree?*

# Topic 1 – Using measurements

## Working with small and large areas

**AN 42**

Foundation/Intermediate/
Advanced
Element **1.2,2.2,3.2**
Performance criteria
**1,2,3,4,5**
Range **Techniques**
(Number; Shape, space and measures);
**Levels of accuracy**

Smaller areas, such as areas of printed text on pages, or areas of diagrams, are measured in square centimetres (sq. cm or $cm^2$), or square inches (sq. in. or $in.^2$).

$1 in.^2 \approx 6.5 cm^2$ ( not 2.5 as some might think). This diagram shows why this is so.

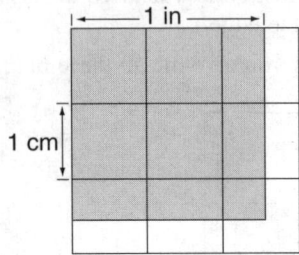

In the same way,

$1 m^2 = 10\ 000\ cm^2$ (square centimetres), $= 100$ cm by $100$ cm.

$1 cm^2 = 100\ mm^2$ (square millimetres) $= 10$ mm by $10$ mm.

For very large areas,

1 hectare (ha.) $= 10\ 000\ m^2$, that is, a hectare is the area of a square 100 m by 100 m, roughly the area of a football pitch.

As with floor areas, finding any area is based on counting squares. You can short-cut this counting of squares by looking for rectangles.

For instance, instead of finding the area of the large rectangle above right by counting the centimetre squares (there are 42 so the area is $42\ cm^2$), you can just find $42\ cm^2$ by working out 6 cm $\times$ 7 cm (6 columns of 7 squares).

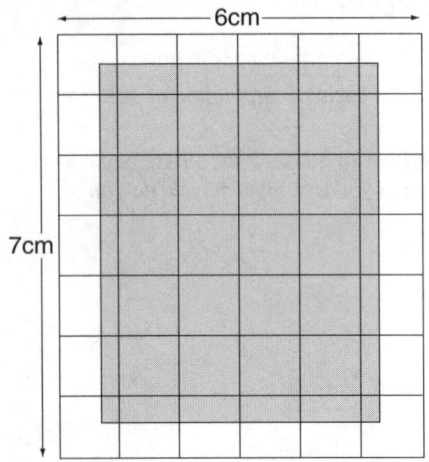

The area of a rectangle is given by finding length $\times$ breadth.

The area of this sheet of paper (A4 size) is

$21.0$ cm $\times$ $29.7$ cm $= 623.7\ cm^2$

$\approx 1/16\ m^2$

(1/16 of $10\ 000\ cm^2 = 625\ cm^2$)

(A3 size is twice this size, so the area of an A3 sheet $\approx 1250\ cm^2$ or $1/8\ m^2$.

The area of A2 is $2 \times$ A3 $\approx 2500\ cm^2$ or $1/4\ m^2$).

So here, the area of the shaded rectangle can be found exactly by finding length $\times$ breadth – no need to estimate parts of squares.

Shaded area $= 4.8$ cm $\times$ $5.8$ cm

$= 27.84\ cm^2$

$\approx 28\ cm^2$.

or area $= 48$ mm $\times$ 58 mm

$= 2784\ mm^2$

$\approx 2800\ mm^2$.

You can find the areas of some other shapes by imagining fitting them together to make rectangles, or by using special formulae.

### Key points to remember

You can find areas of triangular shapes by cutting rectangles in half and of complicated shapes by splitting them up into simpler shapes.

### Putting it into practice

*On squared paper, mark out a complicated shape. Find its area using different methods. Check that the methods all give about the same estimate for its area.*

### Activity

Find the areas of the three shapes.

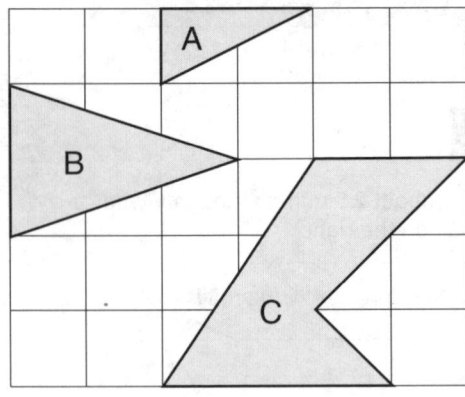

■■ *Area A is half of $2\ cm^2 = 1\ cm^2$.*

*Area B is $1.5 + 1.5 = 3\ cm^2$.*

*Area C is $3 + 0.5 + 2 = 5.5\ cm^2$.* ■■

# Topic 1 – Using measurements

## Finding areas

**AN 43**

Foundation/Intermediate/
Advanced
Element **1.2,2.2,3.2**
Performance criteria **2,3,4,5**
Range **Techniques**
(Number; Shape, space and measures)

In a car park each car needs a space measuring 9 ft. wide by 18 ft. long.

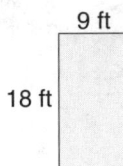

If the space available for parking is 18 ft. by 54 ft. then the best design is shown below.

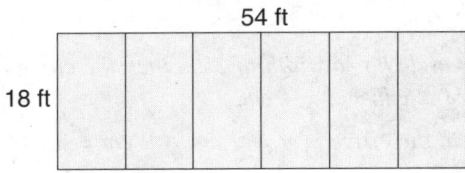

You can see there are six parking spaces if they are to be 9 ft. wide.

### Activity

A field measuring 90 ft. by 60 ft. is to be used as a car park. Each car requires a space of 18 ft. by 9 ft. Design a layout for the field to park as many cars as is sensible and give an estimate of the number which could be parked.

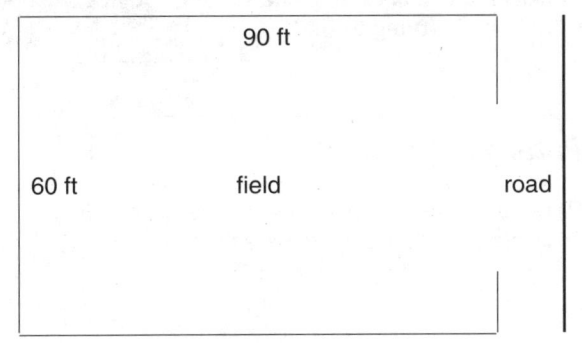

This is one possible design for 18 cars.

Area of a rectangle is length × width.

### Activity

A section of the room at an exhibition needs to be fenced off for a crèche as is shown in the diagram. You must allow 8 square metres of space per child. The fencing available is 26 m long.

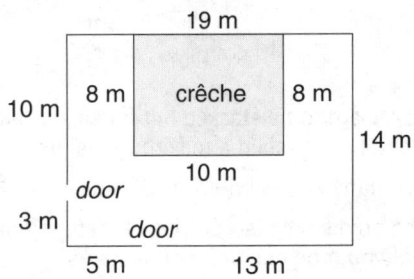

**1** How many children can this crèche accommodate?

**2** Rearrange the fencing to hold as many children as possible. Draw a sketch to show your idea.

*1  Area is 80 m². Number of children is 80 ÷ 8 = 10 children.*

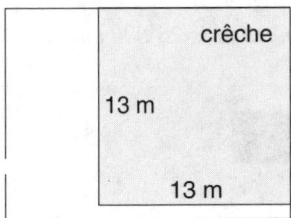

*2  Area is 169 m². Number of children is 169 ÷ 8 = 21.125.    21 children.*

### Key point to remember

Area of a rectangle is length × width.

### *Putting it into practice*

*Measure the length and width of a car parking space and design a car park and find the area of land used.*

# Topic 1 – Using measurements

## Working with shapes

**AN 47**

Foundation/Intermediate/Advanced
Element 1.2, 2.2, 3.2
Performance criteria 1,2,3,4,5,6,7
Range **Techniques** (Number; Shape, space and measures); **Checking procedures**

The size of shapes is important if the shapes are to be packaged or stacked in a confined space.

### Activity

This is a box of size 40 cm × 50 cm × 45 cm.

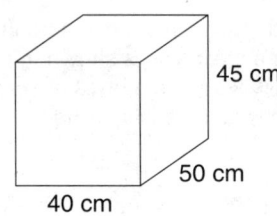

Fifty boxes are to be stacked but for safety reasons the stacks must not exceed a maximum height of 2 m.

1. How many stacks will be required?
2. If the boxes are stacked close together what floor area would be needed for the stacks?

■ $1 m = 100 cm$

1. Height of each stack is 200 cm.
   Maximum number of boxes in each stack is
   $200 \div 45 = 4$ boxes (180).
   Number of stacks needed is $50 \div 4 = 13$

2. Base area of each box is $40 \times 50 = 2000$ cm$^2$
   Total floor area is $2000 \times 13 = 26\,000$ cm$^2$
   
   $10\,000$ cm$^2$ = 1 m$^2$
   Floor area needed is 26 000 cm$^2$ or 2.6 m$^2$. ■

### Activity

**Cards**

A rectangular card needs to have a hole cut into it, as in the diagram.

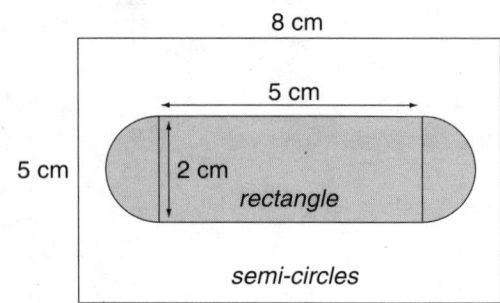

1. Find the area of the card after the hole has been cut by considering the separate shapes involved.
2. Find the weight of each card if the card weighs 0.25 g per cm2.

■

1. The area of the rectangle before the hole is cut is
   $8$ cm $\times 5$ cm $= 40$ cm$^2$
   
   Add together the two semi-circles to form one circle for the calculation.
   
   If the rectangle has a width of 2 cm then the circle has a radius of $2$ cm $\div 2 = 1$ cm.
   
   The area of the circle is $\pi \times 1$ cm $\times 1$ cm $= 3.14$ cm$^2$.
   
   The area of the rectangle is $5$ cm $\times 2$ cm $= 10$ cm$^2$.
   
   The total area of the hole is
   $3.14$ cm$^2$ + $10$ cm$^2$ = $13.14$ cm$^2$.
   
   Area of the final card is $40 - 13.14 = 26.86$ cm$^2$.

2. Weight of the card = area $\times 0.25$ g
   $= 26.86 \times 0.25$ g $= 6.715$ g. ■

### Key points to remember

Consider the shapes separately. Think logically about what you are trying to find.

### Putting it into practice

Design a card similar to the one in the second activity. Calculate the area of card you need to use.

# Topic 1 – Using measurements

## Volumes of simple shapes

**AN 48**

Foundation/Intermediate/
Advanced
Element **1.2,2.2,3.2**
Performance criteria
**1,2,3,4,5,6**
Range **Techniques**
(Number; Shape, space and measures); **Checking procedures**

You will often find that some complex designs are various cuboids fitted together.

> Volume of a cuboid is found by multiplying length × breadth × height.
>
> Volume is measured in cubic units for example $cm^3$ or $m^3$.

### Activity

An aquarium shop offers to provide a variety of shapes of tanks. They need to calculate the volume of the tanks in order to determine the strength of the stand needed to support the weight of the water contained in it.

The basic models are,

1 a cuboid measuring 1.2 m by 0.3 m with a depth of 0.5 m

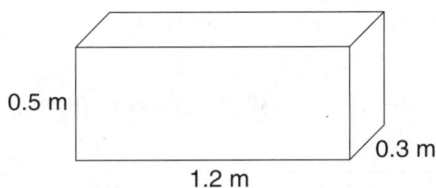

2 an L-shaped tank, which is shown below. (This view is from above and the depth of the tank is 0.7 m)

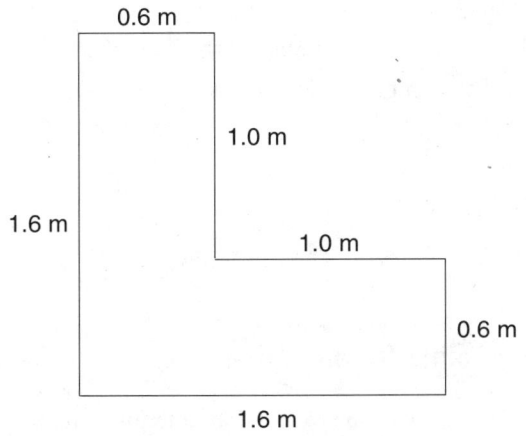

Calculate the volume of each tank.

∎

1 Volume of cuboid = $1.2 \times 0.3 \times 0.5 = 0.18 \ m^3$

2 Volume of L-shaped tank =
   $1.6 \times 0.6 \times 0.7 + 0.6 \times 1.0 \times 0.7 = 1.092 \ m^3$ ∎

### Activity

This diagram is a plan of the floor space of a factory in which the height of the room is 4.5 m. For health and safety reasons you need to calculate the volume of the room.

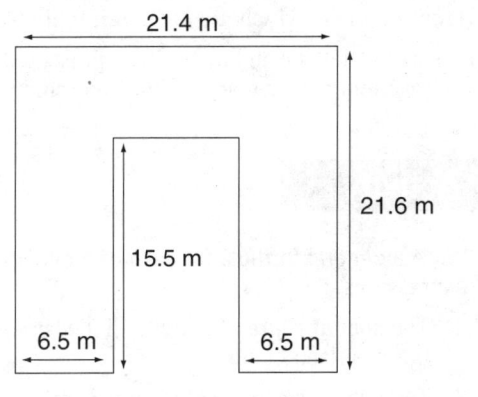

∎ *Volume*

Left-hand volume:    $6.5 \times 15.5 \times 4.5 = 453.375 \ m^3$

Right-hand volume:    $6.5 \times 15.5 \times 4.5 = 453.375 \ m^3$

Top volume:    $21.4 \times 6.1 \times 4.5 = 587.43 \ m^3$

Total volume:    $453.375 + 453.375 + 587.43$
                $= 1494.18 \ m^3$. ∎

### Key point to remember

The volume of combined solids can be found by adding together the volumes of each part of the shape.

### *Putting it into practice*

*Find the volume of your classroom.*

# Topic 2 – Useful techniques

## Using simple formulae

**AN 54**

Foundation/Intermediate/Advanced
Element **1.2,2.2,3.2**
Performance criteria
**1,2,3,4,5,6**
Range **Techniques (Number); Checking procedures**

### Addition and subtraction

Your friend is three years older than you and you are eighteen. You can easily find the age of your friend by adding, $18 + 3 = 21$ years.

Your friend will always be three years older than you, no matter what your age. If we let your age be represented by $x$ years then the age of your friend is $x + 3$ years at any time.

> An expression is a mathematical term for a collection of symbols (such as $x + 3$).

This type of expression is often used on a spreadsheet to give a general formula which can be applied to the various different numbers which are entered into the spreadsheet.

It is usual to let the unknown be represented by an italic lower-case letter; $x$ or $y$ are the most common letters used.

### Activity

Write a general formula for each of the following expressions.

1 The cost of a litre of petrol $C$, if it cost $xp$ last week but has risen by 6p.
2 The cost of a can of cola $K$, which originally cost 45p but has been reduced by $yp$.

■

1 $C = x + 6$ pence.
2 $K = 45 - y$ pence. ■

### Multiplication

If you buy six compact discs costing £7 each, to calculate the total cost involved you multiply the number purchased by the cost of the compact disc, $6 \times £7$. If the price of the disc was changed to £$x$, the total cost would be $6 \times £x$.

We call $6 \times x$, or $6x$ an expression for the cost of six discs at £$x$.

### Activity

Write a general expression for the total of each of the following,

1 3 pairs of shoes at £$y$ per pair.
2 5 pairs of socks at £$x$ per pair.
3 $x$ bottles of orange at 45p a bottle.

■

1 $3 \times £y = £3y$.
2 $5 \times £x = £5x$.
3 $x \times 45p = 45x$ pence. ■

### Division

You are told that the cost of ten posters is £20. If you wished to share the posters and the cost between friends, you would quickly work out that each poster costs £2. To do this you have divided the cost of the posters by the number of posters.

$£20 \div 10 = £2$

If your posters came in a bargain pack, number unknown, then the same calculation would be,

$£20 \div x$

This would be the general expression to find the cost of a poster.

### Activity

Find the general expression for the cost of one item in each case.

1 The cost of one tropical fish, if $x$ of them cost £200.
2 The cost of one floppy disk if ten of them cost £$y$.

■

1 $£200 \div x$ or $\frac{£200}{x}$
2 $£y \div 10$ or $\frac{£y}{10}$ ■

### Key points to remember

Always think of the expression in terms of real numbers. Consider what you would do in each case. Then write the expression.

### Putting it into practice

*You will find that algebra is necessary when designing spreadsheets in the projects you are involved with. Think of a situation when you would need to use a formula and work out what it would be.*

# Topic 2 – Useful techniques

## Writing equations

**AN 56**

Foundation/Intermediate/Advanced
Element **1.2, 2.2, 3.2**
Performance criteria
**1, 2, 3, 4, 5, 6, 7**
Range **Techniques**
(Number; Handling data);
**Checking procedures**

Sometimes when you need to do the same calculation several times using different numbers, it helps to write it down in the form of an equation.

### T-shirt printing

A printer works out his charges for printing logos on T-shirts like this:

fixed charge for setting up machine £20, plus £2 per T-shirt.

This can be written as an equation ($x$ is the number of T-shirts printed):

cost of order = £20 + £2$x$

#### Activity

1. Use the equation to work out how much he would charge for 30 T-shirts.
2. What would he charge for 100 T-shirts?
3. If the printer found a receipt for £44.00 while he was sorting out his records, how many T-shirts would he have printed for that amount? (Try using an equation to work this out.)

■■

1  £20 + £2 × 30 = £80

2  £20 + £2 × 100 = £220

3  This time, the thing you didn't know was the number of T-shirts, so you should have written a slightly different equation.

   $44 = 20 + 2y$

   $2y = 44 - 20$

   $y = 12$

So he printed 12 T-shirts. ■■

### Hiring a photocopier

Suppose you wished to hire a photocopier. The cost of hiring it is £1000 per year and in addition to this, electricity and paper costs are 1p per page. You need to calculate how much to charge for each page copied in order to cover your costs for the year. This can be solved by using a simple equation.

#### Activity

1. Write an expression for the total costs per year, if $n$ is the number of pages copied.
2. If the charge for one copy is $x$ pence, write an expression for revenue collected during the year. ($n$ is still the number printed.)
3. Find how many copies need to be printed to cover the total costs for the year if the cost per page, $x$, is set at 5p.

■■

1  The units must all be the same. We shall work in pounds.

   The cost of hiring is £1000.

   The cost per page is 1p, this is £0.01.

   $n$ copies at £0.01 = £0.01$n$.

   Total costs per year,
   £1000 + 0.01$n$.

2  $0.01nx$ pence = £0.01$nx$.

3  The outgoing costs match the incoming money when,

   $nx = 1000 + 0.01n$.

   When $x = 5p$,

   $0.05n = 1000 + 0.01n$

   $0.04n = 1000$

   $n = 1000 / 0.04 = 25\,000$.

   25 000 copies need to be printed.

■■

### Changing costs

#### Activity

The electricity and paper costs are increased, so that the cost per page for electricity and paper is 3p. How many copies need to be printed to cover the costs for the year if the cost per page is left at 5p?

■■ *The equation becomes,*

$0.05n = 1000 + 0.03n$

$0.02n = 1000$

$n = 50\,000$. ■■

#### Key points to remember

- Equations can be used to solve practical problems.
- They are useful if you have to work out the same calculation several times on different numbers.

#### *Putting it into practice*

*Investigate the cost of hiring an item for one of your projects. Write an equation to express your costs.*

# Topic 2 – Useful techniques

## 'Less than' and 'greater than'

**AN 57**

Foundation/Intermediate/Advanced
Element **1.2,2.2,3.2**
Performance criteria **1,2,3,4,5,6,7**
Range **Techniques (Number); Levels of accuracy; Checking procedures**

If you were hiring a Bouncy Castle to keep children amused at an exhibition you would need to make sure that the children are safe. You would need to set restrictions on who could use it perhaps the children between the heights of 120 cm and 130 cm. This can be expressed as an inequality.

Children must be taller than 120 cm,

children, height > 120 cm,

and children must be less than 130 cm,

children, height < 130 cm.

We can combine this and write

120 cm < height of children < 130 cm.

---

< means less than
> means greater than.

---

### Activity

Write inequalities to express these statements:

1 Children must weigh less than 45 kg.
2 Children must be older than 18 months of age.
3 Children must be younger than 10 years.
4 Children must be older than 18 months but younger than 10 years.
5 Children must be 125 cm or less in height.
6 Children must be 105 cm or greater in height.

■

1 Children, weight < 45 kg.
2 Children, age > 18 months.
3 Children, age < 10 years.
4 18 months < Age of children < 10 years.
5 Children, height < 125 cm.
6 Children, height > 105 cm. ■

---

$\leq$ means less than or equal to.
$\geq$ means greater than or equal to.

---

### Activity

You are to order biscuits to resell. You know that you will be able to sell the chocolate ones for more than the plain ones. A manufacturer could state that in a tin of mixed biscuits, at least 20 per cent but less than 25 per cent are chocolate.

The tin of biscuits contains 200 biscuits. Find the possible number of chocolate ones, and write this as an inequality.

■ *First find 20% of 200,*

$\frac{20}{100} \times 200 = 40.$

*Then 25% of 200,*

$\frac{25}{100} \times 200 = 50.$

*The number of chocolate biscuits is given by the inequality,*

$40 \leq$ number of chocolate biscuits $< 50.$

*This means there are at least 40 but less than 50 chocolate biscuits.* ■

Inequalities are often used in spreadsheets, when you need to sort entries that come into certain categories. For example, in a business you might want a list of all customers who have spent more than £100 in the last year, so that you could send them details of a special offer you were arranging. A health clinic might want to send a leaflet to all patients over 60, or to everyone who had made more than three visits to the clinic in the last six months. All these things could be done by writing a formula which contained an inequality and instructing the spreadsheet to sort out the entries to which it applied.

### Key points to remember

< means less than.
> means greater than.
$\leq$ means less than or equal to.
$\geq$ means greater than or equal to.

### *Putting it into practice*

Analyse answers to a survey. Divide the age group of the people questioned into less than 15 years, 15 to 20 years, and so on.

# Topic 2 – Useful techniques

**AN 60**

Foundation/Intermediate/Advanced
Element **1.2,2.2,3.2**
Performance criteria
**1,2,3,4,5,6**
Range **Techniques**
(Handling data)

## Conversion rules

When you gather measurements or other data, you will use the most convenient units for measuring.

But these may not be the units you should use for recording the data. So you may have to convert the data from one set of units to another.

For instance, you may have a tape measure marked in feet and inches, but need to record the measurements in metres and centimetres.

Or you may have weighed a parcel using ounces but need to convert this to grams to find the cost of posting.

## Converting within the same 'family' of units

Plans for buildings sometimes show measurements in millimetres only.

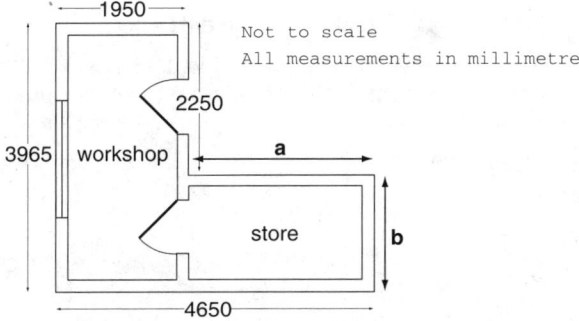

You have to convert the measurements to metres and centimetres to make them easier to visualise so they are like these:

4 m 68 cm, 11 m 20 cm

### Activity

1. Convert the measurements on the plan to metres and centimetres.
2. Find the two other measurements 'a' and 'b' in millimetres. Then convert these to metres and centimetres as well.

■

1. 1000 mm = 1 m and 10 mm = 1 cm so 1950 mm = 1 m 95 cm, others are 4 m 65 cm, 2 m 25 cm and 3 m 96.5 cm.

2. 'a' = 4650 − 1950 = 2700 mm = 2 m 70 cm
   'b' = 3965 − 2250 = 1715 mm = 1 m 71.5 cm. ■

If you can visualise the situation you are dealing with, it can be a big help in checking your work.

For instance, because you know this plan is of a workshop and store, and because you can see the doors on the plan, you can be pretty sure that the length of the building is between 4 m and 5 m, and not between 40 m and 50 m, nor between 40 cm and 50 cm.

Using your common sense like this helps prevents your making big errors.

## Approximate conversion rules

### Activity

Try using these rules

'1 oz. is about 30 g'

'10 cm is about 4 in.'

to convert these amounts:

- a parcel weighing 6½ ounces into grams;
- a piece of wood 3 feet 7 inches long into cm;
- a pack of currants weighing 150 g into ounces;
- a skirt waistband of 73 cm into inches.

■ *The parcel: 6 oz ≈ 6 × 30 = 180 g, ½ oz. ≈ 15 g so 6½ ounces is about 195 g.*

*The wood: 3 ft. (36 in.) = 9 × 4 in. ≈ 9 × 10 cm = 90 cm, 7 in. ≈ 10 + 7.5 = 17.5 cm so 3 ft. 7 in. ≈ 107.5 cm.*

*The currants: 150 g ÷ 30 = 5 oz.*

*The waistband: 10 cm is about 4 in., so 70 cm ≈ 28 in. The extra 3 cm is a little over 1 in., so the waistband is a little over 29 in..* ■

### Key points to remember

- You are multiplying or dividing in each case. Use your common sense to decide which to do.
- There is no one right method. Choose one you understand.
- Always check your results by asking:
  - Does this seem right?
  - Does it fit with what I know already?

### *Putting it into practice*

*Practise measuring a variety of items using the rules above. Check your results by measuring the items again, directly in the other units.*

## Topic 2 – Useful techniques

### Use a mean of a set of data

**AN 65**

Foundation/Intermediate/Advanced
Element **1.2, 2.2, 3.2**
Performance criteria **1, 2, 4**
Range **Techniques**
(Number; Handling data)

## The mean

The mean is the straightforward average found by adding together all the results and dividing that total by the number of results used. Almost every time a set of figures is given in a newspaper article, magazine article or factual report, a mean is usually given to summarise a set of results.

### Activity

Read through this list of 'features of the mean' and decide which ones are true and which are false.

|   |   | True | False |
|---|---|---|---|
| 1 | The mean is always a whole number | ☐ | ☐ |
| 2 | The mean is always one of the results on the list | ☐ | ☐ |
| 3 | The mean is always exactly in the middle of the list of results | ☐ | ☐ |
| 4 | You can work out what the results on the list must have been | ☐ | ☐ |
| 5 | If you know how many results there were you can work out the total | ☐ | ☐ |
| 6 | It gives you a rough idea of what the results were | ☐ | ☐ |
| 7 | Most of the results will equal the mean | ☐ | ☐ |
| 8 | All the results will lie within six either side of the mean | ☐ | ☐ |
| 9 | The results above the mean will balance the ones below it. | ☐ | ☐ |

■■ *Do the next activity before you check your answers.* ■■

### Activity

1 These are the weights of five friends:

A: 47 kg   B: 54 kg   C: 59 kg
D: 62 kg   E: 135 kg

Find their mean weight.

2 Go back to the first activity and see whether you want to change any of your answers.

■■
1  71.4 kg
2  The following are TRUE from the first activity:
   no. 5     no. 6     no. 9. ■■

If you are not sure about number 9 here are the weights in kg of the friends and the differences from the mean (71.4 kg).

| Person | Weight | Difference from mean |
|---|---|---|
| A | 47 | 24.4 |
| B | 54 | 17.4 |
| C | 59 | 12.4 |
| D | 62 | 9.4 |
| E | 135 | +63.6 |

### Activity

1 Add up the 'negative differences' for the people A, B, C and D on the list above.
2 What is the total for all five differences?
3 Write down five numbers of your choice. Find the mean. Find the differences from the mean and the total of these.

■■
1  63.6
2  Zero
3  The total for differences should be zero. ■■

## The mean in industry

The mean is often used in the manufacturing industry to monitor the sizes or weights of items being made. So, for instance, in a chocolate factory samples of about five bars of chocolate will be weighed at intervals throughout the day. The mean for each sample is calculated, and may be plotted on a graph, (called a quality-control chart). The mean should be very close to the weight printed on the chocolate wrapper. If a sample mean is not close to the right value, the production line may have to be stopped or the machinery adjusted.

### Key points to remember

- The mean gives a rough idea of where the results in the data set lie.
- It does not give any idea about variability in results.
- It is useful for monitoring weights and measurements of manufactured items.

### Putting it into practice

*Work out the mean measurement (such as the weight or length) for some manufactured goods that are used in your college or work placement.*

# Topic 2 – Useful techniques

## Finding the mode

**AN 66**

Foundation/Intermediate/
Advanced
Element **1.2,2.2,3.2**
Performance criteria
**1,2,3,4,5,6**
Range **Techniques**
(Number; Handling data)

When you are looking at the results of a survey or another piece of research, the result which occurs most often is known as the mode. This result is described as having the highest frequency. The mode is simple to find and is useful to know.

The owner of Jack's Bistro has employed a consultant to do a thorough survey of the company and to produce a report. Part of this survey concerned customers' complaints:

Customers' complaints,
2 June – 8 June

| Nature of complaint | Frequency |
|---|---|
| food took a long time | 14 |
| poor choice on menu | 2 |
| tablecloth dirty | 1 |
| food was cold | 4 |
| waitress rude | 2 |
| bill took too long | 1 |

### Activity

Which type of complaint occurred most frequently? This is called the mode.

▪▪

*The modal type of complaint is 'food took a long time'.* ▪▪

Data which consists of categories like this cannot be used to find any kind of numerical average. If you want to give a typical result to a survey of this kind, it is best to use the mode.

Another part of the survey was a profile of customers – what kinds of people use the bistro and why?

Here are the results of a question on the ages of customers at two different times of day.

| Age of customer | Frequency | |
|---|---|---|
| | lunchtime | evening |
| 0 – 9 years | 2 | 0 |
| 10 – 19 years | 0 | 3 |
| 20 – 29 years | 4 | 25 |
| 30 – 39 years | 5 | 4 |
| 40 – 49 years | 8 | 2 |
| 50 – 59 years | 9 | 0 |
| 60 – 69 years | 3 | 0 |
| 70 – 79 years | 0 | 0 |

### Activity

1. Find the modal age group
   a. at lunchtime
   b. in the evening.
2. What sort of people were eating
   a. at lunchtime
   b. in the evening?

▪▪

1. The modal age groups are:
   a. 50–59 years
   b. 20–29 years

2. a. At lunchtime most of the customers could be described as 'middle-aged'. Perhaps the bistro is used by office workers at lunchtime, with older workers and senior staff probably better able to afford to eat there in the middle of the day.

   b. In the evening most of the customers are under 30. The bistro seems to attract a different 'crowd' in the evenings – perhaps a more fashionable younger group. ▪▪

### Key points to remember

- The mode is the result with the highest frequency.
- The mode is especially useful for qualitative (non-numerical) data for which no other kind of average or type of typical value can be found.

### *Putting it into practice*

*Find the mode for some data you have collected. Your survey could be about customer complaints, suggestions for improvements or the means of transport people use to get to work.*

# Topic 2 – Useful techniques

## Finding the median

**AN 67**

Foundation/Intermediate/
Advanced
Element **1.2, 2.2, 3.2**
Performance criteria
**1, 2, 3, 4, 5, 6**
Range **Techniques**
(Number; Handling data)

The median is often used as a representative or typical value for a set of results. It is the value which occurs exactly half way through the results. In everyday language it could be called the 'middling' value.

The owners of a small guest house are thinking of redecorating and upgrading the accommodation they provide. They decide to do some research on what other guest houses in the area charge per night for bed and breakfast.

Here are the results they found:

£12.50
£18
£19.50
£15
£20

### Activity

1. Write down those five amounts listed in order.
2. Pick out the result in the middle. This is the median value.

■■

1. £12.50, £15, £18, £19.50, £20
2. The median is £18. ■■

Some time later, the owners of the guest house hear that someone else is opening for bed and breakfast in the area and will charge £17.50 a night. What will the median be now?

### Activity

1. Write the six amounts down in order.
2. Can you pick out a middle value now?

■■

1. £12.50, £15, £17.50, £18, £19.50, £20
2. There is no longer a result in the middle.

As the median position is now a 'gap' in the middle of the results, the median is found by taking the average of the two middle results:

$$\frac{(£17.50 + £18)}{2} \quad \frac{(£35.50)}{2} = £17.75$$

So the median is now £17.75. ■■

The guest house owners look back over their bookings for the previous month to see how many nights each guest had stayed.

| Number of nights | Frequency |
|---|---|
| 1 | 4 |
| 2 | 5 |
| 3 | 3 |
| 4 | 2 |
| 5 | 12 |
| 6 | 11 |
| 7 | 8 |
| 8 | 3 |
| 9 or more | 1 |

### Activity

How many guests had stayed at the guest house during the previous month?

■■ 49 – This is the total for the frequency column. ■■

To find the median – you could write down a list for the number of nights for each of these 49 guests:

1 1 1 1 2 2 2 2 2, etc.

An easier way is to make a running total of the frequencies, so that you can pick out the middle result.

| Number of nights | Frequency | Running total |
|---|---|---|
| 1 | 4 | 4 |
| 2 | 5 | 9 |
| 3 | 3 | 12 |
| 4 | 2 | |
| 5 | 12 | |
| 6 | 11 | |
| 7 | 8 | |
| 8 | 3 | |
| 9 or more | 1 | |

### Activity

1. Fill in the running total (this is called the cumulative frequency).
2. As there are 49 guests, which result is in the middle?
3. What is the median number of nights?

■■

1. The running totals should be:
   4, 9, 12, 14, 26, 37, 45, 48, 49
2. The 25th
3. 4 nights ■■

Notice that both the examples on this resource sheet have been for numerical data (i.e., cost in £s or number of nights). If you want to find a median your results must be numerical. If your data consists of categories, e.g., types of customer complaints or reasons for staying in the guest house (holiday, business, etc.) the only kind of typical result you can give is the mode.

### Key points to remember

- The median can be found only for numerical data (i.e. not for qualitative data as in 'type of complaint' or 'reason for journey').
- When you put the results in order, the middle result (or average of the two middle results) is the median.

### Putting it into practice

*Find the median for some data you have collected. Your survey could be about distances people travel to work or college, time taken for journeys to work, amounts of money spent by customers, times taken to serve customers.*

# Topic 3 – Number problems

## Addition 1

**AN 68**

Foundation/Intermediate/Advanced
Element **1.2, 2.2, 3.2**
Performance criteria **1, 2**
Range **Techniques**
(Number)

Following a service at a local garage, the bill for parts is shown in the activity below. Check the bill.

### Activity

Find the total cost of the following:

Plugs £8.40
Oil filter £5.89
Washer 98p
Brake fluid £5.34
Engine oil £16.08

■■ To add these together, we must either list all the items in pence or list them all in pounds. It is more convenient to convert 98p to £0.98 than to change all the other items.

| Plugs | £8.40 |
| Oil filter | £5.89 |
| Washer | £0.98 |
| Brake fluid | £5.34 |
| Engine oil | £16.08 |
| Total | £36.69 |

Notice that the numbers are lined up from the right. ■■

### Activity

Find the cost of small novelty items purchased to fill Christmas crackers.

Tape measure 56p
Compass 84p
Necklace 29p
Plastic penknife 38p

■■ This time all the items are in pence. Add the pence,

56p
84p
29p
38p

The total is 207p or £2.07. ■■

### Activity

A van has a maximum weight allowance of one ton.

112 hundredweight = 1 ton

Find the total weight of the following items and decide whether they can all go into the van.

Engine parts 57.6 hundredweight
Wheels 20.7 hundredweight
Seats 8.9 hundredweight
Tools 15 hundredweight

■■

Again the numbers must be lined up from the right-hand side.

15 is the same as 15.0.

| Engine parts | 57.6 hundredweight |
| Wheels | 20.7 hundredweight |
| Seats | 8.9 hundredweight |
| Tools | 15.0 hundredweight |
| Total | 102.2 hundredweight |

The items weigh less than 112 hundredweight so the van can be loaded. ■■

### Key points to remember

- Before numbers can be added together, the units must be the same.
- The numbers are lined up from the right-hand side.

### Putting it into practice

*Calculate a budget for a project. Make a detailed list of the items you require. Make sure your numbers are all in the same units, either all in £s or all in pence, and line up your numbers from the right-hand side.*

# Topic 3 – Number problems

## Addition 2

**AN 69**

Foundation/Intermediate/
**Advanced**
Element **1.2,2.2,3.2**
Performance criteria
**1,2,3,4,5,7,8,9**
Range **Techniques
(Number); Checking
procedures**

You will find that it is often useful to display data in tables. A set of scores from a questionnaire on five hotels is shown below.

### Activity

A group of four judges visited five hotels. They filled in questionnaires and gave marks to each of the hotels. The maximum mark possible in each case was 20 so that the five hotels could score a maximum of 80 marks.

|  | Hotel | | | | |
|---|---|---|---|---|---|
|  | 1 | 2 | 3 | 4 | 5 |
| Name | | | | | |
| Alison | 18 | 12 | 17 | 15 | 19 |
| Chaz | 16 | 13 | 13 | 18 | 20 |
| Graeme | 15 | 11 | 15 | 12 | 20 |
| Nicki | 15 | 16 | 12 | 17 | 19 |

1  How many marks did each of the judges give, in total?
2  Which hotel scored the highest marks overall?

■

1  Alison 81
   Chaz 80
   Graeme 73
   Nicki 79

2  The total scores for each hotel were,

| Hotel | 1 | 2 | 3 | 4 | 5 |
|---|---|---|---|---|---|
|  | 64 | 52 | 57 | 62 | 78 |

*so the highest-scoring hotel is number 5.* ■

In a work situation, stock control is often done on computer. Remaining stock is counted and the results are stored on a spreadsheet. This makes it easy to compare stock levels over a long period of time. Although spreadsheets will do calculations automatically, you must always be able to check them yourself. This will help you check whether mistakes have been made when typing in the information.

### Key points to remember

- Tables can be used to store information effectively.
- It is important to check information entered into spreadsheets.

### Putting it into practice

*Design a table to control stock in your college or work placement.*

### Activity

An advice centre had seven different leaflets for clients to pick up. One hundred of each were put in the display at the beginning of the month. The numbers left in stock at the end of the month were counted and put onto a spreadsheet.

| Leaflet | Number left in stock |
|---|---|
| 1 | 29 |
| 2 | 53 |
| 3 | 48 |
| 4 | 52 |
| 5 | 80 |
| 6 | 15 |
| 7 | 60 |

1  Which has been the most popular leaflet?
2  If 50 more of each are delivered, write the new stock list.
3  When you come to display the new leaflets, you find that there are more of leaflet 3 left than you expected. You count them up, including the new leaflets, and find that there are 134. What mistake do you think was made when typing the information into the spreadsheet?

■

1  Leaflet 6.
2  
| Leaflet | Number in stock |
|---|---|
| 1 | 79 |
| 2 | 103 |
| 3 | 98 |
| 4 | 102 |
| 5 | 130 |
| 6 | 65 |
| 7 | 110 |

3  *134 is 50 + 84. Somebody typed the figures the wrong way round when they entered 48 into the spreadsheet.*
■

# Topic 3 – Number problems

**AN 70**

Foundation/Intermediate/Advanced
Element **1.2, 2.2, 3.2**
Performance criteria **1, 2**
Range **Techniques**
(Number)

## Large numbers

A patient is told that he must count calories and fibre each day to keep to a diet. He is told to try to keep fibre intake as high as possible, but keep calorie intake down to around 1000 calories per day. This involves careful calculations with calorie control and fibre charts.

### Activity

Use the list given below.

|  | Calories per portion | Fibre g per portion |
|---|---|---|
| Bread | 160 | 2 |
| Margarine | 105 | 0 |
| Muesli | 205 | 4 |
| 1 apple | 50 | 2 |
| 1 banana | 90 | 4 |
| 1 sausage | 130 | 0 |
| Baked potato | 170 | 5 |
| Peas | 60 | 9 |
| ½ pint milk | 150 | 0 |

1. Find the calorie and fibre content of a meal of three sausages, a baked potato and a portion of peas.
2. If the meal is now changed to one sausage, two baked potatoes and peas, what would the calorie and fibre content be? Which meal would be more beneficial to the diet and why?
3. If 1000 calories a day are allowed, would it be possible to eat muesli for breakfast with ¼ pint of milk as well as bread, margarine and a banana for lunch in addition to the meal in question 1?

*1* 620 calories. Fibre 14 g.
*2* 530 calories. Fibre 19 g.
   This meal would be better because the calories are less and the fibre content has increased by 5 g.
*3* No, this would total 1255 calories.

## Pools win

Have you ever seen a newspaper headline such as,

### Pools win – 1.2 million!

If you were lucky enough to win this, what figures would you expect to be added to your bank account?

A million has six noughts. You need to be able to consider place value to write numbers accurately. Here are the important numbers.

| 1 million | 1 000 000 |
|---|---|
| 100 thousand | 100 000 |
| 10 thousand | 10 000 |
| 1 thousand | 1000 |
| 1 hundred | 100 |
| 1 ten | 10 |
| one | 1 |

We would write 1.2 million as 1 200 000.

1 000 000 + 200 000 =
$$\begin{array}{r} 1\ 000\ 000 \\ 200\ 000\ + \\ \hline 1\ 200\ 000 \end{array}$$

### Activity

Write the following numbers in figures.
1. Three hundred and seventy five thousand.
2. Fifty thousand and sixty.
3. One hundred thousand and eight.
4. Four million, two hundred thousand.
5. Two point three million.

*1* 375 000.
*2* 50 060.
*3* 100 008.
*4* 4 200 000.
*5* 2 300 000.

### Key point to remember

Remember place value when writing numbers.

### Putting it into practice

Practise reading and writing large numbers with a partner as though you were taking messages over the phone.

# Topic 3 – Number problems

**AN 71**

Foundation/Intermediate/
Advanced
Element **1.2, 2.2, 3.2**
Performance criteria **1, 2**
Range **Techniques**
(Number)

## Negative numbers

In winter, temperatures are often negative. For example −3 °C or even −9 °C on a very cold night. The negative sign means that the temperature is below 0 °C. In the case of −9 °C it is 9° below zero.

### Activity

1. If the temperature overnight dropped to −8 °C at midnight but was 10 °C by mid-day, what is the rise in temperature from midnight to mid-day?
2. The temperature on Monday midnight is recorded as −6°, but by Tuesday midnight it is −10 °C. Which night is colder and by how much?

■

1. 18 °C.
2. Tuesday by 4 °C. ■

You can enter negative numbers into your calculator by using the +/− button.

To enter −23 follow these instructions.

Calculator: 23 +/−   Display −23.

If the display reads −15 and you require it to read 15 the +/− can be used in the following way.

Calculator: Display −15 +/−

### Activity

Use your calculator to complete the following exercise.

1. Enter −256. Add 70 to this and read the display.
2. Enter −37. Subtract 20 from this and read the display.
3. Enter −3. Multiply this by 5 and read the display.

■

1. Display −186.
2. Display −57.
3. Display −15. ■

## Bank accounts

Some bank statements have the letters DR after the balance. This indicates that the account is overdrawn. CR shows that the balance is in credit.

### Activity

The balance of an account is displayed as shown below.

| Balance | £53 | DR |

1. If the overdraft facility on this account is set at £200, how much more could be withdrawn from the account?
2. £100 is deposited into the account, what is the new balance?

■

1. £147.
2. £47 CR. ■

Some companies send out statements to their customers in which money paid by the customer is recorded as a minus figure.

### Activity

Here is part of a quarterly telephone bill for a customer who pays a regular amount each month. Fill in the missing figure at the bottom. Do you think the customer should increase or reduce her monthly payment?

| | |
|---|---|
| Call charges | 216.77 |
| Advance charges | 20.16 |
| Other charges & credits | 25.05 |
| Subtotal ex VAT | 261.98 |
| VAT at 17.5% | 45.84 |
| Total charges | 307.82 |
| Payments you have made | −420.00 |
| Credit from last statement | −12.24 |
| Credit on your budget account | _____ |

■ The missing figure is −124.42. This represents an overpayment, so the customer should probably talk to the telephone company about reducing her monthly payment to them. ■

### Key points to remember

- Negative numbers are ways of expressing values below zero.
- To put a negative number into your calculator use the +/− button.

### Putting it into practice

Design a chart to show a small loan being repaid to a bank. Show details including DR to indicate when the account is overdrawn.

# Topic 3 – Number problems

## Subtraction

**AN 72**
Foundation/Intermediate/Advanced
Element **1.2,2.2,3.2**
Performance criteria **1,2,5,6**
Range **Techniques** (Number);
**Checking procedure**

In shops it is common to have notices such as,

and in order to find out how much the item costs it is necessary to take the 30p away from the quoted price.

### Activity

Find the cost of each of the following items in a sale, if the saving quoted is to be made.

1. Envelopes, originally 45p, reduced by 10p.
2. 1000 pens originally £25, reduced by £6.
3. 10 reams of printer paper £37, reduced by £9.
4. Three files, originally £15 for three, reduced by £3 each.

■ *Notice that the numbers must be lined up from the right before subtraction can take place.*

```
1   45p        2   £25       3   £37
    10p –          £6 –          £9 –
    ───            ───           ───
    35p            £19           £28
```

4 *Original cost £5 each. Reduced by £3 each to £2 each. Cost of three files £6.* ■

## Stock control

If you are selling anything, you need to keep an up to date stock list.

### Activity

This is a stock list for some of the items in a High Street chemist's shop. The numbers in stock early Monday morning are shown below.

| Item | Number in stock |
|---|---|
| 1 | 200 |
| 2 | 250 |
| 3 | 150 |
| 4 | 125 |
| 5 | 135 |
| 6 | 99 |
| 7 | 63 |

The items sold over five days are shown below. Adjust the stock list to show the numbers in stock on each of the five days.

| Item | Mon | Tues | Wed | Thurs | Fri |
|---|---|---|---|---|---|
| | *Number sold* | | | | |
| 1 | 21 | 13 | 7 | 9 | 12 |
| 2 | 32 | 9 | 9 | 10 | 11 |
| 3 | 14 | 10 | 12 | 13 | 15 |
| 4 | 8 | 17 | 14 | 13 | 12 |
| 5 | 9 | 12 | 11 | 7 | 6 |
| 6 | 7 | 9 | 10 | 11 | 10 |
| 7 | 12 | 21 | 9 | 7 | 6 |

Find the totals sold of each item over the five days and check by addition that the final number in stock is correct.

■

| Item | Mon | Tues | Wed | Thurs | Fri |
|---|---|---|---|---|---|
| | *Number in stock* | | | | |
| 1 | 179 | 166 | 159 | 150 | 138 |
| 2 | 218 | 209 | 200 | 190 | 179 |
| 3 | 136 | 126 | 114 | 101 | 86 |
| 4 | 117 | 100 | 86 | 73 | 61 |
| 5 | 126 | 114 | 103 | 96 | 90 |
| 6 | 92 | 83 | 73 | 62 | 52 |
| 7 | 51 | 30 | 21 | 14 | 8 |

| Item | 1 | 2 | 3 | 4 | 5 | 6 | 7 |
|---|---|---|---|---|---|---|---|
| Total sold | 62 | 71 | 64 | 64 | 45 | 47 | 55 |
| Total remaining stock | 138 | 179 | 86 | 61 | 90 | 52 | 8 |

*The total sold plus the remaining stock should add up to the original number.*

| Original number | 200 | 250 | 150 | 125 | 135 | 99 | 63 |

■

### Putting it into practice

*Keep a stock control list for a project. Use subtraction to keep it up to date.*

### Key points to remember

- Notice that the numbers must be lined up from the right before subtraction can take place.
- When counting stock, check your result by adding the total of items sold to the remaining stock.

# Topic 3 – Number problems

## Working with subtraction

**AN 73**

Foundation/Intermediate/Advanced
Element **1.2,2.2,3.2**
Performance criteria **1,2,5,6**
Range **Techniques (Number); Levels of accuracy; Checking procedures**

### Journeys

Suppose you are on a train journey. You know that the train is due to arrive at 17.50 and the time at present is 14.33. You can then find out how much longer you have to spend on the train, by subtracting 14.33 from 17.50.

You must take care when you do this. You cannot put this into a calculator as 17.50 − 14.33, because,

> there are 60 minutes in each hour.

From 14.33 to 15.00 there are,
60 − 33 = 27 minutes,
17.00 − 15.00 = 2 hours,

and there are 50 minutes from 17.00 to 17.50.

In total this is,
27 minutes + 2 hours + 50 minutes
= 3 hours 17 minutes.

### Activity

1. A train is due to arrive at Manchester at 12.15. If the time is 11.17, find how much time the train still has to travel if it is to arrive on time.
2. An aircraft is due to leave the airport at 19.45. Passengers are advised to be at the airport 2 hours before the flight is due to leave. If the journey to the airport for Melanie takes 1 hour 20 minutes, find the time she needs to leave home.
3. To travel from Cardiff to Stafford, it is necessary to change trains at Birmingham. If the Cardiff to Birmingham train arrives at Birmingham at 16.18 and the Birmingham to Stafford train leaves at 17.06, find how much time is spent at Birmingham.

■
1  58 minutes.
2  16.25.
3  48 minutes. ■

You will have met a similar type of problem with a video tape. Most tapes last 3 hours. This is 3 × 60 = 180 minutes.

### Activity

1. A programme is recorded on a three-hour video tape. If the programme is a film lasting 1 hour 35 minutes, how many minutes are left on the tape?
2. A half-hour comedy programme is added to the tape. Is there enough room left on the tape to record a one hour play?

■
1  85 minutes.
2  No. There are only 55 minutes left. ■

It is frequently necessary to calculate length of service for employees in years and months.

> There are 12 months in a year.

### Activity

A company's Christmas bonus payments are going to be awarded on length of service to the 31 December 1995. You are required to calculate the length of service for each employee in an office.

Find the length of service to the 31 December 1995 in each case giving your answer in years and months.

| Employee | Starting date |
|---|---|
| Mark | 1 June 1987 |
| Serjit | 1 September 1990 |
| Mary | 1 February 1972 |
| Fred | 1 August 1960 |

■
Mark   8 years 7 months.
Serjit  5 years 4 months.
Mary   23 years 11 months.
Fred    35 years 5 months. ■

### Key points to remember

There are 60 minutes in each hour. You cannot subtract time directly using a calculator.

### Putting it into practice

Plan a journey using rail or bus timetables.

# Topic 3 – Number problems

## Addition, subtraction and multiplication

**AN 74**

Foundation/Intermediate/
Advanced
Element **1.2,2.2,3.2**
Performance criteria
**1,2,3,4,5**
Range **Techniques**
(Number);
**Levels of accuracy**

## Change

When you go into a shop, you do not always have the correct amount of money. Suppose you buy a compact disc costing £6.99 and a blank tape costing 90p. You give the shop keeper a £10 note. What change would you expect?

90p is the same as £0.90, so calculate,

£6.99 + £0.90 = £7.89

change,

£10 − £7.89 = £2.11.

You would expect to have £2.11 change given to you.

### Activity

In each case find the change given when the following purchases are made.

1. Items costing £2.80 and 56p. Find the change from a £5 note.
2. Items costing £6.60 and 99p. Find the change given from a £10 note.
3. Items costing 84p and 12p. Find the change from a £1 coin.

■

1 £1.64.

2 £2.41.

3 4p. ■

### Activity

A computer can be purchased for £1000 cash.

Alternatively it can be repaid over

a twelve monthly instalments of £100 per month or

b twenty-four monthly instalments of £60 per month.

Find the cost of the system using methods **a** and **b** and compare these with the cash price of £1000.

■

a Cost £1200. This is £200 more expensive than the cash price.

b Cost £1440. This is £440 more expensive than the cash price. ■

### Activity

1. Compare the price of two notepads, costing 90p for the two in a college shop against the cost of purchasing two at the usual price of 48p each.
2. A pack of large envelopes cost £1.80 for six. Another pack costs £2.30 for 9. What is the difference in price if 18 envelopes are required?

■

1 96p − 90p = 6p. The college shop is cheaper by 6p.

2 *You would need to buy three packs of the £1.80 envelopes,*
£1.80 + £1.80 + £1.80 = £5.40,
*or two packs of the £2.30 envelopes,*
£2.30 + £2.30 = £4.60.

*The second option is cheaper by,*
£5.40 − £4.60 = £0.80 or 80p. ■

Suppose you wanted to put up some shelves to display goods for sale at an exhibition.

### Activity

The shelving is supplied in 2 m lengths.

1. If each shelf is to be 80 cm long, how many lengths of wood would you require to make 10 shelves?
2. How much wood is wasted from each length?

■

1

> 100 cm = 1 m

80 cm + 80 cm = 160 cm
*Two shelves can be cut from each piece of wood.*
*Five lengths of wood are required.*

2 *40 cm are left from each length of wood.* ■

### Key points to remember

Make sure your units are the same before you add or subtract.

### Putting it into practice

*Investigate and cost the best way of buying materials for your course. For example, compare the most economical and practical method of purchasing computer disks.*

# Topic 3 – Number problems

## Time – addition and subtraction

**AN 75**

Foundation/Intermediate/Advanced
Element **1.2, 2.2, 3.2**
Performance criteria **2, 3, 4, 5**
Range **Techniques**
(Number)

It is possible that you may need to fill in a time sheet for work completed. You would need to check in and check out. Look at the time sheet below. Remember that,

> there are 60 minutes in each hour.

### Activity

This is a time sheet for a student on a work placement. The student is required to clock in and out at lunch time as well as the beginning and end of the day.

|       | Mon   | Tues  | Wed   | Thurs | Fri   |
|-------|-------|-------|-------|-------|-------|
| in    | 8.15  | 8.20  | 8.17  | 8.10  | 8.06  |
| out   | 12.20 | 12.30 | 12.35 | 12.40 | 12.45 |
| *Lunch* |     |       |       |       |       |
| in    | 13.10 | 13.35 | 13.20 | 14.05 | 13.15 |
| out   | 17.45 | 18.37 | 18.06 | 17.50 | 17.55 |

1. On which day did she leave work the earliest?
2. On which day did she have 1 hour 25 minutes for lunch?
3. How long did she work on Friday morning?
4. How long did she work in total on Monday?
5. On which day did she have the shortest lunch break?

■

*1  Monday.    2  Thursday.    3  4 hours 39 minutes.*
*4  8 hours 40 minutes.    5  Friday.* ■

### Activity

Use the bus timetable from Avonbury to Oldport to answer the questions.

| Avonbury    | 7.50 | 8.10 | 9.15  | –     | 10.35 |
|-------------|------|------|-------|-------|-------|
| Bedworth    | 8.05 | 8.25 | 9.30  | –     | 10.50 |
| Hospital    | 8.42 | –    | 10.07 | –     | 11.27 |
| Wellington  | 8.45 | 9.00 | 10.10 | 10.40 | 11.30 |
| Shockham    | –    | –    | –     | 10.57 | –     |
| Telford     | 9.00 | 9.15 | 10.25 | –     | 11.45 |
| Gaol Square | 9.05 | 9.20 | 10.30 | –     | 11.50 |
| Chapel Gate | 9.12 | 9.27 | 10.37 | –     | 11.57 |
| Churton     | 9.20 | 9.35 | –     | –     | 12.05 |
| College Lane| –    | –    | 10.50 | 11.15 | –     |
| Oldport     | 9.30 | 9.45 | 10.55 | 11.20 | 12.15 |

1. What time does the 8.10 bus from Avonbury arrive at Telford and how long is the journey?
2. How long is the journey of the 10.07 bus from the Hospital to College Lane?
3. What time does the 11.30 bus from Wellington arrive at Churton and how long was the journey?
4. Nimita is to catch the bus from Telford to Churton. Which bus does she need to catch in Telford to be in Churton by 9.50?

■

*1  9.15. 1 hour 5 minutes.*
*2  45 minutes.*
*3  12.05. 35 minutes.*
*4  9.15.* ■

### Key points to remember

Take care when adding or subtracting if time is involved. Always remember that there are 60 minutes in each hour and you cannot just enter the times into your calculator.

### Putting it into practice

- Use bus or train timetables to plan a journey.
- Keep a time-sheet on your work placement, or project progress.

# Topic 3 – Number problems

## Working with addition and subtraction

**AN 76**

Foundation/Intermediate/Advanced
Element 1.2, 2.2, 3.2
Performance criteria 2, 4, 5, 6, 7
Range **Techniques** (Number); **Checking procedures**

## Mileage charts

When planning a journey it is often useful to use mileage charts. These can be found in any road atlas.

### Activity

This is an example of a typical mileage chart.

To find the distance between two towns, follow the horizontal line from one town and the vertical line from the other. At the intersection, read off the mileage. For example the distance between Derby and Glasgow is 277 miles.

**Mileage Chart**

| Ayr | | | | | | | |
|---|---|---|---|---|---|---|---|
| 200 | Bradford | | | | | | |
| 366 | 213 | Cardiff | | | | | |
| 272 | 75 | 145 | Derby | | | | |
| 441 | 275 | 119 | 200 | Exeter | | | |
| 134 | 308 | 473 | 380 | 544 | Fort William | | |
| 33 | 205 | 371 | 277 | 446 | 103 | Glasgow | |
| 238 | 67 | 227 | 90 | 282 | 351 | 243 | Hull |

Use the chart to answer the following questions.

1. What is the distance between Ayr and Hull?
2. If you travel from Ayr to Glasgow via Fort William, what is the total length of the journey?
3. Find the total journey form Bradford to Fort William via Derby and Glasgow.
4. If you need to travel from Cardiff to Hull and then discover that you need to go to Bradford on the way, how much does this add to the journey?

■
*1  238 miles.     2  237 miles.*
*3  455 miles.     4  53 miles.* ■

## Meter readings.

To calculate cost it is necessary to keep a check on meter readings.

### Key point to remember

- Charts can be used to set out addition and subtraction problems.

### Putting it into practice

*Plan a journey. Use a mileage chart.*

### Activity

A car hire firm keeps a log of the mileometer readings on its hire cars. This is recorded at the end of each month.

|  | Initial reading | Month 1 | Month 2 |
|---|---|---|---|
| Car A | 2578 | 3625 | 5998 |
| Car B | 5223 | 5999 | 7982 |
| Car C | 2589 | 2832 | 5998 |
| Car D | 128 | 245 | 889 |
| Car E | 2578 | 5689 | 6999 |

Find the mileage covered by

1. Car C in two months,
2. Car D in the first month,
3. Car B in the second month.

Which car covered the greatest number of miles in the two months?

■
*1  3409 miles.    2  117 miles.    3  1983 miles.*
*Car E covered the greatest number of miles in the two months.* ■

## Designing charts

A chart is a good way of recording information so that you can add and subtract numbers later.

### Activity

A group of four friends share a telephone. They have bought a telephone which displays the amount each call costs and have a rule that everyone writes down what they've spent at the time so that they can divide up the bill later. Design a chart for them to record this information on.

■ *Your chart should have had four columns, one for each of the friends. You may have decided to have an extra column so that they can write down other information, such as the time each call was made – but this isn't really necessary. When you are designing a chart that you want people to fill in, keep it as simple as possible.* ■

# Topic 4 – Solving problems

**AN 77**

## Use of a calculator

Foundation/Intermediate/Advanced
Element **1.2, 2.2, 3.2**
Performance criteria **2, 5, 6, 7, 8, 9**
Range **Techniques** (Number);
**Checking procedures;**
**Levels of accuracy**

When dealing with decimal quantities it is useful to use a calculator. Be careful to enter the numbers correctly – it is easy to press the wrong button by mistake. Always question whether the answer given by the calculator is a sensible size for the question set.

For example, if we wish to find 1.2 + 2.3 and the answer we get is 24.2, then we know that we must have made a mistake.

1.2 is almost 1 and 2.3 is almost 2.

1 + 2 = 3 so the answer should be between 3 and 4. Try again!

The sequence into the calculator is

**1 . 2 + 2 . 3 =**

1.2 + 2.3 = 3.5

Care must be taken entering figures into a calculator if they are given in different units. For example, to total £1.24, £2.36, 96p and £3.25, the 96p must be changed to pounds and entered as £0.96. The total would be £7.81. This answer then is reasonable. If you had entered 1.24 + 2.36 + 96 + 3.25 the answer would be 102.85. This is unreasonable.

### Activity

You are in charge of a fish and chip shop. Fish are £1.50 each and chips 75 pence per bag. Find the total charge for three fish and five bags of chips.

■ *75 pence = £0.75*

*Total charge for the fish is £1.50 × 3*
**1 . 50 × 3 = 4.50**

*Total charge for the chips is £0.75 × 5*
**0 . 75 × 5 = 3.75**

*Total = £4.50 + £3.75 = £8.25.*
*This seems a reasonable answer.* ■

### Activity

You are asked to keep the weekly records for the sales of a small confectionery stall and total the week's taking before handing the records to the next person with responsibility for the stall.

|       | Crisps | Chocolates | Drinks | Total |
|-------|--------|------------|--------|-------|
| Sun   | £3.52  | £4.27      | £1.67  |       |
| Mon   | £4.56  | £3.18      | £3.08  |       |
| Tues  | £1.76  | £2.90      | £1.96  |       |
| Wed   | £2.53  | £3.24      | £2.95  |       |
| Thurs | £3.12  | £2.85      | £2.86  |       |
| Fri   | £2.75  | £1.94      | £3.42  |       |
| Sat   | £1.92  | £4.01      | £1.95  |       |
|       |        |            |        | ?     |

### Key points to remember

When using a calculator always make a quick check that the answer seems sensible and that all figures are in the same units.

### *Putting it into practice*

*Budget how much you would spend on books and materials.*

■ *Total the rows and columns to double check that the final total is the same value for the rows and columns.*

|       | *Crisps* | *Chocolates* | *Drinks* | *Total* |
|-------|----------|--------------|----------|---------|
| *Sun*   | *£3.52*  | *£4.27*      | *£1.67*  | *£9.46*  |
| *Mon*   | *£4.56*  | *£3.18*      | *£3.08*  | *£10.82* |
| *Tues*  | *£1.76*  | *£2.90*      | *£1.96*  | *£6.62*  |
| *Wed*   | *£2.53*  | *£3.24*      | *£2.95*  | *£8.72*  |
| *Thurs* | *£3.12*  | *£2.85*      | *£2.86*  | *£8.83*  |
| *Fri*   | *£2.75*  | *£1.94*      | *£3.42*  | *£8.11*  |
| *Sat*   | *£1.92*  | *£4.01*      | *£1.95*  | *£7.88*  |
|         | *£20.16* | *£22.39*     | *£17.89* | *£60.44* |

■

# Topic 4 – Solving problems

## Multiplication and division 1

**AN 78**

Foundation/Intermediate/
**Advanced**
Element **1.2,2.2,3.2**
Performance criteria
**1,2,3,5,6,7**
Range **Techniques**,
(Number; Handling data);
**Checking procedures;**

Multiplication is a quick method for totalling several items of equal amount, for instance, if you buy five books of stamps and each book has four stamps then altogether you have bought

$4 + 4 + 4 + 4 + 4 = 20$. It is far quicker to say 5 times 4 or $5 \times 4 = 20$. This is a fairly easy calculation. If decimals are involved it may be easier to use a calculator.

### Activity

You are going to supervise a stationery stall in the reception of an exhibition. You have to total the value of the stock at the beginning and end of the day in order to calculate the amount of cash taken for goods sold.

**Stock at 9 a.m.**    Total
36 pencils at 20p
24 ballpoint pens at 50p
52 small notepads at 45p
18 erasers at 25p
15 bookmarks at 30p

**Stock at 5 p.m.**
28 pencils at 20p
15 ballpoint pens at 50p
43 small notepads at 45p
12 erasers at 25p
13 bookmarks at 30p

■ *Total at 9 a.m. = 5160p = £51.60.*
*Total at 5 p.m. = 3935p = £39.35.*
*Amount of cash taken is £12.25.* ■

### Activity

You have a part-time job at your local cinema which is divided into two small theatres.

Cinema 1: This is used for adult films and has 100 seats at £3.00 per seat.

Cinema 2: This is used for children's films and it has 80 seats at £1.50 per seat.

If every seat was taken on one evening how much would you expect the takings to amount to?

■ *$100 \times £3.00 = £300$*
*$80 \times £1.50 = £120$*
*Total takings = £420* ■

### Activity

You have to put together the wages for some staff. The correct change is required.

List the notes and coins that you would use in each case if the bank have supplied only £10 and £5 notes as well as £1, 50p, 20p, 5p and 1p coins. Use the least number of coins in each case.

1   £30.18,
2   £25.34,
3   £17.12.

■

*1   $3 \times £10 + 3 \times 5p + 3 \times 1p = £30.18.$*
*2   $2 \times £10 + 1 \times £5 + 1 \times 20p + 2 \times 5p + 4 \times 1p = £25.34.$*
*3   $1 \times £10 + 1 \times £5 + 2 \times £1 + 2 \times 5p + 2 \times 1p = £17.12.$* ■

### Key points to remember

- If you need to find the total of several equal numbers, it is quicker to use multiplication than addition.
- Remember to change pence to pounds or pounds to pence if necessary.

### *Putting it into practice*

*Keep records of the materials used in a project. Total and cost the items.*

# Topic 4 – Solving problems

## Multiplication and division 2

**AN 79**

Foundation/Intermediate/Advanced
Element **1.2, 2.2, 3.2**
Performance criteria **2, 3, 5, 6, 7**
Range **Techniques** (Number); **Checking procedures; Levels of accuracy**

When dealing with numbers it is very useful to be able to make a rough approximation.

For example if you wanted to purchase 5 novels at £4.99 each, first find the cost of 5 at £5. This is £25, so that,
$5 \times £4.99 = 5 \times £5$ minus $5 \times 1p = £25 - 5p = £24.95$

### Activity

You decide to go on a shopping spree with £45 to spend. You wish to buy three bargain videos at £5.99 each and two compact discs at £12.99 each. If you need £1.50 for the bus fare home, calculate without a calculator whether you can afford to buy the three videos and two CDs and have enough money left to catch the bus.

■ $3 \times £5.99 = 3 \times £6 - 3 \times 1p = £18 - 3p = £17.97$.
$2 \times £12.99 = 2 \times £13 - 2 \times 1p = £26 - 2p = £25.98$.
Total $(£18 - 3p) + (£26 - 2p) = £44 - 5p = £43.95$.
Change $= £1.05$ which is not enough for the bus fare. ■

When multiplying decimals without a calculator try to work with convenient amounts and then add or subtract the small differences.

Division is the opposite process to multiplication. For example, if I am to set out the seating for a group of people in 4 rows with 9 chairs in each row then there will be $9 \times 4$ chairs. 36 chairs are available. If I wanted the same number of chairs set into 3 equal rows I would need to divide 36 by 3 to find that there are 12 chairs in each row.

### Activity

You have been asked to set out the seating for 72 people in equal length rows.

1. What would be the number of chairs in a row if there are to be 8 rows?
2. How many rows will there be if there are to be 24 chairs in each row?
3. What would be the number of chairs in each row if there are to be between no less than 11 rows but no more than 14 rows – and you want to have an equal number of chairs in each row?

■
1. $72 \div 8 = 9$.
2. $72 \div 24 = 3$.
3. $72 \div 12 = 6$. (The other numbers between 11 and 14 don't give you a whole number of chairs in each row.)
■

### Activity

You have been asked to organise the drinks at a reception. The drinks are delivered in litre bottles. There are 100 guests. A litre bottle will fill eight glasses. Three drinks per guest are to be allowed. How many litres do you order?

■ *Glasses required* $100 \times 3 = 300$.
*Number of bottles* $300 \div 8 = 37.5$.
*Order 38 litres.* ■

### Key points to remember

- When totalling several items of the same value (whether using a calculator or not) it is quicker to multiply rather than to add.
- When multiplying or dividing without a calculator, work in round numbers and add or subtract the small differences afterwards.
- When you use a calculator remember to check that the answer is of a sensible size.

### *Putting it into practice*

*Design four different seating arrangements for a hall if there must be chairs provided for 120 people.*

# Topic 4 – Solving problems

**AN 81**

Foundation/Intermediate/Advanced
Element **1.2, 2.2, 3.2**
Performance criteria **2, 3, 5**
Range **Techniques**
(Number);
**Levels of accuracy**

## Fractions

Fractions are a part or a share of an item.

You will probably have shared a pizza with friends and had to work out the share that each person would eat. Some fractions occur more often than others in everyday life. In the case of the pizza, if there are two of you then each has a half which is written as ½. In the same way if there were three people then each has ⅓ (a third) and if there were four each has ¼ (a quarter) and so on.

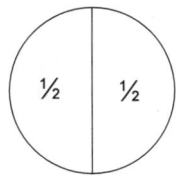 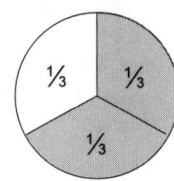 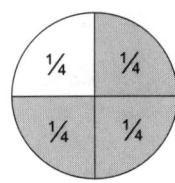

We can see from the diagrams above that the shaded parts would be ⅔ and ¾.

In a fraction such as ⅔ the bottom number tells us how many parts the whole was divided into and the top number tells us how many of them we have.

### Activity

You have invited a group of friends for tea and you decide to bake a cake. You decide to make a square cake.

Draw a sketch in each case to help you solve these problems.

1. Which would be the larger piece, a half or a third?
2. Half of the cake would be the same as how many quarters?
3. Divide the cake into eight equal parts so that each part is an eighth. How many eighths are equal to one half?
4. If the cake is divided into fifths and someone eats three fifths, how much of the cake is left?

■

1. A half is larger than a third.
2. Two quarters are the same as one half.
3. Four eighths are the same as a half.
4. Two fifths are left. ■

It is very common to use fractions when talking about time. For instance, we talk about half past one or a quarter to five and so on.

one hour = 60 minutes.

½ an hour 60 ÷ 2 = 30 minutes.

¼ of an hour = 60 ÷ 4 = 15 minutes.

¾ of an hour = 60 ÷ 4 × 3 = 45 minutes.

### Activity

1. Change the following times into hours and minutes.
   a. Three and a quarter hours.
   b. Four and three quarter hours.
   c. Six and a half hours.
2. Three students share access time on a computer taking one third of the time each. The machine is available for 2 hours this afternoon. How much time can they each have on it?

■

1. a. 3 hours 15 minutes.
   b. 4 hours 45 minutes.
   c. 6 hours and 30 minutes.
2. ⅓ of 60 minutes = 20 minutes.
   They can have twice this time (40 minutes) each. ■

## Money

It is also sometimes useful to use fractions with money.

### Activity

How many pence do these fractions represent?
a. £½   b. £¼   c. £¾   d. £⅓.

■ a. 50p, b. 25p, c. 75p, d. 33.33 p (or 33p, to the nearest penny) ■

### Key points to remember

- In a fraction such as ¾ the bottom number tells us how many parts the whole was divided into and the top number tells us how many of them we have.
- It is useful to remember common fractions of time and money.

### Putting it into practice

*Write down some fractions you could use when measuring the height or length of things.*

# Topic 4 – Solving problems

**AN 82**

## The calculator fraction button

**Foundation/Intermediate/ Advanced**
Element **1.2,2.2,3.2**
Performance criteria **6,7,8,9**
Range **Techniques** (Number); **Checking procedures**

There is a button on your calculator which can help you when you are working with fractions. The button looks like this

$a^{b/c}$

You would enter a fraction, say $\frac{2}{4}$ into your calculator in the following way:

**2 $a^{b/c}$ 4**

the screen shows 2 ⌋ 4 this is the calculator's way of showing fractions.

If you now press the equals sign something impressive should happen:

**2 $a^{b/c}$ 4 =**

Screen shows: 1 ⌋ 2

This means that the calculator has changed your fraction $\frac{2}{4}$ into its easiest form $\frac{1}{2}$.

$\frac{2}{4} = \frac{1}{2}$.

### Activity

Use your calculator to work out the following problems.

**1** $\frac{2}{5} + \frac{1}{3} =$

**2** $\frac{7}{9} - \frac{3}{5} =$

**3** $\frac{1}{4} \times \frac{2}{3} =$

**4** $\frac{5}{6} \div \frac{7}{8} =$

■

*1* ***2 $a^{b/c}$ 5 + 1 $a^{b/c}$ 3 =*** *11 ⌋ 15 = $\frac{11}{15}$.*

*2* ***7 $a^{b/c}$ 9 – 3 $a^{b/c}$ 5 =*** *8 ⌋ 45 = $\frac{8}{45}$.*

*3* ***1 $a^{b/c}$ 4 × 2 $a^{b/c}$ 3 =*** *1 ⌋ 6 = $\frac{1}{6}$.*

*4* ***5 $a^{b/c}$ 6 ÷ 7 $a^{b/c}$ 8 =*** *20 ⌋ 21 = $\frac{20}{21}$.* ■

Your calculator can deal with numbers that are greater than one, such as $3\frac{1}{2}$. As this is a mixture of whole numbers and fractions it is called a mixed number. We would put $3\frac{1}{2}$ into the calculator as

**3 $a^{b/c}$ 1 $a^{b/c}$ 2** and it would look like 3 ⌋ 1 ⌋ 2 on the screen.

If you put a top heavy fraction into your calculator not only will it change it to its easiest form but it will change it into a mixed number. Try $\frac{15}{12}$.

**15 $a^{b/c}$ 12** = 1 ⌋ 1 ⌋ 4

This equals $1\frac{1}{4}$.

We say that this number is written in its lowest terms.

### Activity

You are working in a local factory. The rates of pay are as follows:

Basic pay of £3.20 per hour up to 35 hours.

Evening overtime is paid at time and a quarter.

Saturday is paid at time and a half.

Sunday is paid double time.

Find your take-home pay in a week in which you work 35 hours at basic rate, 5 and a half hours in the evening, four and three-quarter hours on a Saturday and six and a half hours on a Sunday.

■ *Basic pay £3.20 × 35 = £112.*

*Evening overtime*
*£3.20 × $1\frac{1}{4}$ × $5\frac{1}{2}$ = £22.*

*Saturday overtime*
*£3.20 × $1\frac{1}{2}$ × $4\frac{3}{4}$ = £22.80.*

*Sunday overtime*
*£3.20 × 2 × $6\frac{1}{2}$ = £41.60.*

*Total £198.40.* ■

### Key points to remember

- The fraction button on your calculator looks like $a^{b/c}$
- If you put a top-heavy fraction into your calculator and press the = sign your calculator will give you an answer that is a mixed number in its lowest terms.

### *Putting it into practice*

*Find out the rates of pay at your work placement. Practise using fractions on your calculator by working out what pay someone would receive if they worked various hours at different times of the week.*

# Topic 4 – Solving problems

## Fractions and decimals

**AN 84**

Foundation/Intermediate/Advanced
Element **1.2, 2.2, 3.2**
Performance criteria **2, 3, 5, 6**
Range **Techniques** (Number);
**Levels of accuracy**

For many years money has been decimalised and most units are now based on hundreds or thousands. For example, we write 3 metres 26 centimetres as 3.26 m as there are 100 cm in 1 m.

5 kilometres 17 metres is written as 5.017 km as 1000 m = 1 km.

### Activity

We are used to thinking of some common fractions in terms of decimals.

Use your calculator to find these fractions as decimals. The first one is done for you.

1. A half, ½.
   Calculator: 1 ÷ 2 =
   Screen display: 0.5
2. A quarter, ¼.
3. Three quarters, ¾.
4. A third, ⅓.

■
2   0.25.
3   0.75.
4   0.3333333
*This is called a recurring decimal as it is never ending.* ■

Money is always written to the nearest penny, this means to two decimal places.

### Activity

Find, correct to two decimal places

1. ½ of £5.00.
2. ¼ of 9 kg.
3. ¾ of 1 m.
4. ⅓ of £4.00.

■
1   ½ × £5.00 = £2.50.
2   ¼ × 9 kg = 2.25 kg.
3   ¾ × 1 m = 0.75 m.
4   ⅓ × £4.00 = £1.33. ■

Notice that for question 3 the answer was 0.75. The zero is important. It is usual to have at least one figure before the decimal point. We don't start a number with the decimal point such as .75 in case the decimal point gets missed and we would think the answer was 75 instead of 0.75. Sometimes if we want to write a whole number such as five pounds we just write £5 rather than £5.00 although both are correct.

### Activity

You have been taking several measurements and you wish to change them into more convenient units remembering that there are,

100 cm in 1 m        100 pence in £1
1000 m in 1 km       1000 g in 1 kg

Change
1. 752p to £
2. 8634 cm to m
3. 750 g to kg
4. 5254 m to km
5. 6 000 000 cm to km

■
1   752p ÷ 100 = £7.52.
2   8634 cm ÷ 100 = 86.34 m
3   750 g ÷ 1000 = 0.750 kg
    or 0.75 kg
4   5254 m ÷ 1000 = 5.254 km
5   6 000 000 cm ÷ 100 =
    60 000.00 m or 60 000 m
    60 000 m ÷ 1000 = 60.00 km
    or 60 km ■

In answers 3 and 5 you can omit the zeros after the decimal point, without altering the value of the number.

### Key points to remember

- Common decimals are ½ = 0.5, ¼ = 0.25, ¾ = 0.75 and ⅓ = 0.33333.
- All decimals must have a number before the decimal point.
- If a decimal point is followed by zeros and no other numbers (e.g. 15.00) then these zeros could be omitted without altering the value of the number.
- Decimal units such as money, metric lengths and metric weights can be easily changed from small units to large.

### Putting it into practice

*Keep a record of everything you spend for a week and add up the total. Take care to ensure that all your figures are written in correct decimal form.*

# Topic 4 – Solving problems

## Use decimals to describe

**AN 85**

Foundation
Element **1.2**
Performance criteria **2,3,5**
Range **Techniques**
(Number);
**Levels of accuracy**

Most of the units you use for measuring length and weight are in metric or decimal form. Decimals are easy to use. Look at the scale below. It shows the value 2.6. The distance between the 2 and the 3 is divided into ten spaces by short lines. The pointer is pointing to the sixth short line from the 2, so the value is at $2^6/_{10}$.

$2^6/_{10}$ is the same as 2.6.

### Activity

The diagram below represents a ruler marked in centimetres. Write as decimals the lengths marked A, B, C, D and E.

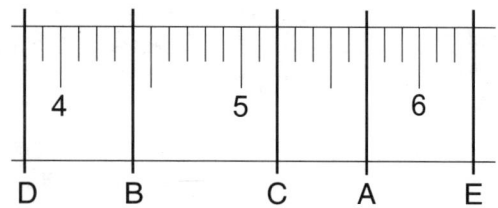

■

A is 5 units and 7 tenths = 5.7 cm

B is 4 units and 4 tenths = 4.4 cm

C is 5 units and 2 tenths = 5.2 cm

D is 3 units and 8 tenths = 3.8 cm

E is 6 units and 3 tenths = 6.3 cm ■

Some measurements, especially weights are measured on a dial. Some scales are very accurate and can measure a difference as small as one hundredth of a unit. (This kind of accuracy would be necessary for a chemist measuring drugs, for example.) Metric measurements can also be easily changed to a decimal. For example, 1 unit and twenty seven hundredths can be written as

$1^{27}/_{100}$ = 1.27.

You can check this on your calculator:

$1 + {}^{27}/_{100} =$

or **1 $a^{b/c}$ 27 $a^{b/c}$ 100 = $a^{b/c}$**

When reading a dial or ruler, if the reading lies between two marks on the scale then take the reading to the closest mark.

### Putting it into practice

*Use your ruler to measure the sizes of some paper and envelopes, giving the answers to one decimal place.*

### Activity

Different levels of accuracy are needed in different situations.

How accurate do you think you would have to be if you were weighing the following:

**1** a new-born baby

**2** yourself – to see if you had lost weight on a diet

**3** a parcel you needed to put stamps on.

■ *The baby would be weighed to the nearest gram. Bathroom scales usually measure in tenths of a kilogram. You would need to know the weight of the parcel in grams.* ■

### Activity

The diagram below shows scales to measure quantities from 0 to 1 kilogram. Take the readings for the weights A, B, C and D giving the reading correct to the nearest hundredth of a kilogram, this means to two decimal places.

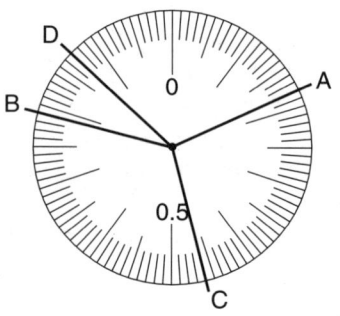

■

A is eighteen hundredths = 0.18 kg

B is seventy-nine hundredths = 0.79 kg

C is forty-six hundredths = 0.46 kg

D is eighty-eight hundredths = 0.88 kg. ■

### Key points to remember

- Measurements can be read from scales such as rulers and dials where the reading is taken to the nearest mark.

- If the scale is marked in tenths then the measurement is to one decimal place, if it is in hundredths then the reading is to two decimal places.

# Topic 4 – Solving problems

**AN 86**

Foundation/Intermediate/Advanced
Element **1.2, 2.2, 3.2**
Performance criteria **2, 3, 4, 5**
Range **Techniques** (Number); **Levels of accuracy**

## Use decimals

Sometimes you have to correct decimals to a set number of places. This happens most often when dealing with money. For instance, if you wanted to share £2.49 equally between two people then, £2.49 ÷ 2 = £1.245 this means one pound and 24½ pence. You cannot have half pence and so this would be rounded up to £1.25. The same thing would happen for £1.246, £1.247, £1.248 and £1.249 as they are all nearer to £1.25.

Any quantities below £1.245 such as £1.243 would become £1.24. All money terms must be written correct to the nearest penny.

### Activity

You had arranged the finances for several trips run from your local youth club and now you have to refund the excess money paid for each trip to the members of the club. Give all your answers correct to the nearest penny. Share:

1. £13.78 between 4 people.
2. £7.54 between 6 people.
3. £17.52 between 7 people.

■
1 £13.78 ÷ 4 = £3.445 = £3.45 to the nearest penny.
2 £7.54 ÷ 6 = £1.2566667 = £1.26 to the nearest penny.
3 £17.52 ÷ 7 = £2.5028571 = £2.50 to the nearest penny. ■

## Reading Scales

Some measurements are read from a dial. Sometimes the pointer lies between the marks on the scale and you have to find an approximate reading. If the pointer lies half way between marks then a half-way reading can be taken. For example, if the pointer lies between 1.2 and 1.3 this is between 1.20 and 1.30 so then 1.25 is the half way mark. If the pointer lies between 0.36 and 0.37 then the reading is 0.365.

### Activity

You have a part-time job weighing fruit, vegetables and spices in your local store. You need to make the reading as accurate as possible. If you mark the weight too high the customer will complain to your employer and if you read it too low your employer may well end your employment. The scales below each measure in kilograms. Find the reading as accurately as possible.

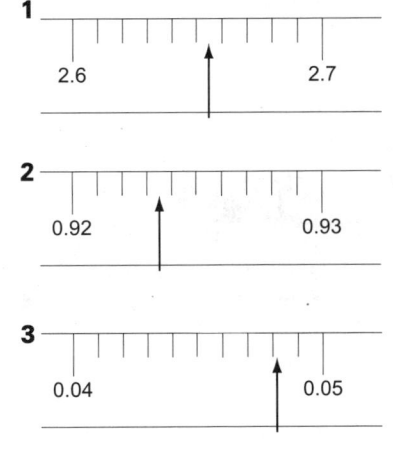

■
1 Half way between 2.65 and 2.66 = 2.655 kg
2 Half way between 0.923 and 0.924 = 0.9235 kg
3 Just over 0.048 kg and this would be the best approximation. ■

### Activity

Different levels of accuracy are needed in different situations.

How accurate do you think these different types of scales would have to be in a large chemist's shop?

1. used by the pharmacist to weigh out drugs
2. provided for people to step on and weigh themselves
3. in the postroom.

■ The pharmacist's scales would measure to the milligram (thousandth of a gram). The scales for people to weigh themselves would probably measure to a tenth of a kilogram. The scales in the postroom would measure to the nearest gram. ■

### Key point to remember

When dealing with decimal numbers you must give a realistic and practical answer and sometimes this means making a correction to a calculated value or a value read from a scale.

### Putting it into practice

Weigh some packages and letters ready for mailing. Use the Royal Mail postage rates to decide on the postage to be paid.

# Topic 4 – Solving problems

## Percentages

**Foundation/Intermediate/Advanced**
Element 1.2, 2.2, 3.2
Performance criteria 4, 6, 7, 8, 9
Range **Techniques (Number); Checking procedures; Levels of accuracy**

You will have noticed that sale prices often offer 10% off, or VAT is charged at 17½%.

> One per cent is the same as $1 \div 100$ or 0.01.

If an item costing £10 is reduced by 12% in a sale, we can find the 12% reduction as follows,

$12 \div 100 \times £10 = £1.20$

It can also be found by using the % button on your calculator.

Calculator: **10 × 12 %** Display 1.20

### Key points to remember

- One per cent is the same as $1 \div 100$ or 0.01.
- Interest is added on.
- Discount is subtracted.

### Activity

1. Find 17% of £20.
2. Find 25.6% of £400.
3. Find 52.5% of £3000.
4. Find 12.5% of £80.

∎
1  £3.40.   2  £102.40.
3  £1575.   4  £10. ∎

## Interest

If you borrow money, it is usual to charge interest on the amount borrowed. For example, if you borrow £400, interest could be charged at 20%. In this case you would have to pay back both the £400 and the 20% interest on the £400.

The interest would be 20% of £400 = £80, so the total to be paid back would be,

£400 + £80 = £480.

### Activity

Find the total to be paid back on the following loans. The interest to be charged is given in each case.

1. £1500, interest 10%.
2. £260, interest 15%.
3. £20 000, interest 20%.

∎
1  £1650.
2  £299.
3  £24 000. ∎

## Discount

When a sale price is given, a discount is made on the original price. If you see a pair of jeans with a 20% discount on the original price of £35, the sale price of the jeans is,

£35 − 20% of £35,

£35 − £7 = £28.

### Activity

Find the sale price of the following items if the percentage discount is given.

1. Shoes, original price £45, discount 15%.
2. Shirt, original price £30, discount 50%.
3. Holiday, original price £450, discount 25%.

∎
1  £38.25.
2  £15.
3  £337.50. ∎

### Putting it into practice

- Find the rate of interest charged at your local bank on money borrowed.
- Calculate the reduction on sale goods when a percentage discount is given.

# AN – Interpret and present data

**Element 3**

## Topic 1 – Diagrams, maps and plans

- AN96   Describing two-dimensional shapes
- AN97   Describing three-dimensional shapes
- AN98   Using flow charts to convert measurements
- AN99   Use simple maps

## Topic 2 – Representing and displaying data

- AN104  Counting your results
- AN106  Finding the mean (discrete data)
- AN110  Bar charts
- AN111  Pie charts
- AN113  The range
- AN115  Line graphs
- AN118  Choosing the right diagram
- AN119  Two-way tables

## Topic 3 – Interpreting graphs and tables

- AN120  Reading tables
- AN121  Reading bar charts
- AN122  Reading pie charts
- AN126  Misrepresenting data – 1
- AN127  Misrepresenting data – 2

# Topic 1 – Diagrams, maps and plans

## Describing two-dimensional shapes

**AN 96**

Foundation/Intermediate/Advanced
Element **1.3, 2.3, 3.3**
Performance criteria **1, 2**
Range **Techniques** (Shape, space and measures);
**Explain the main features**

It is useful (and sometimes necessary) to be able to describe shapes accurately using the correct words. Most of the shapes shown on this resource sheet appear in buildings and structures in our everyday surroundings.

### Activity

Look first at the diagrams showing the most common two-dimensional shapes.
Next try to find as many of these shapes as you can in each picture on the other side of this sheet.

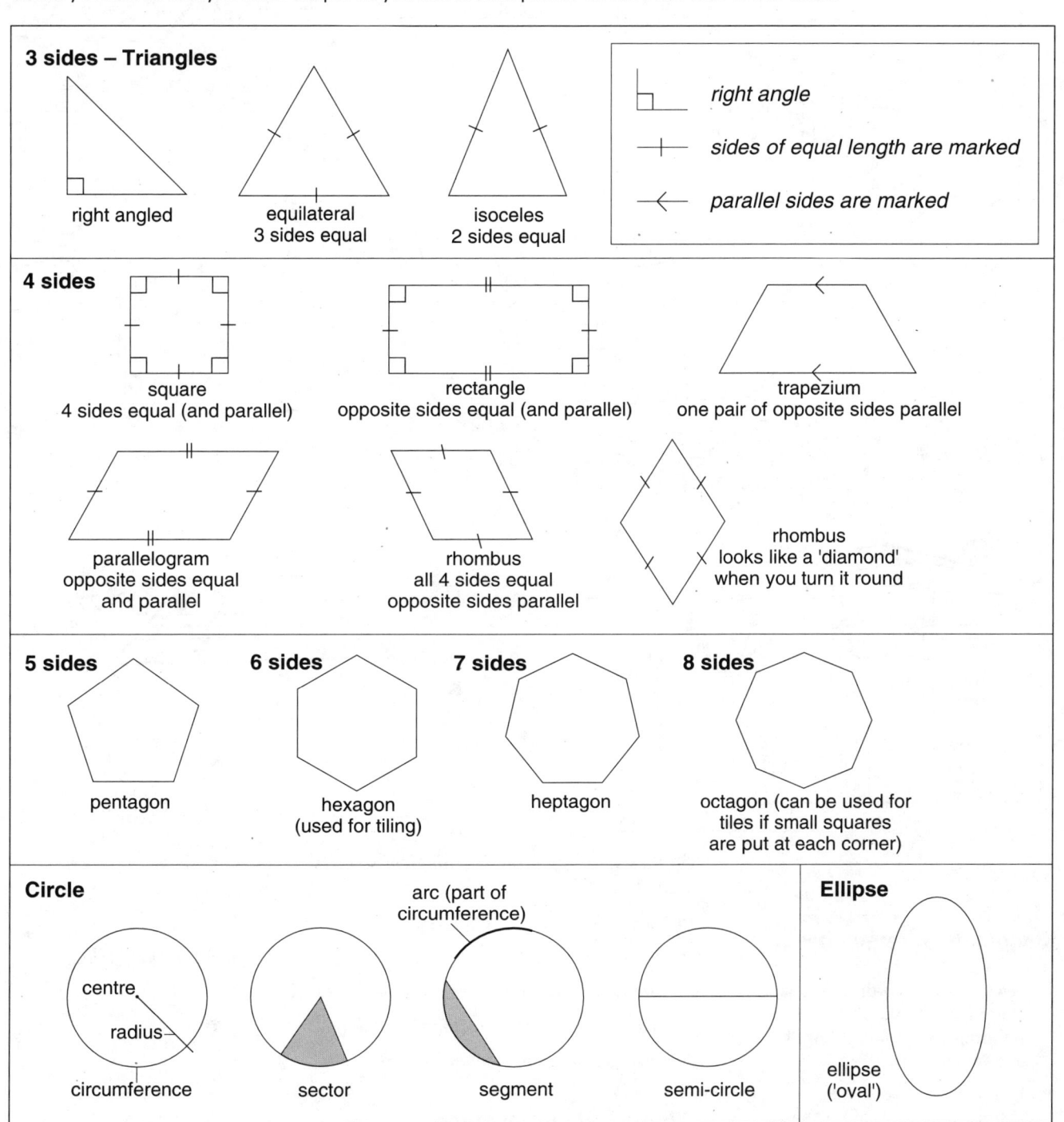

# Topic 1 – Diagrams, maps and plans

## Describing two-dimensional shapes (continued)

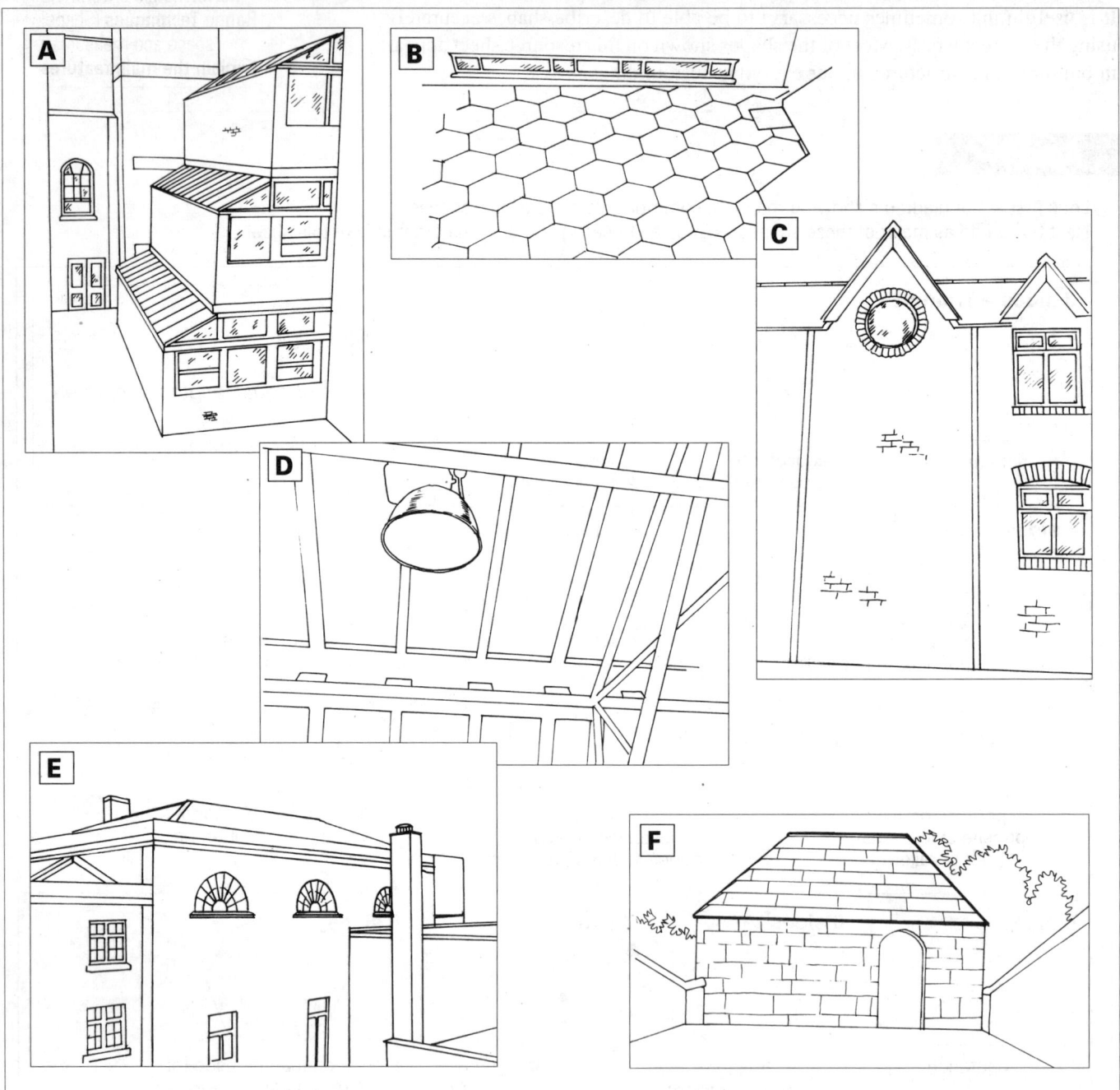

■ *Picture A: right-angle triangles; squares; rectangles; segment (on top of arched window.*

*Picture B: hexagons; rectangles.*

*Picture C: isosceles triangles; circle; rectangles; segments or arcs (slight arch).*

*Picture D: circle; rectangles; triangles.*

*Picture E: semi-circles; rectangles; triangles.*

*Picture F: trapezium; rectangles.* ■

### Key points to remember

- A variety of two-dimensional shapes can be seen in buildings, furnishings, signs and logos.
- Describing these shapes simply and accurately is an important skill in a variety of jobs, including design work, catering, interior design, building and retailing.

### Putting it into practice

What two-dimensional shapes can you see in your immediate surroundings? Are there any unusual shapes in buildings that you see every day?

## Topic 1 – Diagrams, maps and plans

**AN 97**

Foundation/Intermediate/Advanced
Element **1.3, 2.3, 3.3**
Performance criteria **1, 2**
Range **Tecnhiques** (Shape, space and measures);
**Explain the main features**

### Describing three-dimensional shapes

While everyday objects may have flat two-dimensional sides (the sides of a box may be a rectangle) they actually occupy space in three dimensions. It is important to know the names of three-dimensional shapes so that you can accurately describe three-dimensional objects and buildings.

## Three-dimensional objects

Three-dimensional (3D) shapes occur in buildings, furniture and packaging. Virtually all goods sold in shops are packaged in some way. Packages which will fit together neatly in larger cartons are the most popular. Think about this problem as you work through this sheet.

### Activity

The most common 3D shapes are shown in the diagrams here. (It is quite an interesting problem to decide how to represent a 3D object in a 2D diagram!)

All prisms have uniform cross-sections (they can be cut across in slices which are all the same).
Cubes and cuboids are prisms; so are the following shapes.

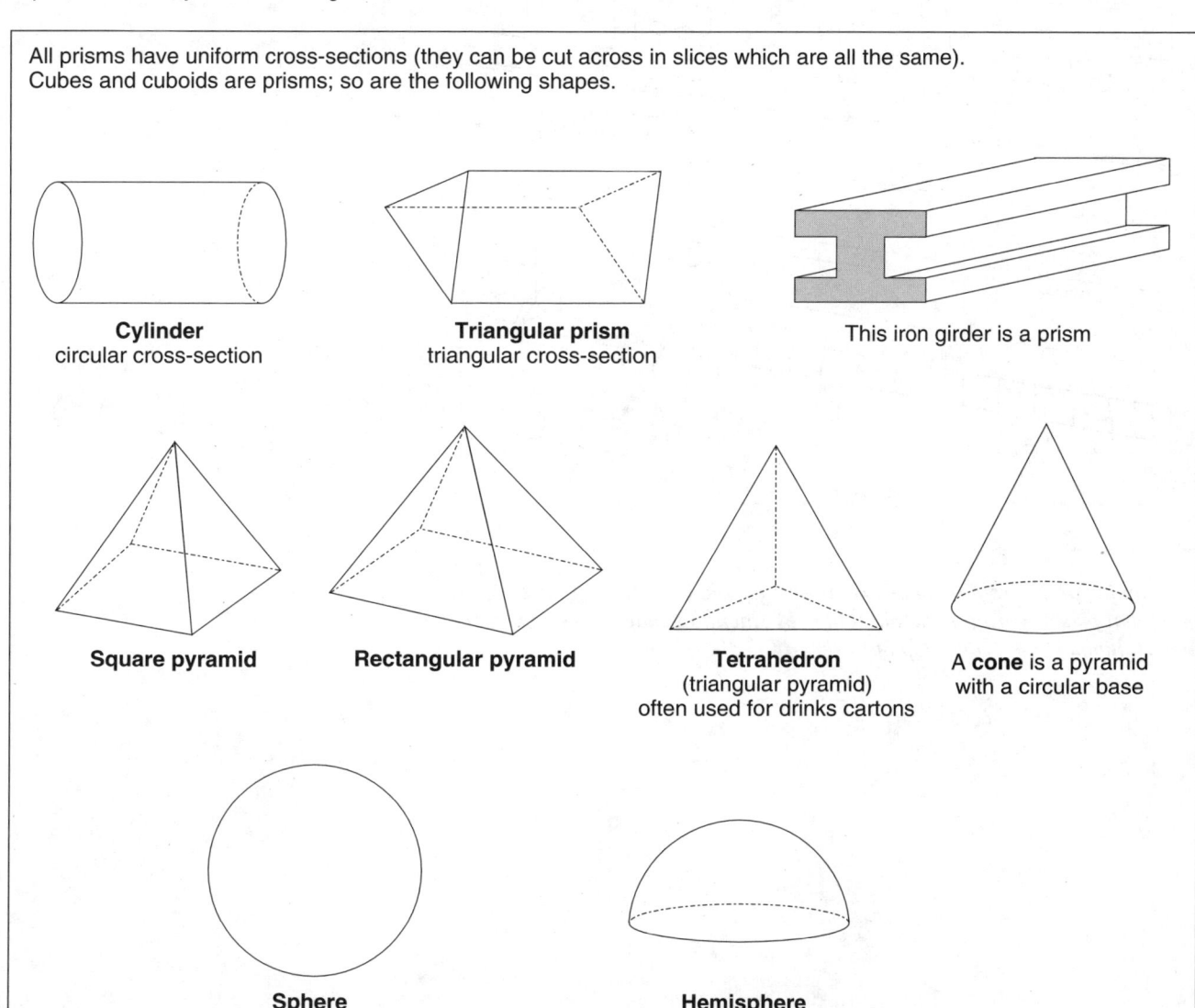

**Cylinder**
circular cross-section

**Triangular prism**
triangular cross-section

This iron girder is a prism

**Square pyramid**

**Rectangular pyramid**

**Tetrahedron**
(triangular pyramid)
often used for drinks cartons

A **cone** is a pyramid with a circular base

**Sphere**

**Hemisphere**

# Topic 1 – Diagrams, maps and plans

## Describing three-dimensional shapes (continued)

### Activity

Look at the drawing. How many 3D shapes can you find in it? You should be able to find at least six different shapes.

▌▌ *triangular prism (roof on back extension); cuboid (extension to house); pentagonal prism (garage); cuboid (chimney stack); cylinder (tower on roof); cylinder (chimney pot); cone (top of tower).* ▌▌

### Key point to remember

Workers in the building industry, catering, interior design and retailing need to be able to identify and describe 3D shapes.

### *Putting it into practice*

- What 3D shapes can you identify around you now?
- Where on buildings are you likely to find pyramids, hemispheres or cones?
- Which 3D shapes can you find used as packaging for food or for stationery items?

# Topic 1 – Diagrams, maps and plans

## Using flow charts to convert measurements

**AN 98**

Foundation
Element **1.3,2.3,3.3**
Performance criteria **1,2,3,4**
Range **Techniques**
(Number; Handling data);
**Levels of accuracy;**
**Explain the main features**

Very often you have to use a formula to convert one kind of measurement to another, e.g., miles to kilometres or degrees Centigrade to degrees Fahrenheit for temperatures. (There are more resource sheets on other ways of converting measurements in Elements 1 and 2.)

If you find it difficult to use formulae you can make it easier by breaking the process down into smaller steps. A flow diagram can help you do this.

Kilometres to miles
1 kilometre = 5/8 miles

To change kilometres to miles you need to multiply by 5 and divide by 8. This can be shown on a simple flow chart.

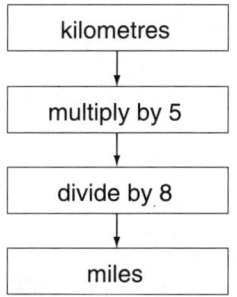

### Activity

1 Use the flow chart to change
   a 12 kilometres to miles
   b 160 kilometres to miles

2 Can you think how you could use the flow chart to change miles back to kilometres?
   Try out your idea on an answer you already know.

3 Draw a new flow chart to change miles to kilometres.

■ *1a*

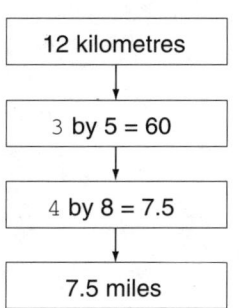

*1b*

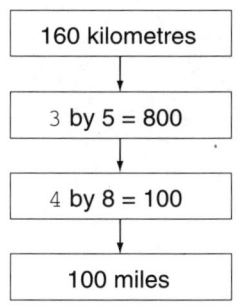

2 To use the flow chart to change miles back to kilometres, you could go backwards through the steps in the flow chart. But you would have to multiply by 8 (not divide), and divide by 5 (not multiply). So each step will have to be done the opposite way round.

3

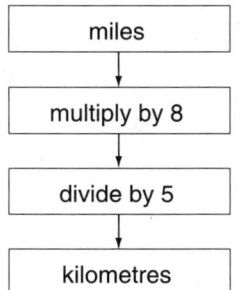

### Activity

You are told that 1 litre = 1¾ pints.

1 Change 1¾ to quarters.
2 Explain why it is true that 1 litre = ⅞ pints.
3 Use this to draw a flow chart to change litres to pints.
4 Change 8 litres into pints.
5 Draw a flow chart to change pints into litres.

■
1  1¾ is 7 quarters
2  So 1¾ = ⅞
3

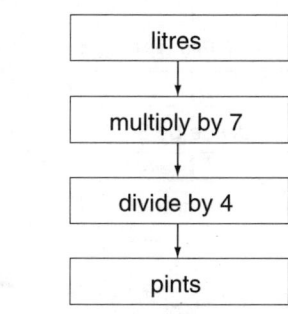

4  14 pints
5

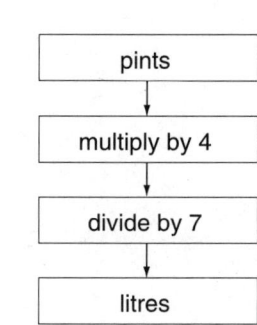

■

Here is a harder flow chart. It changes temperatures from Centigrade to Fahrenheit.

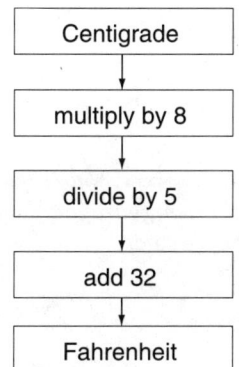

### Activity

1 Use this flow chart to change 10°C to Fahrenheit.
2 Can you draw the flow chart to change Fahrenheit to centigrade (this is harder!)

• 115 •

# Topic 1 – Diagrams, maps and plans

## Using flow charts to convert measurements (continued)

■

1  $10\ C = 48\ F$

2

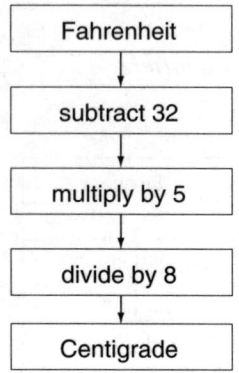

■

### Key points to remember

Each part or step in the working out of a formula is shown separately. To reverse the calculation, you must do the OPPOSITE calculations in REVERSE order.

### Putting it into practice

*If 1 kg = 2.2 lb. draw a flow chart to change it to pounds. Try to draw a flow chart to show a formula which you use in your vocational studies.*

# Topic 1 – Diagrams, maps and plans

## Use simple maps

**AN 99**

Foundation
Element **1.3, 2.3, 3.3**
Performance criteria **1, 2**
Range **Techniques** (Shape, space and measures);
**Explain the main features**

Simple maps and diagrams are often used to explain how to get to places. Here is a map showing how to get to a tile warehouse (selling floor and wall tiles). This map was printed as part of an advert in a local newspaper.

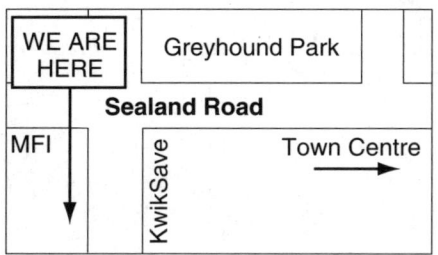

### Activity

Explain how you would find the tile warehouse if you were coming from the town centre.

■ *To find the tile warehouse you need to travel out of the town centre on the Sealand Road. Go past the Greyhound Park (on your right). At the crossroads near Kwik Save turn left. The tile warehouse is on the right.* ■

It is much clearer to have these instructions in the form of a map. Somebody once said, 'A picture is worth a thousand words'. That is certainly true here.

### Activity

Look at this second map (also from an advert in the local paper). Explain the easiest route to the shop from the M53.

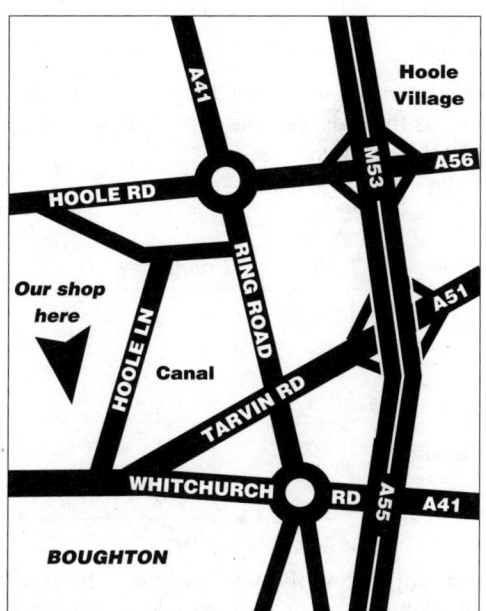

■ *The easiest route from the M53 is to leave the motorway at the junction with the A51 (Tarvin Road). Cross the ring road driving straight on. At the T junction with Whitchurch Road turn sharp right then turn right again into Hoole Lane. The shop is on the left-hand side.* ■

There are other slightly more complicated routes from the M53 leaving the motorway at the junction with the A56.

### Activity

Draw a simple map showing how to reach your school or college from the town centre. Show the bus or train station giving the easiest route for someone travelling on public transport.

### Key points to remember

- A simple map need not necessarily be drawn to scale.
- It should show useful landmarks to enable people to identify where they are.

### Putting it into practice

- *Try to find examples of maps in your local paper. Do they show enough detail?*
- *Are they accurate? Does this matter?*
- *Draw a map showing how to get from your school or college to your work placement.*

# Topic 2 – Representing and displaying data

## Counting your results

**AN 104**

Foundation/Intermediate/Advanced
Element **1.3,2.3,3.3**
Performance criteria **1,2,3**
Range **Techniques** (Handling data); **Conventions**; **Explain the main features**

This resource sheet shows how simple data can be summarised as a table. Data (or results) which have been counted (rather than measured) are usually called **discrete data**. These results will be very simple as it is possible only for whole numbers to occur.

The director of Basset's Buses has employed a consultant to produce a report on the workings of the company, its customers and other aspects of the service it provides.

Here is some of the information collected as the consultant recorded the number of passengers on each bus as it arrived back at the bus station.

**Number of passengers on buses arriving back at bus station**

| 8 | 1 | 4 | 0 | 3 | 3 | 7 | 0 | 3 | 0 |
|---|---|---|---|---|---|---|---|---|---|
| 5 | 4 | 2 | 4 | 6 | 7 | 6 | 5 | 1 | 1 |
| 7 | 6 | 6 | 4 | 5 | 4 | 5 | 6 | 7 | 7 |
| 0 | 0 | 8 | 2 | 5 | 7 | 6 | 6 | 4 | 3 |

This information will be easier to understand if it is recorded on a table.

### Activity

The first column in the table below lists all the results that came up when the number of people on the buses was counted. The second column is used for marking how many times a particular result occurs. Go through the list above. Every time you get to a particular number, make a tally mark in the second column of the chart, like this: | . When you have five results for one number, make your fifth line go through the other four, like this: ||||. When you have made tally marks for all the buses in the list, count them up for each number of passengers and fill in the third column. 'Frequency' means 'how often' – it tells you how often each result came up.

| Number of passengers | Tally | Frequency |
|---|---|---|
| 0 | | |
| 1 | | |
| 2 | | |
| 3 | | |
| 4 | | |
| 5 | | |
| 6 | | |
| 7 | | |
| 8 | | |

Your completed table should look like this:

| Number of passengers | Tally | Frequency |
|---|---|---|
| 0 | ||||  | 5 |
| 1 | ||| | 3 |
| 2 | || | 2 |
| 3 | |||| | 4 |
| 4 | |||| | | 6 |
| 5 | |||| | 5 |
| 6 | |||| || | 7 |
| 7 | |||| | | 6 |
| 8 | || | 2 |

### Activity

In another part of the survey, the consultant asked passengers on a bus (route 15), 'What is the destination of your journey?' Here are their replies:

| shopping | school | catch train |
| school | school | catch train |
| catch train | catch train | work |
| visiting friend | work | work |
| shopping | work | school |
| shopping | shopping | school |
| school | catch train | work |
| school | school | work |

Make a table to summarise this part of the survey. What was the most popular reply? What time of day do you think it was?

| Destination | Tally | Frequency |
|---|---|---|
| shopping | |||| | 4 |
| school | |||| ||| | 8 |
| catch train | |||| | 5 |
| visiting friend | | | 1 |
| work | |||| | | 6 |

The most popular reply was 'school'. It was probably around 8.30–8.45 a.m. as most people on the bus were travelling to school or work.

# Topic 2 – Representing and displaying data

## Counting your results (continued)

### Key points to remember

- Discrete data is usually obtained by counting.
- To make a table for discrete data
  - make a list of all possible results
  - use tally marks to record the results of your survey
  - last of all, say how many times each result occurred. This is the frequency.

### *Putting it into practice*

*Make a frequency table to summarise the results of a survey you have conducted.*

# Topic 2 – Representing and displaying data

**AN 106**

Foundation/Intermediate/Advanced
Element **1.3,2.3,3.3**
Performance criteria **2,3,4,5**
Range **Techniques (number); Conventions; Levels of accuracy**

## Finding the mean (discrete data)

The mean is the straightforward average of a set of results. It is the total for the results divided by the number of results in that set. The mean is the most used statistic given to summarise a set of results. Company reports will certainly include averages or means for such things as costs per unit, time taken to deal with customer enquiries, weekly stoppages due to breakdowns in machinery, and so on.

Here are the number of enquiries dealt with each day at a health advice centre.

15   9   27   23   18   25

### Activity

1  Find the total number of enquiries for the week.
2  Find the mean number of enquiries per day.

*1 94, 2 18.8*

## A formula for the mean

As $x$ is used to stand for the values of the variable (or measurement) being used the mean is shown by the symbol $\bar{x}$ (known as x bar). The symbol $\Sigma$ is used for total so that:

$$\bar{x} = \frac{\Sigma x}{n}$$

where $n$ is the number of results.

You will find these symbols used on a scientific calculator so it is useful to know them.

## Finding the mean for a frequency table

Here are the number of enquiries about vaccinations over a longer period of 25 days.

| Number of enquiries | Frequency |
|---|---|
| 0 | 3 |
| 1 | 2 |
| 2 | 2 |
| 3 | 3 |
| 4 | 8 |
| 5 | 5 |
| 6 | 2 |
| 7 | 0 |
| 8 or more | 0 |
| **Total** | **25** |

In order to find the mean number of enquiries we need to find the total for all enquiries on all 25 days and then divide that total by 25.

Notice that the total of the frequency column is 25; this gives the total number of days.

In order to find the grand total for the number of enquiries you need to multiply each result by its frequency.

| Number of enquiries ($x$) | frequency ($f$) | $fx$ |
|---|---|---|
| 0 | 3 | $3 \times 0 = 0$ |
| 1 | 2 | $2 \times 1 = 2$ |
| 2 | 2 | $2 \times 2 =$ |
| 3 | 3 | $3 \times 3 =$ |
| 4 | 8 | $8 \times 4 =$ |
| 5 | 5 | |
| 6 | 2 | |
| 7 | 0 | |
| 8 or more | 0 | |
| | Total = | Total = |

### Key points to remember

- The mean is found by first finding the total of all the results. Then divide this total by the number of results.
- If the data has been given as a frequency table, the grand total for the results will have to be found by multiplying each result by its frequency.

### Putting it into practice

*Conduct a survey at your work placement. Your data should be 'discrete data' obtained by counting. Here are some ideas:*
- *numbers of letters arriving each day*
- *number of telephone enquiries each hour*
- *number of staff absent each day.*

*Find the mean of your results.*

# Topic 2 – Representing and displaying data

## Bar charts

**AN 110**

Foundation/Intermediate/Advanced
Element **1.3,2.3,3.3**
Performance criteria **1,2,3,4,5**
Range **Techniques** (Handling data); **Conventions; Levels of accuracy**

A bar chart can be used to illustrate qualitative or categorical data, such as type of complaint, favourite food, method of transport, and so on. The height of each bar is used to show the frequency and so different categories can be compared very easily.

A large sample of passengers travelling on Basset's Buses on weekday mornings between 10 a.m. and 11 a.m. were asked what their destination was. Their replies are shown below.

| *Destination* | *Frequency* |
|---|---|
| shopping | 16 |
| railway station | 7 |
| visiting friends | 9 |
| medical or other appointment | 7 |
| school | 3 |
| work | 8 |
| **Total** | **50** |

### Activity

Finish the bar graph shown here:

■ *Your finished bar graph should look like this:*

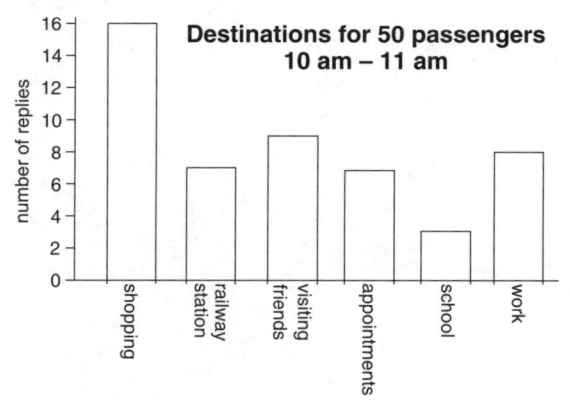

## Bar line graphs

A bar line graph is sometimes used to illustrate discrete data (numerical results obtained by counting, such as number of enquiries per day). The height of each line represents the frequency. The fact that thin lines are used instead of bars emphasises the idea that only whole number values are possible.

Here is a bar line graph drawn to show the numbers of passengers on buses (route number 2) coming into this bus station.

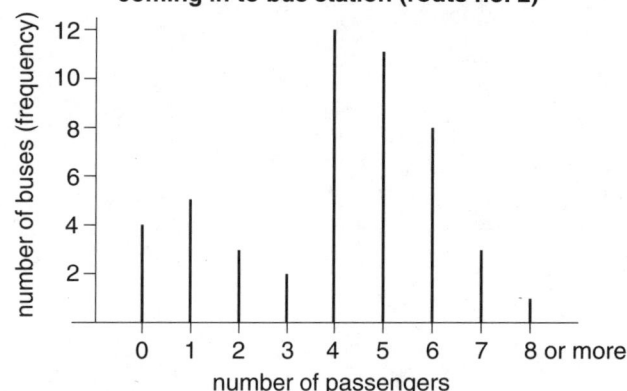

### Activity

1. Draw up a frequency table from this graph.
2. What is a typical number of passengers for a number 2 bus returning to the bus station?

■

1. No. of passengers  0 1 2 3 4 5 6 7 8 or more
   Frequency         4 5 3 2 12 11 8 3 1

2. 4 is the mode (the result with the highest frequency) so 4 or 5 would be a good answer. ■

For a bar line graph you will need discrete numerical data (obtained by counting). Ideas for this include:

- the number of employees absent every day
- the number of letters received every day
- the number of complaints received each month.

# Topic 2 – Representing and displaying data

## Bar charts (continued)

### Key points to remember

- A bar graph is used to illustrate discrete data of some kind.
- The height of each bar represents the frequency for each result.

### *Putting it into practice*

*Draw a bar graph to illustrate some data which you have collected. Some ideas for categorical data are:*

- *How do employees travel to work?*
- *Which services provided by a company are used most often by customers?*
- *What new services would customers like introduced?*

# Topic 2 – Representing and displaying data

## Pie charts

**AN 111**

Foundation/Intermediate/Advanced
Element **1.3, 2.3, 3.3**
Performance criteria **1, 2, 3, 4, 5**
Range **Techniques** (Number; Handling data); **Conventions; Levels of accuracy**

A pie chart is a circular diagram which shows how a large group of results is divided up. So, for instance, you can draw a pie chart showing the reasons for customers complaining at a restaurant. The pie chart will clearly show which type of complaint occurs most often and what proportion it is of the total.

Here are the results of a survey of customers' complaints to Jack's Bistro for one month:

| Nature of complaints | Frequency | Proportion of total | Degrees on pie chart |
|---|---|---|---|
| food took a long time | 31 | 31/50 = 0.62 | 0.62 × 360 = 223 |
| poor choice on menu | 6 | 6/50 = 0.12 | |
| tablecloth dirty | 4 | 4/50 = | |
| food cold | 3 | | |
| waitress rude | 4 | | |
| bill took too long | 2 | | |
| | Total = | | |

■■ *Your finished pie chart should look like this:*

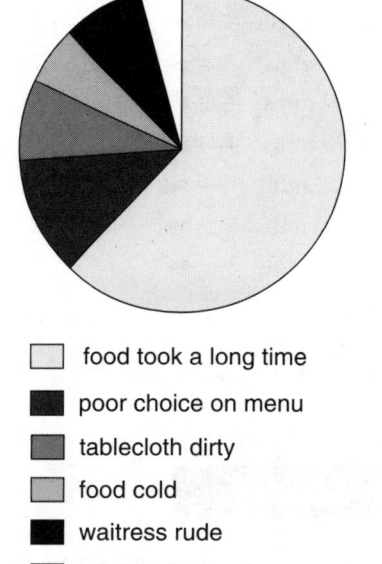

☐ food took a long time
■ poor choice on menu
▨ tablecloth dirty
▢ food cold
■ waitress rude
☐ bill took too long

It is clear that the majority of customers' complaints are about the length of time for the food to arrive. Is this group ½ of the total? ¾? More? A pie chart will show this clearly.

First we need to find out how many complaints there were, then find out what proportion of the total each group is.

Proportion = $\frac{\text{frequency for that section}}{\text{total}}$

The last step is to divide up the circle by multiplying each proportion by 360.

## Drawing a pie chart

1. Draw a circle carefully marking the centre.
2. Draw a line out from the centre to the circumference (anywhere you like).
3. Draw the angle for your first section.
4. Move the protractor round for the next section.

### Activity

Finish drawing this pie chart.

☐ Food took a long time
☐ Poor choice on menu

## How to construct a pie chart

1. Find the total for the frequencies on your table.
2. Find the proportion of the total for each section.
3. Divide up the circle by multiplying each proportion by 360°.

### Key points to remember

A pie chart is best used for qualitative (or categorical) data as in the example here. It allows you to compare the proportion of results in each category. The pie chart here clearly shows that 'food took a long time' was a larger proportion of complaints than all the others put together.

### Activity

1. Complete the table
2. Find the total frequency
3. Find the proportion for each section
4. Find the degrees on the pie chart.

■■
2   50

3   Proportions are: 0.62, 0.12, 0.08, 0.06, 0.08 and 0.04

4   Degrees are: 223, 43, 29, 22, 29, 14 (all given to the nearest degree) ■■

### Putting it into practice

*Try drawing a pie chart to illustrate some data you have collected.*

• 123 •

# Topic 2 – Representing and displaying data

**AN 113**

Foundation/Intermediate/
Advanced
Element **1.3,2.3,3.3**
Performance criteria **2,3,5**
Range **Techniques** (Number;
Handling data); **Conventions**

## The range

The manager at a laboratory which tests blood samples decides to investigate the reliability of the service provided by two different courier services, 'Speedy Deliveries' and 'Rocket Couriers'. She records the number of minutes late for deliveries by both firms.

| Late deliveries | Speedy Deliveries | Rocket Couriers |
|---|---|---|
| −30 mins* → | 1 | 5 |
| 0 mins → | 1 | 16 |
| 30 mins → | 7 | 33 |
| 60 mins → | 10 | 25 |
| 90 mins → | 12 | 12 |
| 120 mins → | 3 | 6 |
| 150 mins → | 2 | 0 |
| 180 mins → | 5 | 0 |
| | 41 | 97 |

\* i.e., up to 30 minutes early

### Activity

1. Decide upon a typical amount for the lateness of deliveries by
   a  Speedy Deliveries
   b  Rocket Couriers.
2. Explain how you decided upon your answer.

■■

1. You may have given any one of these answers:

   a  Speedy Deliveries
   mode 90–120 mins
   mean 98.4 mins
   median just over 90 mins

   b  Rocket Couriers
   mode 30–60 mins
   mean 57.75 mins
   median between 30 and 60 minutes closer to 60 minutes.

2. You may choose any of these as a typical value. The mode is the easiest to find. Because the data is grouped, it is difficult to find the median. ■■

## Variability

Clearly samples brought by Speedy Deliveries tend to arrive later than those brought by Rocket Couriers. But which of the two companies is more consistent? Which is less variable?

One of the simplest measures of variability is the range. The range is the difference between the smallest and the largest results in each sample.

| Range = | largest value − smallest value |
|---|---|

To find the range for these results we will have to take the largest possible result consistent with the frequency table as we do not know it exactly (likewise for the smallest).

For Speedy Deliveries the range is

Largest possible result 210 mins (just under)

smallest possible result −30 mins (i.e., 30 minutes early)

Range = 210 − (−30) = 240 mins

### Activity

1. Find the range for Rocket Couriers.
2. Are Rocket Couriers more reliable or less reliable than Speedy Deliveries?

■■

1. Range = 150 − (−30) mins
   = 180 mins

2. Rocket Couriers are more reliable.
   * their times are less variable
   * they arrive earlier than Speedy Deliveries (i.e., they are less late!). ■■

### Key points to remember

* The range is a simple measure of variability.
* It is the largest result minus the smallest.

### Putting it into practice

*Find the range for distances of students' journeys to college and their work placements.*

# Topic 2 – Representing and displaying data

## Line graphs

**AN 115**

Foundation/Intermediate/
Advanced
Element **1.3,2.3,3.3**
Performance criteria **1,2,3,4,5**
Range **Techniques** (Handling data); **Levels of accuracy; Conventions**

Bob Munroe the office cleaner at Darton Printing has been complaining about the temperature when he arrives for work at 6 a.m.

As part of the company survey, the consultant decides to collect data on working conditions, so she monitors the temperature in the office for 24 hours. Here are the results:

| Time | *Midnight* 12 p.m. | 2 a.m. | 4 a.m. | 6 a.m. | 8 a.m. | 10 a.m. |
|---|---|---|---|---|---|---|
| Temp | 6° | 4° | 3° | 2° | 8° | 10° |

| Time | *Noon* 12 a.m. | 2 p.m. | 4 p.m. | 6 p.m. | 8 p.m. | 10 p.m. |
|---|---|---|---|---|---|---|
| Temp | 12° | 12° | 12° | 10° | 9° | 8° |

These temperatures can be shown on a line graph.

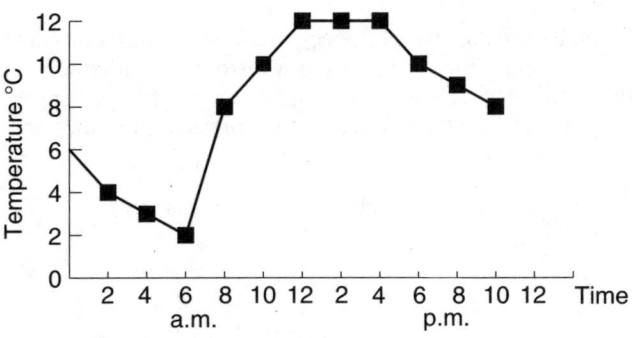

### Activity

1. When is the coldest time in the office?
2. When do you think the heating is turned on?
3. When is it turned off?

▌▌

1. 6 a.m.
2. between 6 a.m. and 8 a.m.
3. between 4 p.m. and 6 p.m. ▌▌

### Key points to remember

- A line graph can be used to show how the same measurement changes over time.
- Each point is joined to the next one using a straight line.
- The time scale is shown on the horizontal axis.
- A line graph should not be used to join unrelated measurements from different places or samples.

### Activity

A wholesaler has obtained a record of the number of customer complaints month by month about deliveries.

1. Draw a line graph to show the number of customer complaints.
2. When do most complaints occur?
3. Can you think of any reasons for this?

| Month | JAN | FEB | MARCH | APRIL | MAY | JUNE |
|---|---|---|---|---|---|---|
| complaints | 53 | 60 | 49 | 43 | 38 | 35 |
| Month | JULY | AUG | SEPT | OCT | NOV | DEC |
| complaints | 42 | 28 | 41 | 39 | 47 | 48 |

▌▌

1. Your line graph should look like this:

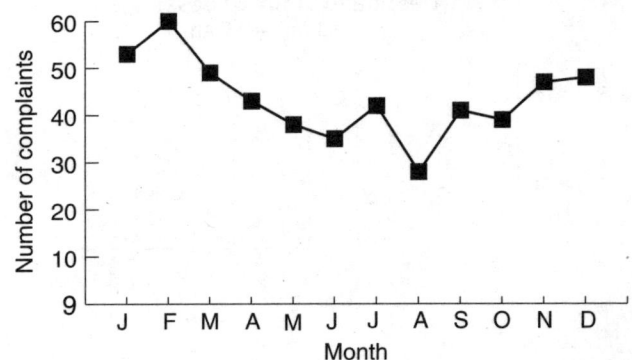

2. Most occur in February
3. This is in winter, when the weather is likely to be very bad, causing delays. ▌▌

### *Putting it into practice*

*Draw a line graph to illustrate some data you have collected – you must have measurements of the same kind collected over several time periods. Your data could be*

- *customer enquiries each month*
- *letters arriving each week*
- *phone calls each hour of the day.*

# Topic 2 – Representing and displaying data

## Choosing the right diagram

**AN 118**

Foundation/Intermediate/Advanced
Element **1.3,2.3,3.3**
Performance criteria **1,2,3,4,5**
Range **Techniques** (Number; Handling data); **Levels of accuracy; Conventions; Explain the main features**

It is important to choose the right diagram according to
- what you want to show
- what kind of data you have.

Look at your data and decide what you want to show or do. Here is a list of ideas to think about. Do you want to
- compare unrelated items (show which ones have the highest frequencies)
- compare items which form parts of a whole (data may have percentages adding up to 100%)
- look at a single set of measurements
- see if two sets of measurements are related
- make predictions
- follow a set of measurements or results over time.

## Comparing unrelated items – bar graph

If you have items or groupings which have been counted (discrete data) and you wish to show which groups have the highest frequencies you can draw a bar graph.

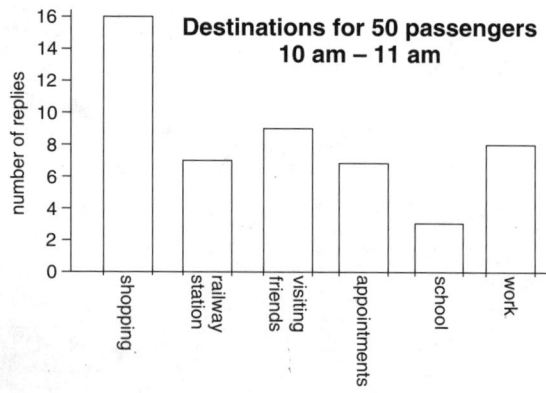

## Comparing items which form part of a whole – pie chart

You may have items which form a sensible 'whole' or total such as
- time spent in a whole day
- items bought spending your whole salary or wages
- total manufacturing costs split into raw materials, wages, energy costs, rent, etc.

Alternatively, you may have data presented as percentages which add up to a total 100%. In these situations a pie chart will show how the total is divided up. You can see which parts form the largest sections. Because the diagram is circular it is not easy to read off actual frequencies. If the frequencies must be clearly shown, a bar graph is better.

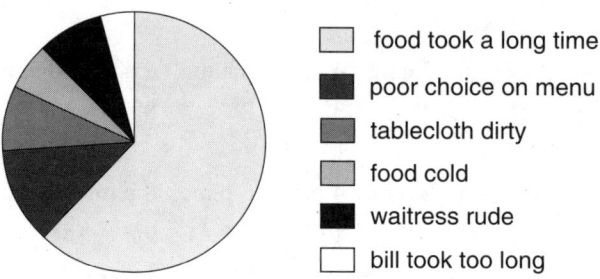

## Looking at a single set of measurements – histogram

If you have data which has been measured (continuous data) you can show the results using a histogram. Suitable measurements for a histogram might be: heights or lengths, weights, temperatures, prices, blood pressure (or other pressures) and so on.

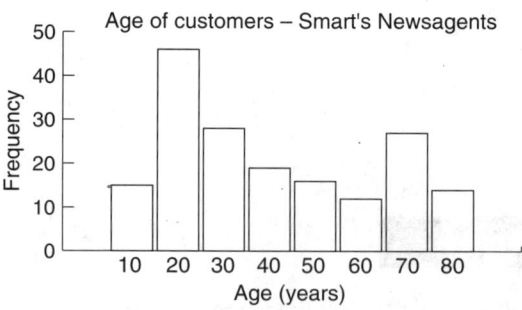

## Investigating a relationship between two sets of measurements – scatter diagram

If you think two measurements may be related, obtain results for a group of people (or items) and plot a scatter diagram. Here are some ideas for pairs of measurements which are related: height of a person and weight; age of a tree and height; price of an item and number sold; time taken to do a job and price charged.

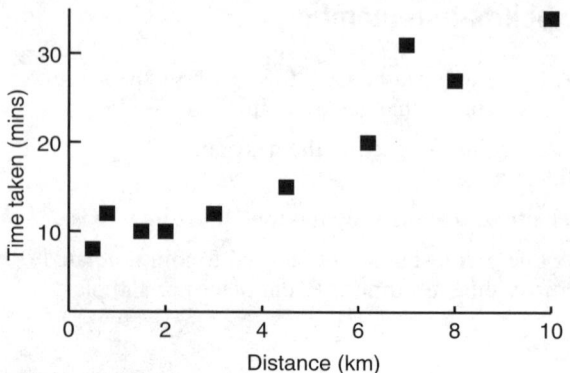

# Topic 2 – Representing and displaying data

## Choosing the right diagram (continued)

## Making predictions – best-fit line

If your scatter diagram shows a strong relationship between the two sets of measurements you can use the results to make predictions. A best-fit line can be drawn onto the graph so that predicted results can be taken from the line.

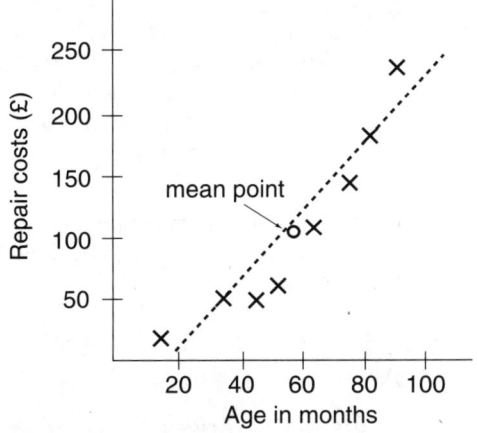

## Following a set of results over time – line graph

If you have measurements taken at different times over a period of time these can be shown on a line graph. This is similar in some ways to a scatter diagram but unlike a scatter diagram the points can be joined together using straight lines. Time is always shown on the horizontal axis. If you decide to make predictions you can try to draw in a best-fit line. In this situation the line is sometimes called a trend line.

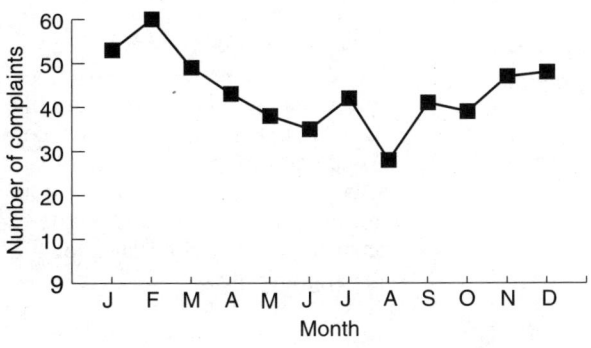

### Activity

A group of students have various sets of data from a survey on elderly people to present in a report. Try to decide which graph they should use for each set of data.

1. how Mrs Smith spends her pension
2. ages of elderly people and blood pressure
3. Mrs Smith's blood pressure every week
4. pensions every year 1980–95
5. blood pressures for 200 patients
6. cost of a loaf of bread in six shops
7. predicting heating cost for a one-bedroom flat
8. size of flat and heating costs
9. favourite brands of coffee for elderly people

a. line graph
b. pie chart
c. histogram
d. scatter diagram
e. best-fit line
f. bar graph

■ *Your answers should be:*
*1b; 2d; 3a; 4a; 5c; 6f; 7e; 8d; 9f.* ■

### Key points to remember

- Use bar graphs to compare the frequency of discrete data (data you have counted).
- Use histograms to show continuous data (data you have measured).
- Use pie charts to compare items which form part of a whole.
- Use scatter diagrams to look at the relationship between two sets of measurements.
- Draw a best-fit line onto a scatter diagram if there is a strong relationship between the measurements.
- Use line graphs to show a set of results over time.

### *Putting it into practice*

*Think about the data you might gather from a survey. Which type of diagram should you use to display it?*

# Topic 2 – Representing and displaying data

**AN 119**

Foundation/Intermediate/Advanced
Element 1.3, 2.3, 3.3
Performance criteria 2, 3
Range Techniques (Handling data); Conventions

## Two-way tables

Two-way tables are used to show how two classifications or groupings are inter-related. They are found in newspaper and magazine articles and in *Social Trends*, and other government publications.

> *Social Trends* is a collection of statistics about life in this country which is published by the government. Most libraries have copies.

A two-way table might show whether different kinds of customers require or use different services. Here is an example where two students have gone to a leisure centre to see which facilities are used by different age groups.

Instead of using separate questionnaires they have recorded the answers straight onto this sheet using tally marks.

| Age | Swimming | Karate | Weight training | Squash | Badminton |
|---|---|---|---|---|---|
| 10 & under | ⅢⅢ ⅢⅢ II | I | | | |
| 11–16 | ⅢⅢ IIII | ⅢⅢ ⅢⅢ II | | | III |
| 17–29 | ⅢⅢ II | ⅢⅢ IIII | ⅢⅢ ⅢⅢ I | II | ⅢⅢ I |
| 30–49 | IIII | III | II | ⅢⅢ I | III |
| 50 & over | ⅢⅢ IIII | | I | IIII | IIII |

### Activity

1. What were the two questions the students asked people going into the leisure centre?
2. Fill in this copy of the two-way table, but write in numbers instead of using tally marks, showing the frequency of each of the results.

| Age | Swimming | Karate | Weight training | Squash | Badminton |
|---|---|---|---|---|---|
| 10 & under | | | | | |
| 11–16 | | | | | |
| 17–29 | | | | | |
| 30–49 | | | | | |
| 50 & over | | | | | |

3. How many children aged 10 and under went into the sports centre?
4. What was the most popular sport for children up to 10?
5. What was the most popular sport for people aged 17–29?
6. What was the least favourite sport for people aged 50 and over?

■■

1. 'How old are you?' (or 'Which of these age groups do you fit into?'), and 'Which sport(s) will you be taking part in today?'
3. 13   4. Swimming   5. Weight training   6. Karate. ■■

### Activity

1. If you wanted to know whether vegetarians are less likely to be satisfied with the choice of food in the college canteen, which two questions would you ask?
2. Draw up the framework for a two-way table which could be used to record people's answers.

■■

1. Are you a vegetarian?
   Are you satisfied with the standard of food in the canteen?
2. Your table should look something like this:

|  | Vegetarian | Meat eater |
|---|---|---|
| Satisfied | | |
| Not satisfied | | |

■■

### Key points to remember

A two-way table is used to see whether the answers to two questions are related. The possible answers to each question must be listed and grouped in a sensible way. Answers to the first question are listed across the table, while answers to the second question are listed going down.

### Putting it into practice

Think of two related questions you could ask to test a theory or hypothesis you may have. Ask the people in your group and record your results on a two-way table.

Some suggestions are

- time taken to get to school or college and means of transport
- gender and leisure interests.

• 128 •

# Topic 3 – Interpreting graphs and tables

## Reading tables

**AN 120**

Foundation/Intermediate/Advanced
Element **1.3,2.3,3.3**
Performance criteria **1,2,3,4,5**
Range **Techniques** (Handling data); **Explain the main features; Conventions**

Important information is often presented as a table of numbers. Such tables appear daily in newspapers, magazines and even on television. Company reports will certainly contain tables of sales and profits. Tables are used to present numerical information in a summary form. The information should be fairly easy to understand once you have had some practice at reading and interpreting tables.

The main things to do when looking at a table of numbers are
- don't panic
- try to think of some questions, then look for the answers.

Here is a table from the annual report of a lending library.

> Columns are vertical.
> Rows are horizontal.

| Year | Borrowings – Percentages | | | | | | | | | |
|---|---|---|---|---|---|---|---|---|---|---|
| | *Romance* | *Science fiction* | *Mystery* | *Other fiction* | *Children's* | *Biography* | *Health & beauty* | *Manuals* | *Science* | *Other non-fiction* |
| 1990 | 13.6 | 12.5 | 9.9 | 19.6 | 10.2 | 5.7 | 7.4 | 4.2 | 3.4 | 13.5 |
| 1991 | 13.4 | 13.1 | 8.4 | 17.3 | 12.2 | 5.9 | 7.9 | 3.8 | 3.7 | 14.3 |
| 1992 | 12.3 | 13.7 | 8.2 | 16.4 | 13.5 | 6.2 | 8.7 | 3.6 | 4.2 | 13.2 |
| 1993 | 11.8 | 14.3 | 7.4 | 15.7 | 13.8 | 6.1 | 9.2 | 3.4 | 5.8 | 12.5 |
| 1994 | 10.8 | 14.5 | 7.2 | 16.1 | 14.3 | 6.7 | 9.0 | 3.3 | 4.6 | 13.5 |

### Activity

The above table may look quite fearsome at first, but when you try out some simple questions, it won't seem at all bad.

1. What is the information about?
2. What does each row add up to? There is a word near the top which will give you a big clue.
3. Does it make sense to add up each column across?
4. Which types of books have become more popular as a proportion of the total borrowed over the period of five years?
5. Which types of book have become less popular?
6. Can you work out how many science fiction books were borrowed in 1993?

▐▐
1. It is about different types of books borrowed from a library.
2. 100%
3. No
4. Science fiction, Children's, Biography, Health and beauty, Science.
5. Romance, Mystery, Other fiction, Manuals.
6. No – you have no information about actual numbers, only about percentages of the total. ▐▐

### Key points to remember

When you look at a table try to decide
- What the table is about.
- Are the figures percentages or actual counts?
- If they are percentages do the columns add up to 100%? Or the rows? Or neither?
- Look for the biggest categories or groups.
- Look for changes (if you have figures for two or more years).

### Putting it into practice

*Find a table of data. Social Trends should be available in your library. It has information on a wide variety of interesting topics including sport and leisure, households and families and spending habits. See if you can write half a page saying what the table is about.*

# Topic 3 – Interpreting graphs and tables

## Reading bar charts

**AN 121**

Foundation/Intermediate/Advanced
Element **1.3,2.3,3.3**
Performance criteria **1,2,3,4,5**
Range **Techniques** (Handling data); **Levels of accuracy; Conventions; Explain the main features**

Bar charts are often used to illustrate data so that different categories can be compared. They appear daily in newspapers. As they are simple to read, they should make numerical information easier to understand. Here is a bar chart from a local survey showing what percentage of 16–19-year-olds used certain types of leisure facility in March 1995.

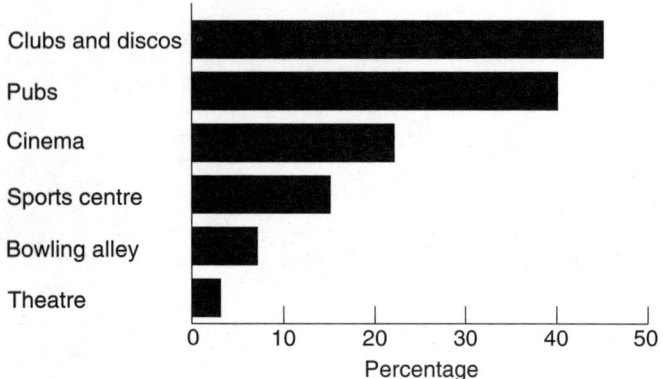

From that point of view, it is similar to a pie chart but being on a straight line it is easier to read than a pie chart.

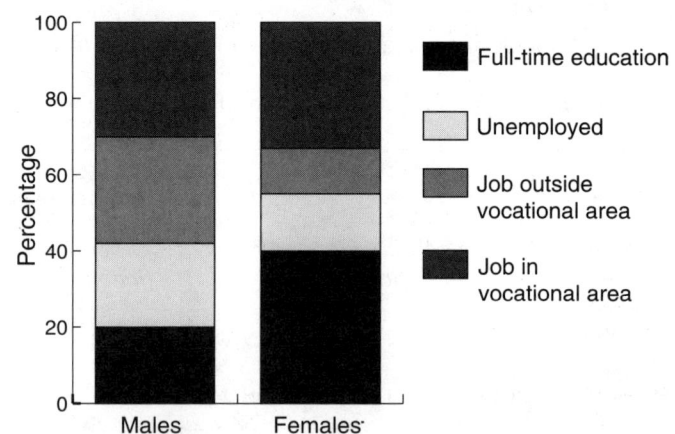

### Activity

1. What is the bar graph about?
2. What are the figures on the horizontal axis?
3. Can you tell how often 16–19-year-olds use these facilities?
4. Can you tell which facility 16–19-year-olds use most often?
5. Which facility has the smallest percentage of 16–19-year-olds using it?
6. If you did a survey on the leisure facilities used by young people can you think of a different way of drawing this bar graph?

### Activity

1. Which group had more people working in their vocational area?
2. Which group was more likely to be unemployed?
3. Can you tell how many ex-students were still involved in full-time education 12 months after they completed their GNVQ course?

■■ *1 Females, 2 Males, 3 No* ■■

■■

1. The bar graph is about the 16–19-year-olds' use of leisure facilities.
2. Percentages of 16–19-year-olds.
3. No.
4. No – you can just tell what percentage of 16–19-year-olds used these types of facility at some time or other during the month of the survey.
5. Theatre.
6. You could draw a bar graph showing how many times 16–19-year-olds used facilities in a month, or what percentage of their leisure time was spent at each type of facility. ■■

Here is a slightly different kind of bar graph called a component bar graph. Each bar is the same size and represents 100%. It shows the percentage of each group.

### Key points to remember

- The length of each bar represents the frequency or percentage on a bar graph.
- Check the scale shown at the side. If percentages are used you may not be able to convert these to actual amounts.

### Putting it into practice

*Try to find a bar graph in a newspaper or magazine. If not, look in Social Trends in the library. Try to write half a page about the information in the graph.*

# Topic 3 – Interpreting graphs and tables

## Reading pie charts

**AN 122**

Foundation/Intermediate/Advanced
Element **1.3,2.3,3.3**
Performance criteria **1,2,3**
Range **Techniques** (Handling data); **Conventions**;
**Explain the main features**

Pie charts are often used in books and newspapers to show proportions or percentages. Because they are more difficult to read than bar graphs they tend to be used less often. Pie charts are very useful if two (or more) different groups are to be compared, then two or more pie charts can be drawn.

Here are some pie charts drawn to illustrate some data from a survey about how male and female students at a particular college spent their time in a typical week.

**Time use in a typical week**

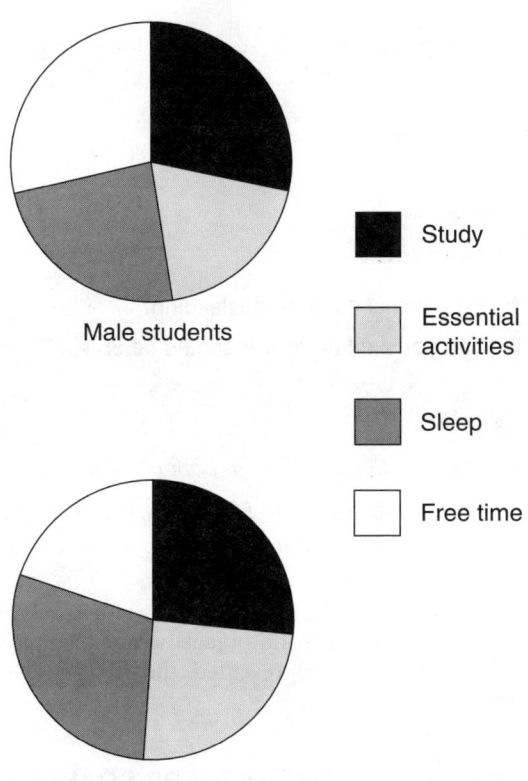

Essential activities are things like shopping, personal care, cooking, domestic work and child-care.

### Activity

Look at the pie chart for male students.
1  **a**  Which activity takes up most time?
   **b**  Which activity takes least time?
2  Answer question 1 again with reference to female students.
3  Who spends most time on 'essential activities'?
4  Who spends most time on leisure activities/free time?
5  Can you tell how many hours on average a female student has as free time per week?

■■

1  **a**  It is difficult to tell which activity takes the most time, as study, sleep and free time are all very close. (In fact, sleep is slightly more than the others.)
   **b**  Essential activities take the least time.
2  Sleep takes the most time, free time the least.
3  Female students spend most time on essential activities.
4  Male students have most free time.
5  Not easily! (You would need to work out how many hours in a week (7 × 24) then measure the angle on

### Key points to remember

- A pie chart is a circle divided into sections to show proportions or percentages for each group or result.
- The angle for each section shows how big that group is relative to the others.
- The largest group (or result) has the largest angle.
- It is difficult to work out the actual frequency for each result.

### Putting it into practice

Find a pie chart in a magazine, newspaper or in Social Trends. Try to write a half page about the information in it.

# Topic 3 – Interpreting graphs and tables

## Misrepresenting data – 1

**AN 126**

Foundation/Intermediate/Advanced
Element **1.3,2.3,3.3**
Performance criteria **2,3,4,5**
Range **Techniques** (Handling data); **Conventions; Levels of accuracy**

This resource sheet looks at ways in which diagrams may be drawn to exaggerate a particular effect and mislead the person looking at the diagram. These kinds of diagrams sometimes appear in newspapers and magazines. Look at this graph:

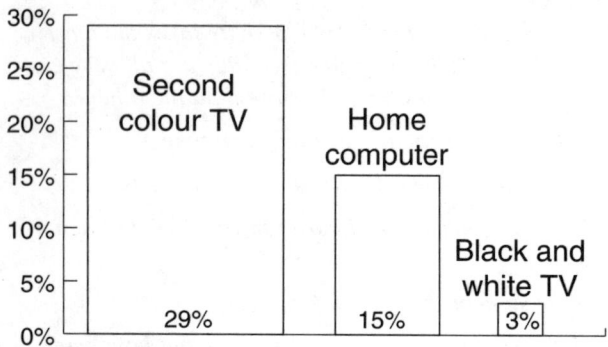

### Activity

1. What impression does the graph give?
2. Is the vertical axis correctly drawn?
3. Is there anything wrong with the shape of the blocks?
4. Try re-drawing the three blocks the same width across.

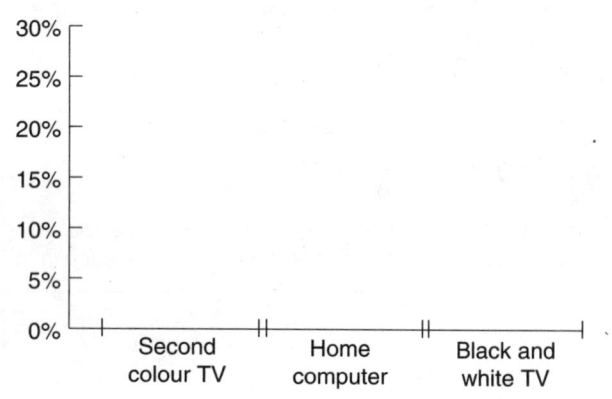

5. Is this fairer?
6. Why?

■

1. It shows that many more homes have a second colour television than a black and white television.
2. Yes
3. The blocks are different widths
4. Graph correctly drawn
5. Yes
6. The blocks on the first graph exaggerated the results by having different areas. Really, the height should show the frequency on a bar graph. ■

## Picture graphs

Picture graphs can be very misleading

**VALUE OF A FIVER HALVED!**

£5 note
Worth £5 in 1979

£5 note
Worth only £2.50 in 1989!

### Activity

1. Why is this diagram misleading?
2. Can you explain how it should be drawn?

■

1. The £5 note has 'shrunk' in both directions!
2. The area (or size) of the £5 note should be half the first one, not a quarter as it is here. ■

The last example used incorrect areas to mislead you. Even worse is the misuse of solid objects which have volume. If these volumes are misrepresented, the effect is even more pronounced.

**OWNERSHIP OF DISHWASHERS SOARS!**

Percentage of households owning a dishwasher

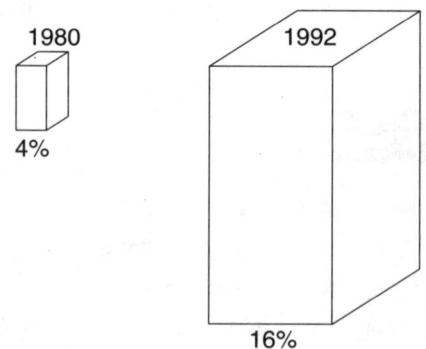

### Activity

1. Re-draw this as a simple bar graph
2. Explain what is wrong with the picture.

# Topic 3 – Interpreting graphs and tables

## Misrepresenting data – 1 (continued)

**2** *The second dishwasher should only have 4 times the size. Instead it is 4 times taller, 4 times wider and 4 times deeper. So it appears to be 4 × 4 × 4 = 64 times bigger!*

Even if a three-dimensional object is drawn as a 'flat' two-dimensional object our brains will interpret it in three dimensions.

### Key points to remember

- If a bar graph is drawn, the vertical scale should start at zero, and all the bars should be the same width.
- If pictures are used, they should not be exaggerated. Two-dimensional shapes must have the correct areas. If three-dimensional objects are drawn they must have the correct volumes.

### Putting it into practice

*See if you can find some exaggerated diagrams in newspapers and magazines. Draw them again correctly if you can, or change them to bar graphs.*

# Topic 3 – Interpreting graphs and tables

**AN 127**

Foundation/Intermediate/Advanced
Element **1.3,2.3,3.3**
Performance criteria **2,3,4,5**
Range **Techniques** (Handling data); **Conventions; Levels of accuracy**

## Misrepresenting data – 2

Unfortunately you will sometimes see graphs which have been deliberately drawn wrongly in order to emphasise a particular point. If you look through some newspapers you are very likely to find similar examples to the ones shown here. Sometimes incorrectly drawn graphs even appear on TV news, but these have been shown less often recently. (Perhaps due to viewers like yourself writing letters!)

Here is a typical newspaper headline:
INFANT MORTALITY PLUNGES!

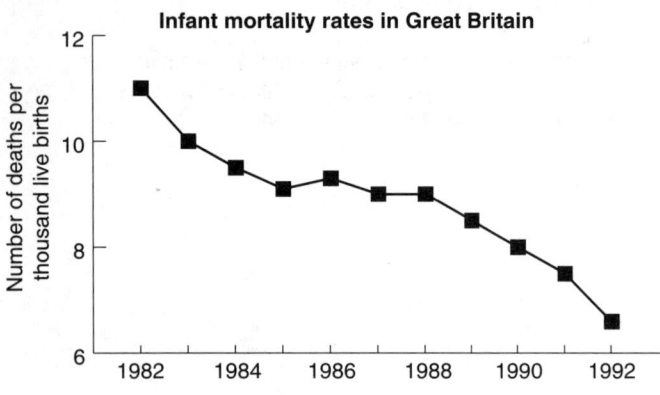

### Activity

1. Look closely at the vertical axis. What is the number at the bottom?

2. Re-draw this line graph, using the diagram on the right. This time, it starts with zero at the bottom of the vertical axis. Fill in the missing points as best you can and join them up with straight lines.

3. Does the graph give a different impression to the first one? In what way?

4. Look carefully at the vertical axis. It has been changed in two ways. What two changes have been made?

5. Explain two things which could be done (but should not!) to change a graph, to make it look steeper.

■■

1. *It starts at 6*

2.

3. *Yes. The graph still shows a decrease but it does not look so dramatic.*

4. *It starts at zero. The scale is smaller (the numbers go up in 2s so they are closer together).*

5. *To make a graph look steeper a writer might:*

   **a** *start the scale higher than zero  this is not really acceptable on a line graph, and*

   **b** *change the scale by making it larger (numbers spaced wider apart)  this is acceptable.* ■■

Line graphs and bar graphs should always be drawn with the vertical axis starting at zero. Sometimes the starting points on both axes of a scatter graph may be moved to avoid having a big empty space at the bottom left hand side of the graph. This is acceptable providing it is indicated clearly on the graph what has been done.

### Key points to remember

- On line graphs and bar graphs the vertical axis should start at zero.
- If the vertical axis does not start at zero, the graph may produce a misleading impression.

### *Putting it into practice*

*Look in a newspaper or magazine for a line graph (or a bar graph) which has been drawn with a scale that misrepresents the results. See what effect it has when you re-draw the graph correctly.*

# GNVQ Core Skills:
# Communication

Janet Byatt and Karen Davies
Hugh Hillyard-Parker
Cathy Lake
Sheila White

## COMMUNICATION – Take part in discussions
### Element 1

### Topic 1 – Discussion basics

- C1    Know you audience
- C2    Know your purpose

### Topic 2 – Types of discussion

- C6    Face-to-face discussions
- C7    Meetings
- C12  Discussions on straightforward or routine matters
- C13  Using the phone

### Topic 3 – Skills for successful discussions

- C16  Good listening
- C17  Checking understanding
- C21  Asking questions
- C22  Giving and receiving feedback
- C24  Using body language
- C29  Using your voice
- C30  Ending discussions

# Topic 1 – Discussion basics

## Know your audience

**C 1**

Foundation
Element **1.1**
Performance criteria **2**
Range **Audience;
Situation**

### What is your audience?

When you read the word 'audience' you probably think of people attending a concert or the theatre. So do you have an audience?

The answer is yes: every time you talk to someone – in a discussion group or on the telephone, for example, you are talking to an audience.

### Activity

In each of these situations, who is your audience?

1 You say something in a discussion group at school/college.
2 You are telling some friends about something funny that happened to you.
3 You answer a question that your teacher has asked you.
4 You have just started work and want to ask a colleague a question.
5 Your boss at work asks you to describe what you did today.

Your audience can be anything from a group of close friends to a boss at work.

■■ As you think about these situations and you identify the audience, you will be aware of the differences between talking directly to a person (a one-to-one conversation) and talking to several (a group conversation). In one-to-one conversations you are able to gain feedback such as words of agreement, nods, facial expressions. These may be less obvious in a group as individuals may not directly respond to the speaker. ■■

■■ You might reply that it depends on the individual – and you'd be right. But clearly there are right and wrong ways of addressing different people. For example, you are much less likely to be jokey with a work supervisor or teacher than with friends. It is better to be respectful with people in senior positions, e.g. a work supervisor. ■■

Which of these people would you call by their first name? That can be a good test of how you should address people.

In the example below, Dan gets it completely wrong . . .

**Sharon:** Hello Dan, I'm your work supervisor, Sharon Brook.

**Dan:** Wotcha, Shaz, great to meet you!

Don't forget that it is not just the words you use which is important – it is also the tone of voice you use. Think carefully about tone – the sound and manner of what you say and make sure it matches the impression you want to make.

### Your audience at work

All jobs involve talking to a wide range of different people. You have to judge what tone and manner is suitable with different people.

### Activity

1 Think of a typical job in your chosen vocational area. Make a list of all the people you would come into contact with, if you had that job.
2 Next to each person in your list, say what would be a suitable way of talking to them.

■■ At work, you would usually aim to be friendly and polite. With each individual, however, you have to judge how far you can go, in terms of being formal or informal. ■■

### Key points to remember

- Whenever you talk (or write) to someone, you are addressing an audience.
- Make sure your tone and manner are appropriate to that audience.
- At work, it is better to be formal with colleagues and bosses – at least to start with.

### Putting it into practice

List three different projects you are doing for your GNVQ which involve discussion or meetings.
For each one, note down:
- who your audience is
- what is a suitable tone and manner for you to use with that audience.

### Talking to your audience

Think again about the audiences you identified in the last activity.

### Activity

When you are talking to the people listed below would you try to be:

|  | polite | friendly | respectful | jokey | bossy |
|---|---|---|---|---|---|
| other students | ☐ | ☐ | ☐ | ☐ | ☐ |
| friends | ☐ | ☐ | ☐ | ☐ | ☐ |
| work colleagues | ☐ | ☐ | ☐ | ☐ | ☐ |
| a work supervisor | ☐ | ☐ | ☐ | ☐ | ☐ |
| teacher / lecturer | ☐ | ☐ | ☐ | ☐ | ☐ |

## Topic 1 – Discussion basics

### Know your purpose

**Foundation**
Element **1.1**
Performance criteria **1**
Range **Subject; Purpose**

## What is your purpose?

Whenever we communicate, we usually have a reason for doing this – we have some purpose in mind. This is true whether we are communicating on the phone, by letter or face to face with other people.

### Activity

What would be the purpose of your communication in these situations?

1. You get back from a holiday and give your best friend a call.
2. You are travelling by train to see a show in a town nearby. You ring your local station.
3. You call into your local newsagent to cancel the newspaper delivery for the week your family is away.

■ *In the first situation, your purpose would be to catch up and exchange news. In the second situation, your purpose is quite clear – to gain information. The purpose of the communication in the third situation is also clear – to ask someone to do something.* ■

Knowing what your purpose is is important. It makes it easier to choose the best way of communicating and saves you wasting time and effort.

### Activity

Think of a situation where you found yourself in a discussion with someone (or several people), but you weren't quite sure why…

1. Describe the situation.
2. What did you, or the other person/people, achieve?
3. What did you feel during and after the discussion?

Often it is important to state your purpose early on in any communication. For example:

- In a phone call, you start: 'I'm ringing… (to make an appointment, or whatever)'.
- In a discussion, you agree on an agenda and what you all hope to achieve by the end of the meeting.

## Communicating at work

In most jobs people are busy – they don't have time to waste in pointless communication. You are busy too – you need to know what you have to achieve.

### Activity

1. Think of five situations at work where you might have to communicate with others. Think of a job in the vocational area you are interested in.
2. In each situation, what would your purpose be?
3. How would you try to achieve your purpose?

■ *It's important to remember that your colleagues will have their own goals, too, which may conflict with yours. If you deal with people outside the organisation, you may have to give more consideration to their goals. For example, customers are 'always right'! Your goal may be to get them to make up their mind as quickly as possible; they may need time to think. Learning to achieve your goals, while respecting other people's, is an important part of all communication at work.* ■

### Key points to remember

- Whenever you communicate, be aware of your purpose.
- If you don't know what your purpose is, you waste your own and other people's time.
- It often helps to state your purpose at the start.

### *Putting it into practice*

*List three different tasks you have to do for your GNVQ which involve discussion or meetings. For each one:*

1. *Note down what your purpose is. How do you make sure other people are aware of your purpose?*
2. *Think about the other person/people you are talking with. What is their purpose? How do you find out what it is?*

# Topic 2 – Types of discussion

## Face-to-face discussions

**C 6**

Foundation
Element **1.1**
Performance criteria **1.4**
Range **Purpose; Situation**

## What are face-to-face discussions?

When we describe a discussion as being 'face-to-face', this means we are talking in person to one or more people.

In your studies the discussions you have probably range from individual tutorials, to projects you do as part of a small team or discussions with your whole GNVQ group. All these discussions involve communication on a personal level with other people. They all involve taking turns to speak and listen.

There are differences, though. For example, in a one-to-one discussion, you may make 50 per cent of the contributions. In a larger group, you may play a much smaller part – making only a small proportion of the contributions.

> **Hint**
> Be careful not to dominate discussions, but don't opt out either!

Different forms of groups have different purposes, too. In a one-to-one discussion with a tutor your aim may be to discuss your personal progress or any difficulties – you would hardly want to discuss these things in the presence of the whole group.

## Discussions at work

In many vocational areas a lot of talking is done! Again this could be in:

- individual discussions – e.g. with colleagues, customers or visitors
- small group discussions – e.g. between colleagues in a department
- large group discussions – e.g. staff meetings, workshops, conference seminars.

## Successful face-to-face discussions

A bit of thought – and practice – can make discussions much more successful.

### Activity

Below is a list of hints that can help make face-to-face discussions successful. How good are you at doing each one?

- At the start of the discussion, say what your purpose is, e.g. 'I'm trying to find out...' or 'I want to discuss...'
- Give other people opportunity to make their contributions.
- Show you are listening, e.g. by nodding your head.
- Look interested and attentive – it gives encouragement to other people.
- Be aware of other people's feelings, ideas and opinions.
- Look at other people's body language – what are they telling you?
- If you don't understand what someone is saying, ask them to explain.
- At the end of the discussion, repeat the key points or check what you have agreed.

▌▌ *Several of these points relate to body language. This is an important aspect of face-to-face discussions – communicating not just through words, but with expressions and gestures, too.* ▌▌

### Key points to remember

- To communicate well in discussions takes skill and practice!
- Use positive body language – and be aware of the other person's body language too.
- Talking is an essential skill for work – in some jobs it's the most essential skill.

### *Putting it into practice*

*The next time you take part in discussions for your GNVQ, make a point of assessing:*

- *what the purpose of the discussion was*
- *why the discussion took the form it did (e.g. small or large)*
- *how you contributed to the discussion*
- *how you used the skills listed above.*

# Topic 2 – Types of discussion

## Meetings

**C 7**

Foundation
Element **1.1**
Performance criteria **1,2,3,4**
Range **Subject matter; Purpose**

### What makes a meeting?

People often talk about 'going to meetings' or 'being in a meeting', especially at work. The word 'meeting' can sound rather grand. So what is a meeting?

### Activity

Which of the following would you describe as a meeting?

**A** You meet up with a group of friends and sit chatting in a local café.

**B** Three students get together to discuss how to set about a project.

**C** The members of one department of a company discuss schedules over a cup of coffee.

**D** A group of GNVQ students meet to hear a talk given by someone from a local company.

▌▌ *A 'meeting' suggests a formal get-together, so you may not regard A as a meeting. However, all the rest are meetings. If the speaker in D just talked to the group, and didn't encourage discussion, then that would probably be a lecture, not a meeting!* ▌▌

Meetings are an important part of working life. Many workplaces are big organisations, with lots of different people carrying out different tasks – meetings are a good way of discussing aspects of work.

### Features of meetings

Here are some of the features which are typical of meetings.

- There should be a common purpose.
- People often behave more formally than in casual discussions.
- The meeting may be organised formally, with an agenda.
- People may have particular roles, e.g. someone leads or 'chairs' the meeting.
- Everyone has a part to play and a contribution to make.

This final point is very important: all discussions involve taking turns – turns in speaking and turns in listening. In meetings you have to strike the right balance – make your contribution, but don't dominate the discussion.

### Skills for meetings

In meetings, you need certain skills to get your message across effectively.

### Activity

For each of the skills listed below, think of an example of how you have done this in a meeting.

- Listened attentively.
- Shown you were alert in the way you sat or in your expression.
- Contributed actively to the meeting – sharing your ideas and opinions.
- Shown you were listening when others were talking, e.g. by nodding.
- Encouraged other people to contribute, e.g. by asking them questions.
- Maintained eye contact with other people.

What do you find difficult about meetings? What do you enjoy about meetings?

▌▌ *If you couldn't think of an example for each skill, make an effort to use that skill next time you take part in a meeting.* ▌▌

### Key points to remember

- Meetings are an important part of working life.
- Be aware of the purpose of any meeting.
- Meetings are often formal and may have a formal structure.
- Play your part in any meeting – take your turn.

### *Putting it into practice*

*Draw up a checklist of skills needed to communicate in meetings. This could take the form of a Dos and Don'ts list. Use this list next time you take part in a meeting. Make an effort to do as many of the Dos as you can, while avoiding the Don'ts.*

# Topic 2 – Types of discussion

**C 12**

Foundation
Element 1.1
Performance criteria 1,2,4
Range **Subject; Purpose; Audience; Situation**

## Discussions on straightforward or routine matters

In every work situation you have to communicate about all sorts of things. Many of these things are straightforward or routine matters. Others are not. Routine matters are:

- frequent – they crop up on a regular basis
- predictable – you know roughly what will happen.

## Routine matters at work

Every job has its share of routine matters. There are many tasks that you will have to do on a regular basis.

### Activity

Which of the following situations involve discussion on 'routine matters'?

**A** A customer rings up and asks to be sent a catalogue or brochure.

**B** On Monday morning, you and your supervisor discuss the work coming up that week.

**C** Your department is having a meeting to discuss the theft of some equipment.

**D** A customer rings up to complain about your organisation.

■ *Clearly A and B are fairly routine situations. They are a normal part of the working routine. C is definitely an unusual, non-routine matter. D, too, is a non-routine situation – we would hope!* ■

In work situations it is important to recognise non-routine matters. If it is a matter that falls outside your normal area of work, then someone else should be dealing with it. For example, complaints are usually dealt with by someone fairly senior.

Remember, matters are non-routine if

- you don't understand the subject being discussed
- the situation is one you have not met before
- the subject is complicated, difficult or sensitive
- the matter lies beyond your authority.

## Skills for routine discussions

When discussions are routine, we expect them to be predictable. However, don't take any situation for granted. Discussions may be routine, but they are never identical! So:

- use suitable language and vocabulary;
- be aware of your audience;
- remember your purpose;
- treat each discussion individually;
- listen closely to what is being said to you.

### Jargon

In routine discussions, people tend to use a lot of jargon.

### Activity

Think about all the different words you have met for the first time in your GNVQ studies. You may use these terms routinely with other students.

- List four or five words or expressions that are 'jargon' relating to GNVQs.
- How would you explain these words to people unfamiliar with them?

This example should show how easy it is to pick up and use jargon. Be aware of the danger of using it routinely.

### Hint

When you start work in a new job, what is routine to other people is not routine to you. Don't be afraid to ask if you need someone to explain something to you.

### Key points to remember

- Treat each discussion individually.
- Really listen to what the other person has to say – not what you expect them to say.
- Use good communication skills at all times.

### *Putting it into practice*

*Keep a log of the next three meetings or discussions you have where subject matter is routine. Note down:*

- *what the subject matter was*
- *how you dealt with the subject matter.*

## Topic 2 – Types of discussion

### Using the phone

C 13

Foundation/Intermediate/
Advanced
Element 1.1, 2.1, 3.1
Performance criteria 2
Range Audience; Situation

## The power of the phone

In all areas of work and life in general, the phone has become an indispensable way of communicating directly with other people.

### Activity

Think about the last five phone calls you made.

1. Why did you choose to use the phone in this situation?
2. Was the phone the best way of communicating in this situation?

You probably identified the following advantages of using the phone:

- speed – you can reach people very quickly
- distance – the phone is ideal when people are too far to contact by other means
- convenience – you don't have to move from your home/office/chair.

### Using the phone: good practice

The phone can have its drawbacks, too, especially when it is not used

### Activity

Have you experienced any of these problems when using the phone?

A  You can't relate as well to the other person, because you can't see them.

B  You can't assess their reaction to what you are saying except through voice.

C  It is easy to be distracted while speaking on the phone.

D  You sometimes can't hear them properly and may mis-hear important details.

Now work through this list again. This time, make a list of ways of overcoming these problems.

■■ *All these are problems which most people experience from time to time. D is a technical problem. Others are to do with the fact that phone conversations can only be voice-to-voice, not face-to-face.* ■■

When you use the phone...

- Give the other person your full attention.
- Listen carefully to their tone of voice.
- Speak clearly yourself, without shouting.
- Avoid distractions.
- Don't try to do something else when speaking on the phone.
- If you can't hear something, ask them to repeat it.

### The phone at work

The phone is an essential piece of equipment in almost all work settings.

### Activity

How is the phone used in jobs in the vocational setting you are interested in? Give some examples of how it is used and why it is important.

Jobs vary enormously in how much work is done on the phone. However, the advantages already mentioned apply especially to work settings.

### Personal phone calls

One area which sometimes causes problems in work settings is the issue of personal phone calls at work. Long personal calls cost money and a massive telephone bill can hit an organisation hard. They may also cause resentment among your colleagues who see you avoiding work.

### *Putting it into practice*

*The next few times you make phone calls think about:*

1. *why you chose to use the phone on this occasion rather than any other form of communication*
2. *how well you used your voice.*

# Topic 3 – Skills for successful discussions

## Good listening

**C 16**

Foundation
Element **1.1**
Performance criteria **1.3**
Range **Purpose; Subject**

## What is listening?

There are two sides to communication.

- When we talk to people, we are sending messages.
- When we listen to people, we are receiving messages.

For good communication, listening is just as important as talking.

### Activity

Think about all the situations where you listened to someone yesterday. Make a list of the situations. For each situation, why were you listening?

A  to gain information

B  to receive instructions

C  to get to know other people

D  to give other people encouragement or support

E  just for fun – because you were enjoying a conversation.

■■ *You need to listen in all sorts of situations. In relaxed situations, **E** is a good reason for listening, but all the others may be important too. In situations involving work and study, **A** and **B** are often particularly important.* ■■

Listening is not the same as hearing. Good listening means hearing and understanding. Then you can respond in the most suitable way to what you have heard.

## Showing you are listening

Good listeners show that they are listening. This can be done both by the things you say and how you use your body (body language). You can nod your head from time to time, smile, raise your eyebrows and look the speaker directly in the eyes. Try not to look around you, fidget or look at your watch. This body language will tell the other person that you are bored by the conversation.

You can show you are listening in other ways.

- Make shorts remarks such as 'really', 'uh huh' or 'mmm'.
- Pick up on what the other person has said, e.g. 'you mentioned...'

### Listening at work

Listening is an essential communication skill for work.

### Activity

Below are three situations you might meet at work. Why is it important to listen in each case? What would happen if you didn't listen carefully?

A  A colleague is describing to you how to use the photocopier.

B  You have a meeting with colleagues to discuss work coming up.

C  Someone you don't know comes into your office; she tells you her name and that she has come for a meeting with your boss.

■■ *It is important to listen so that:*

A  *you learn how to use the machine safely and efficiently*

B  *you know what you will be expected to do and what other people will be doing*

C  *you can pass on accurate information to your boss about the visitor.* ■■

If you don't listen carefully things can go wrong. You won't know what you are supposed to be doing. This creates a bad impression and wastes time – your own and other people's.

### Key points to remember

- In discussions, listening well is just as important as talking.
- Listening means hearing and understanding what someone is saying.
- Show you are listening.

### Putting it into practice

*For the next three discussions you have relating to your GNVQ, take the following steps:*

1  *Decide what the purpose is of the communication: why did you need to listen carefully?*

2  *Describe how you showed you were listening: what feedback did you give?*

## Topic 3 – Skills for successful discussions

**C 17**

Foundation
Element **1.1**
Performance criteria **3**
Range **Situation;
Subject**

### Checking understanding

# Successful communication

For communication to work, people have to understand each other. However, there are many situations where you may not understand fully what someone tells you.

For example:

- They are talking about something which you don't know much about.
- You may not hear what they are saying because they mumble or you are distracted for a moment.
- They don't express themselves clearly.

In these situations, it is important to check what they mean. It is especially important in situations which are new to you, such as when you start work or a new course of study.

### Activity

Imagine you are in the following situation: you have been working in an organisation for a week or so and are just getting familiar with the way things work. Your supervisor, Wendy, has the day off and her manager, comes in and asks you to look through the files for a lot of information about some projects. You are not quite sure about the names of one or two of the files. Your boss is in a hurry.

What do you do?

**A** Say: 'Yes, right away', and hope you can make sense of the files once you start looking.

**B** Say: 'I'm sorry, I'm not familiar with some of the file names. Could you repeat them, so I can check I've noted them down correctly?'

**C** Say: 'I think you'll have to wait for Wendy to get back on Monday, because I really don't understand the filing system.'

▌▌ The best approach is probably **B**. The manager will be far happier to spend a minute repeating them now, rather than waste much more time later when you make a mess of the task. ▌▌

### Hint
**Don't pretend you have understood something, if you haven't or are not sure. It will cause you more trouble in the long run.**

## Ways of checking understanding

There are many ways of working out that you understand what people mean. Two good approaches are:

- Repeat what they say, e.g. 'You think that I ought to ring him now?'
- Ask questions, e.g. 'Shall I ring him now or wait until tomorrow?'

Both of these approaches encourage the other speaker to say more or explain what he or she actually means.

### Hint
**Don't be afraid to ask questions – most people don't mind being asked.**

### Key points to remember

- Discussions fail if people don't understand each other – so check that you do understand.
- Don't pretend you have understood something if you haven't.
- Asking questions is often the best way of checking whether you have understood something.
- Repeating the other person's words is a good way of getting them to explain further what they mean.

### *Putting it into practice*

*When you next have discussions with people, make a point of checking anything you don't understand. What do you find is the best way of checking your understanding?*

# Topic 3 – Skills for successful discussions

## Asking questions

**C 21**

Foundation
Element **1.1**
Performance criteria **1,4**
Range **Subject; Purpose**

Asking questions is useful for all sorts of reasons:
- You can find out information from other people.
- You give other people the chance to speak.
- You can check that you have understood something.
- You can draw people out – especially if they are shy or nervous.

## Open and closed questions

Some questions encourage people to open up and talk – these are called 'open' questions. They often start with how, when, what, where, why. Questions are called 'closed' if you can answer them with just a yes or no, or a similar short answer.

'What did you think of the film?' can be answered with 'It was great – what I really enjoyed was ...' and is an example of an open question.

'Did you like the film?' 'No.' illustrates a closed question.

❙❙ *We would use closed questions in A, C and E. In B and D, open questions would be better.* ❙❙

**Hint**
Be careful with closed questions – they can shut down the conversation altogether.

### Activity

Are these questions open or closed? Tick the appropriate box.

|   | | Open | Closed |
|---|---|---|---|
| A | What are you studying? | ☐ | ☐ |
| B | Would you come into my office, please? | ☐ | ☐ |
| C | Is that an IBM over there? | ☐ | ☐ |
| D | How is that project going? | ☐ | ☐ |
| E | How old are you? | ☐ | ☐ |

**Key points to remember**
- Asking questions is a good way of gaining information and encouraging communication.
- Open questions encourage people to talk.
- Closed questions are useful for gaining specific information.

❙❙ *A and D are open questions: the person being asked has the chance to give a lot of information. C is a closed question, needing only a yes or no answer although the person being asked could follow up with more details. E is closed as well, as it only requires a short answer, i.e. your age. B is a trick question – it's not really a question at all; it's an instruction.* ❙❙

In most situations open questions are most useful, as they encourage people to communicate. However, in some situations closed questions are just as useful, especially when you need to get precise information.

### *Putting it into practice*

*Watch a TV news or current affairs programme that contains interviews. Note what sort of questions the interviewer asks. Write down some of the questions. How do the questions encourage the interviewee to talk and give information?*

*You may find it helpful to record a programme on video so that you can watch it more than once.*

### Activity

Look at the following situations described below. If you were in this situation, would you choose an open or a closed question? Tick the appropriate box. It will help you to think what questions you could actually ask.

| Imagine you want to: | | Open | Closed |
|---|---|---|---|
| A | ask a customer for details in order to fill in a holiday booking form | ☐ | ☐ |
| B | find out how a client of yours is feeling after her operation | ☐ | ☐ |
| C | ask a supervisor whether a particular computer program can do certain things | ☐ | ☐ |
| D | get ideas from colleagues about where to hold the Christmas party | ☐ | ☐ |
| E | find out if a meeting is still going to go ahead | ☐ | ☐ |

# Topic 3 – Skills for successful discussions

## Giving and receiving feedback

**C 22**

Foundation
Element **1.1**
Performance criteria **3,4**
Range **Subject; Situation**

# What is feedback?

In many discussions we have to give our ideas, opinions or views about what someone else says or does. Describing our thoughts in this way is often called giving feedback.

### Activity

Think about discussions you have had recently where you have to express your own view about something that someone else has said or done. Describe the situation and what you said. How did you feel as you gave the feedback?

Many people find it difficult to give feedback, especially when you know the other person won't like what you have to say. A lot of people also find it embarrassing to give praise to others.

There are good and bad ways of making comments and giving feedback.

## Guidelines for giving feedback

- be specific – mention specific examples of what the person said or did
- back up your comments with good reasons
- be friendly and willing to praise
- be helpful – offer useful suggestions, if appropriate
- be tactful, if you have to – never be abusive or unkind.

### Activity

Below are comments made by two people about a poster produced by one GNVQ student. Which is more useful?

**A** That's a brilliant poster, Sam. Fantastic. Wow, I wish I'd done one as good as that.

**B** I really like your poster, Sam. The colours are great and the overall design is really eye-catching. That drawing is excellent.

▐▐ *Person A obviously likes the poster, but doesn't explain why. Person B praises the poster and also explains why the poster is so good.* ▐▐

Feedback is most helpful when it is

> **Hint**
> Even when you have something unpleasant to say to someone, try to think of something good to say first.

Sometimes it is best to give feedback in private, if you are talking to just one person. This makes it easier to be honest and not feel embarrassed.

> **Hint**
> Use positive body language when giving feedback. It helps get your message across.

## Receiving feedback

Receiving feedback can be just as difficult as giving it. Many people find it hard to accept praise and it is never easy to feel we are being criticised. It's hard not to take criticism personally. Ideally, we should try to be open and see criticism as something helpful. We should try to learn from what other people tell us.

### Key points to remember

- Giving feedback means giving your views, ideas and opinions.
- Always be helpful when giving feedback.
- Be sensitive – never be critical just for the sake of it.
- Be willing to accept praise!
- Be willing, too, to accept criticism and learn from it.

### *Putting it into practice*

1. Practise giving feedback to other people in as many different situations as possible. Follow the guidelines given above. Be aware, too, of feedback you receive. What do you find most useful?

2. Watch how other people give feedback in work situations. How well do they do it? When does it work best?

# Topic 3 – Skills for successful discussions

**C 24**

**Foundation**
Element **1.1**
Performance criteria **2**
Range **Audience; Situation**

## Using body language

## What is body language?

The way we receive messages from people's expressions and gestures is called body language. Some people refer to it as non-verbal communication – this is because you are communicating without words.

### Activity

Look at the four illustrations shown below. Which of the four words listed best describes each picture?

**A** interested

**B** bored

**C** angry

**D** delighted to see you

• 148 •

# Topic 3 – Skills for successful discussions

## Using body language (continued)

■ *We can tell from their expressions and gestures what these people are feeling or thinking. 1 looks delighted to see you, 2 looks very angry, 3 seems interested and 4 is clearly bored.* ■

You can use virtually every part of your body to send messages. You can communicate through

- your eyes – e.g. how much eye contact you make
- your face – the expressions you make
- gestures – how you use your arms, hands, head
- body posture – how you sit or stand
- tone of voice – how you say something (rather than what you say).

Even the clothes you choose to wear are a form of body language. They tell other people what sort of person you are or even how you are feeling on a particular day.

### Activity

Imagine you are talking to someone. Assuming that they don't say anything, how could you tell that they

1. are really interested
2. agree with you
3. disagree with you
4. don't understand you.

■ *You should have found it very easy to think of ways people show all these things. Practise making the gestures and expressions you described – do it to a mirror to check what effect they produce!* ■

### Key points to remember

- Body language is a way of communicating without using words.
- Body language includes eye contact, expressions, gestures, posture, your tone of voice – even the clothes you wear.
- Be aware of your own body language and the messages you are sending.
- Be aware of the messages other people send you through their body language.

### *Putting it into practice*

*Next time you have any discussion or conversation connected with your GNVQ, be aware of the body language you use. Make an effort to use encouraging, positive body language. Look at the other person or people you are talking with. What does their body language tell you?*

# Topic 3 – Skills for successful discussions

## Using your voice

**C 29**

Foundation
Element **1.1**
Performance criteria **1,2**
Range **Subject; Purpose; Audience; Situation**

# The voice as communication tool

When you are talking to people, what you have say is important, but how you say it can be vital.

### Activity

How well do you use your voice?
- Do you ever mumble or speak unclearly?
- Can people always hear what you are saying?
- Do you sometimes gabble or speak too quickly?
- How 'interesting' would you say your voice is?

Most of us are quite lazy about how we speak. We tend to think that our voice is just the way it is. But with training and practice we can dramatically improve its quality.

## Using your voice at work

There are many jobs in which the voice is an important tool of the trade. In fact, anyone who has a job which involves communicating with people needs to think carefully about how they use their voice.

### Activity

Below is a list of different people for whom the voice is an important 'tool of the trade'. What sort of tone of voice would each of them use in the situation described? Think of one or two words for each example.

- salesperson trying to sell a product to a customer
- politician addressing a conference
- nurse reassuring an anxious patient
- receptionist talking to a visitor.

*Here are our suggestions:*
- *salesperson – confident, persuasive*
- *politician – forceful, confident*
- *nurse – calm, reassuring*
- *receptionist – welcoming, friendly.*

### Activity

Think about a job in the area of work you are interested in. What aspects of the job involve using your voice effectively?

You may not have to give speeches in public or deal with anxious customers or clients, but you will have to communicate with a range of people, including colleagues and supervisors. In every situation, if you speak clearly and with a varied, lively tone, you are more likely to get your message across – and impress people.

In situations where you are nervous, you can make an effort to relax physically.

- Take deep breaths – breathe in deeply and blow the air out.
- Take a drink of water.
- Aim to speak more slowly and clearly than normal.

All these help to keep your voice relaxed and working smoothly.

### Key points to remember

- How you say something can be just as important as what you say.
- Try to make your voice clear and easy to listen to – aim for an interesting, varied tone.
- Your voice may be an important tool for your work.
- Make a special effort to relax your voice in situations where you are nervous.

### *Putting it into practice*

1. Make a note of how you speak in the next discussions you take part in. Pay particular attention to any of the points in the first Activity which you felt you were weaker on.
2. Observe how other people use their voices in a work context, such as receptionists or telephonists you speak to, people who serve you in shops, etc.

# Topic 3 – Skills for successful discussions

## Ending discussions

**C 30**

Foundation
Element 1.1
Performance criteria 3,4
Range **Subject; Situation**

## A good ending

Like most things in life, discussions have beginnings, middles and endings. The beginnings of discussions often start with introductions and 'hello's. The middles are the main part, when you get down to talking about what's important. So what happens at the end of discussions?

### Activity

Think about the last time you were involved in:
1. a group discussion with other students
2. a one-to-one chat with a friend
3. a tutorial with your teacher.

How did the discussion end?

All too often discussions just stop suddenly or fizzle out. You may remember times when someone says: 'Oh look at the time – I must go' or 'There goes the bell, we'd better stop.'

This is fine if it is an informal discussion or chat with friends. However, in more formal situations, it is important to end discussions properly.

On the other hand you may remember discussions which ended in a better way. For example, you may have ended by making decisions about what to do next or by fixing a date for another meeting. You may have left the meeting feeling satisfied and encouraged.

The end of a discussion is when you can settle some very important points.

- You can summarise the main points of what you have discussed.
- You can agree what action you and other people will take.
- You can arrange a time when you will meet again for the next discussion.

These are things you can do no matter what sort of discussion you are involved in – one-to-one, group discussion, or whatever.

## Making notes

Often it is important to have a written record of what you agree during a discussion or meeting. A good way of doing this is by making notes for yourself. You may also make notes during the discussion, but it is at the end of the meeting that you have the chance to check what you have agreed.

### Hint

In meetings at work, it is often vital to make notes. This gives you a record of any action you are expected to take.

### Key points to remember

- The end of the discussion can be very important. It is the point where you can
  - summarise the main points of what you have discussed
  - agree on action you and other people will take
  - make future arrangements, e.g. when to meet again.
- At the end of the discussion, check the main points, e.g. if there is any action you have to take.
- Make notes to remind yourself of things agreed during the discussion.

### Putting it into practice

1. On the next three occasions when you are involved in discussions relating to your GNVQ, pay attention to what happens at the end of the discussion. Make a point of noting down, and checking, what is agreed during the discussion and any action that you and others have to take.
2. If possible, do the same thing for three discussions in a work setting, e.g. when you are on a work placement.

# COMMUNICATION – Produce written materials — Element 2

## Topic 1 – Grammar and punctuation

- C32  Full stops and commas
- C34  Capital letters
- C36  Sentences
- C37  Checking spelling

## Topic 2 – Improving your writing skills

- C41  Deciding what to write
- C42  Writing a rough draft
- C43  Taking notes
- C46  Drafting
- C47  Your final draft

## Topic 3 – Formats for writing

- C49  Introduction to filling in forms
- C51  Introduction to writing memos
- C53  Writing standard letters
- C55  Writing a CV
- C57  Writing leaflets and brochures

# Topic 1 – Grammar and punctuation

## Full stops and commas

**C 32**

Foundation
Element **1.2**
Performance criteria **2,3**
Range **Conventions**

Full stops and commas
- help other people to understand what we have written
- make it easier for us to read what other people have written
- help us to avoid misunderstandings.

Look at this example from a badly written letter. Misunderstandings can happen very easily if full stops and commas are not used correctly:

> Three members of staff will attend the meeting on 13 March weather permitting they will also take part in the excursion to the open air theatre.

▇▇ *If you received this letter would you be able to tell whether the members of staff were going to the meeting or not? It could mean that they were going to attend only if the weather was good. You would probably have to check. This kind of confusion wastes time and costs money. If the letter had full stops and commas there would be no chance of a misunderstanding:* ▇▇

> Three members of staff will attend the meeting on 13 March. Weather permitting, they will also take part in the excursion to the open air theatre.

Using full stops and commas incorrectly also makes a poor impression on other people.

## Full stops

. This is a full stop. Most sentences end with a full stop. For example: We got back from the conference late last night. The office doors were locked.

### Activity

Imagine you are given this phone message at work:

'Pete rang delivery will arrive tomorrow at 3 when the van gets here give him a ring.'

What would you think the message meant?

1. Pete rang. Delivery will arrive tomorrow at 3. When the van gets here give him a ring.

2. Pete rang. Delivery will arrive tomorrow at 3 when the van gets here. Give him a ring.

▇▇ *As you can see, these are completely different messages. Without full stops, you can't tell whether you are expected to ring Pete immediately or tomorrow.* ▇▇

## What is a comma?

, This is a comma. Two of the more common uses of commas are in lists and to separate parts of a sentence to make it more understandable.

### In a list

For example: We have arranged meetings in London, Birmingham, Manchester and Edinburgh.

You only need a comma before the 'and' at the end of the list if the meaning is unclear without a comma. For example: They want coffee, bacon and eggs, and cereal.

### Separating parts of a sentence

For example: The photocopier, which had broken down the week before, went wrong again as soon as she began copying.

You can use commas like this if the words between the commas – which had broken down the week before – are not needed for the meaning of the sentence. You can see in this example that if you take out the words between the commas the sentence still makes sense. 'The photocopier went wrong again as soon as she began copying.'

> **Hint**
> If you are not sure about whether to use a comma, say the sentence out loud to yourself and put commas in where you pause naturally.

### Activity

Read the text which follows and add full stops and commas.

The sales conference was a great success we had over 250 visitors to our stand including nine Americans four Germans and three Australians There was a great deal of interest in our new product Focus 2000 and we received 43 new orders As there was so much interest I would suggest that next year we double the size of our stand and increase the number of staff to six

▇▇ *The sales conference was a great success. We had over 250 visitors to our stand including nine Americans, four Germans and three Australians. There was a great deal of interest in our new product, Focus 2000, and we received 43 new orders. As there was so much interest, I would suggest that next year we double the size of our stand and increase the number of staff to six.* ▇▇

Did you remember to put a full stop at the end of each sentence? Did you use commas in the list of types of visitor? Did you try saying the sentences out loud to decide where to put commas?

# Topic 1 – Grammar and punctuation

## Full stops and commas (continued)

### Key points to remember

- We need full stops and commas to make sense of what we write and read.
- The most common use of the full stop is at the end of a sentence.
- The two most common uses of commas are in lists and to separate parts of a sentence to make it more understandable.
- Say a sentence out loud to help you decide where to put commas.

### *Putting it into practice*

*Imagine you are writing a job application letter. Write a few sentences listing your interests using full stops and commas correctly.*

# Topic 1 – Grammar and punctuation

## Capital letters

**Foundation**
Element **1.2**
Performance criteria **3**
Range **Conventions**

Use capital letters:

- at the beginning of sentences, e.g., Please send me five rolls of fax paper as soon as you can.
- for names of people, places, job titles, films, books and plays (except for short words like 'the', 'a' etc.), e.g., Meera Patel, Computer Services Manager, Manchester, England, Three Men and a Little Lady
- for nationality words, e.g., India, Ukrainian
- for names of days, months and special days (but not for 'autumn', 'summer' etc.), e.g., Tuesday, March, Easter Day, Diwali
- for 'I' (but not for 'me', 'my', 'mine' and 'myself' unless they are at the beginning of a sentence), e.g., On Saturday I went to work with my brother.

Many people find the use of capital letters confusing but it's important to get this right. It's easy to create a bad impression or offend someone if you do not use capital letters correctly. It's especially important to get it right when you are using capital letters for people's names and job titles at work.

Here's an example of capital letters not being used where they should be:

There will be a presentation on Friday 15 March to mark the retirement of the chairman, Mr david lowes.

The Chairman would probably be offended by this note. He would expect a capital letter not only for his name but also for his job title.

### Key points to remember

- Capital letters can help to make sense of what we write and read.
- People can be offended if capital letters are used incorrectly, particularly for their names and job titles.
- The most common uses of capital letters are at the beginning of a sentence, for names of people, job titles, places, films, books and plays, for nationality words, for names of days, months and special days, and for 'I'.

### Putting it into practice

*Write a list of the names of the people in your work placement and their job titles using capital letters correctly.*

### Activity

Rewrite these sentences using capital letters where you think they are needed. Remember to give job titles capital letters if they are important.

1. please notify your supervisor if you have an accident.
2. All letters of application should be sent to james bowman, managing director, in the glasgow office.
3. Delivery from france will take three days.
4. The factory will be closed for easter from friday 4 april to monday 7 april inclusive.
5. Please discuss with me what time you want to take off for Christmas or diwali.

▮ 1  *Please notify your Supervisor if you have an accident.*

2  *All letters of application should be sent to James Bowman, Managing Director, in the Glasgow office.*

3  *Delivery from France will take three days.*

4  *The factory will be closed for Easter from Friday 4 April to Monday 7 April inclusive.*

5  *Please discuss with me what time you want to take off for Christmas or Diwali.*

*It is important to use capital letters for both Christmas and Diwali.* ▮

# Topic 1 – Grammar and punctuation

## Sentences

**C 36**

**Foundation**
Element **1.2**
Performance criteria **2,3**
Range **Conventions**

This is a sentence:

*You can start work any day you choose except Friday.*

This is not a sentence:

*No matter which day.*

A sentence is a group of words which stands alone.

### Activity

Decide which of the following are sentences.

|   |                                  | Yes | No |
|---|----------------------------------|-----|----|
| 1 | In the office.                   | ☐   | ☐  |
| 2 | Can you come over immediately?   | ☐   | ☐  |
| 3 | We may need to order them soon.  | ☐   | ☐  |
| 4 | Immediate delivery.              | ☐   | ☐  |

■ *1 No 2 Yes 3 Yes 4 No* ■

### Activity

Rewrite 1 and 4, making them complete sentences.

■
1 stayed in the office until 10pm.
2 Immediate delivery of the parts is essential. ■

When we are talking, we don't always need to speak in sentences. We can often use our voice and body language to get across what we are saying. But when we write things down, we need to write in complete sentences so that what we are writing make sense to someone else. At work, this can be especially important. Writing in complete sentences creates a good impression and helps avoid any misunderstandings.

Look at these two examples:

*Example 1*

**Geeta**: How many cables do you need?

**Paul**: Not sure yet.

**Geeta**: More than six?

**Paul**: Probably – I'd order more anyway.

*Example 2*

Paul,

I would be grateful if you could let me know how many cables you need. If you need more than six I will have to order further supplies.

Geeta

In *Example 1*, Geeta and Paul are talking to each other and so they are able to understand each other and agree on what to do without using complete sentences. But in Example 2, when Geeta is writing to Paul, she needs to be more formal and organise her words into complete sentences.

### Activity

Imagine you are writing to someone to explain to them how your company arranges delivery. Make up complete sentences using the following phrases:

1 immediate delivery guaranteed
2 receive order
3 insurance not included
4 postage and packing extra
5 if any problems.

■ *Immediate delivery is guaranteed when we receive your order. Insurance is not included and postage and packing are extra. Please ring me if you have any problems.* ■

### Key points to remember

- A complete sentence is a group of words which makes sense on its own.
- You should always use complete sentences when you are writing.
- You do not have to use complete sentences when you are talking.

### *Putting it into practice*

*Using complete sentences, write an account of a meeting recording who said what.*

# Topic 1 – Grammar and punctuation

## Checking spelling

**C 37**

Foundation
Element **1.2**
Performance criteria **2,3**
Range **Conventions**

At work, where you need to be accurate and create a good impression, it's especially important to get spellings right. Most of us have difficulties with spelling.

### Using a dictionary

If you are not sure about the spelling of a word you can look it up in a dictionary. Decide how you think the word is spelt, and look for that spelling first. If you have got the spelling nearly right, you might find the word somewhere on that page. If you can't find it there, try other possible spellings. If you can't find it at all, ask someone who might know the correct spelling or who might be able to find the word in the dictionary for you. Don't be afraid to ask people at work how to spell a word – it's better to get the spelling right if you can. Or you might be able to use a spellcheck on a computer.

### Activity

Imagine your friend on a work placement has asked you to check the spelling in this letter before she sends it out. Using a dictionary to help you, write out the correct version on a separate piece of paper.

I am writing in conexion with your order for 45 minature cathedrels. These will be redy for you to colleck on Thursday 15 Febuary. Please bring with you a check for £13.50. Please also note that the faktory will be clozed for one week from 12 March. It will reopin on 19 March.

■■ *I am writing in connection with your order for 45 miniature cathedrals. These will be ready for you to collect on Thursday 15 February. Please bring with you a cheque for £13.50. Please also note that the factory will be closed for one week from 12 March. It will reopen on 19 March.* ■■

### Spelling names

If you have to spell the names of products, organisations and people you will probably not be able to find these in a dictionary or a spellcheck. Check spellings by looking at letterheads, packaging and signatures on letters. If you are at work, make sure you get the spellings of people's names right before you write to them. If necessary, telephone their departments or organisations and check how their names are spelt.

### Key points to remember

- It is important to spell correctly.
- Use dictionaries or spellchecks to check your spelling.
- Use letterheads and packaging to check your spelling of company names, etc.
- Always check the spellings of people's names.

### *Putting it into practice*

1. With a partner and a dictionary, check the spelling in something you have written for a GNVQ project.
2. Every time you come across a spelling mistake, write down the correct spelling from the dictionary. At the end, learn all the correct spellings and test each other.
3. Have you made the same kind of mistake several times? If so, there might be a basic spelling rule that you need to learn. Talk to your tutor.

# Topic 2: Improving your writing skills

## Deciding what to write

**C 41**

Foundation
Element **1.2**
Performance criteria **1,2,4**
Range **Subject; Format; Audience**

Decide what you want to write before you start writing. This is an especially important skill at work where people will be relying on you to provide information so that they can make decisions and take action.

### Think first

Before you write anything, think about:

- Whom am I writing to? It's surprising how many people forget to ask themselves this. The style you choose to write in will depend on whom you are writing to. For example, if you are writing to an employer for a job you should use a formal style but if you are writing to a friend you can be quite informal.

- What do I want to say? Make sure that you have worked out what your main points are. Concentrate on these and don't get sidetracked.

- What do they need to know? If you are writing to an employer for a job, he or she will only want information which is strictly relevant to you, the job and the company.

- What do they know already? There is no need to include anything that they already know. It can be very irritating to have to wade through lots of extra information in order to find the

▌▌ *You might have included:*

- *the reason for writing – invitation to the sales conference*
- *the date, time and venue of the conference*
- *how to get there*
- *where to reply to.*

*You wouldn't include information about menus or entertainments. The people you are writing to don't need to know these things in order to decide whether or not to come to the conference.* ▌▌

### Activity

Imagine you are helping to organise a sales conference and you have been asked to write a list of the main points to be included in a letter to invite people to the conference.

### Key points to remember

- Before you start writing you should decide whom you are writing to, what you want to say and what the person you are writing to needs to know.

- Don't include anything which the person you are writing to already knows or doesn't need to know.

### Putting it into practice

*Write a list of the main points about yourself that you would want to tell a potential employer in a letter of application.*

# Topic 2 – Improving your writing skills

**C 42**

Foundation
Element **1.2**
Performance criteria **1,2,3**
Range **Subject**

## Writing a rough draft

A rough draft is a first attempt at writing something. It usually contains all the main points you want to make but it is not in its polished, final form. When you fill in a form or write a letter at school, college or work, write a rough draft first.

- Sort out exactly what you are going to say and how and where you are going to say it before you write your final draft.
- Check that what you have written is clear, logical and about the right length.
- Write the introduction and conclusion after you have written the main text.
- Concentrate on what you are writing about and worry about punctuation, spelling and so on afterwards.
- Show it to someone else for their comments and ideas before you write your final draft.

> **Hint**
> In some work situations, you might be asked to write a rough draft to show a colleague or supervisor for approval before you produce the final draft.
> In this case, you will probably want it to be more polished than if it is just for your own use.

**DON'T** worry about your style, spelling or punctuation too much.

**DON'T** spend time checking your information at this stage – make a note of anything that needs checking and do it before your write your final draft.

**DO** write as fast as you can without re-reading as you go.

**DON'T** redraft too much – this can be especially tempting if you are working on a word processor.

### Activity

Imagine you are filling in a questionnaire about the catering facilities in your school or college. Write a rough draft for your answer to the last question in the questionnaire:

'Finally, we'd like to have your ideas about how we could improve our services. Please use this space to tell us about any changes you think we could make to the choice of meals provided or the organisation of the canteen.'

Think first about the main points you want to make and write a sentence for each one. Then put your sentences in an order. Aim to write about 75 words.

## Checking your rough draft

When you have written your rough draft you should check it before going on to write your final draft.

### Activity

Check what you have written.

1. Have you covered all the main points you thought of? If not, go back to your list, identify any which you have missed out and add sentences to cover them.

2. Was your draft easy to read back and did it make sense to you? If not, go back to your list of points and try to rearrange them so that what you have written is more logical.

3. Was there anything you weren't sure of? If so, you will need to do some extra research before you write your final draft.

4. Have you written much more or less than 75 words? If you have written more, you will need to go through what you have written, crossing out anything which is not essential. If you have not written enough, you will need to think of some more comments.

### Key points to remember

- Writing a rough draft allows you to sort out what you want to say before you start writing a final draft.
- You might need to write a rough draft for a colleague or supervisor to approve.
- Think first about the main points you want to make then write a sentence for each one.
- Group your sentences together in a sensible order.
- Check your rough draft carefully before going on to write a final draft.

### *Putting it into practice*

Write a rough draft for part of one of your GNVQ projects. Aim to write about 250 words.

# Topic 2: Improving your writing skills

## Taking notes

**Foundation**
Element 1.2
Performance criteria 1,4
Range **Subject;
Audience; Format**

We need to take notes to remember things we might otherwise forget. Here are some notes which someone has taken from a recorded telephone train timetable:

Kings Cross dep 11.15
Arrive York 16.00

York dep 21.30
Arrive KX 23.30

### Taking notes

1. Pick out the most important points and jot them down, for example,

    11 packs arr 15 March.

2. Shorten words and use abbreviations if you can, for example,

    'KX' for 'Kings Cross', '&' for 'and' etc.

3. Use headings to group points if you can, for example,

    Overtime, Every other Sat, Start Sat 12 Dec, Time + 1/2.

4. List points using bullets, asterisks or numbers, for example,

    Bring identification:
    - passport
    - driving licence
    - student card

5. Don't worry about writing in sentences, for example,

    Delivery no gd. Ring supplier. Money back on return.

6. Start new lines frequently, for example,

    first interviews 15 Feb
    shortlisting 18-20 Feb
    second interviews 25 Feb
    job starts 1 Mar

7. Underline or use capital letters to highlight important points, for example,

    REPORT TO MRS GRIDLEY 9AM THURSDAY

There are two main kinds of notes:

- notes on what someone is saying, for example, when you are being given instructions
- notes from other pieces of writing, for example, when you are collecting information.

When you make notes you need to be clear about why you are making them. For example, at a meeting you might need to have a record of what everyone is going to do and by what date, and whom they should report back to. You won't have time to write everything down that is said.

### Activity

Imagine your boss is about to go on holiday. She quickly gives you some instructions for while she is away and you have to make notes on anything you'll need to know and you think you won't remember. This is what she says:

'I'll be away for a fortnight – until September 9th. I'm back in the office on the 10th. You can contact me on 0223 654789 but only in an emergency. If you're not sure or worried about anything, talk to Julie or Mena. They can make any decisions. Make sure the letters about the sales conference go off by Friday but don't worry about the minutes for the meeting until I get back. I'm sure you'll be fine – it'll be good for you to have the run of the place for a couple of weeks. And we'll have a two-day handover period before you go on your holiday.'

Write your notes on a separate piece of paper, include anything you think you'd need to know and may not remember. You don't need to write in complete
sentences – just jot down the key words to remind you of the main points of the instructions. Try to write no more than 20 words.

▐▌ *Back Sept 10*

*0223 654 789 – emergency*

*Julie or Mena*

*Sales letters by Friday*

*Minutes wait till back* ▐▌

# Topic 2: Improving your writing skills

## Taking notes (continued)

### Activity

Your boss has asked you to find out about the climate in India so that he can plan a sales trip. You find this information in a travel guide:

> The heat starts to build up from around February and by April or May it's unbearably hot. The rains usually reach southern India by the beginning of June and gradually work their way up through the country until they reach northern India by the middle of June. The monsoon ends around October and this is probably the best time of year to travel in India. The temperatures are not too hot and not too cool, although Delhi and other northern cities can become quite crisp at night.

Make notes, concentrating on what your boss needs to know to plan his trip. Make sure that what you write down is accurate and use note form rather than complete sentences.

▌▌ *Oct – best time to travel*

*Hot season starts Feb*

*April May too hot*

*Monsoon starts June – travelling difficult – ends Oct* ▌▌

Read through your notes again. Do you think they would give your boss a clear indication of the best and worst time to travel in India?

### Key points to remember

- Making notes is an important skill to develop at work.
- You need to be clear about your purpose for making the notes.
- You might need to make notes on what someone says or on what you have read.
- Your notes should be accurate and relevant.
- Don't use complete sentences when making notes.

### Putting it into practice

*Ask a friend to imagine they are preparing for a job interview. Ask them to talk to you about their qualifications, work experience and outside interest. Make notes on what they say which might help them to prepare for the interview. Read the notes back to your friend and ask them whether they think your notes are accurate and cover all the main points relevant to the interview.*

# Topic 2: Improving your writing skills

## Drafting

**C 46**

Foundation/Intermediate/Advanced
Element **1.2, 2.2, 3.2**
Performance criteria **1, 2**
Range **Subject**

When you are writing something simple and straightforward, you don't usually need to write a rough draft. But if you are writing something more complex or sensitive, especially in a work situation, you usually need to produce a first draft. This letter is an example of something which should have been drafted out first:

> Dear Mr ~~Pallet~~ Patel
>
> ~~I hope you don't mind my writing~~ I am writing to say that I ~~can't~~ am no longer able to work for you on Saturdays as I am ~~too tired~~ finding it difficult to fit in my college work.
>
> I will work for two more weeks as agreed so I will finish ~~the week after next~~ Saturday 15 March. ~~Sorry~~ I hope you understand and that you can find ~~someone else~~ someone to replace me soon.
>
> Yours ~~faithfully~~ ~~sincerely~~ sincerely
>
> Paula

### Step-by-step approach to drafting

1. Think about your audience.
2. Think about why you want to say what you are saying, i.e., the purpose of what you are writing.
3. Decide what you want to say – write a list of the main points you want to make.
4. Group your points together under headings.
5. Write a sentence for each point and group them into paragraphs corresponding to your headings.
6. Write linking sentences between paragraphs.
7. Write an introductory sentence at the beginning.
8. Write a concluding sentence at the end.
9. Give your draft a title if it needs one.

### Activity

Draft a report on your first week of work experience for your tutor. Use the step-by-step approach to help you structure your draft. Write about 500 words.

## Any problems?

When you were writing your rough draft, you might have encountered some of the problems listed below.

### It's too clumsy

Don't worry too much about creating something too polished at this stage. Your aim is to establish what you want to say and how you are going to say it. You will be able to improve it when you write your final draft.

### I haven't checked the spelling

Unless your first draft is going to be seen by a colleague or supervisor, you can check spellings after you have finished roughing it out, rather than stopping to look words up in the dictionary as you write. Keep a list of all the spellings you're not sure of so that you can check them at the end.

### I'm not sure if I've got the punctuation right

Again, you can check the punctuation after you have produced your first draft.

### It's too long

You can delete some sentences or paragraphs when you have finished.

### I'm not sure about some of the information

Make sure you have time between writing the rough draft and the final draft to check any facts you are not sure of. Keep a list of anything you need to check so that you can do all the extra research at the end.

### I can't decide what to put in the introduction

It's often easier to write the introduction once you have written the main text – then you can be sure of the main points you are going to include.

### I'm not getting anywhere

If you are having real trouble writing a rough draft, go back to your list of points and make sure that you understand each of them and that they are grouped together in a logical way.

# Topic 2: Improving your writing skills

## Drafting (continued)

### I'm on my fifth draft and it's still not right

Don't be tempted to redraft too much – especially if you are working on a word processor. You are only aiming to sort out what you are going to say and how you are going to say it at this stage.

## Checking a rough draft

After you have written your rough draft you should check it carefully before going on to write your final draft. Check for:

- **content** – is it relevant, accurate, clear and complete? Make sure you have included all the points in your list and that what you have written is logical and easy to read.
- **purpose** – does it do what it is meant to do? Remember that other people will want to use the information you are providing to make decisions and take action.
- **tone** – is it suitable for the people you are writing for? Try to imagine that you are the reader rather than the writer and decide whether you have got the tone right for them.
- **length** – is it overlength or too short? Do a rough word count by adding up the average number of words per line (roughly) and multiplying this by the number of lines per page. Or use a word count if you are working on a word processor.

### Activity

Check the rough draft you wrote earlier for:
- content
- purpose
- tone
- length.

### Key points to remember

- Writing a rough draft allows you to sort out what you want to say and how you want to say it before you start writing the final draft.
- Use a step-by-step approach to write a rough draft.
- Make sure you know your audience.
- Check a rough draft for content, purpose, tone and length before going on to write a final draft.

### Putting it into practice

*Write a rough draft for a report on one of your GNVQ projects for next year's students or prospective employers. Write about 500 words. Follow the step-by-step approach and check your rough draft when you have written it. Make sure you select a tone that is appropriate for your audience.*

# Topic 2: Improving your writing skills

## Your final draft

**Foundation**
Element 1.2
Performance criteria 1,2,3
Range **Subject;**
**Conventions**

### Writing a final draft

Once you have written and checked a rough draft, you are ready to write your final draft. This is easier to do if you are working on a computer because you can easily change your rough draft. If not, you will have to retype it or write it out by hand very carefully. Before you start:

1. Add anything you have forgotten to include.
2. Delete anything which you think isn't essential; if in doubt, cut it out.
3. Change the order of what you have written if it doesn't seem clear.
4. Correct any spellings or punctuation.
5. Check your facts and figures and make any changes.

### Presenting your final draft

It is important to present your final draft carefully, especially if you are writing it for your GNVQ or in a work situation. Check that it is

- clear
- easy to read
- accurate
- neat and tidy.

### Activity

Compare these two final drafts for a report on fire drills. Write down as many reasons as you can why Draft B is not as good as Draft A.

### Draft A

Fire drills

All staff have been involved in at least one fire drill this year. There were no major problems in any drill although we identified a number of minor problems:

- some fire doors had been propped open
- some staff did not know how to use fire extinguishers
- the evacuation area (the staff car park) is too near the main building.

I would recommend the following action:

1. A memo to all staff instructing them not to prop fire doors open.
2. Training from the fire department on how to use fire extinguishers.

I will investigate other possibilities for the evacuation area and report back.

### Draft B

FIRE DRILS
~~Most~~ All staff have been involved in at least one fire drill this year. There were no major/~~hiccups~~/problems in any dril although some fire doors had been proped open, some staff ~~didn't~~ did not know how to use fire extinguishers, the evacuation area (the staff car park) is to near the mane building.
I'd send a memo to all staff, telling them not to ~~prop~~ fire doors open training from the fire department on how to use fire extinguishers.
I'll ~~investigate~~ look at the evacushun area.

# Topic 2: Improving your writing skills

## Your final draft (continued)

■ *Draft B is unlikely to create a good impression or get much attention. Did you note down the following:*

- *The points are not set out in a logical and clear order. (In Draft A the main points are clearly listed using bullet points.)*
- *The handwriting is messy and difficult to read. (Draft A is neatly typed.)*
- *It is too cramped. (Draft A has wide margins and double spacing between lines.)*
- *It contains crossings out. (Draft A has been carefully checked at rough draft stage and there are no crossings out in the final draft.)*
- *It is full of spelling mistakes, for example, dril, proped, mane, to, traning, posibilities. (The spellings in Draft A have been carefully checked.)* ■

### Tips on writing a final draft

1. Use a typewriter or word processor, or write clearly and neatly.
2. Set your points out in a clear and logical order. Use lists and bullet points • or numbering if it helps.
3. Leave plenty of space in the margins and between lines.
4. Try not to have any crossings out if you are writing by hand. It's better to produce another final draft than to hand something in which is full of mistakes.
5. Check the spelling of any words you are not sure of in a dictionary.

### A word about proof-reading

One of the most important skills to develop when you are writing is proof-reading. This means reading something you have written slowly and carefully to make sure that it does not contain any spelling, punctuation or other mistakes. It's surprising how many mistakes can creep in unnoticed.

### Activity

Proof-read this passage and try to find eight mistakes.

James McIntosh is a well-known ontraprenor in the Glasgow area with investments in shiping, forestry, turism and and catering. Mr Macintosh spends most of the week London but returns most weekends to his home in Troon. Every weekend he can be seen at Troon golf course with his wife, Susann.

■ *Did you find the following:*

*McIntosh spelt Macintosh – particularly important to check the spelling of people's names carefully. Entrepre-neur, shipping, tourism spelt wrongly; Susann is probably wrong but you would need to check it as it might be an unusual spelling of Susan.*

*Two 'ands' before 'catering'; no 'in' before London. Mr McIntosh spends 'most weekends' at home in Troon but 'every weekend' on the golf course – one of these must be wrong.* ■

It is often more difficult to proof-read your own writing because you are so familiar with it by the time you have finished writing it. You might like to arrange with a friend to check each other's work.

### Key points to remember

- It is important to produce a good final draft, especially in your studies and in a work situation.
- A final draft should be clear, easy to read, accurate and neat and tidy.
- Proof-read your final draft carefully for spelling and punctuation errors and other mistakes.

### *Putting it into practice*

*Write a final draft for a report on one of your GNVQ projects. If you have worked on the resource sheet, 'Writing a rough draft', use the rough draft you wrote. Check and proof-read it carefully. Write about 250 words.*

# Topic 3: Formats for writing

## Introduction to filling in forms

**C 49**

Foundation
Element 1.2
Performance criteria 2,4
Range Format; Audience

Forms are used when information is needed on a routine basis or in a set format. Examples of forms include application forms, order forms and school or college reports. You may also have to fill in forms at work, for example, to

- order stationery
- report on progress
- provide a record of your hours, holidays or sick leave.

When you are filling in a form, it's important to answer all the questions clearly, fully and accurately. Here's an example of a form about work experience which has been badly filled in by a student. The notes in the margin show you what she has done wrong.

*surname and first name should have been given separately*

*should have checked whether plc or Co Ltd*

*postcode missing*

*should have found out*

*too vague – should have given day as well as month*

*two weeks since when? should have given full date*

*not enough detail*

*doesn't answer the question which is about the work experience itself and not about how comfortable she was*

**WORK EXPERIENCE PROGRESS SHEET**

Student's surname: Jane Robertson    First name: _____

Employer's name: Smithson & Grainger plc or Co Ltd

Employer's address: *(include post code)*
_____
49 Beacon Way, Reading

Employer's telephone number: _____

Date started: June 1994

Date finished: two weeks ago

Details of work done: Technical drawing

Any comments on the work experience you received:
_____Office too cold_____

People often find filling in forms difficult because

- the questions are too complicated
- the form is badly designed and difficult to follow
- there is not enough space to answer the questions
- they don't think carefully enough about the questions before they write their answers.

### Activity

List any forms you have filled in and what they were for. Try to include forms you have filled in on a work placement or at school or college. Beside each one write down anything you found difficult about filling in the form.

In the rest of this resource sheet you will be looking at ways in which you can make form-filling easier for yourself.

# Topic 3: Formats for writing

## Introduction to filling in forms (continued)

### How to fill in forms

1. Before you start to fill in a form, think about what it is for and what information is needed by the person you are filling it in for.

2. Read through the whole form carefully to find out whether there are any questions you will find particularly difficult to answer or for which you will need to do some extra research.

3. Deal with each question in turn:
   - Read the question carefully and make sure you understand what it is asking.
   - Think about your answer.
   - Write a rough version of your answer on a separate piece of paper (unless it is something very straightforward). Make sure what you have written will fit in the space on the form. You might have to cut it down.
   - Write your answer carefully in the space on the form. Make sure you copy your rough answer out word for word – it's easy to miss out a vital word or sentence.

4. When you have answered all the questions, read through the form again and check that what you have written answers the questions properly. Check your spelling, grammar and punctuation and that your handwriting or typing can be read easily.

### Key points to remember

- Forms are used to collect routine information or information that is needed in a set format.
- When you fill in a form, take it step-by-step, making sure you read through the whole form first. Answer each question carefully and check your answers.
- It is important to make sure your answer will fit in the space provided on the form.

### Activity

Imagine you work for a company called Electron. The office photocopier breaks down while you are using it. You are asked to fill in a form telling the engineer what has happened. You have the following information:

1. The photocopier is a Canon Model 200. It broke down on Tuesday 18 May at 11 a.m.
2. The paper jammed suddenly while you were copying a 100-page report.
3. You tried to get the paper out using the correct lever but the lever jammed too.
4. This also happened two weeks ago but then you were able to release the lever yourself and get the paper out. The photocopier has worked since then.
5. The photocopier was last serviced in January.

---

Name of company _____
Model number of machine _____
When did the fault occur? _____
What was the machine being used for when the fault occurred? _____
Was any corrective action taken? _____
What was the outcome? _____
Has this fault occurred before? _____ If yes, when? _____
When was the machine last serviced? _____

---

Your answer might have looked something like this:

Name of company _Electron_____
Model number of machine _Canon Model 200_____
When did the fault occur? _Tuesday 18 May 11 am_____
What was the machine being used for when the fault occurred? _Copying 100-page report_
Was any corrective action taken? _Yes – tried using lever to unjam paper_
What was the outcome? _Lever jammed too_
Has this fault occurred before? _Yes_____ If yes, when? _2 May_
When was the machine last serviced? _January_

Look through your answers and check that you have included all the relevant information and that the engineer would be able to read and understand your answers.

### Putting it into practice

*Copy out the form on the previous page and fill it in properly. Use your own details if you have done work experience. If you haven't, make up all the extra details you need.*

| Topic 3: Formats for writing |

## Introduction to writing memos

Foundation
Element **1.2**
Performance criteria **3,4**
Range **Format; Audience**

## What is a memo?

The word 'memo' is short for 'memorandum'. A memo is a written message which is usually sent within an organisation, often as a reminder to someone else to do something. There is no 'Dear X' at the top and no 'Yours sincerely' or 'Yours faithfully' at the bottom.

Some organisations use standard pre-printed paper for memos. You may have come across this in one of your work placements. A standard memo looks like this:

---

### MEMORANDUM

To: Geraldine Poole        Date:    4 March 1995
From: Winston Smith

Subject:

Just to let you know that the next school visit will be on Wednesday 9 April. Please make sure that you will be available to welcome the children when they arrive at 11 am.

*Winston Smith*

---

Standard memos are mostly used for information about routine matters such as sick leave, information about parking spaces and so on.

### Writing a memo

Most memos contain

- the word 'memo' or 'memorandum'
- who it is to (first name only if you know them well)
- who it is from (first name only if you know them well)
- date
- heading
- text – what you want to say
- signature (full name, first name or initials).

### Activity

Use this preprinted paper to write the following memos.

---

### MEMORANDUM

To:                              Date:
From:

Subject:

---

**Memo 1**

Memo dated 14 June 1995 from Gupta Wareham, Personnel Director, asking all staff to give details of the annual leave they have booked for the rest of the year and how many days' leave they still have to book.

# Topic 3: Formats for writing

## Introduction to writing memos (continued)

---

### MEMORANDUM

To:                                      Date:
From:

Subject:

---

**Memo 2**
Memo dated 16 June 1995 from Vanessa Brookes giving the following details:
Holidays booked 15 August to 29 August and 11 September to 13 September.

---

### MEMORANDUM

To: All staff                          Date:    4 March 1995
From: Gupta Wareham, Personnel Director

Subject: Annual Leave

Please let me have written details of all the annual leave which you have booked for the rest of the year.

Thank you

G.W.

---

### MEMORANDUM

To: Gupta Wareham                      Date:    16 June 1995
From: Vanessa Brookes

Subject: Annual Leave

I have booked annual leave from 15 August to 29 August and from 11 September to 13 September. I have five more days to book.

Vanessa

---

### Key points to remember

- A memo is a written message, often sent as a reminder.
- Some organisations use standard preprinted paper for memos.
- Memos are less formal than letters or reports.

### Putting it into practice

*Write a memo to your supervisor in a work placement saying when the next school or college holidays are and explaining that you won't be at work then.*

# Topic 3: Formats for writing

## Writing standard letters

**C 53**

Foundation/Intermediate/
**Advanced**
Element **1.2,2.2,3.2**
Performance criteria **4**
Range **Format; Audience**

We use standard letters to
- acknowledge receipt of something
- ask for information
- order something
- confirm information
- give instructions.

Standard letters are usually in a set format which may be stored on a computer. All you have to do is fill in the details. Here is an example of a standard letter which you might send if you worked in a library:

**Pemshire County Council Libraries**

*name, address and telephone number of person or organisation sending the letter*

Bredwith Library
PO Box 154
Market Street
Bredwith GM4 9PH
Telephone: 0433 356989

*date*

30 July 1995

*name and address of person receiving the letter*

Ms G R Slight
43 The Acres
Bredwith
GM4 7HY

*reference number*

Your ref: 087765

*salutation*

Dear Sir/Madam

*subject heading*

Requested item: 358.2311 Lavender, T. I. The Life of Bradley

*the text*

The book listed above, which you requested, is now at the library. Please collect it within ten days of the date of this letter. Please bring your library ticket and, if the request has not been prepaid, your reservation fee.

*closing*

Thank you

Yours faithfully

*signature*

*Simon Woods*

*full name of person sending letter – pp means 'in the place of' and is used if someone signs a letter on behalf of someone else*

pp Susan Greene
County Librarian

# Topic 3: Formats for writing

## Writing standard letters (continued)

For standard letters, you can use either:

- Dear Sir/Madam and Yours faithfully or
- Dear...(the name of the person) and Yours sincerely.

If you know the person you are writing to well, you can use their first name and sign your first name but you should still type or write your name in full under your signature as not all signatures are easy to read.

### Activity

Imagine you work in the fabric department of a large furnishings shop. Write a standard letter telling a customer that the curtains that have been made for her are ready to collect. Make up any details such as the date, names and addresses. Sign the letter from yourself. Make sure that all the information the customer needs is included and that the information you give is accurate.

### Key points to remember

- Standard letters can be used to acknowledge receipt of something, ask for information, order something, confirm information and give instructions.
- Standard letters can be stored on a computer.
- Letters should include the name, address and telephone number of the person or organisation sending the letter; the date; the name and address of the person receiving the letter; any reference numbers; a salutation; a subject heading; the text; a closing; a signature; and the full name of the person sending the letter.

### Putting it into practice

*Write a standard letter which you could use when you write to companies for application forms for jobs you have seen advertised.*

■ *Your letter might be similar to this:*

**Avalon Furnishings**

Mrs G Patel  
107 York Road  
Straden TR5 9GV

4 High Street  
Porloth TR3 7KJ  
Telephone: 0224 098765

7 August 1995

Order number: 547

Dear Mrs Patel

**Curtain making service**

I am writing to let you know that the curtains you ordered are now ready to collect. The store is open from 9 to 5.30 Monday to Friday and from 9 to 7 on Saturday.

Yours sincerely

*Joanna Kirtle*

Joanna Kirtle  
Fabric Department

# Topic 3: Formats for writing

## Writing a CV

**C 55**
Foundation/Intermediate/Advanced
Element **1.2, 2.2, 3.2**
Performance criteria **1, 4**
Range **Format; Audience**

## What is a CV?

A CV is a summary of personal details, education, previous employment and other skills and interests, which you are often asked to send if you apply for a work placement or a job. (CV stands for 'curriculum vitae' which comes from the Latin meaning 'course of life'.)

## Structure

This example shows how a CV should be structured:

---

### CURRICULUM VITAE

| | | |
|---|---|---|
| NAME | Kelly Maguire | |
| ADDRESS | 12 Smithson Road London NW5 4TL | |
| TELEPHONE | 0181 765 9889 | |
| DATE OF BIRTH | 14 August 1979 | |

**EDUCATION**

| | | | |
|---|---|---|---|
| Sept 1990-July 1996 | Sparrowfield School London NW5 | *GCSEs* English Mathematics Science Craft, design & technology | C C B B |

**EMPLOYMENT**

| | | |
|---|---|---|
| July 1996 to date | Sales assistant Bollingmore's Photo Development | Main duties Serving customers, despatching film and checking prints |

**VOLUNTARY WORK**

Since I was 14 I have worked with families with children with disabilities. I visit two families and spend time with the children, taking them out for walks and playing with them at home.

**OTHER SKILLS**

Typing 30 wpm (word processor)
Basic French
I plan to learn to drive as soon as I am 17.

**INTERESTS**

Synchronised swimming, riding, cinema.

**REFERENCES**

Mr Kraft
Bollingmore's Photo Development
121 High Road
London NW5 4DE
Tel: 081 765 8876

Mr Prentice
Headteacher
Sparrowfield School
London Road
London NW5 7RF
Tel: 081 765 4213

---

*Personal details*
Give details of name, address, telephone number and date of birth. Give your first name and surname in full but don't give middle names. Highlight your name so that an employer can see at a glance who you are. Include your full address, postcode, telephone code and number.

*Education*
Give the dates you attended, names and locations of schools and colleges. Only list secondary education. If you have attended more than one school or college, put details of the first one first. Give details of any examinations you have passed – don't list any examinations you have failed. If you obtained a distinction or merit of some kind, give information about that too.

*Employment*
Give dates, names and locations of employers, title of job held and main duties. Start with your current or most recent job. Use note form to list your main duties as you need to keep the CV as short as possible.

*Voluntary work*
Give details of any voluntary work which might be relevant. Voluntary work is seen by many employers as useful work experience.

*Other skills*
Only give details of skills which might help you get the job.

*Interests*
Give details of hobbies, sport and leisure activities. These do not have to be work-related – you want to show the employer that you are a well-rounded person with a full life outside work.

*References*
Give names, addresses and telephone numbers of two people who will provide information about you to a prospective employer. Include one from your school or college and one from an employer if you can. Check with them first that they are willing to be your referees.

# Topic 3: Formats for writing

## Writing a CV (continued)

Employers often use CVs to decide whether or not to call you to interview. Your CV may be all the information they have about you so it is important for your CV to highlight your good points and to encourage them to read it by making sure it is:

- brief
- clear
- relevant
- accurate
- well-presented.

It takes time and effort to produce a good CV but it's well worth it because it can really improve your job prospects.

If you are called for an interview for a work placement or job, you should be familiar with your CV and take a copy with you as the interviewer may want to discuss the information it contains during the interview.

### Key points to remember

- A CV is a summary of personal details, education, previous employment and other skills and interests.
- A good CV is essential – when an employer first sees it he or she usually knows nothing about you and only has the CV to make a judgement about whether to interview you or offer you work experience.
- A CV should be clear, simple and well-presented and should fit on no more than two pages of A4 paper.

### *Putting it into practice*

*Write your CV, using the CV on the previous page as a model. If you already have a CV that you are happy with, offer to produce a CV for a friend.*

# Topic 3: Formats for writing

## Writing leaflets and brochures

**Foundation/Intermediate/Advanced**
Element **1.2, 2.2, 3.2**
Performance criteria **1, 4, 5**
Range **Subject; Format; Audience**

Leaflets and brochures are very similar. The main difference is that leaflets are shorter – sometimes no longer than a single page.

Leaflets are used to publicise events, advertise new products, tell people about issues and campaigns – or sometimes to give basic information about a place or perhaps a service that is offered to people. Leaflets are cheap to produce. You can't tell people everything in a leaflet. You should try to tell them only enough to get them interested in finding out more.

Brochures are longer than leaflets. They are often used by companies to advertise a whole range of products. They usually try to give people all the information – such as prices, details of different models – that they need to know. Because they are quite expensive to produce they are often aimed at people who are already quite interested in the subject.

### Key points to remember

- Get your readers' attention on the cover.
- Break your text up into manageable chunks.
- Get your readers interested in the first five words.

### Getting attention

The front cover of a leaflet or brochure has to make people look at it. A picture or a bright colour is often used to do this. You can also use words to get people's attention – such as a slogan or an at-a-glance description of what's inside (or both).

**Activity**

Try writing the words to go on the cover of:

- a brochure about holidays for young people in Spain this summer
- a leaflet for a campaign against the destruction of the rain forests.

■■ *You could have written a slogan for either of these examples. The holiday brochure would also need some facts – the date, the age range and the destination.* ■■

### Breaking it up

People rarely read a leaflet or a brochure all the way through at once. They may start at the back – or open a page at random and look at anything that seems interesting. You have to write your text in separate chunks that make sense on their own. Have a look at a leaflet or brochure to see how this is done.

Remember when you are writing a leaflet or brochure, you have to keep persuading people to read on. In any block of copy, the first few words are really important. You should try to catch your readers' interest in the first five words of your copy.

**Activity**

Try writing the first sentence of a paragraph introducing a leaflet on:

- a new playgroup
- the sports facilities at a college.

■■ *Here are some suggestions:*

1. *Have you got children under 5? Children will love Play Space!*
2. *Fit people will have more fun.*
3. *The gym is free for all students.* ■■

### What do you want people to do?

Every leaflet or brochure must have some way in which readers can respond to what they have read. This could be a form to fill in – or a telephone number or an address where they can get more information.

### Putting it into practice

*Plan and write a leaflet to encourage local businesses to provide work placements for students at your college.*

# COMMUNICATION – Use images — Element 3

## Topic 1 – Making and finding images

- C59 What can images do?
- C60 Choosing images
- C61 Finding images
- C62 Copying images
- C63 Thinking about your audience
- C64 Using and making images

## Topic 2 – Types of image

- C71 Symbols
- C72 Diagrams
- C73 Graphs and tables
- C74 Photographs
- C75 Drawings and cartoons
- C78 Maps and plans

## Topic 3 – Using images

- C82 Planning your work
- C83 Posters
- C84 Leaflets

# Topic 1 – Making and finding images

## What can images do?

C 59

Foundation/Intermediate/Advanced
Element **1.3,2.3,3.3**
Performance criteria **2**
Range **Images; Audience; Situation**

When you are explaining things to others it is often useful to use a picture, a diagram, a symbol, or some other image to show what you mean.

### Activity

This diagram was at the end of a questionnaire. It shows how to fold the leaflet for posting.

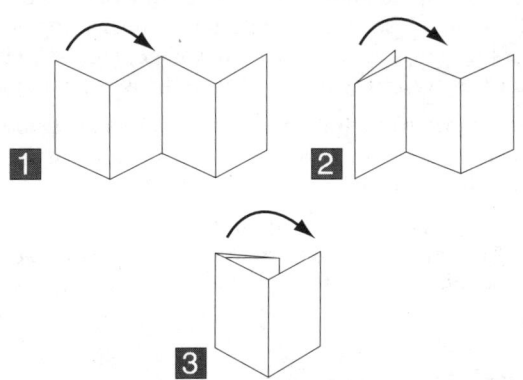

Try using words to explain how to fold the questionnaire.

▌▌ *You probably found this very difficult. Even if you managed it, your explanation is unlikely to have been as clear as the diagram. There are some things that it is much easier to explain with a diagram than with words. Diagrams are also good at showing the order in which things have to be done.* ▌▌

### Activity

This image was on the door of the IT room in a college. The circle and the diagonal bar were printed in red. What do you think it means?

▌▌ *This symbol is a reminder not to bring drinks into the IT room in case they spill and damage the computers. You may never have come across a symbol exactly like this before but you could probably guess what it meant. Most people are familiar with the 'language' of symbols and know that a circle with a bar across is an instruction not to do something. Symbols are a way of giving instant information.* ▌▌

### Activity

What images could you use in these situations to get your point across?

1 You are organising a work rota and want everybody to be clear about when they are on duty.
2 You have helped to organise a very successful open day and want some good publicity in the local paper.
3 A new student asks how to get to the Principal's office.

▌▌ *The best way to explain your rota would be to put a chart on the notice board. You could show how successful the open day was by giving the local paper a photograph of the event.*

*In the third situation you would probably want to show the new student a* map. ▌▌

The chart, photograph and the map all show things that would be quite hard to put into words.

The *chart* sets out information in a clear way so that people can find the details they need quickly. The *photograph* gives an impression of what it was like at the open day. The *map* shows how the college site is arranged, so that people can find their way around.

There are many other types of image which you can use.

*Graphs* let you compare different figures.

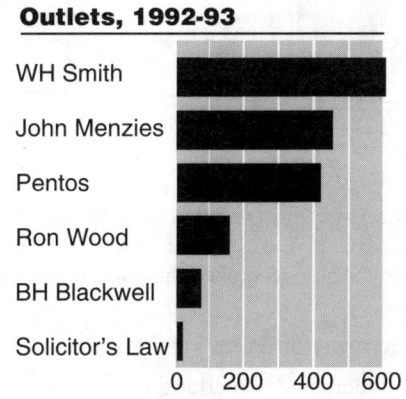

This graph shows you at a glance how many shops each chain of booksellers had in 1992–93.

# Topic 1 – Making and finding images

## What can images do? (continued)

*Cartoons* can be used to say something in an amusing way.

This cartoon is from a booklet about buying computers. It makes a useful point – that size is something to think about when you are choosing a computer notebook – and helps to make a technical subject seem more human and approachable.

*Illustrations* can give a feeling of what an object, a person, a place or a situation looks like and can also create a mood.

This illustration was on the front of a leaflet produced by a GPs' practice. It looks a bit like a picture from a children's storybook and makes the surgery seem attractive and friendly.

Images can do many different jobs. They can

- help you understand something
- help you recognise something quickly
- tell you what to do
- make you want to read something
- affect what you feel about something.

### Activity

Look through a copy of a newspaper. How many different types of images can you find in it? What job do you think each image is doing?

You should have been able to find examples of all the types of image mentioned on this sheet, and probably some others as well, such as strip cartoons and company logos. The headlines in the paper are a kind of image, too. The size of the letters, as well as what they say, tells us something.

In your project work for your vocational subject you will need to show that you understand how images can be used – and use them yourself.

These days, you don't have to be an artist to produce images. Modern technology – particularly the computer and the photocopier – mean that everyone can use images.

### Key points to remember

- Images can give information that is very difficult to put into words.
- There are many different types of image, including photographs, graphs, maps, symbols, illustrations, diagrams and cartoons.
- You should use images in your project work.

### *Putting it into practice*

*Start making a collection of different kinds of image that you see in newspapers and magazines. They may give you ideas that you could use in your project work.*

# Topic 1 – Making and finding images

## Choosing images

When you are looking for a photograph, a diagram – or any kind of image, there are some questions which you should think about.

- What information do I need to give?
- What's available?
- Can I copy the image?

## What information do I need to give?

Start by thinking about what you want the image to show. This may sound obvious, but it is very easy to pick an image which gives *too much* information, *too little*, or even the *wrong* information altogether.

### Activity

You have been asked to come for an interview by a company called ASB Ltd which is in another town. They send you this map.

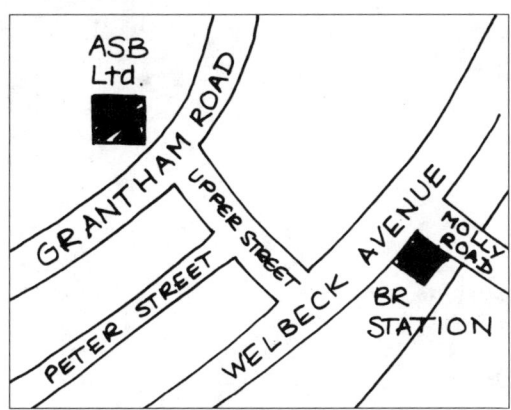

Does it give you all the information you need?

▌ *The map shows you how to get to their building from the station, which is useful if you are coming by train. However, it doesn't show how far it is from the station to their offices, so you have no idea how long it would take to walk there. And the map only shows a few streets, so it would not be much good if you were driving to the interview.* ▌

When you are choosing a map or any other sort of image, try to put yourself in the place of the person who will be using it. What information will they need?

### Activity

What was the problem with the image chosen in this situation?

Richard was in charge of the photocopier in an office. He was fed up with people always coming to him for help when the paper got jammed, so he pinned on the wall next to the photocopier a page from the technical manual, that contained a very complicated diagram showing all the inside parts of the machine. Everybody still kept coming to him for help.

▌ *Richard gave far too much information – nobody could understand the diagram. He should have found a much simpler diagram just dealing with paper jams. If there wasn't one in the manual, he could have drawn one himself – or marked the diagram from the manual to show which parts of the photocopier people should look at.* ▌

Don't confuse people by using images which are too complicated or technical. Try to find something simpler that gives the information they need. If you can't find a simple image, you may be able to adapt a more complicated one.

Sherie was preparing a leaflet for tourists in Yorkshire and wanted to include pictures of local scenery. She found a good photograph of a waterfall and sent it off to the printers. When the leaflet was printed, several people wrote in and pointed out that this waterfall was actually in Lancashire.

In this situation, the image Sherie used gave the wrong information. She should have checked the details of the photograph properly before she used it.

### Hint
**Always check that an image gives the information you think it does.**

## What's available?

In a work situation, your employers may provide

- leaflets for customers and clients
- instruction manuals, maps and other reference information for staff.

Outside organisations, such as those promoting safety, often provide posters and leaflets.

# Topic 1 – Making and finding images

## Choosing images (continued)

You may find other useful images in magazines – particularly magazines for your vocational area.

While you are studying, there are a lot of ready-made images that you can use.

### Activity

Here's a list of places where you may find useful images:
- books
- magazines and newspapers
- instruction manuals
- CD-Roms
- catalogues
- leaflets.

Where could you get access to these things?

*Your library is probably the best source of pictures.*

## Can I copy the image?

Sometimes you will find an image that you want to make copies of. This may be because you want lots of people to see it, or because it isn't usable in its present form – it could be the wrong size or in a book you don't want to destroy.

> An office supplier produced a very good (and expensive) planning chart. One organisation liked the chart so much that they wanted everyone in the office to have their own copy – but didn't want to pay for twenty charts. They made photocopies and covered them with clear plastic. When the officer supplier's representative came round he noticed the copied charts on the walls and told his managing director, who wrote to the organisation and insisted that they replace all the copies with full price genuine charts – or he would take them to court.

Never make multiple copies of other people's images without checking that they don't mind first – it can cause a lot of bad feeling and can be expensive. It is best to ask permission in writing.

Assuming it's OK to copy an image, there are also some practical things to consider. You can't make a clear black and white photocopy of a colour picture or a photograph, for example.

### Key points to remember

- Put yourself in the place of the person who is using the image. What do they need to know? How much do they need to know?
- Check that the image gives the information you think it does.
- Be aware of where you can get hold of useful images.
- Don't make multiple copies of an image without getting written permission first.

### *Putting it into practice*

*Find a map that would be helpful to show new students how to get to your school or college. (Think about the kind of transport they would use to get there.) If you wanted to make copies of the map to go in a leaflet, how would you get permission?*

# Topic 1 – Making and finding images

## Finding images

**C 61**

Foundation
Element **1.3**
Performance criteria **1**
Range **Images; Points**

When you are doing your project work, you will sometimes need to find images to illustrate what you are saying or writing. There are a lot of ready-made images available that you can use.

## Useful organisations

Many organisations produce posters, leaflets and reports which are designed to be displayed in the workplace or read by people at work. These often contain useful pictures, diagrams and charts.

Some of these are government organisations, such as the Health and Safety Executive, the NHS, the Department of Trade and Industry or the British Tourist Authority.

Many types of work have their own national bodies who organise training and set standards. They sometimes produce careers information, too.

### Activity

1. Look at the posters, leaflets and careers information on display in the part of your college or school where you do your vocational course. Who publishes this material?
2. Ask your tutor or people at your work placement for the names of the national organisations in your vocational area.

Build up a list of organisations who might be able to supply useful posters and leaflets. Find out their addresses. If you write to them, explaining what you are studying and what you need, they may be able to help.

## Employers

Large employers are another useful source of material. Look out for

- brochures and advertisements aimed at the general public
- careers information
- information for people already at work.

### Activity

Find out who the large employers are in the type of work you are interested in. Who are the big national employers? Who are the local employers in your own area?

Add these employers to your list of useful organisations. You may want to write to them, too.

Large suppliers of equipment also produce catalogues, posters and other information.

## Newspapers and magazines

You can also find useful pictures, graphs, headlines and cartoons in ordinary newspapers and magazines. Keep an eye out for them.

Special trade magazines are published for people doing most types of job. You won't find many of these magazines in the newsagents, but you may see them in college or at your workplace.

### Hint
**If you cut out anything from a newspaper or magazine, make a note of where it came from. Include the name of the newspaper or magazine, the page number and the date.**

Your school or college library will contain books and magazines with useful images. You won't be able to cut these out, but may be able to copy them to use them in your projects.

Your library or resource centre may have an encyclopaedia on CD-Rom from which you can print pictures. Check with the member of staff in charge that it's OK to use them in the way you want.

### Key points to remember

- Build up a list of organisations who could supply useful images.
- Use the resources at your school or college.
- Keep your eyes open for useful images.

### *Putting it into practice*

*Start a collection now of images that are relevant to your GNVQ. Keep them together in a folder for future use. Remember to note down where all the images came from.*

# Topic 1 – Making and finding images

## Copying images

**C 62**

Foundation
Element **1.3**
Performance criteria **1,2**
Range **Images; Points**

## What will and won't photocopy

Some things photocopy better than others.

### Activity

Tick the boxes to show whether you think these things will come out well on a photocopy.

| | Can photocopy | Can't photocopy |
|---|---|---|
| Text | ☐ | ☐ |
| Diagram drawn with lines only | ☐ | ☐ |
| Diagram with grey shading | ☐ | ☐ |
| Colour picture | ☐ | ☐ |
| Photograph | ☐ | ☐ |
| Large areas of black | ☐ | ☐ |

▌▌ *Text copies well, as long as it is printed on a plain white background. Diagrams and pictures which are drawn with lines also work well. Illustrations which contain grey shading are sometimes OK – but the grey can come out lighter or darker and spoil the picture.*

*You can't usually make good photocopies of colour pictures. All the colours come out as shades of grey, but some colours which look light to the eye come out looking darker than you would expect.*

*Photographs (whether they are black and white or colour) don't come out well on a photocopier. Some photocopiers can't copy large areas of solid black – they make the inside of the area white.* ▌▌

### Hint

If you photocopy something you want to keep for reference, check you haven't lost any important information on your copy.

The easiest way to copy an image is to use a photocopier.

## What are you allowed to photocopy?

### Activity

Do you think it would be all right to photocopy these things for these reasons?

1. a graph from a newspaper – to use in a report you are writing as part of a project.
2. a page from a textbook which contains a helpful chart – for everyone in your group to put in their folders.
3. a cartoon from a magazine – to put on the front of a leaflet you are handing out at an open day.

▌▌ *It's OK to make **one copy** of something you need for your studies, so **1** is fine. However, you should not make more than one copy of anything that has been published without asking permission in writing, so **2** and **3** are not all right, unless you write to the publishers of the textbook or the magazine first and they agree.* ▌▌

## What you can do with a photocopier

If you draw an illustration or a cartoon, it may look much better if you *reduce* it in size on the photocopier. Professional illustrators and cartoonists usually draw their pictures larger than the size they will appear in print.

Some images can look better if they are *enlarged*. You can do this in several stages if you need to, photocopying and enlarging your photocopies. You can get some very interesting results if you make some things – such a typewritten word or part of a picture – much bigger than they are normally shown.

You can make *alterations* to a picture – whiting out some sections or adding more details and then photocopying your new version.

### Key points to remember

- You are allowed to make a single copy of a picture for use in your studies.
- If you want to make more copies of something that has been published, get written permission first.
- Photographs, colour pictures and large areas of black don't come up well in photocopies.
- Try reducing or enlarging your images.

### *Putting it into practice*

*Find a picture of your college or school that will photocopy well. Try reducing and enlarging it.*

# Topic 1 – Making and finding images

## Thinking about your audience

**C 63**

Foundation/Intermediate/Advanced
Element **1.3, 2.3, 3.3**
Performance criteria **2**
Range **Images; Audience; Situation**

In any situation, the key to choosing the right image to use is to think about whom the image is for.

At work, and when you are studying, you will come across people who know

- about the same as you
- more than you
- less than you

about any subject. You may have to explain things using images to any of these groups.

### Activity

Imagine that you were designing a wall display about the types of job your course is preparing you for. It will be seen by the groups listed below.

Tick the boxes to show how much knowledge you would expect the groups to have about the subject of your display.

|   | Same as you | More than you | Less than you |
|---|---|---|---|
| 1 Other students on the course |   |   |   |
| 2 Local employers |   |   |   |
| 3 Your tutor |   |   |   |
| 4 Children from local schools |   |   |   |

Now think which group it would be most difficult to choose the right images for.

▌▌ *You probably decided that group 1 knew about the same as you, groups 2 and 3 knew more and group 4 knew less. It is usually more difficult to choose images for people who know less about a subject than you.* ▌▌

▌▌ *Ali was bewildered by the diagram. It does tell him what he needs to know, but also gives a lot more unnecessary information as well. Ali only wanted to put some oil in his car – he didn't want to give it a full service.* ▌▌

If you are explaining something that you are very interested in or know a lot about, remember that other people may not find it as easy to understand as you.

### Activity

Carole was a receptionist at a factory. One of the directors, who was new to the district, had to visit a supplier on the other side of town. He asked for directions and she gave him a street map. Two hours later he phoned up, saying he had been going round and round the one-way system and was lost. What did Carole do wrong? How could she have avoided this situation?

### Activity

Ali had just bought a second-hand Range Rover. He didn't know much about engines and went to ask a friend (who did) how to put the oil in. The mechanic showed him this page from the manual. What do you think Ali felt?

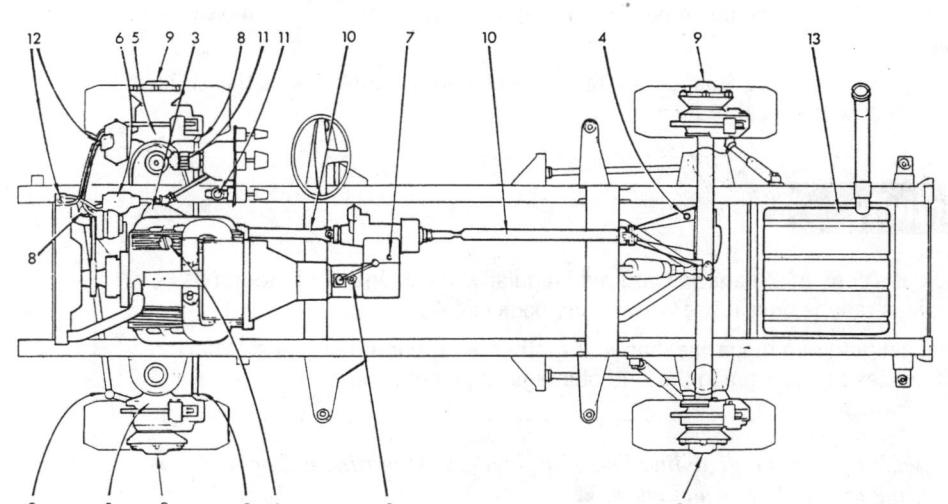

### Recommended lubricants and fluids

| Component or system | Lubricant type/specification | Duckhams recommendation |
|---|---|---|
| 1 Engine | Multigrade engine oil, viscosity SAE 20W/50 to API SE | Duckhams Hypergrade |
| 2 Main gearbox*<br>Early 4-speed with limited slip differential | Hypoid gear oil, viscosity SAE 80EP to API GL4 | Duckhams Hypoid 80 |

# Topic 1 – Making and finding images

## Thinking about your audience (continued)

❚❚ *Carole did not think about the director's lack of knowledge of the town's one-way system. It would have been helpful if she could have marked it on the street map.* ❚❚

## What other messages does the image give?

### Activity

Here is a business card sent out by a local electrician. What do you think of it? Would it encourage people to give him work?

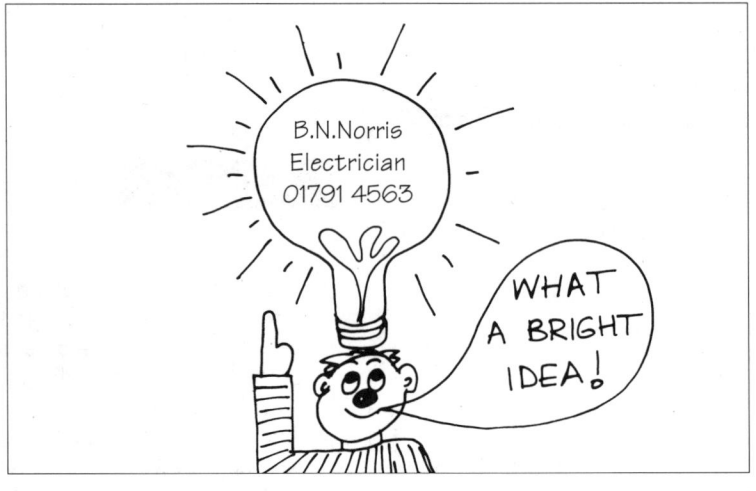

❚❚ *This card looks very amateurish. Wrongly or rightly, people might assume that his work as an electrician was very amateurish, too.* ❚❚

If your diagrams, cartoons, maps or other images are to be seen by people you want to impress, such as potential employers or customers, make them as professional as you can.

When you are choosing images for the general public, think about the style of picture which will appeal to them.

### Activity

Look at a copy of a magazine you read regularly. What kind of photographs and illustrations does it use? How is the page laid out?

Now get hold of a magazine that your mother or grandmother reads. What differences can you see in the kind of images and the layout?

❚❚ *You were probably able to find lots of differences. Magazine editors are very aware of the tastes of their audience.* ❚❚

If you are choosing images to appeal to the public and you pick a style that is too
- old fashioned
- exciting
- childish

for your audience, they won't respond.

### Key points to remember

- Put yourself in the place of the person who is using the image. What do they need to know? How much do they know already?
- If your image is meant to impress, is it professional enough?
- Think about whether your image will appeal to your audience.

### Putting it into practice

Find a leaflet that gives information to the public on a topic that has something to do with your GNVQ area. Look at the images and decide what kind of audience it is intended to appeal to. Decide how you would change the appearance of the leaflet to make it appeal to a completely different audience.

# Topic 1 – Making and finding images

## Using and making images

> **C 64**
> Foundation/Intermediate/Advanced
> Element **1.3, 2.3, 3.3**
> Performance criteria **2, 3**
> Range **Images; Audience; Situation**

If you need to use an image, you have to decide whether to

- use a ready-made image
- make an image yourself
- adapt a ready-made image.

## Ready-made images

Many *government and trade organisations* produce posters, leaflets and reports which are designed to be displayed in the workplace or read by people at work. These often contain useful pictures, diagrams and charts.

*Large employers* are another useful source of material, including brochures and advertisements, careers leaflets, information for people already at work.

Special *trade magazines* are published for people doing most types of job. You won't find many of these magazines in the newsagents, but you may see them in college or at your workplace.

### Activity

1. Look at the posters, leaflets and careers information on display in the part of your college or school where you do your vocational course. Who publishes this material?
2. Ask your tutor or people at your work placement for the names of the national organisations in your vocational area.

■ *Build up a list of organisations who might be able to supply useful posters and leaflets. Find out their addresses. If you write to them, explaining what you are studying and what you need, they may be able to help.* ■

> **Hint**
> If you cut out anything from a newspaper or magazine, make a note of where it came from. Include the name of the newspaper or magazine, the page number and the date.

Your school or college library will contain books and magazines with useful images. You won't be able to cut these out, but may be able to copy them to use them in your projects.

Your library or resource centre may have an encyclopaedia on CD-Rom from which you can print pictures. Check with the member of staff in charge that it's OK to use them in the way you want. You can also use computer clipart.

## Making your own images

If you can't find an image that's right you may have to make your own, either by hand or using a computer.

Your decision about whether to make an image will depend on

- the time and resources available
- your own skills
- how important the job is.

### Activity

Would you make your own images in these situations?

- You'd like to have a cartoon on a poster about an open day at the college.
- You would like to take a flowchart drawn on the computer to an initial discussion about a project with other students.
- You want to present your design for a running-shoe to your tutor for assessment.

■ *Your answers to the first two questions will depend on your skills and the time and resources available. If you are good at drawing cartoons, you would probably decide to draw one for the poster. If you have access to a computer program that draws spreadsheets and know how to use it, and you can spare the time before the meeting, your answer will probably be yes.*

*However, it is pointless to spend hours learning about a new program when you could make a handwritten sketch that would do just as well for a first meeting. In the third situation, you would almost certainly have to make your own images. However difficult or time-consuming you find it to draw your design, your tutor will need your sketches if he or she is to assess your work.* ■

It is easy to spend a very long time indeed preparing images, especially if you enjoy doing it. While you are at school or college, you may have the time available to do this. However, when you get to work, time becomes much more precious. Your employer probably would not be very happy if you spent a whole morning at the computer drawing up a perfect chart for a rota. Also, many of the jobs you would tackle yourself at college may be done by specially trained professionals at work.

# Topic 1 – Making and finding images

## Using and making images (continued)

### Adapting images

Quite often, you can alter an image that you find so that it fits your own needs. You can do this by

- using only part of the image
- adding extra information
- using the image as a reference to make a new one.

#### Activity

A furniture shop is selling off last year's range of kitchen cupboards in a sale. Only a few types of cupboard remain. They have run out of brochures, but they do have some copies of a colour advertisement that shows a kitchen with all the cupboards in place. How could a salesperson adapt the photograph to show a customer

1. the cupboards they still had in stock
2. the measurements of a cupboard he was thinking of buying and needed to check would fit into his kitchen
3. how a combination of cupboards could be arranged to fit in a corner in a different way from that on the photograph.

*In 1, the salesperson could cross out the cupboards that were out of stock, using only part of the image.*

*In 2, the measurements could be marked on the photograph, adding extra information to the image.*

*In 3, a diagram could be drawn, using the photograph to help get the proportions right.*

### Key points to remember

- Decide whether you need to use a ready-made image, make a completely new one or adapt an existing image.
- Consider the time and resources available, your skills, the importance of the job.

### *Putting it into practice*

*Decide on an image you could use for a leaflet about your college. Would you make your own image or use or adapt a ready-made one?*

# Topic 2 – Types of image

## Symbols

Foundation/Intermediate/Advanced
Element 1.3,2.3,3.3
Performance criteria 1,2
Range **Images; Points**

A symbol is a picture or design that has a definite meaning. Symbols are good for getting a simple message across very quickly. They are useful when you want people to react immediately to something.

### Activity

The shape of road signs mean something. Can you match these shapes and meanings?

- information
- prohibition (don't!)
- warning

If you are not sure, take a look at some signs when you are next out.

You often see symbols on cardboard boxes used for packing things which say how the boxes must be handled.

### Activity

If you worked in the packing department of a company and had labels with these symbols:

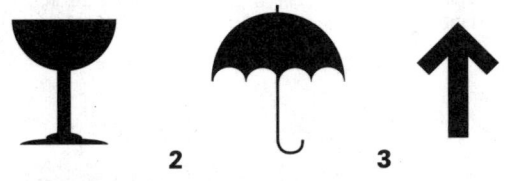

1   2   3

Which symbols would you use for a box

a   which must be kept the right way up
b   containing a breakable piece of equipment
c   which must not get wet.

▌▌ *The answers are a3; b1; c2.* ▌▌

## Icons

A lot of computer software uses symbols known as icons to represent the things you can do with the program.

For example

 means cut out

 means paste in.

Some of these icons are easy to understand, but you may have to check some in the manual. Books, especially those that tell you how to do things, often use icons.

## When not to use symbols

Symbols are not very good at giving complicated messages.

### Activity

Would you use a symbol in these situations? If you would, what would it be?

1   to warn people not to touch a panel of a machine that got very hot
2   to mark a series of 'bright ideas' in a manual
3   to tell people to leave their name with the receptionist before they sat down in the waiting room.

▌▌ *In **1**, you could use a warning triangle with a picture of a hand. In **2**, you could use an exclamation mark ! or a picture of a light bulb or even a picture of Einstein. **3** is too complicated to explain with a symbol.* ▌▌

## Logos

Most organisations and businesses have their own symbol – called a logo – which they put on all their products and stationery. Logos sometimes have a meaning but their real purpose is to make people notice the organisation's name whenever they see it.

### Key points to remember

- Symbols are a good way of getting people to react quickly.
- Symbols are good at giving simple messages, but not so good for complicated ideas.

### *Putting it into practice*

*Design a logo for an employment agency that specialises in the type of work you are interested in.*

# Topic 2 – Types of image

## Diagrams

**C 72**

Foundation
Element **1.3**
Performance criteria **1,2**
Range **Images; Points; Audience; Situation**

Some diagrams are like simple drawings, with all the unnecessary details left out. They can be a good way of showing how to use things.

### Activity

Think of three examples of diagrams that you have seen recently. How useful were they?

*Your examples might have included:*

- *assembly instructions*
- *labelled diagrams showing the features of a piece of equipment*
- *step-by-step diagrams in a manual.*

Diagrams are particularly useful when you want to show the order in which to do things.

### Activity

You want another student to go to a shop and buy a stapler just like the one in the office. Would you give him:

- a colour photograph from a brochure
- a diagram showing how to put new staples in the office stapler.

*In this situation, the photograph would probably be better than the diagram. Diagrams are good at showing how things work, but because they leave out a lot of details they may not give a full idea of what things actually look like.*

Diagrams can also explain ideas. For example, a flowchart is a diagram which shows the order in which things must be done. This flowchart shows how to use a car park.

Find a parking space
↓
Insert 20p in machine
↓
Remove ticket from machine
↓
Display ticket in your windscreen

When you need to explain a series of steps to someone else, it can be very useful to sketch out a simple flowchart for yourself first. If you find it difficult, this may be because you aren't completely clear about all the steps and the order they need to be done in. A flowchart will also help the person you are talking to.

Another type of diagram that you will probably see at work is the organisational diagram. This shows how the various parts of the organisation fit together.

### Activity

Use this chart to explain to the office assistant how he fits into the organisation and who will tell him what to do.

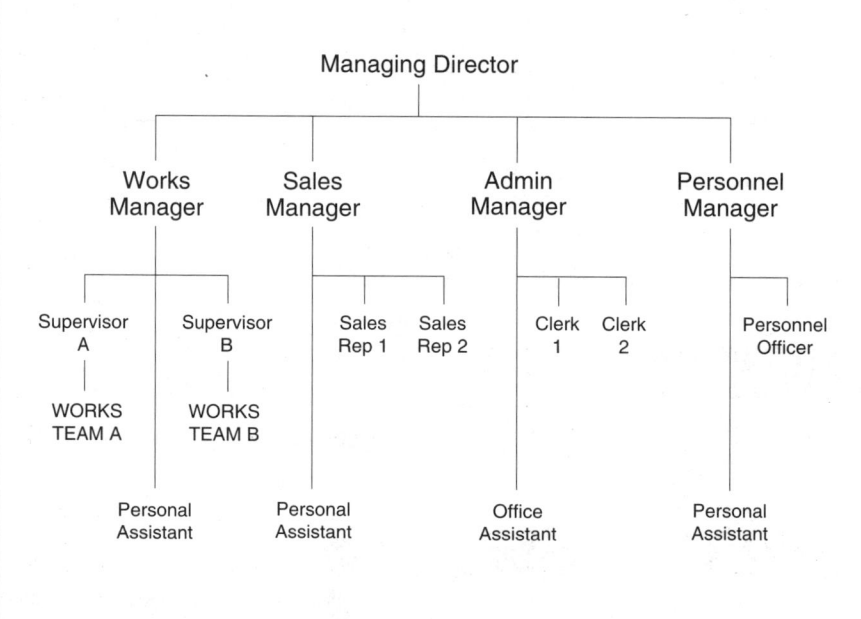

*Did you notice how jobs are on different levels in the chart, to show their importance? The lines connecting the jobs show who reports to whom.*

Some people find diagrams like this quite difficult to understand. However, if you talk them through, the diagram can be a useful reminder of what you've said.

### Key points to remember

Diagrams can show

- what to do
- the order in which to do things
- the structure of something (like a company).

It can be helpful to talk someone through a diagram.

### Putting it into practice

*Draw up a flowchart showing the stages to go through to find a job.*

# Topic 2 – Types of image

## Graphs and tables

**C 73**

Foundation
Element **1.3**
Performance criteria **1,2**
Range **Images; Points; Audience; Situation**

## Graphs

Many people find numbers quite difficult to understand. Graphs can give a clear picture of what numbers mean.

This bar graph shows the numbers of women and men employed in a factory.

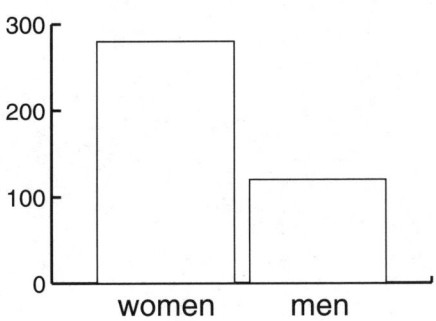

This pie chart shows how people at a factory travel to work.

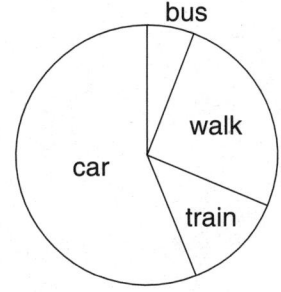

This line graph shows a company's profits over the last few years.

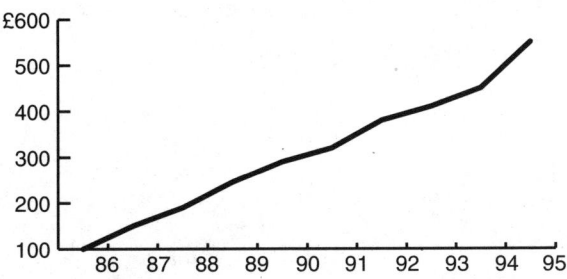

### Activity

Look quickly at the graphs and answer these questions.

1. Are there more men or women working at the factory?
2. How do most people go to work at the factory?
3. How do you think the company will do in 1996?

▐▐ 
1. It's easy to see that there are more women than men.
2. It's clear that most people go to work by car.
3. Things look good for 1995! ▐▐

### Activity

Of the three types of graph shown here, which would you use to show

1. how student numbers have changed over the last three years
2. what percentage of students are on various courses
3. what number of students are on various courses.

▐▐ You would use a line graph for **1**, a pie chart for **2** and a bar graph for **3**. ▐▐

(You will find more information about graphs in the Application of Number resource sheets.)

## Tables

Tables are used to present numbers or facts so that you can refer to them quickly. You can't see what the figures in a table mean as quickly as you can on a graph, but tables give exact numbers, which is sometimes important.

### Activity

A tasting session was held to see what people thought of two new cola drinks.

This table was drawn up to show the results:

|  | Age 11–16 | | Age 17–21 | |
| --- | --- | --- | --- | --- |
|  | Male | Female | Male | Female |
| Prefer drink A | 74 | 82 | 51 | 48 |
| Prefer drink B | 46 | 52 | 23 | 18 |
| No preference | 94 | 56 | 19 | 16 |
| Dislike both | 6 | 10 | 7 | 18 |
| **Total** | 200 | 200 | 100 | 100 |

Explain the table to another student. Together, decide which of the two drinks the company should make and whom they should advertise it to.

▐▐ Did you notice that the totals for the two age groups were different? This means that drink A (which was everybody's favourite) was actually more popular with the 17–21 year olds. You have to read tables carefully. ▐▐

# Topic 2 – Types of image

## Graphs and tables (continued)

### Key points to remember

- Graphs are a good way to give a general picture of a set of numbers.
- Bar graphs show things you can count, line graphs show how things change over a period of time and pie charts show how something is divided up.
- Tables are used to present numbers – read them carefully.

### Putting it into practice

When you have some numbers to present as part of a project, decide whether it would be better to present them in a chart or a graph. Which type of graph would be suitable?

## Topic 2 – Types of image

### Photographs

Foundation/Intermediate/Advanced
Element **1.3,2.3,3.3**
Performance criteria **1**
Range **Images; Points**

You may have heard people say that the camera never lies – but it does! You can use photographs to give useful information about a person, a place or an event. You can also make things look much better – or worse – than they really are.

## Choosing photographs

Sometimes you will use photographs which have been taken by other people. You may find them in newspapers or magazines – or perhaps they have been taken by other people at your college.

It is more difficult than you might think to re-use a photograph. This is because every photograph is taken for a reason and the reason affects the way the photograph looks.

### Activity

Look through a newspaper or magazine that contains lots of photographs. Try to decide *why* each of the photographs was taken. Here are two ideas. Try to think of some more.

- to make you want to buy something
- to make you feel angry about something
- 
- 

■■ *Photographs can be taken to make people look attractive, important or ridiculous. They can make organisations look successful or run-down and jobs look interesting or boring. They can make places look frightening or beautiful. It all depends on what the photographer wanted to show.* ■■

### Activity

A college principal was putting together a brochure to attract new students. She looked around the office to find any photographs to put in. She found:

1  a black and white photograph of the college gates taken for an anti-litter campaign
2  a glossy advertising photograph of the IT equipment supplied by the company that installed it
3  some photographs taken on the last day of term by a lecturer who wanted a record of her students dressed in silly clothes.

What would you advise the principal to do?

■■ *None of these photographs sounds suitable. 1 and 3 could put people off the college and 2 would not tell them anything about what it was like to study there. It would be much better to take a new set of photographs, showing what she wanted to show.* ■■

## What makes a good photograph?

### Activity

Look at the two photographs below, which are both taken from a tourist brochure. Which place would you rather visit?

■■ *You probably chose the second photograph. It has people in it – and that makes it easier to imagine what it would be like to be there.* ■■

Most photographs that make us *feel* something have people in them.

# Topic 2 – Types of image

## Photographs (continued)

## Taking photographs

Decide whether you want a wide shot or a close up. Wide shots give a better idea of the situation and what is going on in the background. Close ups usually have more impact, however.

Vary the angle at which you take photographs. We are used to looking at the world from about five to six feet above the ground. Things can look more interesting sometimes if you go lower or higher.

Try to get the person or thing you are photographing in the middle of your picture, not at the edge.

If you can, learn how to use a flash-gun. Even with outside shots, it can make the details in the foreground come alive. One famous photographer said that this is the single most important thing for getting better results.

Practise taking photographs. Shoot off a whole roll and hope to get two or three good pictures. The more relaxed you are when taking photographs, the more relaxed and natural your subjects will be.

## Using parts of photographs

You don't have to use the whole of a photograph. Professionals often crop (cut off) the edges. Use pieces of paper to cover up the parts you don't want to decide where to crop your photograph.

You can also make cut-outs.

Cut-outs can make photographs look more interesting. They are also a good way of getting rid of details you don't want to include.

### Key points to remember

- If you are using a photograph taken for another purpose, think about whether it is giving the message you want to give.
- People in photographs make them look more interesting.
- Think about your technique – use the tips on this sheet.
- You can crop photographs or make cut-outs.

### *Putting it into practice*

*Take a series of photographs for an open day at college showing the sorts of thing you are learning on your GNVQ course.*

### Activity

Here is another photograph from the tourist brochure.

Make a copy of it and cut off the background around the chimney. It should look much more dramatic now.

# Topic 2 – Types of image

## Drawings and cartoons

**C 75**

Foundation/Intermediate/Advanced
Element **1.3, 2.3, 3.3**
Performance criteria **2, 3**
Range **Images; Audience; Situation**

You may need to produce drawings as part of your GNVQ course, especially if your studies involve designing things which you will make. You may need to show your tutor several stages of the process – from your earliest ideas to a finished design.

### Activity

Think of something you could be asked to design as part of your course. It could be an object to be manufactured or perhaps a stand for an exhibition.

Make a list of questions your tutor might want the drawings to answer. We've suggested one question to start you off.

- How big is it?

❚❚ *Your questions will depend on the type of work you do in your course, but they could include: What colour is it? What do all the parts do? How do you make it? What's it made from? Where did you get the idea from? Your drawings, and the labels you put on them, should give the information your tutor will need.* ❚❚

You may be very skilled at drawing. If not, you can improve your results by:

- tracing parts of photographs
- adapting published drawings
- using clipart
- using drawing programmes on the computer.

These techniques are not 'cheating'. It is OK to use them to get your ideas across – as long as you acknowledge how you did it.

## Drawings at work

People who work in small businesses and organisations sometimes illustrate their own leaflets and brochures. Unfortunately, the results often look very amateurish. At work, it is best to leave drawings which will be seen by the public to professionally trained illustrators. Unless you are very talented indeed, your own drawings could reflect badly on your organisation.

## Cartoons

Cartoons can give a fresh viewpoint on a subject and make it seem more human and less daunting. They are used a great deal in many different kinds of publication – including some which give very serious information. However, you do have to be careful when using cartoons, as the rest of this resource sheet makes clear.

Single cartoons usually tell a joke or make an amusing point. If you see a cartoon that is relevant and which you think is funny, you may want to include it in your project work. Before you do:

- check that other people understand the joke and think it's funny
- consider whether anybody would be offended by it
- look at it again yourself after a little time – do you still think it's funny?

Humour is a very personal thing. Cartoons that make you laugh may not work on other people.

A strip cartoon can be a very effective way of telling a story. Here is an example taken from a leaflet about substance abuse:

# Topic 2 – Types of image

## Drawings and cartoons (continued)

### Activity

Would it be a good idea to use a strip cartoon in these situations?

1. a leaflet for students explaining how to register at college
2. a leaflet advising young people about depression
3. a leaflet for elderly people explaining how to keep warm in winter.

▌▌ *You could use a strip cartoon in **1** and **2**, but probably not in **3**. Even quite unexciting or very serious subjects can be treated in this way, as long as you are sensitive.*

*However, you should consider whether your audience is used to looking at strip cartoons. Many middle-aged and elderly people think they are childish.* ▌▌

### Activity

Get hold of a comic and discuss it with a friend. Look at how the artist has built up the story. How are speech bubbles used? What different angles are the pictures drawn from? How much information is in each frame? Are the frames different sizes and shapes?

▌▌ *You can use these techniques in your own strip cartoons.* ▌▌

### Key points to remember

- When doing drawings for your project work, think about what your audience needs to know.
- At work, drawings are probably best left to the professionals.
- Cartoons can make a subject easy to understand, but think about whether they will be appreciated by your audience.

### Putting it into practice

Plan and draw a cartoon strip to tell other students what to do on their first day at work placement. Would you be happy to let your employer see what you have drawn?

A caricature is a cartoon in which somebody's characteristics (such a bald head or bushy eyebrows) are exaggerated.

Here is a caricature of the actor Jimmy Nail:

*Reproduced by kind permission of TV Times*

### Activity

Suppose that you looked like Jimmy Nail. What would you feel if someone put this picture in the college magazine? Would you be:

- embarrassed?
- hurt?
- amused?

▌▌ *Celebrities learn to accept seeing caricatures of themselves – it's part of being famous. However, ordinary people can be quite upset by this kind of cartoon. Caricatures can also make use of sexual and racial stereotypes that may be offensive – so use them with care.* ▌▌

# Topic 2 – Types of image

## Maps and plans

**C 78**

Foundation/Intermediate/Advanced
Element **1.3, 2.3, 3.3**
Performance criteria **1,2,3**
Range **Images; Points; Audience; Situation**

There are many different kinds of maps and plans.

### Activity

Look at this map. It shows the National Trust's Associations and Centres in the London area. It comes from a brochure encouraging people to join their local association.

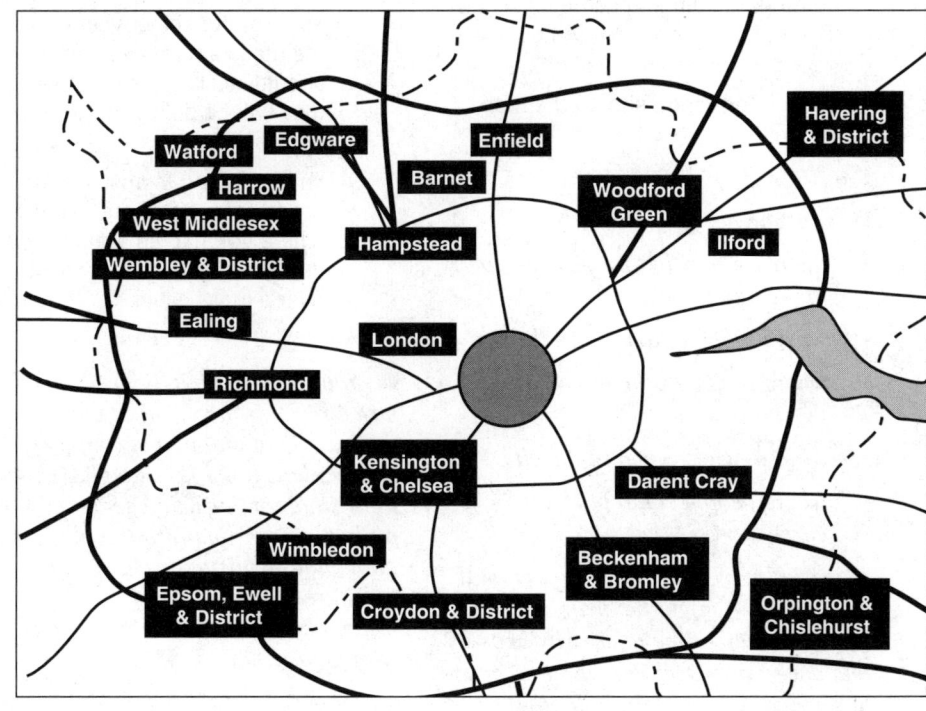

What do you think the purpose of this map is?

1 to show you how to get to your local association (if you live in London)

2 to show that there is a local association near you (if you live in London)

3 to show you which association you should join if you live in a particular part of London.

❚❚ *The right answer is 2. All the map does is show that there are lots of associations in London. The National Trust hopes that people will look at where they live on the map, see the name of the nearest association and look for further details elsewhere in the leaflet.* ❚❚

Maps and plans can
- give information about particular areas
- show where places are
- show how to get to places
- give exact measurements.

Here are two maps from a leaflet provided by a local doctor. As you can see, they do very different jobs. The first map shows you whether you are in the doctor's area. If you don't live in the shaded part of the map, you probably won't be taken on as a patient. The second map shows you how to get to the surgery. It is on a much bigger scale and gives the names of the surrounding streets.

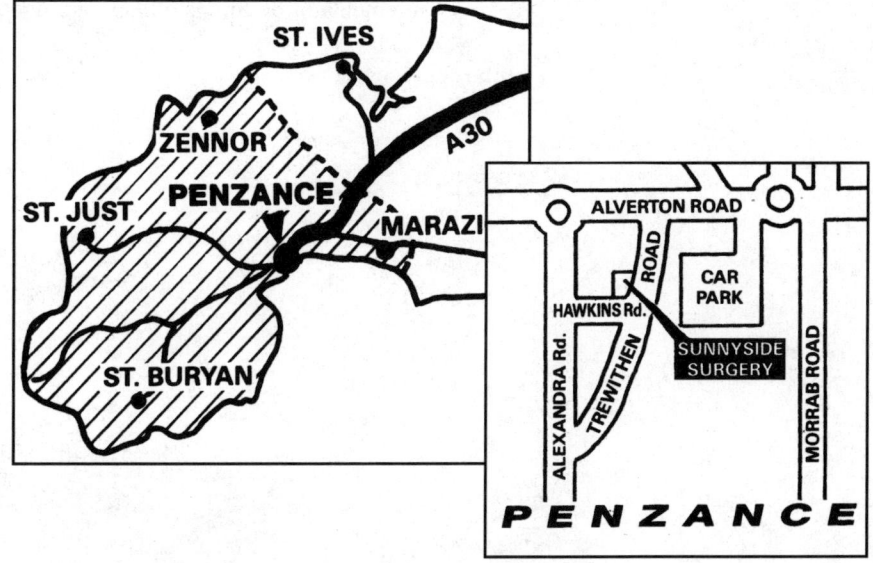

# Topic 2 – Types of image

## Maps and plans (continued)

### Activity

Find out what area is served by the local branch of a trade union you could join when you start work. Mark it on a map.

Draw another map to show how to get to the trade union offices.

▌▌ *Your two maps were probably similar in many ways to the maps on the doctor's leaflet.* ▌▌

You need to think about which type of map to use in any situation. Questions you may need to ask yourself are:

- How much detail should I put in?
- What scale should the map be drawn to?
- Does it matter if the measurements are exact?

### Activity

Corinne was organising a meeting to which people from all over the country were invited. She wanted to send out a map to show how to get to the building, which was in the middle of the city. Some of them would be coming by train and some by car. The station was a ten-minute walk away.

What information should the map show?

▌▌ *Corinne needs to show:*

- *the route to walk from the station to the building*
- *where to get a taxi at the station*
- *where to get off the motorway or the main road*
- *the one-way system in the city*
- *where people could park their cars.*

*This is a lot of information to get on a single map. It might be clearer if she drew one map of the motorway exits and one-way system and another larger-scale map to show the route from the station and where to get taxis and park cars.* ▌▌

Plans are drawn on a larger scale than maps. They show a smaller area in more detail. Some plans are drawn to an exact scale and show detailed measurements of buildings. Others are not so precise.

### Activity

If you were drawing a plan in these situations, would you need to take exact measurements?

1. You need to take a plan of the office to furniture suppliers to see if a certain model of desk will fit.
2. You want to show where in the office a removals firm should stack a load of boxes they will be delivering over the weekend.
3. You are filling in an accident report form and want to show where you had an accident in the office when you tripped over a loose cable.

▌▌ *You would definitely need exact measurements in your first plan. In the second situation, a very rough sketch plan would be enough. In the third situation, exact measurements probably aren't important, unless you think that the distance between the furniture (or some other measurement) had something to do with your accident.* ▌▌

### Key points to remember

- Maps and plans can do many different jobs.
- Think what people will need a map to tell them.

### *Putting it into practice*

*Draw a plan of your college which gives information that you think would be useful to new students.*

# Topic 3 – Using images

## Planning your work

This resource sheet explains how you can use diagrams and charts when you are planning your work. You could find these ideas useful in your project work and in many situations you may meet at work.

## Developing your ideas

At the beginning of a project, you probably don't have a very clear idea of all the things you have to do. A diagram called a *mind map* can help.

1. Start with a large, blank sheet of paper. In the middle, write what you are planning.

2. Around this, write all the things you can think of that are involved.

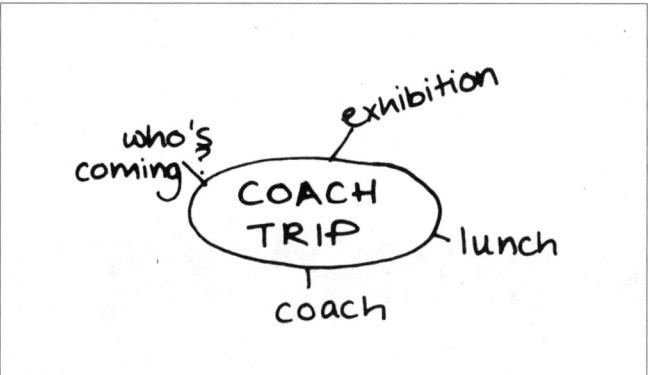

3. Then think about each of the branches, and add more detail.

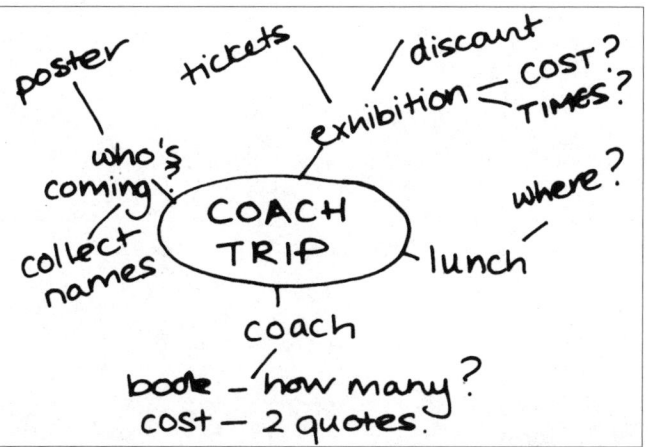

It doesn't matter how untidy the mind map gets. It is just a way of writing down your thoughts in a way that makes sense to you. When you've finished, you should have an overview of all the things you have to do.

### Activity

Make your own mind map about planning a party with friends. When you've finished, use coloured pens to divide up the tasks among three people.

■ *The shape and contents of your map will be very much your own but it might have included branches dealing with where you held the party, music, food and drink and whom to invite. Did you find that the mind map helped you to think of things you might have forgotten?* ■

## Making a plan

A simple flowchart can help to work out the best order in which to do things. Start at the end and work backwards, thinking of what has to be done before each job can be started.

Here is a flowchart showing the preparations for the coach trip in the mind map.

# Topic 3 – Using images

## Planning your work (continued)

### Activity

Make a flowchart showing the preparations for the party.

▐▌ *A flowchart can prevent holdups because you haven't thought of something that should have been done much earlier.*

*When you write a flowchart, you may find that you've left something out. Most people have to have a few tries at a flowchart before they get everything in the most logical order.* ▐▌

### Key points to remember

- Mind maps can help you get an overview of a project.
- Flowcharts help you get things in the right order.

### *Putting it into practice*

*Use a mind map and a flowchart to plan how you would set up an exhibition or tackle a project that you are involved in at the moment.*

# Topic 3 – Using images

## Posters

**Foundation/Intermediate/Advanced**
Element **1.3, 2.3, 3.3**
Performance criteria **1, 2, 3**
Range **Images; Points; Audience; Situation**

Posters are a way of spreading information to a lot of people. They can persuade us to

- buy something
- come to an event
- give money
- change the way we behave
- think about something in a new way.

A successful poster has to be noticed. This can be done by using

- bright colours
- an image that surprises people
- large size
- large letters
- being everywhere you go.

As you go around town, notice the posters that stand out. What kind of images do they contain? Some advertisers use images which are designed to attract or sometimes to shock. Some use very large slogans which make us laugh or surprise us.

When you are designing a poster, be aware of whom you are aiming it at. Some things that you find funny or attractive might make other people turn away.

### Activity

If you were designing a poster about a concert for your college noticeboard, how would you make sure it was noticed?

■■ *You could put the name of the band in very big letters (if they were popular) or use a picture that would catch the eye. You could print the poster on coloured (perhaps fluorescent) paper. You could print lots of copies of your poster and put them all over the noticeboard (although this might not be popular). A very large poster might also be unpopular if it didn't leave any room for other notices.* ■■

## How far away?

Some posters are designed to be seen from the other side of the street. Others are designed to be put in shop windows where people will be much closer to them. This affects the size of the type and the image you can use. Your main image and lettering should be large enough for people to notice as they are passing. Other information, which gives more details, can be much smaller. If people are interested in your poster, they will come up to it and read it properly.

## What should a poster tell you?

A poster must contain some information.

### Activity

What information would these posters need to include?

- a poster advertising an exhibition of a famous photographer's work
- a poster advertising a drugs helpline.

What kind of images could they contain?

■■ *The first poster would need to give the photographer's name, where the exhibition was held, when it was on and how much it cost. It would probably use one of the most famous photographs. The second poster would need to give the telephone number and the name of the organisation involved. The image could be a syringe, easily recognisable as something to do with drugs.* ■■

### Key points to remember

- Use an eye-catching image or some other way to get attention.
- Think about where your poster will be displayed.
- Include all the necessary information.

### *Putting it into practice*

*Design a poster for an event at your school or college. Think about whom it is aimed at, how you will copy it and the information it will contain.*

## Topic 3 – Using images

### Leaflets

C | 84

Foundation/Intermediate/Advanced
Element **1.3,2.3,3.3**
Performance criteria **1,2,3**
Range **Images; Points; Audience; Situation**

Leaflets can be used to tell a large number of people about something. They are often used for advertising and to tell the public about services they can use.

> **Activity**
>
> Think of the last three times you took a leaflet.
> What was it about?
> Where did you get it?
> Why did you take it?

You may have picked up your leaflets at college, in a shop or perhaps in a post office or library. You may have been handed them in the street. Whatever the leaflets were about, you will have made a quick decision to take them because you thought they were interesting or useful.

Leaflets are handed out free – but you still have to persuade people to take them.

## AIDA

When advertisers put together leaflets they use a formula, AIDA, which stands for: Attention; Interest; Desire; Action.

### Attention

It is very important to put something on the cover of the leaflet that will attract people's attention and make them want to look inside.

You can attract attention in many ways. You could use

- a good picture
- a large headline that catches the eye
- a bright colour.

### Interest

When people have noticed your leaflet, you want them to see something that will make them want to read it. The kind of thing you choose will depend on the type of people you are trying to interest.

> **Activity**
>
> What images could you use to interest your audience on a leaflet
> - about a fitness club for retired people
> - about a new type of bank account for young people.

■ *You could use a photograph or a drawing of elderly people exercising or looking very fit on the cover of the first leaflet. The second leaflet should probably show people who were obviously students. In each case, you would be using the image to tell people whom the leaflet was for.* ■

### Desire

Inside your leaflet, you should show or describe something that people really want. This could be a picture of the product you are trying to sell. A campaigning leaflet could show an image of something people will really want to stop, such as cruelty to animals.

You can list the benefits of what you are describing and highlight them with bullet points, or other design features, like this:

- free membership for one year
- big discounts at all our stores
- monthly newsletter
- generous credit terms.

### Action

A leaflet should include some way in which people can take action. This could be

- a form to fill in
- a phone number to ring
- details of whom to go and see to get more information
- names of shops which sell what you are advertising.

## Designing a leaflet

Keep the cover of your leaflet as simple as possible. The only job the cover has to do is to encourage people to pick up the leaflet and look inside.

The third page of any leaflet is the one that people look at most carefully. Put your main message there.

Don't put too much information on each page.

> **Key point to remember**
>
> - AIDA!

> **Putting it into practice**
>
> Find a leaflet that you don't think has been well designed. See if you can use the information on this sheet to do a better job with it.

# COMMUNICATION – Read and respond to written materials — Element 4

## Topic 1 – Reading techniques
- C88   Why read?
- C90   Selecting a reading strategy
- C91   Scanning
- C93   Skim reading
- C95   Careful reading

## Topic 2 – Reference skills
- C97   How to use a dictionary
- C98   Using a dictionary at work
- C100 Using an index to find information
- C103 Using a contents list to find information
- C104 Choosing the right reference source
- C105 Using reference sources to find information

## Topic 3 – Reading containing images and graphics
- C107 The use of graphical illustrations in reading
- C108 Getting the main idea from graphical information
- C109 Getting the main idea from graphs and charts
- C112 Reading text containing graphical material

## Topic 4 – Read and respond to different formats
- C114 Reading different formats
- C115 Reading timetables and price lists

# Topic 1 – Reading techniques

## Why read?

**C 88**

Foundation
Element **1.4**
Performance criteria **1**
Range **Materials; Purpose**

When you think about reading you might think about reading books or magazines. There are, of course, many other kinds of reading you will come across.

- reading instructions
- reading letters
- reading bills
- reading posters and advertisements
- looking up information
- reading information from graphs and tables.

Which of these do you already read?

There are many reasons for reading.

- enjoyment
- finding out about new things
- checking information
- giving messages and information.

### Activity

1. Make a list of everything you have read in the last few days
2. Note down which reading was
   - for pleasure
   - for checking information
   - for finding out new information
   - a message.

■ *We read for many different reasons, some connected with home and leisure activities and some connected with work and study.* ■

You do not need to read all the written material you find at work or at home – you can be selective.

### Activity

Look at these examples of reading you might find at work.

Which of them do you need to look at and which of them can you ignore?

|   | | Read | Ignore |
|---|---|---|---|
| 1 | A memo about holidays from your boss. | ☐ | ☐ |
| 2 | A memo about a special course for employees over 55 and about to retire. | ☐ | ☐ |
| 3 | A technical manual about company finance systems. | ☐ | ☐ |
| 4 | Your payslip. | ☐ | ☐ |
| 5 | Safety instructions for your job. | ☐ | ☐ |

■ *Obviously you will read those items which directly concern you and your job. You can safely ignore items which do not concern you or your job, though you might choose to read them out of interest.* ■

## What to read at work

Every business receives letters and documents through the post. A lot of time can be saved if you select what to read and what to ignore.

### Activity

The daily post for a building company employing 25 people included the following items:

- a letter from a customer wanting a quote for some work
- a bank statement
- a cheque from a customer
- an invoice from the suppliers
- a leaflet from the Tax Office relating to companies employing more than 200 people
- a pamphlet from the DSS about child care regulations.

You are given the task of sorting out which ones need attention and if there are any that can be ignored. Be careful not to throw away anything important!

■ *The information from the Tax Office and the DSS can safely be ignored as it is not relevant to this organisation. It would not be wise to ignore any of the other letters, as they all require some action from the company.* ■

### Key points to remember

- You do not need to read everything that you come across.
- You can be selective and choose what to read and what to ignore.
- Think carefully before deciding not to read something, just in case it is important.

### Putting it into practice

Talk to someone who works in your work experience area. Ask them

- what they need to read
- what they can safely ignore.

# Topic 1 – Reading techniques

## Selecting a reading strategy

**C 90**

Foundation/Intermediate/
Advanced
Elements **1.4, 2.4, 3.4**
Performance criteria **1, 2**
Range **Materials; Purpose**

## How do you read?

We don't read everything the same way. We use different reading techniques for different kinds of reading. For instance, you might read a magazine article in a different way from a telephone directory. Three techniques you can use are:

- skimming – this is the technique you use when you read very quickly through the whole of a text to decide whether you are going to bother to read it carefully
- scanning – this is a technique you use when you let your eyes run quickly over something looking for particular pieces of information. You use scanning to pick out names in a telephone directory
- careful reading – reading and if necessary re-reading all the words in a text and making sure that you understand them.

### Activity

Think about which of the three reading techniques you would use when:

1. looking up a word in a dictionary
2. reading a letter from your best friend
3. reading instructions on how to operate a piece of equipment
4. finding an article you want to read in a magazine
5. checking through a chapter in a textbook to see if it's going to be useful for an assignment.

### Hint

You might need to use more than one technique. For instance, when you look up a word in a dictionary you would first scan to find the right area of the page, then skim two or three alternative meanings of the word and finally read carefully the meaning you are looking for.

You probably use all three reading techniques already but it's a good idea to practise them and to consider when is the most appropriate time to use each one. Here are some examples.

- reading a magazine article on your favourite band – careful reading
- looking up your local College's phone number – scanning
- reading Health & Safety instructions for a work placement – careful reading
- reading quickly through an article in a trade journal to see if it will be useful for your next assignment – skimming
- looking through the index of a textbook for a chapter on Health & Safety at Work – scanning.

### Activity

What strategies have you used?

1. Make a list of all the reading you have done in the last day or two – at work and at home. Include everything, adverts, signs, leisure reading, reading at work or outside.
2. What reading strategy did you use?
   - Did you read it carefully?
   - If not, did you skim read it or did you scan it?
3. Did you choose the right reading strategy?
   - Was your first choice of reading strategy the right one?
   - If not, which would have been a better strategy?

### Key points to remember

- You do not need to read everything carefully.
- You can look through pieces of text quickly to decide whether or not you need to go any further – skim.
- You can look quickly for key words that help you locate the information you want – scan.

Remember – you don't need to read the whole telephone directory to find a friend's phone number!

### Putting it into practice

1. Before you start to read something decide how you need to read it.
   - Does it need to be read carefully, word by word?
   - Do you need to skim through it quickly first, in order to decide whether you need to spend time in careful reading?
   - Do you need to scan through the reading simply to find the one piece of information you are looking for?
2. Make yourself a reminder note to choose the right strategy for reading. Stick the note somewhere where it will remind you to think before you start to read.

## Topic 1 – Reading techniques

### Scanning

**C 91**

Foundation
Element **1.4**
Performance criteria **1,2**
Range **Materials; Purpose**

# What is scanning?

When you are looking for specific information in a book or directory you do not have to read every word to find what you want to know. The technique you use, for instance, to find a name in a telephone directory, is called 'scanning'. This means that you decide roughly the right place to look for the information you want, then you let your eyes pick out the word you want. It's the same skill you use when you're looking for someone you know in a crowd.

Remember that skim reading is different. When skim reading you read through all of a piece of writing, skipping through it to get the main idea. You are not just looking for one or two key words as you do in scanning. You might need to use the scanning technique at work or at home when:

- looking up an address in an address book
- looking up information about a particular machine part in a parts inventory
- finding the chapter you want in a manual
- looking at a newspaper article and finding your name in it.

### Key points to remember

- Decide what you are looking for – one key word or phrase.
- Just look for this – don't be side-tracked!
- Use other information such as alphabetical order or an index to help narrow down your search.

### *Putting it into practice*

*Practise the scanning technique by finding names of friends in your telephone directory – see how fast you can do it! You could practise scanning through a newspaper or magazine to find articles relevant to your GNVQ area, for instance,*

- *an article about a new care home opening*
- *an item in the business section about new equipment in a factory*
- *adverts for jobs or training courses.*

### Activity

Find your local *Yellow Pages* and look at the index at the front. Use the scanning technique to find the entry for 'Restaurants'. Use the information here – page numbers – to scan for the telephone number of your favourite fish and chip shop.

# Topic 1 – Reading Techniques

**C 93**

## Skim reading

**Foundation**
Element **1.4**
Performance criteria **1,2**
Range **Materials; Purpose**

## What is skimming?

When you skim a stone across a pond, the stone dips several times into the pond before sinking.

When you read something, you do not always have to read every word. Sometimes you will only need to skip through the reading – or skim it – to pick out the main points. You will miss out a lot but this does not always matter – you will pick up the main points and can go back to read carefully if you need to.

These are some examples of writing you might come across at work where you would not have to read every word, but could skim read:

- a letter from a customer – you could skim read this to check what the letter was about and who would need to deal with it

- a memo from the boss sent to all employees – you could skim read this to see if the memo was about something that concerned you

- a customer record card – you could skim read this if you just wanted to check through it quickly to see if they were making regular orders

### Activity (You will need a highlighter pen)

This is an invoice from a garage for car repairs. Use a highlighter pen to highlight
- the garage name
- their telephone number
- what new parts have been used.

**B-Quik Garage**
Tel: 0171 4567892

Invoice No : 23164
Taxpoint  : 24/02/95
Job No    : 28453
Type/Terms : ER/CR

Claim No    :
Policy      :
Estimate No :

```
623644                        623644
Reg:E554XUJ                   Tri:GREY                        Not:
Mod:N12 NOVA 1200cc           Tra: 4 SPD MANUAL.              S/d:
Col:CARMINE RED               Eng:19860559                    R/d:260388
Cha:96J4099597                Key:
Mil:78908                     Ord:
```

| Description | Qty | VAT | Ext Ret | Total |
|---|---|---|---|---|
| SERVICE AS FOLLOWS:- | | S | .00 | |
| CARRY OUT 81,000 SERVICE. | | S | 30.12 | |
| REPLACED WIPER BLADES | | S | 2.51 | |
| REFIT MOUNTING ON CENTRE EXHAUST | | S | 5.02 | |
| | | | | 37.65 |
| Labour: | | | | |
| 93156954  OIL FILTER | 1 | S | 3.85 | |
| 91126674  SCREENWASH | 1 | S | 1.66 | |
| 93156246  SEALANT (*) | 1 | S | 2.50 | |
| 90444837  WIPER BLADE | 2 | S | 7.14 | |
| 91145664  BULB 245 | 1 | S | 0.52 | |
| | | | | 15.67 |
| Parts: S | | | | 9.78 |
| | | | Total Goods | 63.10 |
| | | | Total VAT | 11.04 |
| | | | TOTAL DUE | 74.14 |

# Topic 1 – Reading Techniques

## Skim reading (continued)

## How to skim read

1. Think about what information you want from the text you are reading.
2. Decide if there are any 'key' words or phrases, or numbers, that you will look for.
3. Have a quick glance at the whole text, then skim through it, missing chunks out but looking for your 'key' words or phrases.
4. You will now know roughly whether the text is useful or interesting and whether to read it carefully or leave it.

### Activity

You are thinking about joining the Army and you want to know how to go about it. You are given this information from an Army brochure. Skim through it and highlight what the steps are; there are at least 4!

### Key points to remember

- You don't need to read every word of a text to get the main idea of what it's about
- Skim reading can be a short cut to helping you decide whether you need to read a text carefully, or ignore it.

### Hint
Try using your finger or a pencil as a guide to help speed up skimming.

### Putting it into practice

- Try skim reading a newspaper article to find out what it is about.
- Practise skim reading information from your GNVQ subject when you do your next assignment.
- Look for some books about your GNVQ subject which are not required reading. Try skim reading parts of them to see if they are useful to you.

If you are aged between 16 and 25 you can enlist in the Army – but there are some restrictions on who may enlist under the age of 16 years 9½ months.

You will need to visit your nearest Army Careers Office (ACIO) – in the phone book under "Army" – and speak to the recruiting staff there. They will brief you on the Army, including what employments are available to you, what the life is like, and will give you some brochures to take away with you. The next step, if you're interested, is to take the Army Entrance Test.

This is computer-based and designed to test your basic intelligence and "trainability". Your score in this test will enable the ACIO staff to brief you on what trades and employments you are suitable for, and to discuss the options open to you.

If you are interested in any of these options, you will then be invited to undergo a medical and later to attend a Recruit Selection Centre where your suitability for both the employment you are interested in and the Army generally is assessed through further tests and interviews. You will also have a more detailed medical and a phsyical fitness assessment test – it will help if you have already started a fitness training programme. If all goes well you will be offered a vacancy and a date when you will start your training.

### Hint
Look for words like 'the next step', 'then', and 'also' which will give you clues that there is an explanation about what is involved in joining up. The word 'test' might also be a clue.

## Topic 1 – Reading techniques

### Careful reading

**Foundation**
Element **1.4**
Performance criteria **1,2**
Range **Materials; Purpose**

# When is careful reading important?

You do not need to read everything carefully. You can use skimming and scanning techniques to help you decide what you do need to read carefully.

### Activity

Look at this list of reading that you might come across in your training or at work. Decide which you would need to read carefully and which you might just need to have a quick look at.

- the details of your next assignment
- the instructions for filling in a passport form
- information for students from your local college
- a work manual, when you are deciding whether it is going to be useful or not
- written comments from your tutor or supervisor about your work

Remember that some texts are important and you will need to read them carefully to make sure you understand them.

### Hints

1. If the text is in small print, try enlarging it on a photocopier. This can make it much easier to read.
2. Try photocopying the text onto pastel-coloured paper. Glaring white paper can be very tiring.
3. Read short sections of the text – don't try to read the whole text in one go if it is difficult.
4. Look up difficult words or ask someone for an explanation. These words can often be the 'key' to the meaning of the passage.
5. You may need to re-read difficult sections at least three times – don't be worried by this as everyone needs to read difficult information several times.
6. Look out for clues in the text:
   - headings
   - sub-headings
   - capital letters
   - italics
   - bold print.

Sometimes careful reading can be a difficult task. This might be because it's

- a bit boring
- difficult to understand
- not very well written or printed
- not particularly useful to you.

Don't waste time reading things that are not useful to you. We can't do much about reading that is boring but here are some hints to make difficult technical information less of a problem to read.

### Activity

Read the information on how to complete an application form for a training scheme. You will need to read the instructions carefully before answering the questions.

#### Tremendous Television Training Scheme

*Completing the form*

1. Please complete the attached form in handwriting with a BALL POINT PEN.
2. Enclose a recent photograph, with your name and address written clearly on the back.
3. The form should be returned to:  Paul Proctor, Human Resources
   Tremendous Television Training Scheme
   Spectre House
   Great Warford TN20 1BV

   by March 27 1996.
4. All applications should be accompanied by copies of qualification/examination certificates.
5. Do not forget to sign your form and to enclose a stamped, addressed envelope for a reply.

- What kind of pen do you need to use to fill in the form?
- When should you return the form?
- What should you enclose with your application form?

# Topic 1 – Reading techniques

## Careful reading (continued)

### Key points to remember

- Decide what you have to read – remember you won't have to read everything carefully.
- Use clues from the text to help your reading.
- Use some of the hints to help you.
- Don't be afraid to take your time.

### *Putting it into practice*

- *Try using some of the hints to help with a difficult piece of reading from your GNVQ subject. Which is the most helpful to you?*
- *Be selective about what you read carefully, but make sure you don't miss anything important.*

# Topic 2 – Reference skills

## How to use a dictionary

**C 97**

**Foundation**
Element **1.4**
Performance criteria **3**
Range **Sources of reference; Subject**

Everyone needs to use a dictionary from time to time – to check the spelling or meaning of a word. Each entry gives the word and its meaning or definition. If there is more than one meaning it will give you the alternatives. Different dictionaries may give you other information which might be useful.

### Activity

Look in a dictionary to see if you can find clues about pronunciation and alternative meanings of words.

### Hint

Not all dictionaries give you this – for example, some pocket dictionaries only give meanings.

Dictionaries are laid out in strict alphabetical sequence from a to z. This is true not just for the first letter of the word, but also for the following letters:

abase

abash

abate

abattoir

### Hint

Most dictionaries have words starting with 'M' about halfway through them.

### Activity

Tick all the words which you would look up in the first half of a dictionary (before 'm')

practice

experience

work

general

clerk

training

As well as being arranged in alphabetical order, dictionaries give us other information to make it quicker and easier to look up words.

There is a word printed, usually in bold, at the top of each page. These words repeat the first word on the left-hand page and the last word on the right-hand page.

We often need to check the meanings of words, particularly when we are reading items which are new to us, such as manuals or reference books. If you start a new job or a new course you might hear or read new words which you need to check. It is very important to be sure that you understand the correct meanings of words, particularly in legal and financial documents, such as those dealing with hire purchase and insurance.

Words often have more than one meaning. Dictionaries will give you alternatives and you have to decide which is the meaning intended in what you are reading. Read the information carefully to get as many clues as you can.

### Activity

Look up the meanings of the word 'drive' as used below.

- The drive to the house was full of weeds.
- The car was French and so had a left-hand drive.
- The student's drive and initiative gained her the prize for best assignment.

A simple word, but it has at least three meanings!

### Key points to remember

- Everyone needs to use a dictionary – keep one handy!
- Dictionaries are arranged in alphabetical order.
- They help you to check the spelling and the meaning of words.
- They can also give you other useful information, e.g., pronunciation.

Using a dictionary needs practice – the more you use one the easier and quicker it becomes!

### *Putting it into practice*

*Look at the dictionaries in the library. Decide which one is best suited to your everyday needs. Does it give all the specialist words you need? If not, where would you go to check on these words?*

# Topic 2 – Reference skills

## Using a dictionary at work

**C 98**

Foundation
Element **1.4**
Performance criteria **3**
Range **Sources of reference;
Subject**

Dictionaries can be enormously useful both at work and when you are studying. A dictionary does not just help us to check spelling or give definitions. It can also tell us how to pronounce a word [dikshonari] and where a word comes from: work is an Old English word!

Dictionaries use alphabetical order to help us to find words quickly and efficiently. We use alphabetical order in work in many other ways, for example in filing.

### Activity

You have to file the following accounts in alphabetical order:

P. Jones
A. Morris
F. Andrews
M. Jones
S. Williams
F. Evans

**Hint**
If the surnames are the same, look at the initials.

### Activity

One of your office staff has filled in an order form – would you need to correct the spelling of the underlined word?

ORDER FORM PS/25
From Ann Stephens
Date 12.9.94
To Stores
Order <u>Stationery</u>
Envelopes – 12 doz.
Copy paper – 2 reams
Typing paper – 2 reams
Carbon paper – 1 box

▋ *A dictionary gives you all the information you need:*

*stationary adj. unmoving, fixed.*

*stationery n. writing materials, especially writing paper and envelopes.* ▋

## Checking spellings

A dictionary can be useful to check spellings – but only if you have a good idea of how to spell a word!

There are other ways to check spelling.

- Ask someone who is a good speller.
- Use a hand-held spell-check machine.
- Use the spell-check facility on a computer.
- Use a special spelling dictionary.

### Key points to remember

- Dictionaries are arranged in alphabetical order.
- Everyone needs to check the meaning of new words and technical or specialist words.

### *Putting it into practice*

*Choose a dictionary that you feel comfortable with. Make a point of using it whenever you are writing or come across a word you don't understand.*

The main reason people use dictionaries is to check the meanings of words.

### Activity

Use the dictionary to find the meanings of the words underlined in this passage:

#### Buying new and used cars

Decide on what you want and how much you can afford. Add on <u>estimates</u> of running costs, insurance, tax, MOT, petrol, repairs and servicing. If you are taking out a loan, add on the repayments. Look at car magazines to see what is <u>available</u> for the price you want to pay, and to check the value of any car you want to trade in. Shop around and see what <u>various</u> dealers have on offer in your price range.

Look for a <u>reputable</u> dealer – ask the advice of friends and look for a trade association sign. This should mean that the dealer follows the <u>requirements</u> of the Code of Practice for the Motor Industry, which could be helpful if you have a complaint.

Does this help you to understand the text?

(Taken from *A Buyer's Guide: Your legal rights* p.37 published by The Office of Fair Trading.)

It is often necessary to check the spellings of words which sound the same.

# Topic 2 – Reference skills

## Using an index to find information

**C 100**

Foundation
Element **1.4**
Performance criteria **1,2,3**
Range **Materials;
Sources of reference;
Subject; Purpose**

## What is an index ?

**index** n. alphabetical list, usually at the end of a book, of names, subjects, etc., with page references.

When you want information about something, you may need to look in a reference book, manual or textbook. Using the index helps you to find what you want to know quickly. It helps to cut down the time it takes to find information.

Check now. Look in the textbook or manual you use most often. Is there an index?

> **Hint**
> They are usually at the back of the book.

### Activity

Find a mail-order catalogue. Look for the index – it may be at the back of the book.

Check the layout of the index:

- Is it in alphabetical order?
- Are there page reference numbers?
- Are there any sub-headings, use of bold print, CAPITAL LETTERS, italics?

Now practise looking for one or two items:

- a CD midi-system
- a spell-check machine

> **Hint**
> You may have to look in two or three different places under different headings, for instance, the CD system could be listed under
> - CD
> - midi-system
> - Hi-fi
> - stereo system

Part of the skill in finding information is to know what word to look up. If you can't find what you want under the first word, try another word which might give some information.

### Activity

Find a textbook or manual relevant to your GNVQ area that has an index. The index will be arranged in alphabetical order.

- Look under 'H' to find any references to Health & Safety
- Look under 'R' to find any reference to Regulations
- Look under 'S' to find any references to Safety at work

Now use the page numbers given and find the references in the book.

A scanning technique will help you to find the words you want. You can then read the information.

> **Hint**
> An index is useful for finding very specific references; a contents list is more helpful for finding chunks of information on particular topics.

### Key points to remember

- An index is usually in alphabetical order
- Use the clues given in the text:
  - sub-headings
  - different print styles
- If the first word you look up doesn't help, try another.

### *Putting it into practice*

*Look at the indexes in different sources*

- *an encyclopaedia*
- *a catalogue*
- *a book of road maps*
- *an A-Z street map*
- *your local Yellow Pages (the index is in the front of this)*
- *Check their layout*
- *Practise finding information using the indexes.*

# Topic 2 – Reference skills

## Using a contents list to find information

**C 103**

Foundation
Element **1.4**
Performance criteria **2,3**
Range **Purpose;
Sources of reference;
Subject**

Many textbooks, pamphlets and manuals will have a contents list. This list will be at the beginning of the text and will show chapter or section headings and page numbers. There will sometimes be some detail under the headings.

This information is useful to help you find your way to the information you need. You should not need to read the whole of a textbook if you are looking for very specific information. Use the contents list as a signpost to the information you need to read.

Contents lists are not listed in alphabetical order – they list the order in which the contents appear in the text. Look out for

- page numbers, in numerical order
- chapter or section headings – perhaps in a different print style
- sub-headings – to help you get exactly the information you need.

### Activity

This is the contents list from a Benefits Agency brochure called *Cash Help while Working*. It gives lots of information on extra help you can get if you are on low wages.

| | | | |
|---|---|---|---|
| 2 | About this leaflet | 23 | **Help with NHS costs** |
| 2 | Rates of benefits and contributions | 23 | NHS prescriptions |
| | | 24 | Prescription season tickets |
| 2 | Free telephone advice service | 24 | NHS dental treatment |
| 3 | Advice in other languages | 25 | NHS sight tests |
| 3 | What is Social Security? | 26 | Help with the cost of glasses |
| | | 28 | NHS wigs and fabric supports |
| **5** | **Help for working parents** | 29 | NHS hospital travel costs |
| 5 | Family Credit | 29 | Free hospital medicines |
| 8 | Disability Working Allowance | 30 | Free hospital appliances |
| | | 30 | Free NHS hearing aids |
| **10** | **Working part-time?** | | |
| 10 | Income Support | **30** | **Bringing up children?** |
| | | 30 | Child Benefit |
| **16** | **Help with rent and Council Tax** | 32 | One Parent Benefit |
| 16 | Housing Benefit | 33 | Tax and the lone parent family |
| 18 | Council Tax Benefit | 33 | Guardian's Allowance |
| **19** | **Help with extra needs** | **35** | **Where to get help or advice** |
| 19 | Social Fund | | |
| 19 | – Maternity Payment | **37** | **Leafleats and where to get them** |
| 20 | – Funeral Payment | | |
| 20 | – Cold Weather Payment | 39 | Order form for leaflets |
| 20 | – Community Care Grant | | |
| 21 | – Budgeting Loans | | |
| 22 | – Crisis Loans | | |

Look at the section headings – in bold print.

- Which section would you need to read if you wanted extra support for children?
- Which page would you look at for information on Income Support?
- Which page would you look at for information on ordering a leaflet on NHS sight tests?

### Hint
**Try skim reading to help you find the information you need.**

Sensible use of a contents list can cut down the length of time you need to spend reading. It can also help to make sure you find the right information.

### Activity

Look at several textbooks or manuals you use in your GNVQ area. Have they all got contents lists? Do the contents lists have the same format – giving headings and page numbers?

Now look at the contents pages and find page reference numbers where you will find information on

- machinery maintenance or
- First Aid or
- work experience.

Did the contents list help you to find the information quickly?

### Hint
**An index is useful for finding very specific references; a contents list is more helpful for finding chunks of information on particular topics.**

### Key points to remember

- Contents lists help you to find information you need more quickly and more efficiently.
- Contents lists give subject headings and page reference numbers.

### Putting it into practice

- *Go to the library and pick out some books which might be useful to your GNVQ area – look at the contents lists to find out if there are any interesting sections.*
- *Make sure you look at the contents lists of texts you use in your next assignment.*

• 215 •

# Topic 2 – Reference skills

## Choosing the right reference source

**C 104**

Foundation
Element **1.4**
Performance criteria **1,3**
Range **Materials;
Sources of reference;
Subject; Purpose**

A reference source can be anywhere you go to get information about something you need to know. You will probably already have used a dictionary, but have you used any of these?

### Activity

Tick off those reference sources you have already used:

- a telephone directory ☐
- *Yellow Pages* ☐
- a GNVQ textbook or manual ☐
- a CD-Rom ☐
- an encyclopaedia ☐
- a thesaurus ☐
- a colleague or friend ☐
- a tutor or supervisor ☐

There are lots of places you can go to find information – where you go will depend on what it is you want to find out.

### Hints

You could try using some of the other reference sources mentioned. Remember, the more sources you know and use, the more likely you are to get the right answer.

You can get information from lots of different sources – you need to make sure you don't waste time by picking the wrong one. Remember you will save time and effort if you take a moment to make sure you're on the right track for the information you need.

## Did you know?

- You can find the correct time by telephone: dial your nearest town code plus 8081.

- You can get information on the weather by dialling 0891-500-400. The code for weather in your local area can be found by looking up 'Weather' in your local directory.

- You can find out about starting up in business for yourself by phoning your local Training and Enterprise Council (TEC) – find the number in your telephone directory.

- Your local library can give you a great deal of help in finding things out – information is their business.

### Key points to remember

- Be clear about what information you need to find out.
- Think carefully what the best source of this information is likely to be.
- Try this source first.

### *Putting it into practice*

*Next time you have an assignment and you need to find information*

- *make a list of what you need to find out*
- *take the list to your library and ask staff to show you where you could find the information you need.*

### Activity

Try the reference quiz!

1. You need to find the time of a train to London next Saturday. Would you
   a ask your Mum?
   b phone the Railway Information Service?
   c look it up in a railway timetable?

2. You need to find the phone number of your local Leisure Centre. Would you
   a look it up in a telephone directory?
   b look it up in *Yellow Pages*?
   c go round there and ask?

3. You need to get hold of information on Health & Safety regulations in your GNVQ area. Would you
   a look it up in a textbook from your GNVQ area?
   b ask someone at work?
   c phone the Health & Safety Executive?

4. You need to find the meaning of a technical term used in your latest assignment. Would you
   a ask your tutor or supervisor?
   b find out from a textbook or manual?
   c look it up in a specialist dictionary?

5. You need to find some information about another country for an assignment. Would you
   a check it out on a CD-Rom?
   b look it up in an encyclopaedia in the library?
   c ask someone from that country?

▌▌ *Trick quiz! You could answer 'yes' to all of these!* ▌▌

# Topic 2 – Reference skills

## Using reference sources to find information

**C 105**

**Foundation**
Element **1.4**
Performance criteria **2,3**
Range **Sources of reference; Subject**

You cannot know everything about everything, so sooner or later you have to find out about something from somewhere else. Even the brainiest people use dictionaries and no-one knows train timetables off by heart.

You can help yourself by knowing the best places to go for particular information. This saves time and effort. Test how well you know your way around the information maze.

### Activity

You have an assignment on the Health & Safety aspects of your GNVQ area. You need to find out as much information as possible.

1. You ask your tutor for ideas. He/she suggests:
   - a GNVQ textbook – go to No. 2
   - the Health & Safety Executive – go to No. 3
   - the library – go to No. 4.

   Which do you choose?

2. The GNVQ textbook might contain the exact information you need – where would you look for it?
   - the contents page – look for a reference to Health & Safety
   - the index – look up Health & Safety, Safety at Work, work regulations
   - flick through the book until you find something that looks relevant.

   Go to No. 5

3. You decide to contact the Health & Safety Executive – how do you find their address and phone number?
   - look up Health & Safety Executive in the telephone directory
   - phone Directory Enquiries (192) and ask for the number
   - find a Health & Safety Executive leaflet and look for their address.

   Go to No. 5

4. The local library might have some information – how would you find exactly what you need?
   - look around the library until you see a shelf with books on your GNVQ area
   - look in the library's reference system – card index file, microfiche or CD-Rom
   - ask a librarian for help.

   Go to No. 5

5. You have found some information. Well done! But you think you might need some extra help and information. What would you do next? Is there anywhere else you could go, apart from the three places already mentioned?

   Think of two other possibilities to find extra information.

■ *Quite often a quick way of finding out information is to ask someone. You need to make sure you ask the right person – you don't want to waste time with the wrong answer or someone who doesn't know.* ■

### Activity

Who would be the right person to ask for information?

- You need to know about grants to students for College places.
- You want to find out how much it would cost to fly from London to Paris.
- You want to ask about work placements.
- You need to find out about booking a driving test.
- You want to find out times and costs of a film you want to see.

### Hint

**Think about who is most likely to know the information you need. Ask them first.**

### Key points to remember

- Know the best place to go to find different kinds of information.
- Always ask the person most likely to know the right answers.
- We are surrounded by an information maze – learn to find your way around.

### Putting it into practice

*Think about all the possible sources of information on your GNVQ area. Investigate all of these and practise using them. Send off for any leaflets or brochures.*

# Topic 3 – Reading containing images and graphics

## The use of graphical illustrations in reading

**C 107**

Foundation/Intermediate/Advanced
Element **1.4, 2.4, 3.4**
Performance criteria **2,3**
Range **Purpose; Sources of reference; Subject**

Quite often in writing it helps to make a point clear if some kind of illustration is used. Remember the old saying about newspaper news items: 'every picture is worth a thousand words'. An illustration of some kind can often be a good way of giving information in a clear and understandable way. Imagine how difficult it would be to read a bus timetable if the whole thing were written out in words!

### Activity

Here are some points to be made in texts. Which graphical illustration matches them?

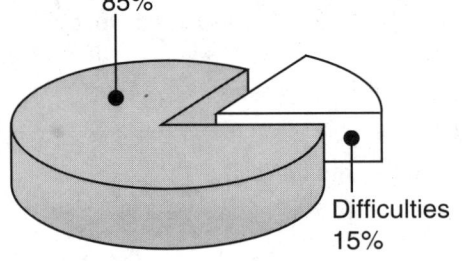

| Built-up areas | Elsewhere | | Motorways |
|---|---|---|---|
| | Single carriageway | Dual carriageway | |
| MPH | MPH | MPH | MPH |
| 30 | 60 | 70 | 70 |
| 30 | 50 | 60 | 60 |
| 30 | 50 | 60 | 70 |
| 30 | 50 | 60 | 70 |
| 30 | 40 | 50 | 60 |

1. Carry only what you can manage safely and easily.
2. The percentage of people who could not work out the change from £20 if they had spent £17.89.
3. Drinking and driving is a waste of money.
4. Rules for driving on motorways.
5. National speed limits for all vehicles.

Did you find any of these graphical illustrations difficult to understand? What would have made them easier?

Usually images and graphical information help to make reading easier. The illustrations are used to make points clearer and they are usually a good way of putting across important messages. If you have problems understanding an image or graphical information:

- Try re-reading the text to make sure you understand what point the author is trying to make.
- Make sure you understand the format or layout of the illustration. This is particularly important for graphs and charts.
- Ask for help or advice if you have real problems understanding the image.
- It may be that the writer's choice of image is not a good one.

# Topic 3 – Reading containing images and graphics

## The use of graphical illustrations in reading (continued)

### Activity

Here is a list of of images or graphical illustrations that you might come across. Tick off any that you have seen.

- a photograph of a news event
- a sketch of a car accident, showing the position of the cars
- a line graph showing average air temperatures for the year
- a block graph showing how many people voted for political parties
- a diagram of how to wire a plug.

These are all things which are easier to understand if they are explained graphically, using an illustration or a diagram to describe them.

Graphical illustrations can take many forms – writers will try to choose an illustration which gives clear and appropriate information.

### Key points to remember

- Images and graphical illustrations can give a lot of information quickly and clearly.
- They can be used to help make difficult points quickly understandable.

### *Putting it into practice*

1. *Look out for examples of logos and graphics in common use in your GNVQ area.*
2. *Make sure you know how to read graphs and charts. They can contain a lot of vital information.*

# Topic 3 – Reading containing images and graphics

## Getting the main idea from graphical information

**C 108**
Foundation
Element **1.4**
Performance criteria **1,2,4**
Range **Materials; Purpose**

Images and graphical illustrations are a useful way of giving important information quickly. They are used everywhere.

- at home
- in schools and colleges
- at work
- in shops
- on roads
- in books, magazines, leaflets.

### Activity

You already know many commonly used signs and logos. Some of these are used across the world. Can you match them with their meanings?

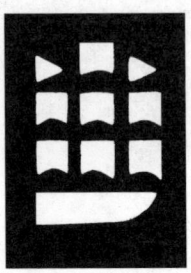

Learner Driver
Keep Britain Tidy
Pedestrian Crossing
Skull and crossbones

Longman
*Yellow Pages*

Each of these signs helps you to recognise particular information quickly. The message might be something to do with safety or it might make you think about a particular company or brand.

There are other ways of giving information using graphical illustrations:

- with cartoons
- using graphs and charts
- using tables of information
- with photographs, drawings or diagrams
- using all kinds of maps.

Looking at the graphical illustrations can often help you to understand important messages in the text.

### Activity

Have a quick look at this passage containing a drawing. Without reading any words can you tell what the passage is about – just by looking at the drawing?

What message or information does the drawing give?

Now check the reading – does the drawing get over the message effectively?

- Trainees using fork lift trucks or other mechanical handling equipment are trained to RTITB (Road Transport Industry Training Board) standard.
- Adequate arrangements include sign posting have been made for vehicle and pedestrian safety.
- There is a safe system of work, including control of keys, parking and battery charging for FLTs and "electric wheelbarrows", and instructions for non-drivers.
- Training has been given in manual handling.

Good illustrations and graphical information can help you to decide the main message of the text.

# Topic 3 – Reading containing images and graphics

## Getting the main idea from graphical information (continued)

### Hint
When you are scanning text or skim reading it, look first at any images or graphical illustrations to give you a clue what the passage is about.

### Key points to remember
- Images and graphical illustrations are a good way of making information
  - more interesting
  - clearer.
- Graphical illustrations can put over difficult or important points quickly.

### Putting it into practice
1. Look out for signs and logos used in your GNVQ area and make sure you know what they are about.
2. Practise finding out information from tables, charts and diagrams.

# Topic 3 – Reading containing images and graphics

## Getting the main idea from graphs and charts

**C 109**
Foundation
Element **1.4**
Performance criteria **1,2,4**
Range **Materials; Purpose**

Graphs, charts and diagrams are often used in texts. They are a useful way of putting across information in a visual way so that it can be understood at a glance though sometimes a little working out will be necessary. Most graphs and charts will have some explanation about how you can get the information you need from them.

The words will usually be on the graph or chart itself, or perhaps underneath. You will need to look for these words to help you understand the information.

### Activity

This chart or table of information gives postal charges for letters posted in this country.

| Weight not over | First Class | Second Class | Weight not over | First Class | Second Class |
|---|---|---|---|---|---|
| 60g | 25p | 19p | 500g | £1.25 | 98p |
| 100g | 38p | 29p | 600g | £1.55 | £1.20 |
| 150g | 47p | 36p | 700g | £1.90 | £1.40 |
| 200g | 57p | 43p | 750g | £2.05 | £1.45 |
| 250g | 67p | 52p | 800g | £2.15 | Not |
| 300g | 77p | 61p | 900g | £2.35 | admissable |
| 350g | 88p | 70p | 1000g | £2.50 | over 750g |
| 400g | £1.00 | 79p | Each extra 250g | | |
| 450g | £1.13 | 89p | or part thereof 65p | | |

How much would it cost to post first class a letter weighing not over 100g?

Can you send a letter weighing 850g second class?

How much would it cost to post a letter second class that weighed 445g?

How much would it cost to post a letter weighing 1,450g?

### Hints

The tricky part of this table is understanding what 'weight not over' means. For example, if a letter weighs 370g it is more than 350g but less than 400g – the weight is therefore not over 400g. The 400g price will be the right one.

You also need to look out for the instructions at the end of the table about the second-class limit and how weights over 1000g

Many graphs and charts work on the same principle. Information is recorded on two axes – often on the left-hand side and across the bottom. An axis is a line along which information is recorded. You need to work out where you are on each axis – where they meet on the graph will give you the information you need.

### Activity

This graph asks 'Are you the right weight for your height?'

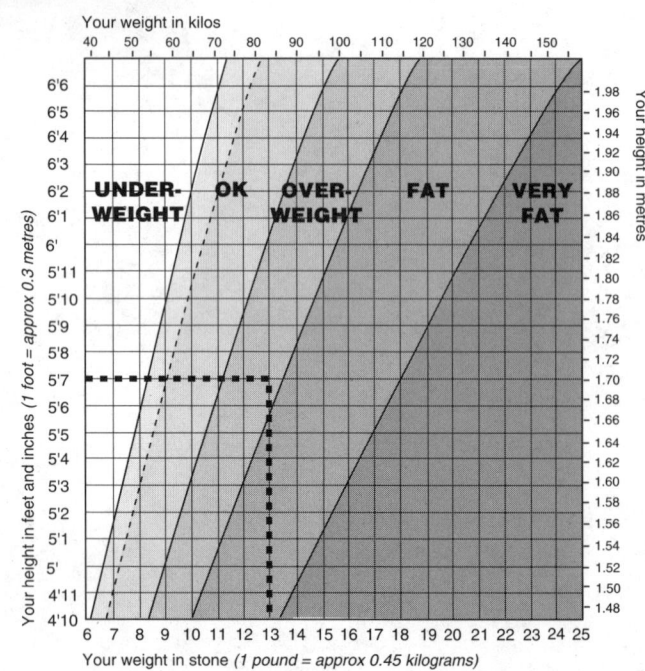

**UNDERWEIGHT**
Maybe you need to eat a bit more. But go for well-balanced nutritious foods and don't just fill up on fatty and sugary foods.

**OK**
Your weight is in the range for health. You're eating the right quantity of food but you need to be sure that you're getting a healthy balance in your diet.

**OVERWEIGHT**
Your health could suffer. You should try to lose weight.

**FAT**
It is really important to lose weight.

**VERY FAT**
Being this overweight is very serious. You urgently need to lose weight. Talk to your doctor or practice nurse. You may be referred to a dietician.

You will notice
- the top axis gives weight in kilos
- the bottom axis gives weight in stones
- the left-hand axis gives height in feet and inches
- the right-hand axis gives height in metres and centimetres.

Kilos, metres and centimetres are metric measures; stones, feet and inches are imperial measures.

**1** Find out where you are on the graph
  – in metric
  – in imperial.

**2** What advice would you give someone who was 5' 2" and 13 stones?

**3** What advice would you give someone who was 1.70 m and 70 kilos?

# Topic 3 – Reading containing images and graphics

## Getting the main idea from graphs and charts (continued)

**Key points to remember**

- Graphs, charts and diagrams often contain important information.
- Make sure you understand how the graph or chart works – read any instructions or explanations carefully.

*Putting it into practice*

1. Look out for graphical illustrations about your GNVQ area. You might look in
   - *textbooks*
   - *manuals*
   - *leaflets and brochures*
   - *magazines.*

   Make sure you know what they mean.

2. Try using images and graphics in your next assignment.

# Topic 3 – Reading containing images and graphics

## Reading text containing graphical material

**C 112**
**Foundation**
Element **1.4**
Performance criteria **1,2**
Range **Materials; Purpose**

Images and graphical material are used to illustrate texts, to give you information in a graphical way to help you understand the words.

- Graphs can help to explain information containing many numbers.
- Diagrams help to explain step-by-step instructions.
- Photographs or drawings are useful to give information which would be difficult to put into words.

You can probably think of many examples from your own experience.

Graphical illustrations are a useful way of explaining information which is complicated, for instance, if it contains many facts and figures.

## Activity

This short piece of text is about the number and type of injuries to workers in the United Kingdom. Read it carefully first.

One graph shows major injuries (amputations and fractures) and how often they happen in different areas of employment. Manufacturing has the highest number of amputations, closely followed by agriculture. For fractures, the service industry has the highest number, with agriculture and manufacturing the lowest.

The other graph shows how often serious sprains/strains and contusions happen in the four main employment sectors. Agriculture and manufacturing have the lowest number of sprains/strains which need more than three days off work. The services sector has the highest number. For contusions the number is highest in the agriculture sector. (A contusion is a serious bruise.) Read the titles of the graphs to help you decide which one is which.

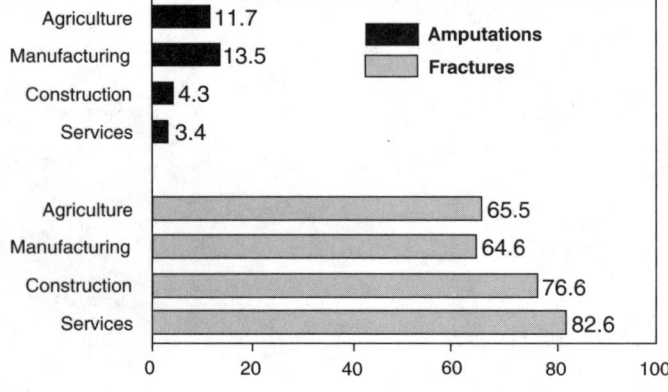

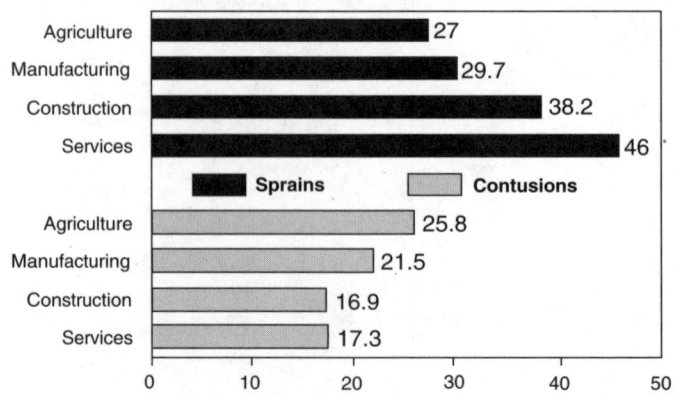

# Topic 3 – Reading containing images and graphics

## Reading text containing graphical material (continued)

### Activity

Look again at the text and check the information in the graphs.

1. What is an 'over-3-day injury'?
   - a an injury that happens for 3 days
   - b an injury that needs 3 days off work
   - c an injury that needs more than 3 days off work.

2. Which is the most dangerous area of employment to work in for breaking bones?
   - a manufacturing
   - b the service industries
   - c the construction industry.

3. Which industry area has the lowest number of amputations?
   - a the construction industry
   - b the services industry
   - c manufacturing industries.

### Key points to remember

- Graphs, charts and pictures help you to understand text.
- Careful reading of text containing graphics is important – to make sure you have understood it.
- Checking information in the text against information in graphs is useful to help you understand points being made.

### Putting it into practice

*Next time you read something that has graphs or charts, check carefully to make sure you understand the text.*

# Topic 4 – Read and respond to different formats

## Reading different formats

**C 114**
Foundation
Element **1.4**
Performance criteria **2**
Range **Purpose**

A great deal of the reading we see at work is in standard formats. Sometimes this is called a pre-set format. If you know that pre-set formats are designed to give the same information, this can help you to get information from them.

## Activity

There are thousands of different forms which ask for your personal details – name, address, telephone number.

Look at these forms and note the different ways they ask for the same information.

---

| Name | Rajiv Patel |
|---|---|
| Job Title | Transport Manager |
| Company | Dolman - Kirby (UK) Ltd |
| Address | Plot 7a, Harling Trading Estate, Swindon, Wiltshire |
| Postcode | SN9 4JK |
| Telephone No | 01793 881921 |
| Nature of Business | foodstuffs exports |
| No of employees | 76 |

---

**You**
Mr ☐  Mrs ☐  Miss ☑  Ms ☐  Other title _____
First names (in full) __Angela Rita__
Surname __Pawluk__
Date of birth __12.2.69__
Number of dependent children __2__
Are you? ☐ Single  ☑ Married  ☐ Divorced  ☐ Widowed
Mother's maiden name
(to be used as a phone call security question) __Jamieson__

---

**YOUR RETURN ADDRESS LABEL**
BLOCK CAPITALS PLEASE-ONE LETTER/No. PER BOX UK-ONLY

Name: J . R O G E R S O N
Address: H I G H W A Y S
H E A T H   R D ,   B O U R N E -
M O U T H    Post Code: B M 1 2 9 2 T

---

**ABOUT YOURSELF**

Surname: Lloyd        Mr/Mrs/Miss/Other: Mr
Forename(s): Brian James
Address: 142, Broadway Road, Hemel Hempstead
Hertfordshire
Postcode: HH3 0PS
Telephone Day: 01442 723985    Telephone Evening: —
Occupation: Student    Date of Birth: 10.11.74    Age: 21

Do you or any person likely to drive suffer from any infirmity, disability, illness or medical condition?    YES ☐    NO ☐
If yes please give details seperately

---

**Surname**
Jones        ~~Mr/Mrs~~/Miss/~~Ms~~
**Other names**
Sharon Louise
**Address**
14 Crown Heights
Sheffield
Postcode: SF14 5BQ
**Daytime phone number**
01742 699421
**Date of birth**
19/04/76

---

Scan the forms for the following information:

How many ways are there of asking for your first name? Can you think of any other ways?

Which one of these forms doesn't tell you whether the person filling in the form is a man or a woman?

How many of these people have a London phone number?

How many of them were born in the 1970s?

Which of their surnames comes first in alphabetical order?

# Topic 4 – Read and respond to different formats

## Reading different formats (continued)

At work you will often have to scan forms to find particular bits of information, usually because you need to do something with the information on the form. You might need to

- send the person further information
- phone them to make an appointment
- fill in their information in the right place
- get a particular piece of information from their form to go in a report or memo
- file the form, or put the information on a computer.

Different standard formats are used for different purposes. They are used to communicate different kinds of information. They are designed to make it easier to communicate particular kinds of information.

### Activity

What kind of information would you expect to find in these standard formats? Match the information to the format.

1 an employee record card
2 a customer record card
3 a local railway timetable
4 a memo to employees about holiday closures
5 machinery record sheet

a the date an employee started work
b a customer's telephone number
c the dates the factory will be closed in the summer
d the times of trains for someone coming for an interview
e the code number of the photocopier to inform the engineer.

■ *1a, 2b, 3d, 4c, 5e* ■

### Key points to remember

- Forms often ask for the same information, though they may use different words.
- Standard or pre-set formats help to make it easier to communicate information.

### *Putting it into practice*

*1 Look out for how standard or pre-set formats used at work ask for information in different ways.*
*2 Practise using these pre-set formats.*

# Topic 4 – Read and respond to different formats

## Reading timetables and price lists

**C 115**

Foundation
Element **1.4**
Performance criteria **2,3**
Range **Purpose; Sources of reference; Subject; Materials**

You will find that a lot of information at home and at work comes in the form of tables of information. This is another kind of pre-set or standard format and is usually a handy way of presenting information, which contains numbers as well as writing, in

- price lists
- catalogues
- timetables
- lists of information
- computer databases.

All of these pre-set formats will have their own layout and you will need to work out how to find the information you want. For example, look at this train timetable and note

### Activity

1. Where would you look on the timetable to find out if there are refreshments on these InterCity trains?
2. Where would you look to find out what 'w' on the timetable means?
3. Where would you look to find a train to Telford next Saturday?

The information is much easier to find when you understand the format and know where to look.

Catalogues and price lists are obviously important for ordering new things and checking information about items. Their layouts vary so you will need to spend time making sure you know what you are looking for and how the information is organised.

### Hint
Use clues like headings, different print styles, columns and boxes. Look out for keys.

## London → Shrewsbury and Telford

Principal train service 4 October 1993 to May 1994

### Mondays to Fridays

| | | London Euston depart | Telford Central arrive | Shrewsbury arrive |
|---|---|---|---|---|
| | | 0635 | 0918w | 0937w |
| | ✕ | 0710 | 1007n | 1027n |
| | ✕ | 0740 | 1107w | 1126w |
| | ✕ | 0840 | 1143w | 1201w |
| R | ✕ | 0940 | 1227w | 1246w |
| | ✕ | 1040 | 1306w | 1325w |
| | ✕ | 1140 | 1443w | 1502w |
| | ✕ | 1240 | 1506w | 1525w |
| | | 1310 | 1606k | 1626k |
| | | 1340 | 1651w | 1712w |
| | | 1440 | 1735w | 1756w |
| | | 1540 | 1815w | 1836w |
| | | 1655 | 1954w | 2013w |
| | ✕ | 1755 | 2047w | 2106w |
| | | 1840 | 2156w | 2217w |
| R | ✕ | 1940 | 2255w | 2314w |
| | | 2040 | 2349w | 0018w |

### Saturdays

| London Euston depart | Telford Central arrive | Shrewsbury arrive |
|---|---|---|
| 0700 | 1007n | 1027n |
| 0830 | 1143w | 1201w |
| 0900 | 1157w | 1218w |
| 0930 | 1227w | 1246w |
| 1030 | 1306w | 1325w |
| 1100 | 1343w | 1403w |
| 1130 | 1443w | 1502w |
| 1230 | 1506w | 1525w |
| 1330 | 1651w | 1712w |
| 1430 | 1735w | 1756w |
| 1530 | 1834w | 1853w |
| 1700 | 1951w | 2012w |
| 1800 | 2047w | 2106w |
| 1830 | 2165w | 2217w |
| 1930 | 2251w | 2310w |
| 2030 | 2349w | 0018w |

### Sundays

| | | London Euston depart | Telford Central arrive | Shrewsbury arrive |
|---|---|---|---|---|
| | | 1140 | 1526w | 1600w |
| | | 1240 | 1622w | 1642w |
| | | 1340 | 1729w | 1750w |
| | | 1440 | 1822w | 1842w |
| | H | 1540 | 1922w | 1942w |
| J | R | 1640 | 1922w | 1942w |
| | H | 1640 | 2029w | 2050w |
| J | R | 1740 | 2029w | 2050w |
| | H | 1810 | 2122w | 2142w |
| J | R | 1840 | 2122w | 2142w |

**Notes**
- H  2 January only
- J   Not 2 January
- k   Changes at Birmingham International
- n   Change at Birmongham New Street
- w  Change at Wolverhampton

[R] Seat reservations recommended
[✕] **Restaurant** (First Class only)
✕ **Restaurant**

All services shown in this table are Intercity unless stated otherwise.

**InterCity trains** offer:
- First Class and Standard accommodation
- Light refreshments, hot and cold drinks (available for most of journey). Meals, where indicated, for most of journey
- Reserved seats available
- Cardphone available for outgoing calls

All times shown are connecting services. Please note that some connecting services are not InterCity and may not convey the full ranfe of InterCity facilities. Please enquire for details.

**Saver and SuperSaver** tickets are not valid for travel on some weekday peak period services. Additionall, SuperSaver tickets are NOT valid on Fridays, ot during the period 17 to 31 December, Thursday 31 March and Saturday 28 May. Departure between midnight and 0229 take the availability of the previous day. Please check your ticket availability before travelling.

For further information on train services, fares and other facilities, please telephone **London 071-387 7070.**

The information is correct at the date of publication but changes may occure.

— three sets of times for weekdays, Saturday and Sunday

— key to the timetable: abbreviations/graphics

— additional information on facilities, tickets, telephone help

• 228 •

# Topic 4 – Read and respond to different formats

## Reading timetables and price lists (continued)

### Activity

Look at this price list. Note that 'h' stands for height.

|          | BOW    |       |        | DOME   |       |        |
|----------|--------|-------|--------|--------|-------|--------|
|          | NET    | VAT   | TOTAL  | NET    | VAT   | TOTAL  |
| 6'x6'h   | £13.00 | £2.27 | £15.27 | £13.95 | £2.44 | £16.39 |
| 6'x5'h   | £11.80 | £2.06 | £13.86 | £12.62 | £2.21 | £14.83 |
| 6'x4'h   | £10.45 | £1.83 | £12.28 | £11.25 | £1.97 | £13.22 |
| 6'x30"h  | £9.00  | £1.57 | £10.57 | £9.95  | £1.74 | £11.69 |
| 6'x18"h  | £6.40  | £1.12 | £7.52  | £7.20  | £1.26 | £8.46  |

Find the total price of a 6' x 4' h bow and a 6' x18" h dome trellis.

### Hint
Look at the headings 'BOW' and 'DOME'. Note that you will only need to look in the 'TOTAL' column.

When you are looking things up in a price list or a timetable you won't need to read everything. Decide what you're looking for and ignore everything else.

### Key points to remember

- Make sure you know what you are looking for in a price list or timetable.
- Check the information in the key if there is one.
- Check through any other writing that could give you important information.

### Putting it into practice

1. Look out for price lists or catalogues concerned with your GNVQ area.
2. Practise using bus and train timetables – you could phone to cross-check this information.
3. Try using a computer database to find information.

# GNVQ Core Skills:
# IT

Ian Kingston
Dot Moore
Anne Rooney

# IT – Prepare information Element 1

## Topic 1 – Word processors

- IT1 Typing text
- IT2 Choosing a format
- IT3 Saving your work

## Topic 2 – Spreadsheets

- IT8 Introducing spreadsheets
- IT9 Getting to know spreadsheets
- IT10 Exploring how spreadsheets work
- IT11 Entering data in an existing spreadsheet
- IT12 Setting up new spreadsheets

## Topic 3 – Databases

- IT14 Introducing databases
- IT15 Getting to know databases
- IT16 Entering data into an existing database

## Topic 4 – Graphics

- IT20 What type of picture do you want?
- IT21 Starting a drawing
- IT22 Starting a painting
- IT23 Lines and line styles
- IT24 Diagrams and plans

# Topic 1 – Word processors

## Typing text

**IT 1**

Foundation/Intermediate/
Advanced
Element **1.1,2.1,3.1**
Performance criteria **2**
Range **Enter; Software**

If you have used a typewriter, you will be familiar with the basic layout of a keyboard. You will find extra keys on a computer keyboard, and may have to modify your way of typing to make the best use of the computer and word-processing program. This sheet looks at typing text to create a text document using a word processor, including:

- looking at the keyboard
- beginning to type
- using the right keys
- using the Return or Enter key.

## The keyboard

Look at the diagram of a typical PC keyboard below. (Your keyboard may look different if you use a different type of computer.)

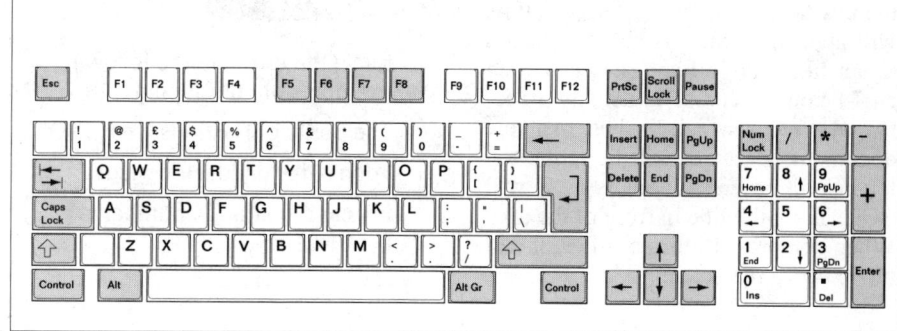

### Activity

Using a coloured highlighter pen, shade in the keys which you can already use.

Check in the table below to find out the function of any group of keys you are not familiar with.

| | |
|---|---|
| Character | Insert the character (letter, number, symbol or punctuation mark) shown on the key. |
| Shift | Hold this down to get upper-case letters (capitals), or the upper character on a key with two characters. |
| Caps Lock | Type only upper-case letters (but not the upper character on a key showing two characters). |
| Tab | Move the caret to the next pre-set tab position. You will need to use this to line up columns of figures or tables. |
| Alt | Hold this down and type numbers on the keypad to get special characters. |
| Cntrl | Hold this down and press one or more other keys to call up special functions (e.g., Cntrl-C to copy a block of text). |
| Option (Mac) | Hold this down and press one or more other keys to call up special functions or characters (e.g., Option- to get –). |
| Command (Mac) | Hold this down and press one or more other keys to call up special functions (e.g., Command-Option-C to copy text). |
| Function keys | Call up a special function; the function called by each key depends on the program you are using. |
| Cursor keys | Move the caret around the document. |
| NumLock | Press this to make the keys on the numeric keypad produce numbers when you press them. With NumLock off, the keys may call up other functions. The keys are probably labelled to show you what these functions are. They may be the same as the functions offered by some of the other keys, such as Page Up and Page Down. |
| Print | Print the screen, or call up a print option for the document. |
| Home/End | Move the caret to the beginning or end of the document. |
| Copy/Insert | Insert text at the position of the caret. |
| Delete/Backspace | Remove the character to the left or right of the caret. |
| Enter | Begin a new line, or send an instruction to the computer. |
| Number keypad | Insert numbers, or call up a function, depending on whether NumLock is on or off. |
| Break | Cancel the current operation; may reset the computer if other keys are held down as well. |
| Escape | Abandon the current operation. |

# Topic 1 – Word Processors

## Typing text (continued)

### Beginning to type

When you start up the word processor, it will probably open a blank document, or file, for you. You can begin typing in this immediately. You will see a caret, or a cursor, which marks the position where characters you type will appear. A caret is usually shaped rather like a large I and may be called an I-beam. A cursor is usually a rectangular block which flashes. In a new document, the caret will be at the top left-hand corner. As you type, it will move along the line in front of the text. When you press Return or Enter, it will move down the screen.

> **Activity**
>
> Find out how to move the caret around a document. The Spacebar is the long key at the bottom of the keyboard. Use this to add spaces between words. Don't use it to line up columns of figures or text in tables, or to move text in from the left-hand side of the page. You should use tabs and indents for this.

### Pressing the right keys

If you have used a typewriter, you may have got into the habit of using lower-case L in place of 1 (one) or I (upper-case i), and upper-case o in place of 0 (zero). In some styles of type, there is little or no difference in the appearance of these. However, when you use the computer, you should be very careful to use l/1/I and O/0 correctly. You should do this when you are using the word processor, or any other application, giving names for your documents and directories, or typing commands. The computer will not recognise l used for 1, for example. You will not be able to use the options your applications offer to find text or numbers if you have confused l/1/I and O/0. On the computer screen, 0 is sometimes drawn with a diagonal line through it to make it easy to tell it apart from O.

This is relevant to finding or searching for text or numbers in a word processor, spreadsheet or database.

> **Activity**
>
> Circle the errors in the following examples of poor typing:
>
> The Battle of Hastings was in 1O66
>
> I don't 1ike daddy-1ong-legs
>
> My car registration number is L451 N0T

■ *The Battle of Hastings was in 1O66: zero, not O*

*I don't 1ike daddy-1ong-legs; capital i, then lower-case Ls*

*My car registration number is L451 N0T: one, then capital o.* ■

### The Return or Enter key

The Return or Enter key moves the caret to the start of a new line. It places a marker in your file which tells the computer to move the following text to the beginning of the next line. This marker is usually invisible, but there may be an option to display paragraph markers. You don't need to – and shouldn't – press Enter or Return when the caret gets to the end of the line you are typing; it will automatically move to the beginning of the next line, taking over the word you are typing if it is too long to fit on the line. You only need to press Enter or Return when you specifically want to begin a new line. For example, when

- you want to start a new paragraph
- you want to insert a blank line
- you want to type a list or an address, with an item on each line.

> **Key points to remember**
>
> - Familiarise yourself with the layout of your keyboard.
> - Make sure you always use the right keys for the characters you want; don't use substitutes.
> - Don't press Return/Enter at the end of a line except to start a new paragraph.
> - Don't use the Spacebar to indent lines or align columns of text or numbers.

> ***Putting it into practice***
>
> *Type the following text, being careful to use the right characters and press Return/Enter only when you need to start a new paragraph.*
>
> *Dear Sirs*
>
> *I hope to complete my current training course on 10 December 1995 and I would like to apply for a grant to follow further training. Please send me an application form. I will be at the address above for the next 20 days.*

# Topic 1 – Word processors

## Choosing a format

**IT 2**

Foundation/Intermediate/Advanced
Element **1.1,2.1,3.1**
Performance criteria **1,2**
Range **Select; Information; Enter; Software**

You need to think about how you want a new piece of writing to look before you start work. Most word processors allow you to choose a format for a new **document**. Format is the term used for the document's appearance – how the text is arranged on the page, the size of the text and the pages, and so on. You will have to make sure you choose the format suitable for the piece you want to create. This sheet helps you to discover:

- the types of document format already set up for your word processor
- how to choose a document format when beginning a new document.

## Why do documents need different formats?

Think for a moment about the different types of text document someone may want to create with a word processor. Make a list.

They may include essays, memos, letters, address labels, lists, invitations and reports. Some will need A4 pages, and some will need to fit onto a different size paper. Some may contain text that is always the same; some may include columns of text or figures; some may need an ornate border or space for illustrations. If people in an organisation produce many documents of a similar type, it is worth setting up a format or template that sets some of the features that are needed each time, such as the page size and the positions for text. Your word processor probably comes with several formats already set up, and someone in your organisation may have set up extra formats for documents you may need to produce frequently.

## Looking at the document formats available

To choose a format suitable for a new document, you need to know what is available.

### Activity

Start the word processor and choose an option to begin a new document. There may be a dialog box or menu from which you can choose existing document types. If so, choose one and look at the document. Close the document without saving it and open another. Look at all the document types offered and try to work out how they are different. Some may have text, lines or boxes already in the document; some may show different page sizes.

Draw up a table to show details of the document types offered by your word processor: Use these headings

**Format name     Type of document     Description**

You will be able to refer to your table later when you need to create documents. You may be able to add to it if you go on to create new formats yourself.

## Choosing a format for a new document

Once you know which formats are available, you will probably be able to find something suitable for most documents you have to create. You will need to make certain you know exactly what is required for each document you begin. Work out which format you would use for each of the following types of document and fill in its name in the box to the right.

- Letter
- Memo
- Set of address labels
- Report that contains tables of figures.

### GLOSSARY
**document** – *a piece of work created on the computer. A word processor is used to create Text documents.*

### Key points to remember

- Document formats help you to produce documents of different types.
- There may be several document formats available for documents you need to create.
- You should be familiar with the document formats available to you.
- Choose a format suitable for the document you are going to create.

### *Putting it into practice*

*When you next need to create a document for your learning or work placement, you should be able to:*
- *review the document formats available*
- *choose a suitable format for your document.*

# Topic 1 – Word processors

## Saving your work

**IT 3**

Foundation
Element **1.1**
Performance criteria **3,4**
Range **Information;
Store input
systematically**

You should save your work at regular intervals, not wait until you have finished your document before saving it. This will protect you against losing all your work if there is a computer failure or power-cut, or if you make a bad mistake. This sheet helps you to find out

- how to save your work following the usual practice in your organisation
- how to store extra information about your document.

## Saving your document

When you have been working on your document for 10 or 15 minutes, you should save it. Save it earlier than this if it would be hard for you to recreate your work. You will probably be able to choose a menu option to save your document.

> **Activity**
>
> Open a document, do a little typing and then save the document. You may have to
> - give a name for the document
> - choose a directory or folder in which to store the document
> - choose a disk on which to store the document.

Sooner or later, everyone learns the hard way about saving their work. Sean explained what happened to him: 'I spent all afternoon working on my assignment. I had to hand it in before 9a.m. the next day, and I had nearly finished it and was going to save it when I had got it all done. At 6p.m. the cleaner came in. She was hoovering around the room, and she knocked the power cable for the computer out of the wall socket. I couldn't believe it – there was just no way to get my work back and I had to do it all again. I hadn't even printed it out, so I just had to remember it as well as I could and start from scratch.'

Your organisation probably already has procedures set up for saving documents in the right place. You will need to know which directories to open so that you can save your documents in the right place.

> **Activity**
>
> If you have a work placement, imagine you have to create a letter to send to a client. Where would you save it? If you don't have a work placement, where would you save a letter to your tutor you had typed on the computer at college?

You will probably have your own work space on a hard disk or on the network. At work, you may need to save work in an area shared by everyone. If you don't save documents in the right place, they will be difficult to find again later.

You can save a document again with the same name after you have made changes to it just by choosing the Save option. You will need to save it with a different name if you want to keep the old version as well.

## Information to store with your document

Many word processors allow you to store some extra information with your document. A box will appear when you save the document with spaces for you to give extra details. These may include the name of the person who created the document, summary information about the document, its topic and some keywords to help you search for it on the disk.

> **Activity**
>
> Can you store extra information with your documents? What information can you give? Find out how to fill in this information following the procedures in place in your organisation.

## Keeping source materials safely

If you are working from source materials on paper that someone has given to you, it is important to file them properly so that your document can be checked against them if necessary.

> **Activity**
>
> Find out where you should file the source materials you have used for the documents you create. Make up a checklist to help you remember what to do if the procedure is complex.

### Key points to remember

- Save your document earlier rather than later – it could save you redoing a lot of work.
- Save your document in the right place so that you can find it easily later.
- Store the correct information with your documents.
- File paper sources away carefully in the right place.

### *Putting it into practice*

*You will need to save your work each time you use the word processor. Follow the procedures you have found out about when saving your work, filing source materials and storing extra information with your document.*

# Topic 2 – Spreadsheets

## Introducing spreadsheets

**IT 8**

Foundation/Intermediate/Advanced
Element 1.1, 2.1, 3.1
Performance criteria 1
Range **Select; Information**

This sheet will introduce you to spreadsheets and give you an idea of the kinds of jobs you can use them for.

Imagine that as part of a presentation to a bank you are making up a **personal budget**. You have worked it out like this:

|  | Jan | Feb | Mar | Apr | May | June | Total |
|---|---|---|---|---|---|---|---|
| Rent | 200 | 200 | 200 | 200 | 200 | 200 | 1200 |
| Community Charge | 50 | 50 | 50 | 50 | 50 | 50 | 300 |
| Telephone |  | 60 |  |  |  | 60 | 120 |
| Electric | 56 |  |  |  | 35 |  | 91 |
| Totals | 306 | 310 | 250 | 250 | 285 | 310 | 1711 |

*Glossary*
**personal budget** – a calculation of what you spend each week or month.

### Activity

How easy would it be to make these changes to the budget?
1. You have found out that Community Charge will cost only £45 per month.
2. You have left out water rates from the budget.
3. Electricity bills are going to be paid in February and June, not in January and May.

■
1. You would have to change the six Community Charge entries, the total for Community Charge at the end of the row, the February total and the overall total.
2. You would have to enter a new set of amounts and add up all of the totals again.
3. These amounts would have to be taken out and new ones put in the right columns. Six totals would have to be added up again.

All these changes would mean that the budget would have to be written out again as it wouldn't be possible to make the changes neatly. ■

Spreadsheets are designed to do jobs like this quickly and without making mistakes. They will help to
- perform **calculations** automatically
- lay out numbers in rows and columns
- change totals automatically when numbers affecting the totals are changed.

*Glossary*
**calculations** – any type of sums; addition, subtraction, multiplication or division.

If you were to use a spreadsheet to calculate your household budget it would be easy to
- make a change to any number, as the totals that it affects will be changed as well
- add new rows or columns of numbers
- change the way things are displayed so that it is easy to follow and looks good.

### Activity

Can you think of any other things that would be made easier if you used a spreadsheet to calculate a personal budget?

■ Any jobs that mean changing the numbers in the budget are made easier. You can change figures to see what would happen if a particular bill were to go up or down and then put them back to what they were to begin with. It is also easy to add new sets of numbers, for example, you could add in a whole new row for water rates. You could add new columns so that the budget covers the whole year. ■

### Key point to remember

- A spreadsheet is useful if you want to lay out numbers in rows and columns and do calculations on them.

### Putting it into practice

Name two tasks for which a spreadsheet would be useful.

# Topic 2 – Spreadsheets

## Getting to know spreadsheets

**IT 9**

Foundation/Intermediate/Advanced
Element **1.1,2.1,3.1**
Performance criteria **2,5**
Range **Enter; Software; Configure software**

Spreadsheets are set up in rows and columns.

|   | A | B | C | D | E |
|---|---|---|---|---|---|
| 1 | Household | Bills | | | |
| 2 | | Jan | Feb | Mar | Total |
| 3 | Rent | 200 | 200 | 200 | 600 |
| 4 | Council Tax | 50 | 50 | 50 | 150 |
| 5 | Telephone | | 60 | | 60 |
| 6 | Electric | 56 | | | 56 |
| 7 | Totals | 306 | 310 | 250 | 866 |

Rows go across the screen and are labelled by numbers.

Columns go up and down the screen and are labelled by letters.

Words or numbers are typed in as cells. A cell is labelled by the letter of the column it is in, followed by the number of its row. This label is known as the **Cell Reference**. In the example above, the cell reference of the cell the arrow is pointing to is E5.

### Activity

In the diagram above:

1 What is the number of the row that has the month headings in it?
2 What is the letter of the column with the figures for March?
3 What is the cell reference of the cell that shows the figure for electricity in January?

▐▌ *1 The month headings are in row 2.*

*2 The letter of the column that has the figures for March is D.*

*3 The cell reference of the cell that has the amount for electricity in January is B6.* ▐▌

Into cells you can type:

**Text:** used for headings and descriptions (for example, the main spreadsheet heading and column and row headings are typed in as text).

**Numbers:** the amounts in the diagram above are typed in as numbers.

**Formulae:** a formula is what you type in when you want to do calculations. It will let you add up a row or column of numbers, subtract one number from another, or multiply or divide one number by another. When any of the numbers that affect the formula are changed, it will change

### Activity

Tick the boxes to show whether these items would be entered as text, numbers or formulae.

|   |   | Text | Numbers | Formulae |
|---|---|---|---|---|
| 1 | The spreadsheet heading | ☐ | ☐ | ☐ |
| 2 | The total amount spent in January | ☐ | ☐ | ☐ |
| 3 | The amount of money spent on the telephone in February | ☐ | ☐ | ☐ |
| 4 | The total amount spent on rent | ☐ | ☐ | ☐ |

▐▌ *Item 1 will be entered as text. Items 2 and 4 need calculations and will be entered as formulae. Item 3 will be entered as a number.* ▐▌

### Key points to remember

- Rows are labelled by numbers, columns are labelled by letters.
- Cells are given a cell reference that has a column letter followed by a row number.
- Cells can contain either text, numbers or formulae.

### *Putting it into practice*

- *Draw up, on paper, a personal budget spreadsheet for any month.*
- *Decide whether entries should be text, numbers or formulae.*

# Topic 2 – Spreadsheets

## Exploring how spreadsheets work

**IT 10**

Foundation/Intermediate/
Advanced
Element **1.1,2.1,3.1**
Performance criteria **2,5**
Range **Enter; Software;
Configure software**

Before you begin to use a spreadsheet you need to learn how to load the spreadsheet program you will be using. There are many spreadsheet programs that do more or less the same things.

### Activity

Find out the name of the spreadsheet program you will be using in your school or college.

■■ *The program you will be using could be one of the following:*

- Excel
- Lotus Improv
- Lotus 123
- CA Complete
- Supercalc
- Plan Perfect  ■■

When you load the spreadsheet program, you will see a screen with letters across the top. These letters label each column. You will also see numbers down the side. These numbers label each row. You type data into cells, which are labelled by a column letter followed by a row number. This label is called a cell reference. At the moment the cursor should be in Cell A1. You can move the **curso**r by using your arrow keys. Pressing the right arrow key once will move the cursor into column B. Pressing the down arrow key once will move it into row 2 and so on.

> **Glossary**
> **cursor** – in spreadsheet programs, the cursor is a rectangular box that is the same size as a cell. Anything you type will be put into the cell where the cursor is.

### Activity

Use the arrow keys to move around the spreadsheet and find the answers to these questions.

1 What is the highest row number?
2 What happens to the column letters when they go above Z?
3 What is the highest cell reference in the spreadsheet?

■■
1 *The answer to this question will change depending on the spreadsheet programme you are using. Most spreadsheet programs have over 1000 rows.*
2 *After Z, the columns in most spreadsheets go on to AA. When AZ is reached the labelling then goes on to BA and so on.*
3 *The highest possible cell reference varies from program to program, but as most programs have over 1000 rows and over 100 columns it will probably be above CA 1000.* ■■

Although spreadsheets have lots of cells that you can put information in, it is not always possible to fill them all up. You will find that the number of cells you can put information into will depend on how much **memory** your computer has.

> **Glossary**
> **memory** – this is the space that the computer uses to keep the information you type in before it is saved on a disk. It is sometimes called RAM. When you switch your computer off the memory is cleared.

To put information into a spreadsheet you need to move the cursor to where you want the information to go. In spreadsheet programs you don't type the information directly into the cell where it is going. There will be a place at the top or bottom of the screen where information is typed. It will be put into the cell only when you press the Return key.

### Activity

Find out how to enter information in the spreadsheet program you are using. Move the cursor into cell A1. Type the word 'Heading' and press the Return key to put it into the spreadsheet.

■■ *You will find that the text you have typed in is shown on the left-hand side of cell A1. This is called left justified.* ■■

### Activity

Move the cursor back to cell A1. Type the words 'This is a Heading' and press the Return key.

■■ *The new text you type will replace what was in there before. You will find that, although it is too long to fit into column A, the text has not been cut off when the column ends. As long as there is nothing in the cell next to it on the right, it will all be shown.* ■■

### Activity

1 Move the cursor to cell B1 and type the number 23 and press the Return key.
2 Move the cursor to cell C1 and type the number 27 and press the Return key.

■■ *The numbers you typed are displayed on the right-hand side of cells B1 and C1, this is called right justified.* ■■

If you want to add these two numbers together, you do not have to do the calculation yourself. You can use a formula to add, subtract, divide or multiply the numbers in the cells. The way you do this will be different in different programs. You will have to find out how to enter a formula in the program that you are using.

# Topic 2 – Spreadsheets

## Exploring how spreadsheets work (continued)

### Activity

Find out how to type the formula to add two numbers together.

Move the cursor to cell D1 and enter the formula to add together the two numbers in cells B1 and C1.

▋▋ If you have done this correctly, Cell D1 will show the answer to the sum, which should be 50. Like numbers, the answers to formulae are right justified.

If you typed the formula in wrongly, you could find that it has been treated as if it is text and what you typed will appear in the cell instead of the answer. If this has happened you will need to look again at how you typed the formula and find out what you did wrong. ▋▋

### Activity

Go to cell B1 and replace 23 with 43. What has happened to the number in cell D1?

▋▋ Because the formula in cell D1 links it to the numbers that are in cells B1 and C1 the answer in it will be added up again when the number in either of the other cells is changed. The new amount in cell D1 should be 70. ▋▋

### Key points to remember

- Most spreadsheets programs have over 1000 rows and over 100 columns.
- Formulae can be entered to add, subtract, multiply or divide numbers.
- Text entered into spreadsheets is left justified while numbers and the answers to formulae are right justified.

### *Putting it into practice*

- *Type a column of five two digit numbers into your spreadsheet.*
- *Type in the formula that adds these numbers up.*
- *Add the same numbers up on a calculator and check to see that your answers match.*

# Topic 2 – Spreadsheets

## Entering data in an existing spreadsheet

**IT 11**

Foundation/Intermediate/Advanced
Element **1.1,2.1,3.1**
Performance criteria **2,3,4**
Range **Enter; Software; Store input systematically**

For spreadsheets that are used all the time, a sheet is set up that holds things like headings and formulae that don't change. This is known as a master sheet. When you want to put data into the spreadsheet, you load the master sheet, fill in the information for the week and then save it under another name. The name you call the spreadsheet will have been decided already. For example, if you were working on spreadsheet files that kept details of expenses and there was one spreadsheet for each month, the files could be called, EXPJAN, EXPFEB, and so on. It is important that you find out the name you are supposed to call the file when you save it. Save your spreadsheet before and after you make important changes.

### Activity

Write in the boxes below, in the right order, the steps you should take to enter data into a master spreadsheet.

1

2

3

▌▌ *You should first load the master spreadsheet that has the headings and formulae. You should then type in any new information. Lastly you should save the spreadsheet under the right name.* ▌▌

When typing data into a spreadsheet that has the headings and formulae, you need to make sure that what you type in is correct and put in the right place in the spreadsheet.

### Activity

This information is to be entered into a spreadsheet for the month of February:

Product 1 – Week 1 – 45, Week 2, – 68, Week 3 – 34, Week 4 – 90

Product 2 – Monday 60, Tuesday 83, Wednesday 59, Thursday 105, Friday 97

Copy the figures above into the right places in the diagram below. If you have been told to name the files using the word SALES, followed by the first three letters of the month, what name would you use to save this file?

|   | A | B | C |
|---|---|---|---|
| 1 | WEEKLY SALES | | |
| 2 | Month: | *Product 1* | *Product 2* |
| 3 | Week 1 | | |
| 4 | Week 2 | | |
| 5 | Week 3 | | |
| 6 | Week 4 | | |

▌▌ *The month should have been put in A2. The entries for Product 1 should have been put in column B, from B2 down to B6, while the entries for Product 2 should have been put in column C, from C2 down to C6. The file should be called SALESFEB.* ▌▌

### Activity

Can you think of two problems if entries are wrong or aren't put in the right cells?

▌▌

- *Any numbers that aren't right will make the totals wrong. You should always check what you type to make sure that it is right.*

- *If you put something in the wrong place it will make the totals wrong. If the amounts for Week 1 and Week 2 for the first product were swapped around, the totals for those weeks would be wrong.*

- *If you put an entry in the wrong place, you can lose information by writing over a formula or piece of text that is already there.* ▌▌

You may need to check on information that has been entered into a spreadsheet. It's possible that an error won't be spotted until some time later. Wherever possible, keep your original source documents on file. Organisations will have their own policies on how much original information to keep.

# Topic 2 – Spreadsheets

## Entering data in an existing spreadsheet (continued)

### Key points to remember

- Master spreadsheets are created, filled in and saved under different file names.
- A system should be used for naming files.
- Entries in a spreadsheet should be made accurately and in the right place.

### *Putting it into practice*

*Over a period of a week, when you are entering information into a spreadsheet, keep a record of*

- *the date when you enter the information*
- *the start and finish time of each session*
- *whether the file has had a back-up copy made.*

# Topic 2 – Spreadsheets

## Setting up new spreadsheets

**IT 12**

Foundation/Intermediate/
Advanced
Element **1.1, 2.1, 3.1**
Performance criteria **2, 4**
Range **Enter; Software;
Store input systematically**

This resource sheet shows you how to set up a new spreadsheet and calls attention to some of the problems you might find.

Formulae are used to perform calculations on any numbers in parts of the spreadsheet, changing the answer if one of the numbers is changed. They work by linking the value in one cell to the values in a range of other cells. A range of cells can be

- a single cell
- a row or part of a row
- a column or part of a column
- a block of cells covering part of several rows and columns.

A range is defined by the cell references of its upper left and lower right cells.

|   | A | B | C | D | E | F | G |
|---|---|---|---|---|---|---|---|
| 1 | **Sales Sheet** | | | | | | |
| 2 | | Mon | Tues | Weds | Thurs | Fri | Total |
| 3 | Hickman | 52 | 30 | 60 | 89 | 47 | |
| 4 | Jenkinson | 65 | 27 | 81 | 103 | 65 | |
| 5 | Ritchie | 49 | 35 | 74 | 76 | 58 | |
| 6 | Varley | 61 | 29 | 57 | 83 | 52 | |
| 7 | **Total** | | | | | | |
| 8 | **Weekly Total:** | | | | | | |

The spreadsheet above shows how many items were sold by salespeople on each day of the week. To calculate the total sales on Monday, the cells to be added up are in the range B3 to B6. The formula for this should be put in Cell B7. To total the week's sales for Jenkinson, the cells to be added up are in the range B4 to F4 and the formula should be put in G4.

### Activity

What range of cells is needed and in what cell would the formula be put in each of these calculations:

1. the total sold on Wednesday
2. Varley's weekly sales
3. the total weekly sales?

■

| Range of cells needed | Formula placed in |
|---|---|
| 1 D3 to D6 | D7 |
| 2 B6 to F6 | G6 |
| 3 B3 to F6 | B8 |

In the case of 3, a block of cells needs to be added up and this is labelled by the top left and the bottom right-hand cell references. ■

There are shortcuts called functions that make some jobs easier. An example of this is when adding up a column or row of figures. To add up the numbers between B3 and B6, you do not have to type B3+B4+B5+B6, a function is available as a shortcut. The exact wording of this will vary between spreadsheet programs but a common form is SUM(B3:B6).

### Activity

Load the spreadsheet program you are using and set up the spreadsheet above. use the SUM function to add up each row and column and find the overall total.

■

- The totals of each column should have been 227, 121, 272, 351 and 222.
- The totals of each row should have been 278, 341, 292 and 282.
- The overall total should have been 1193.

*If you got different answers from these, you should check that you entered the figures correctly and that you used the right formulae.* ■

When you set up formulae in a spreadsheet you should always test that they work properly by entering test data and making sure you are getting the results you would expect.

When you set up a spreadsheet it is important to double check to ensure that the formulae you enter are valid and correct. It is easy to see whether a formula is valid or not as, if it has been entered wrongly, it will not work. Some of the problems you might find are:

**Problem** The formula you enter is treated as text and the formula itself is shown in the cell rather than the result of the calculation.

**Cause** In some spreadsheet programs it is necessary to show that the item you are entering is a formula. It could also be that you have made an error in entering the formula (such as writing 7A instead of A7).

**Problem** When you enter a formula you get an error message that mentions either a 'circular reference' or 'iteration'. In some spreadsheet programs this problem is shown by the number in the cell continually changing and growing when the formula is entered.

**Cause** You have included the cell reference of the cell containing the formula. For example, if you wanted to add up the contents of the cells between A4 and A6 and place the answer in A7, the formula to use is SUM(A4:A6). The above error would occur if you had entered SUM(A4:A7).

# Topic 2 – Spreadsheets

## Setting up new spreadsheets (continued)

In both these cases the problem can be solved if the formula is re-entered properly.

It is more difficult to spot errors in formulae if they are valid but incorrect.

### Activity

Identify the mistake in the following spreadsheet.

|   | A | B | C | D | E | F | G |
|---|---|---|---|---|---|---|---|
| 1 | **Sales Sheet** | | | | | | |
| 2 | | **Mon** | **Tues** | **Weds** | **Thurs** | **Fri** | **Total** |
| 3 | Hickman | 52 | 30 | 60 | 89 | 47 | 278 |
| 4 | Jenkinson | 65 | 27 | 81 | 103 | 65 | 276 |
| 5 | Ritchie | 49 | 35 | 74 | 76 | 58 | 292 |
| 6 | Varley | 61 | 29 | 57 | 83 | 52 | 282 |
| 7 | **Total** | **227** | **121** | **272** | **351** | **222** | |

■ *From just glancing at this spreadsheet it would be easy to assume that the figures are correct. However, the total of the rows added together does not match the total of the columns added together. A mistake must have been made somewhere in one of the formulae that calculate the total of each row or column.*

*To find the mistake, you first need to add all of the numbers from B3 to B6. This will give you the right overall total. You should then add the total of row 7 to find the overall total of all the columns. If this doesn't agree with the right overall total, then there is a mistake in the totals in row 7. If it does match, you should add up the totals in column G to find the overall total of all the rows. In this case it is the total of all the rows that does not match. This means that the error is located somewhere in column G. To find it you need to add up each row and find the one that does not match. The error here is located in Row 4, so the formula adding up that row must have been entered wrongly.* ■

### Activity

How could this mistake have been avoided?

■ *If the spreadsheet had been checked with test data when it was set up, the problem would have been obvious and could have been solved before real data was used.* ■

You can use the spreadsheet to help you make your check by using formulae to add up the total of the rows, the total of the columns and the total of the block of numbers separately. If all three figures agree, it is likely that the spreadsheet has been set up correctly. These check formulae can then be removed from the spreadsheet before it is used for real figures.

### Key points to remember

- Formulae link the value in one cell to the value in a range of other cells.
- Special functions exist that make some operations easier.
- Checks should be made to ensure that formulae entered are both valid and correct.
- Remember to save your spreadsheet before and after making changes.

### *Putting it into practice*

*Using the outline above, set up a spreadsheet to calculate your personal monthly budget.*

# Topic 3 – Databases

## Introducing databases

**IT 14**

Foundation/Intermediate/Advanced
Element **1.1, 2.1, 3.1**
Performance criteria **1**
Range **Select; Information; Software**

This sheet will introduce you to databases and give you an idea of the kinds of jobs you can use them for.

Imagine that as part of a project you did a survey of fifty people who used to go to your school or college. Everyone answering the survey let you know their forenames, surnames, sex and the year they finished the course. They then answered questions about what had happened to them after they left school or college, whether they went on to higher education, found a job or were unemployed and whether the course had proved useful to them.

**SURVEY**
Surname: Clarke
Forename: Wendy
Sex (M or F): F
Year you completed course: 1993

1. Did you successfully complete the course?
   (Y or N)  Y

### Activity

When all the information is collected you will have the answers on 50 sheets of paper. How easy would it be to

1. find out whether someone has answered the survey
2. pick out the sheets of paper from all the people who passed the course last year
3. get a list of everyone who went on to higher education
4. find out the names of people who didn't find the course useful?

■ *As long as the sheets of paper are sorted in order of surnames, finding one person's details would be easy. To do any of the other jobs, you would have to look through all the sheets of paper to find the information you wanted. This would take a lot of time and trouble.* ■

Databases are meant to do jobs like this. They will help you to

- store lots of information
- find bits of information quickly.

If you used a database to hold the results of your survey it would be easy to

- find one person's answers
- get a list of answers people gave to one of the questions
- get a list of all the people who left the course in the same year.

### Activity

Can you think of any other things that would be easier to do if you used a database to hold the survey results?

■ *Any jobs that involve picking out one or more person's details would be easier. An example of this is finding people who gave a certain answer to one of the questions. Using a database makes it simple to sort the answers people gave into any order you want.* ■

Many businesses use databases to hold information on things like

- customers
- employees
- suppliers
- stock

or when lots of information needs to be stored and found quickly.

### Key points to remember

A database is useful if you want to store large amounts of information and find information quickly.

### *Putting it into practice*

*A useful way to use a database is to set up a list of books and resources you are using on your course. Identify jobs that this might help you do.*

# Topic 3 – Databases

## Getting to know databases

**IT 15**

Foundation/Intermediate/Advanced
Element **1.1, 2.1, 3.1**
Performance criteria **1**
Range **Select; Information; Software**

This sheet will let you know some of the different words that you will meet when you use databases.

If you did a survey of 50 people, you would have to make forms with blank boxes for people to enter their answers. A database works in the same way and the blank boxes are called 'fields'. If you set up a database to hold the results of your survey, you would have a field for the person's surname, one for their forenames, one for their sex, one, for example, for the year they finished a course and a field for the answers to each of the other questions.

All the fields for one person make up that person's 'record'. A record holds all the information from one piece of paper.

All the records together make up a 'file'. A file holds all of the information you collected in the survey.

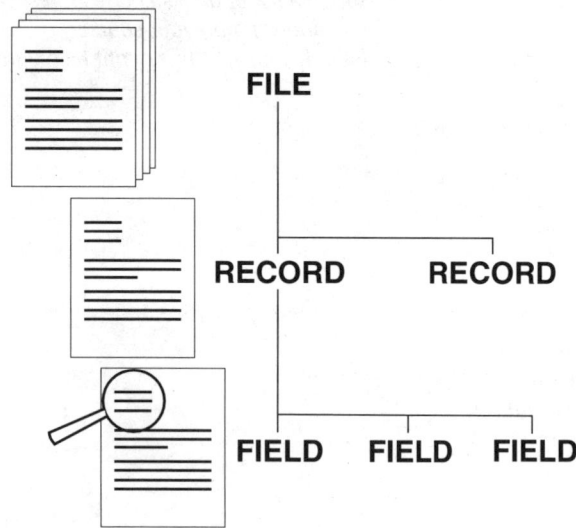

### Activity

Tick the box below to show whether you think each item is a File, Record or Field.

| | File | Record | Field |
|---|---|---|---|
| 1 All the information on one person | ☐ | ☐ | ☐ |
| 2 The space into which you enter a person's forename | ☐ | ☐ | ☐ |
| 3 All the information collected | ☐ | ☐ | ☐ |

■■ *You should have ticked Record for item 1, Field for item 2 and File for item 3.* ■■

Each field is given a label, known as a field name. This lets you know where to put information to be entered.

### Activity

This information is to be typed into a database. Write Sarah's details into the boxes beside the proper field names

Name: Sarah Barnes; Telephone: (01744) 234567; Sex: Female; Hourly Rate of pay: 4.50

Surname: _____
Forename: _____
Sex: _____
Phone: _____
Pay: _____

■■ *The name should have been separated out into surname and forename and written into two boxes instead of one. The other information should have been written in the order it was asked for and not the order given originally.* ■■

### Key points to remember

- Database files are made up of records and fields.
- Each field is given a label known as a field name.

### Putting it into practice

*Look at the database you can use.*
- *Write down a list of the names of the fields that it uses.*
- *Find out how many records there are in the file.*

# Topic 3 – Databases

## Entering data into an existing database

**IT 16**

Foundation/Intermediate/Advanced
Element **1.1,2.1,3.1**
Performance criteria **2,3,4**
Range **Enter; Software; Appropriate intervals; Store input systematically**

Before you put **data** into a database you need to learn how to load the database program you will be using. There are many database programs that do more or less the same things.

> *Glossary*
> **data** – information such as names, addresses, dates or figures entered into a computer

### Activity

Find out the name of the database program you will be using in your school or college.

■ *The program you will be using could be one of the following:*

- *Access*
- *DataEase Express*
- *Equinox*
- *Paradox*
- *Approach*
- *dBase*
- *Foxpro*
- *Superbase*

■

Each database program works differently and you will have to learn how to work with the one you will use. However, the tips below should help you when you start to enter information.

- *Make sure you always enter data into the correct field.* If you don't put data in the correct field, searching for it later becomes very difficult as you do not know where to look. For example, searching for someone with a particular surname would be much harder if the surname has been put into the forenames field by mistake.

- *Take care that typing is correct.* If you type something wrong it is hard to find it later. For example, if you mis-type SALES as SLAES, the database will not include the record in a list of people in the SALES department. This could mean that someone in the SALES department doesn't get paid or doesn't get sent an important letter.

- *Be consistent in the way that you use capital and small letters.* If you start off using all capitals for one field you should do the same thing for that field all the time. If you don't, you may have problems with searching, and you will also make any report done from the database look untidy.

- *Be careful not to reverse numbers (for example, entering 67 instead of 76).* This is one of the most common mistakes made when entering numbers. An invoice sent out for £140 instead of £410 can cost a business dearly if it is not spotted in time.

> *Glossary*
> **printout** – printed copy of information taken from a database or other computer program. This can also be called a 'hard copy'. Printed copy of information.

### Activity

Here is a **printout** made from a database file that stores details of employees.
Pick out five mistakes in the way that the data was entered.

| Surname | Forename | Age | Department | Address1 | Address2 | Town | Postcode |
|---|---|---|---|---|---|---|---|
| JONES | PETER T | 13 | SALES | Rose Cottage | 7 Fore Street | NEWTOWN | NT45 3CD |
| THOMPSON | EMILY | 39 | ADMIN | 2 Sea View Terrace | | WATERTOWN | WT65 3ND |
| Robson | John | 22 | SALES | 4 Park Terrace | | NEWTOWN | NT56 4AA |
| PETERS | MARGARET | 26 | COMPTUER | 94 Newtown Road | WATERTOWN | | WT45 6RB |
| WASIM | ALI | 31 | SALES | 37 Bridge Street | | HOMETOWN | HT32 7PQ |
| PRIOR | SEAN | 44 | ADMIN | 32 Oak Terrace | | NEWTOWN | NT34 5TR |
| PEARCE | CLAIRE | 19 | COMPUTER | Bay View House | 5 Newtown Road | WATERTOWN | WT65 4RP |
| SINGH | GITA | 24 | SALES | 29 HILL STREET | | HOMETOWN | HT34 5MN |

# Topic 3 – Databases

## Entering data into an existing database (continued)

1. A 13-year-old salesman is extremely unlikely and it is probable that Peter Jones is actually 31 and the person who entered the data accidentally reversed the numbers.
2. The surname and forename of John Robson have been entered in a mixture of capitals and small letters while other names have been entered in all capitals.
3. The word COMPUTER has been wrongly spelt as 'COMPTUER'.
4. The town and postcode have been entered into the wrong fields in record number 4.
5. The first line of Gita Singh's address has been entered in all capital letters when other records have been entered in a mixture of capitals and small letters.

To avoid these problems you need to take great care when you enter data.

- Have all the information to hand before you start.
- Write down the details for each record in the same order as you will be entering them into the file. This will make entering the data easier and will cut down the number of mistakes.
- When you enter data, check it carefully for mistakes.
- You might find it easier to enter data accurately if you move a ruler down the page, underneath the line you are entering.
- Always keep the original pages that you are working from when you enter your data. If you don't, it will be impossible to check for mistakes later.

When you have entered your data, you should then make an extra copy of the file on another disk. This is known as making a back-up copy. If you back up your work you will make sure that you have an up-to-date copy of the file you are working with stored safely. This can be useful if

- the original disk becomes faulty
- the file is accidentally damaged.

### Activity

Imagine that a company you are working for holds details of all their customers on a database, including their addresses, telephone numbers and how much money they owe. The company uses this database to print out their customer **invoices**. What problems would there be if the disk holding this database became faulty and there was no back-up copy of the file?

### Glossary
**invoices** – companies send these to customers to let them know how much they owe for things they have bought.

If this database file is lost it could cost the company a great deal of money. They would have no idea of who owed them money and so could not send out any invoices. They would not even have any record of their customers' names and addresses.

Because of problems like these businesses make sure that each time changes are made to a database file, a back-up copy is made. This is a habit you should get into with your own work.

### Key points to remember

- You should enter data into a database carefully and then check to ensure that it is right.
- Copies should be kept of the database on a separate disk to make sure that, if there is a problem with the original disk, there is always a recent copy of the information to hand.

### Putting it into practice

Over the period of a week, when you are entering information into a database, keep a record of

- the date when you enter information into a database
- the start and finish time of each session
- how many records you enter in each session
- whether records are checked for accuracy and consistency
- whether the file has had a back-up copy made.

## Topic 4 – Graphics

### What type of picture do you want?

**IT 20**

*Foundation*
Element **1.1**
Performance criteria **1,2**
Range **Select;**
**Information; Enter;**
**Software**

There are two distinct types of picture you can create on the computer, each suitable for different purposes. These are:

- drawings, also called line art or vector graphics
- paintings, also called raster images or bitmap graphics.

This sheet will help you to decide which type of picture you need to create.

## Drawings

A drawing is a picture built up from a series of lines and shapes. It keeps information about your picture as a description of the parts – a circle, a triangle, a piece of text – and their precise positions. You can alter these parts, changing their shape, size, position, colour and so on.

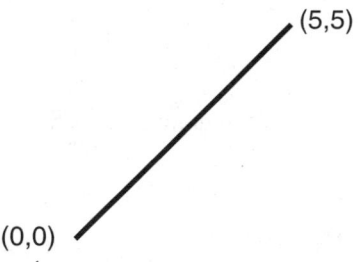

*A drawing stores a line by recording the positions of its ends.*

Because a drawing program can be used very precisely, it is useful for detailed diagrams and illustrations, for charts and graphs, plans and 3D visualisations. Anything you might draw with a traditional drawing board and tools you can draw with a drawing program.

## Paintings

A painting is an image made up of tiny dots of different colours. Your picture is stored as a map of the colours used for the dots. The dots are called pixels (picture elements); they are the smallest possible component of a picture. Each pixel can be only one colour.

Using a painting program is rather like painting: you may choose a 'brush' or some other tool, and spread colour across an area of the screen. The computer holds information about the colour used for each of the pixels, but does not store anything more complex. Shapes are just patches of colour. You can change the picture by painting over it and by moving or copying areas.

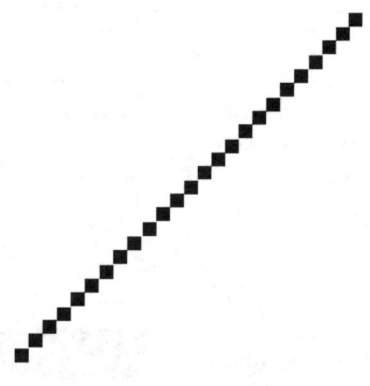

*A painting stores a line as a series of coloured dots.*

A painting is not well suited to precise work, though it can produce very detailed work. It is best suited to freehand art work that you could otherwise create with paints, chalk, crayons or drawing freehand with pen or pencil.

If you scan a picture using a scanner to get an image of it that you can use on the computer, you will have created a painting; the scanner reproduces the picture as a pattern of dots, even if the picture is a diagram or chart.

### Activity

Would you use a drawing program or a painting program for each of these tasks?

- a plan showing the fire exits in the building you work in
- a picture of a sunset
- a graph of an organisation's productivity
- an air-brush style image of a movie star for a poster.

▌▌ *The first and third should be created as drawings; the second and fourth you could create with a painting program.* ▌▌

### Key points to remember

- Drawing programs create precise drawings that consist of parts you can move and change.
- Painting programs create freehand paintings made up of coloured dots.

### *Putting it into practice*

*Find out which programs you have, and whether each is a drawing or painting program. You may need to look in the manuals. The manuals probably have some examples of the type of picture you can produce with the programs; look at them carefully, until you are quite sure you understand which types of picture you can create with a drawing program and which with a painting program.*

*Remember to keep all your source material – such as measurements you have taken or a published picture. You may want to check or change your graphics later.*

| Topic 4 – Graphics | IT 21 |

## Starting a drawing

Foundation/Intermediate/
Advanced
Element **1.1,2.1,3.1**
Performance criteria **2**
Range **Enter; Software**

When you begin a new drawing, you will probably be able to see some or all of the drawing tools you can use on screen. Most drawing programs have a tool panel or toolbox from which you can choose the tool you want to use. There may be other options – such as the thickness for lines – that become available at appropriate points, or that you can choose from menus. This resource sheet looks at how to start a new drawing, and the type of tools you are likely to find.

## Starting a drawing document

When you start the drawing program, it probably opens a new, empty drawing for you. If not, you may need to choose a format for your drawing, perhaps by choosing a page size.

## Drawing tools

The drawing tools are probably in a panel or arranged around one or more edges of the drawing. Many of the tools help you to draw shapes and lines. Typically, you may find any of the tools shown below. You have to click on a tool to select it, and then you can begin using it. Look in your own drawing program's tool panel for tools equivalent to those shown here.

 Draw straight lines, usually connected together. You probably have to click a mouse button at each corner.

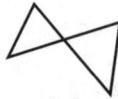 Draw closed shapes made up from straight lines. Again, you probably have to click a mouse button at each corner.

### Activity

Use the straight line and closed shapes tools to copy this arrangement:

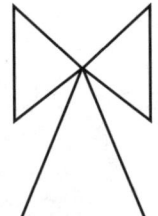

 Draw curved lines. You probably have to click a mouse button for each change of direction.

 Draw closed shapes made up from curved lines. Again, you probably have to click a mouse button for each change of direction.

 Draw circles or ellipses. You probably have to click for the centre and at a point on the circumference.

### Activity

Use the curved lines, closed shape and circle tools to draw a flower like this:

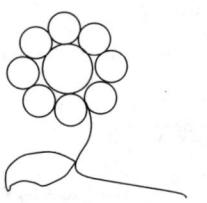

☐ Draw squares or rectangles. You probably have to click at two diagonally opposite corners.

**T** Add text. You probably have to click to position the text, before or after typing it.

### Activity

Use the rectangle and text tools to draw a box with your name in it like this:

| Hannah |

 Select an object in the drawing. Click on the object you want to select. You may be able to select several objects at once by holding down the mouse button and dragging over or around all the objects you want to select, or you may be able to select several objects by holding down a key on the keyboard (such as Shift).

### Key points to remember

- The drawing tools available in a drawing program are usually visible on screen when you open a new document.
- To choose a tool, you have to click on it.
- You have to use the mouse and pointer to draw lines and shapes with the tools.

### Putting it into practice

Create a logo for an imaginary company, or copy a logo you have seen. The sheet on starting a painting asks you to do the same thing; compare the painted and drawn logos.

# Topic 4 – Graphics

## Starting a painting

**IT 22**

Foundation/Intermediate/
Advanced
Element **1.1,2.1,3.1**
Performance criteria **2**
Range **Enter; Software**

When you begin a new painting, you will probably be able to see some or all of the drawing tools you can use on screen. The tools are probably arranged in a tool panel or toolbox. Extra options, such as the shape to use for a paintbrush brush, may become available sometimes or you may be able to choose these from menus. This resource sheet looks at how to start a new painting, and the type of tools your program may have.

## Starting a painting

When you start the painting program, it may open a new, empty painting for you or you may need to choose a size for your painting. A painting takes up more computer memory than a drawing, so your program may not open an A4 painting at first.

There is probably a panel showing blocks of different colours you can choose. You probably need to click on a colour to choose it. Anything you then paint will appear in the colour you have chosen.

## Painting tools

The tools you can use in a painting program help you to draw shapes and lines and to use painting tools such as brushes and spraycans. There are usually some other tools as well. You will need to click on a tool to select it, and then you can begin using it. Look in your own drawing program's tool panel for tools equivalent to those shown here.

 Draw thin lines freehand; you have to use the mouse like a pencil, keeping the button pressed to draw the line.

 Draw thicker lines freehand; again, use the mouse with the button pressed down to draw the line.

### Activity

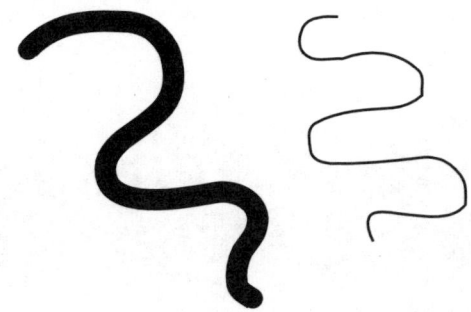

Draw lines like these using the pencil and paintbrush tools. You may find that the lines break up if you move the mouse quickly.

 Draw straight lines, which may or may not be connected together. You have to click a mouse button at each corner.

 Draw filled shapes. You usually have to click a mouse button at two opposite corners to create a rectangle or square, and in the middle and on the circumference to create a circle.

### Activity

Choosing suitable colours, draw a snowman like this using filled shapes:

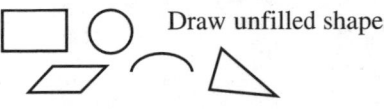 Draw unfilled shapes.

 Fill a closed area with colour. You may be able to change all areas in the colour you click on to another colour.

### Activity

Draw a snowman using unfilled shapes and then use the colour fill tool to fill in the colours.

 Add text. You probably have to click to position the text, before or after typing it.

### Activity

Add your name to your picture of a snowman; compare it with the text you created with a drawing program.

There will probably be tools for making changes to the painting, such as copying or removing areas.

When you are becoming familiar with a drawing program, it is easy to make mistakes, so save your work frequently.

# Topic 4 – Graphics

## Starting a painting (continued)

### Key points to remember

- The painting tools are usually visible on screen when you open a new document.
- To choose a tool or a colour, click on it.
- Use the mouse and pointer to paint on the screen.
- If you paint over an area, the new colour replaces the colouring there before.

### *Putting it into practice*

*Create a logo for an imaginary company, or copy a logo you have seen. The sheet on starting a drawing asks you to do the same thing; compare the painted and drawn logos.*

# Topic 4 – Graphics

## Lines and line styles

**IT 23**

Foundation/Intermediate/Advanced
Element 1.1, 2.1, 3.1
Performance criteria 2
Range **Enter; Software**

Using different thicknesses and styles of line is an important way of marking differences between some of the parts of your drawing or painting. A drawing program generally gives you more choice about line style than a painting program. This sheet helps you to find out about styles of line, join and line ends. It also includes some information on working with curved lines in a drawing program, which can seem unpredictable when you first use them.

## Painting lines

You can probably choose the thickness and perhaps the shape for your brush. You may be able to choose from a selection displayed on screen, or you might have to give a value for the thickness in millimetres or **points**. A point is a unit of measurement used in type and design.

> **Glossary**
> **point** – unit of measurement used for line thickness and text size. A point is about 1/72 of an inch.

You may be able to choose a shaped brush rather than a round one. If you can, you will be able to paint shaped dots, and lines like these:

### Activity

Experiment with different thicknesses of line and different brush shapes, if your program has them. Paint a line using each brush shape in turn.

## Drawing lines

If you are using a drawing program, you will probably have to set the thickness of your line in points. There may be several thicknesses you can choose from, but you will also be able to set a thickness not offered.

### Activity

Experiment with different line thicknesses. You could produce a chart for yourself showing different thicknesses.

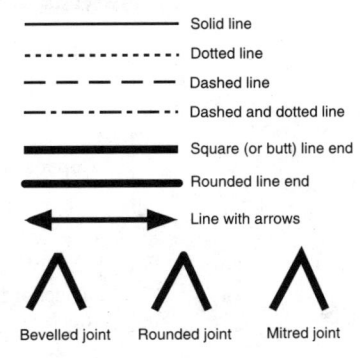

You can probably choose

- a line pattern – such as solid, dotted and dashed lines
- shape of line ends – e.g., rounded ends or arrows
- joins between lines – e.g., butt, rounded or mitred.

### Activity

Try out all the line styles, join styles and line end styles. You may need to look closely to see some of the differences; use the Zoom option to zoom in on lines you want to look at close up.

## Working with curved lines

Straight lines are easy to understand; they are defined by two points, or positions, one at each end – the line is simply drawn between the two points. Curved lines are more complicated.

When you first begin to draw curved lines, you may find that they don't look quite as you had expected or intended. A curved line is controlled by four points: one at each end and two control points which determine how curved the line is. One control point is linked to each end of the line. Here is a curved line with the control points shown. You may sometimes need to alter the curved lines you draw by moving the control points.

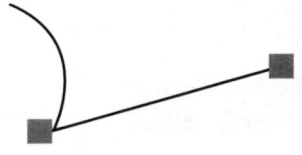

### Activity

Experiment with drawing curved lines. Does the shape of the line alter as you move the mouse around and click the buttons? This is because the position of the second control point is changing the part of the line you have already drawn.

### Key points to remember

- A painting program lets you choose a brush thickness and perhaps a brush shape.
- A drawing program lets you control line thickness, line pattern, the style used for joins between lines and for line ends.
- Curved lines may behave unexpectedly until you are used to them.

### Putting it into practice

*Draw a very simple map of the area around your home to show visitors how to find it from a main road or station. Use thick lines to show roads, and thinner lines for the outlines of buildings and other features.*

• 255 •

# Topic 4 – Graphics

## Diagrams and plans

**IT 24**

Foundation/Intermediate/
Advanced
Element **1.1,2.1,3.1**
Performance criteria **2,5**
Range **Enter; Software;
Configure software**

You can use a drawing program when you need to produce diagrams and plans from simple lines, shapes and text. This sheet helps you to find out about

- planning your drawing
- drawing boxes, shapes and lines
- adding text to a diagram.

## Starting work

It is a good idea to plan out your drawing on paper before you start work on the computer. You may always find this helpful, but it is particularly useful when you first begin using the computer and are not yet used to designing on screen.

### Activity

Using paper and pencil, draw a rough plan of your classroom. Don't worry about exact measurements, just show where everything is. Don't forget the door and windows.

## Drawing lines, boxes and shapes

Most parts of your plan or diagram will usually be regular shapes such as circles, squares and rectangles. You will sometimes want the shapes to be filled with colour, but sometimes you will want them to be just outlines – if they are to be boxes to contain text, for example.

You may want to add lines to show items which you can't show by closed shapes. Sometimes you will want the lines to join shapes together. You may want to add lines with arrows at the end to help you label a diagram.

### Activity

Now begin the plan for your classroom on the computer. Draw the outline of the room using connected straight lines, showing the door open. Add shapes for the furniture and lines with arrows to help you label it (you will add text later).

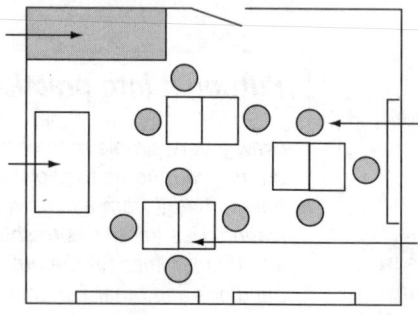

## Adding text

You can probably choose the size and font (style of type) for text you add to your drawing. Text is usually measured in points: a point is about 1/72 of an inch; 10 point is a good size to start with – it is the size of type used in many books.

You may need to draw a special text box to hold your text, or you may be able just to type straight onto the drawing. If you type straight onto the drawing, you will need to press Return or Enter when you want to begin a new line.

### Activity

Add text to label your plan.

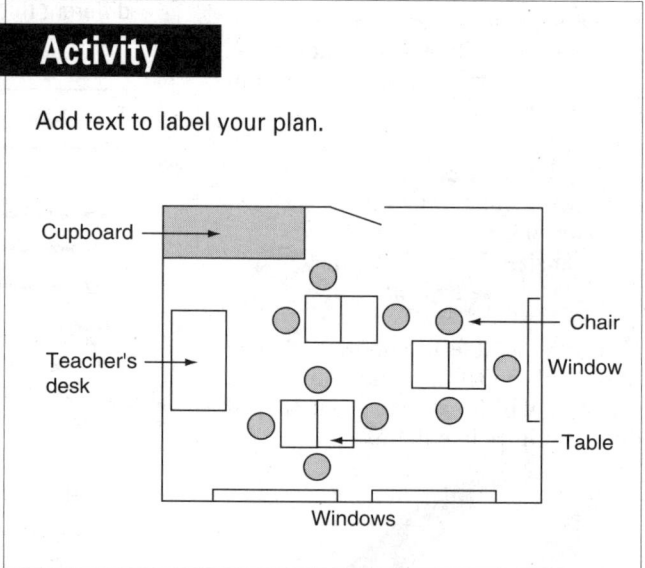

### Key points to remember

- A plan or simple diagram is usually built up from lines, boxes or other shapes and text.
- You can choose a colour or pattern to fill closed shapes.
- You can use lines with arrowheads at the end to label parts of a diagram.
- You can probably choose the font and size for text.

### *Putting it into practice*

*Draw a simple diagram showing new students where the power switches are on the monitor and computer you use.*

• 256 •

# IT – Process information — Element 2

## Topic 1 – Word processors

- IT27 Making simple changes to text
- IT28 Checking your text
- IT29 Cutting, copying and moving text
- IT30 Moving and copying text between documents
- IT31 Moving around a short document
- IT32 Moving around a long document
- IT33 Arranging blocks and tables
- IT34 Finding and replacing text
- IT35 More about finding and replacing text

## Topic 2 – Spreadsheets

- IT38 Changing cell contents
- IT39 Adding and deleting rows and columns

## Topic 3 – Databases

- IT42 Making changes
- IT43 Finding a record
- IT44 Sorting a database

## Topic 4 – Graphics

- IT48 Making simple changes to a drawing
- IT49 Making simple changes to a painting
- IT50 Moving graphics between pictures
- IT52 Using colour and pattern

# Topic 1 – Word processors

## Making simple changes to text

**IT 27**

Foundation/Intermediate/
Advanced
Element **1.2,2.2,3.2**
Performance criteria **2**
Range **Software; Edit; Information**

Sooner or later, you will want to make changes to text you have typed in a word processor, or will need to correct typing mistakes. This sheet explains how to make simple changes by

- deleting (removing) characters
- inserting extra text
- changing text by typing over it.

## Deleting and inserting characters

There will be a Delete key or a Backspace key (or both) on your keyboard. When you press one of these keys once, the character to the left or right of the caret or cursor is removed and the caret moves backwards or forwards.

### Activity

Type some text and then use the Delete or Backspace key to remove some of it. What happens if you keep the Delete or Backspace key pressed down?

■■ *When you keep the key pressed down, it probably repeats, deleting many characters.* ■■

To insert new characters, you can probably move the caret into some text and then begin typing. If your word processor has a cursor instead of a caret, you will need to put this on a character – you can't put it between characters. The existing text is usually pushed along to the right to make room.

### Activity

Type this text using your word processor:

Christmas is on the 35th of December

Now put the caret between the 3 and 5 of 35th and press Delete or Backspace to remove the 3. Now type 2, to correct the line. If your word processor has a cursor instead of a caret, put the cursor on the 5 and then press Delete or Backspace to remove the 3.

## Changing a block of text

If you want to change a block of text, you may be able to **select** it and type over it. The new text you type will probably replace the old text.

### Activity

See if you can select and type over text using your word processor. Type this text:

Easter is at the end of March

Select 'at the end of March' and type 'late in March or early in April'. What happens?

■■ *If you can't do this, your word processor may let you switch between inserting new text and typing over existing text. If so, you can choose an Overtype option and any new text you type will replace old text character for character.* ■■

### Activity

If your word processor lets you switch between inserting and overtyping, type this text with overtype turned on:

I usually go on holiday in June, but not always.

Put the caret before June and type July. What happens? Put the caret before July and type August. What happens now?

■■ *It is important to know whether your word processor starts up in overtype or insert mode – you can type over a lot of text you wanted to keep if you don't notice that it is set to overtype. Choose whichever option you find most convenient for your own work, but do glance at the screen when inserting text just to check that you haven't got it set to overtype.* ■■

### Glossary

**select** – mark a piece of text ready to do something with it. You can usually select text by dragging the pointer over it with the mouse button held down.

### Key points to remember

- You can use the Delete or Backspace key to remove characters.
- You can probably insert text just by positioning the caret and beginning to type.
- You may be able to replace text by selecting it and typing over it.
- You may need to switch between Insert and Overtype mode to control whether you can type over text to replace it.

### *Putting it into practice*

*You will be able to use the techniques you have learned to correct your work as you type. Next time you type a document into the word processor, make simple corrections as you go along.*

# Topic 1 – Word processors

## Checking your text

**IT 28**

Foundation/Intermediate/Advanced
Element **1.2,2.2,3.2**
Performance criteria **2**
Range **Software; Edit; Information**

You will often work from paper documents when using the word processor. It is important that you check the documents you create against the sources you use. This sheet explains

- how to check text on screen or printed out against original sources
- the type of mistakes you should look out for.

## Checking text

If you are working on a short document, you may not need to print it out to check it. For longer documents, many people prefer to check a printed copy. You may need a record of the changes you have made, in which case you will need to mark your changes on a paper copy before making them. If you are checking work on screen, make sure you display it at a scale that is comfortable to read. If you can't, print your document instead.

## Looking for mistakes

The type of mistakes you need to look for will vary to some extent according to the source materials you are working from and the type of documents you are producing. There are some types of mistakes you will always need to look out for.

### Key points to remember

- Check a document carefully against any source materials you have used.
- Check for errors in columns of figures and tables, and check any arithmetic in tables.
- Mark up your corrections clearly and check that you have made all corrections properly.

### *Putting it into practice*

*Print out the last document you created and check it against the source materials you used. Mark up any mistakes in the document, and then correct them. Check your corrections.*

### Activity

Which of these will you need to look out for? Tick the boxes beside any that are relevant to your work.

- Text is accurately copied from the draft. ☐
- Words are spelled correctly and the text is grammatically correct; make sure you have spelled any unfamiliar words or names as they are shown in the draft or sources. ☐
- Figures are correct. ☐
- Tables and columns are lined up correctly (it is particularly easy to make mistakes in tables if some slots are left blank). ☐
- The numbers in tables and formulae add up correctly (e.g., is the VAT correct on all prices?). ☐
- The layout of the page is as you were instructed, or is suitable for the material and effective for its purpose, and is consistent. ☐
- The date, names and addresses are correct. ☐
- You have used the right keys, without confusing zero and upper-case o, for example. ☐

### Hint

Most word processors have spelling checkers to help you avoid typing and spelling mistakes. Some also have grammar checkers.

## Marking up corrections

If you find any errors while checking your document on screen, you can make changes immediately. If you are checking a printed copy of your document, you will need to mark corrections to make later on the computer. This is called marking up your printed copy. There are many symbols that are commonly used to mark-up documents, but it doesn't matter whether you use these or your own way of marking up your work – the important thing is to make sure your mark-up is clear and can be understood by anyone else who may have to look at or type in your corrections.

### Activity

Check the text on the right against the text on the left and mark up any changes (on the right) that are needed to make it the same.

| Dear Gordon | Dear gordon |
|---|---|
| Further to your request for a reference for Ms Ahmed, please find enclosed an account of her work for me over the last three years. I found her a most satisfactory employee and can recommend her to you without reservation. | Furhter to your request for reference for Miss Ahmed, please find enclosed an acount ofher work with me over the last 3 years I found her a most satisfactery employe and can recommnend her without resevations. |

• 260 •

# Topic 1 – Word processors

## Cutting, copying and moving text

**IT 29**

Foundation/Intermediate/
Advanced
Element **1.2, 2.2, 3.2**
Performance criteria **2, 4**
Range **Software;
Information; Edit;
Reorganise**

You will sometimes want to make changes to your documents to delete, move or copy parts of the text. This sheet explains how to do this using the two common methods of moving and copying text:

- cut or copy and paste
- drag and drop.

Moving and copying blocks of text is one of the most useful features of a word processor. It can save you a lot of time. If you were working with a typewriter, you would have to retype material if you wanted to change its order.

## Cut and paste or drag and drop?

Most word processors let you mark or select a block of text and then copy or move it to somewhere else or remove it from your document and throw it away. Many let you do this using a 'clipboard' – you can store a chunk of text on the clipboard temporarily and then 'paste' it back into your document. This is called cut and paste. Some programs let you look at the material on the clipboard, but some don't. Some let you keep several bits of text on the clipboard at once and some allow only one. You will have to find out what your program does.

As well as or instead of cut and paste, some programs let you mark a block of text, pick it up with the mouse pointer and drag it to a new position. When you release the mouse button, the text is dropped into its new place. This is called drag and drop.

## Cutting text to delete it

When you want to remove text from your document, you will need to select the block of text and choose a Cut option from the menu. There may also be a Delete option. Usually, Cut removes the block of text from its current position and stores it on the clipboard so that you can paste it back in, but Delete throws the text away – you can't get it back.

## Moving text

If you want to move text from one place to another in your document, you probably need to:

1. select the block of text
2. choose a Cut option, so that it is removed from the document and stored on the clipboard
3. move the caret to the new position for the start of the block of text
4. choose a Paste option to put the block of text into the document at the new position.

Instead, you may be able to select the block and then drag it to a new position. Some word processors don't let you drag a block off the current page.

### Activity

Load a document that you have already typed into your word processor. Using cut and paste or drag and drop, move the paragraphs around so that they are in a different order. Take care to keep the spacing between the paragraphs the same, and not to run one paragraph into another.

## Copying text

To copy a block of text, you probably need to select the block of text, use Copy to copy it onto the clipboard, position the caret and then use Paste to put the block back into the document. You may be able to use drag and drop instead; you will probably have to hold down a key to tell the computer you want to copy the text rather than move it.

### Activity

Using the document you have loaded, copy the first paragraph to the end; the paragraph should appear in both positions.

### Key points to remember

- You may be able to use cut and paste or drag and drop to move or copy text within a document.
- If you cut or copy text, it is stored on a clipboard and you can paste it back into a document.
- If you delete text it is usually thrown away.

### *Putting it into practice*

*Type your CV and then experiment with moving the different bits of material around until you are happy with the arrangement.*

## Topic 1 – Word processors

### Moving and copying text between documents

**IT 30**

Foundation/Intermediate/Advanced
Element **1.2,2.2,3.2**
Performance criteria **2,4,6**
Range **Software; Information; Edit; Reorganise; Combine**

In many organisations and business settings, people need to create similar documents again and again. To avoid wasting time retyping the same or similar material, you can copy chunks of text between documents. This sheet helps you to decide when you may need to do this and to find out how to do it using your word processor.

### Why copy text between documents?

There are many situations in which you may want to copy or move material between documents. For example:

- You have written a letter to someone, and want to tell someone else the same news; you can copy part or all of the first letter and make any small changes you want.
- You are preparing a report that contains standard paragraphs used in other reports, such as whom to address comments to, or information about confidentiality.
- You have made notes for a presentation, and want to copy or move some material into your final document.
- You have laid out a table of figures in a financial report and want to copy it into a memo to someone.
- You have decided to split a document up, and want to move parts of it to a new document.

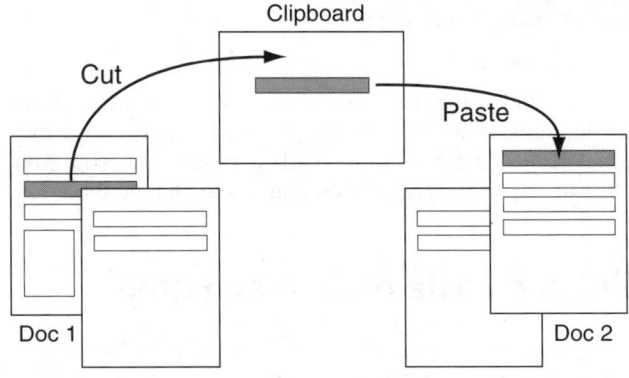

### Activity

When do you think it would be useful for you to copy or move text between documents?

### Using cut and paste to copy or move text between documents

Most word processors let you cut or copy text to a clipboard and then paste it into a different document. If you can do this, you will need to:

1. open the document containing the text you want to copy or move
2. select the appropriate block of text
3. use Cut or Copy to put a copy of the text onto the clipboard
4. open the document you want to put the text in
5. position the caret where you want the text to start
6. use Paste to insert the text into the document.

Depending on the type of computer and word processor you are using, you may have to close one document before you can open the other, or move or minimise its window and choose to view the second document.

### Activity

Load a document you have already typed into your word processor. Select a paragraph and copy it to the clipboard. Now open a new document and paste the paragraph in. Return to the first document and cut a paragraph. It will be stored on the clipboard. Close this document without saving it. Now return to your new document, put the caret after the paragraph you have just added and paste in the text from the clipboard. Tidy up any extra or missing blank lines as necessary.

### Using drag and drop to copy or move text between documents

You may be able to have two documents open side by side and drag a selected block of text from one to another. Only a few programs let you do this. If you can do it, moving and copying text between documents is quick and easy.

### Key points to remember

- You may be able to save yourself time and effort by copying material between documents rather than retyping it.
- You can probably use cut and paste to move or copy material between documents; you may be able to use drag and drop.

### *Putting it into practice*

*Build up one or more documents of material you use frequently. For example, you might include standard paragraphs that you put into a lot of letters. When you need to use one of your pieces of text, copy it into your new document.*

# Topic 1 – Word processors

## Moving around a short document

**IT 31**

Foundation
Element **1.2**
Performance criteria **2,4**
Range **Software; Edit**

When you first begin work on a new document you will start typing and the caret will move forward through the document as you go. However, you will soon need to move around the document because

- you may need to change bits of it
- you may want to check what you have typed already
- you may want to copy or move chunks of text.

You will then need to be able to move around, displaying and working on different areas of the document. This sheet explains how to move the caret around a document.

## Moving the caret

If you spot a mistake in something you have just typed, or want to add something else, you may need to move the **caret** to a different area of the text you can see on screen. Most computers have **cursor keys** which let you move the caret left, right, up and down. If you are using a mouse, you can move the pointer and then click to position the caret.

### Activity

If your computer has a block of cursor keys to the right of the Return or Enter key, experiment with these. Move the caret up, down, left and right. What happens if you keep one of the cursor keys held down? What happens if you move the caret outside the visible area of text?

■ *If you keep a key pressed down, the caret probably continues to move. If you move the caret out of the area of text shown on screen, the text probably scrolls – moves up or down so that you can still see the caret.* ■

### Activity

You may be able to move the caret to the end of the current word or line by pressing a combination of keys. Find out what you can do. You may need to use the manual or on-line help to find out, or ask someone else.

There are some other keys that let you move around the document. Your computer may have any of these:

**Home**
Move to the start of the document
**End**
Move to the end of the document
**PageUp**
Move up one screenful of text, or to the previous page
**PageDown**
Move down one screenful of text, or to the next page
**Next**
Move to the next page
**Previous**
Move to the previous page

Make sure you know how to use these keys.

## Scrolling

If your word processor runs in a window, you can also move around the document using the scroll bars or scroll arrows.

### Activity

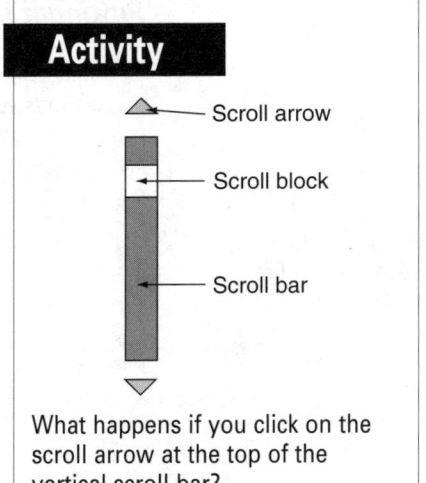

What happens if you click on the scroll arrow at the top of the vertical scroll bar?

What happens if you click in the scroll bar, but not over the solid block?

What happens if you drag the block in the scroll bar?

■ *If you click on the scroll arrows, the document moves through the window in small steps – probably a line at a time. If you click in the scroll bar, the document moves through the window one screenful at a time, so you can see the text immediately before or after that which you have been looking at. If you drag the block in the scroll bar, you can move further through the document. The position of the block in the scroll bar represents your position in the document.* ■

### Glossary
**caret** – marker like an I which shows where the text you type will appear.

### Glossary
**cursor keys** – keys marked with arrows, usually to the right of the typewriter keys. Pressing a cursor key moves the caret in the direction of the arrow on the key.

### Key points to remember

- You can move through a document using the cursor keys or other keys to move the caret.
- You can use the scroll bars and arrows to move your document through the window.

### Putting it into practice

*Whenever you need to type or change a document, you can move the caret around using the techniques you have learned.*

# Topic 1 – Word processors

## Moving around a long document

**IT 32**

*Foundation*
Element **1.2**
Performance criteria **2,4**
Range **Software; Edit; Information**

If you are using a long document, you will find it slow to move around it by using the scroll bars and scroll arrows. It will take a lot of trial and error to find the part of the document you want.

You may want to move around a long document when you are making changes and corrections, when you want to look at part of a document to find out something, or because you want to find parts of it to copy into another document. This sheet explains how to move around a long document more efficiently by

- specifying a page number
- finding text
- pressing a key on the keyboard.

## Moving around by specifying a page number

If your document is more than a few pages long, you will find it useful to be able to specify the page you want to display. Your word processor will have a menu option to let you do this. It may be called Goto page or just Goto. You will find this most useful when you are making changes to a document, working from a paper copy marked up with corrections. If you print page numbers on your document, even when printing a draft copy, you will find it helpful to be able to move around the document on screen using the Goto option.

Many word processors also offer menu options to move to the last or first page of a document, or to display the next or previous page.

### Activity

Find out what Goto page options your word processor offers and tick the boxes below for options that it has.

| | |
|---|---|
| Go to a page specified by number | ☐ |
| Go to the page displayed last | ☐ |
| Move forward a specified number of pages | ☐ |
| Move backward a specified number of pages | ☐ |
| Go to the next page | ☐ |
| Go to the previous page | ☐ |
| Go to the last page | ☐ |
| Go to the first page. | ☐ |

Some word processors offer further options within Goto, allowing you to choose a section, chapter, footnote, reference or other feature of the document.

## Moving around a document by finding text

If you want to find a particular reference in a document, you may be able to use the Find or Search option to move to it. For example, if you know your report contains a section called 'Housing and poverty', you can search for this text.

## Keys on the keyboard to help you move around

You can use the cursor keys and some other keys to move around a document. With a long document, you may want to use Home to move to the very beginning of the document, or End to move right to the end of it.

### Activity

Load a long document and try out the Home and End keys. If you haven't already tried all the keys described in 'Moving around a short document', look at that sheet next and try them out.

### Key points to remember

- It is inefficient to move around a long document using just the scroll bar and scroll arrows.
- Your word processor will have a Goto option; you may be able to specify more than just a page number.
- You can use the Find option to move around the document.

### *Putting it into practice*

*Next time you have to work on an existing document, use the methods you have learned about on this sheet to help you move around the document quickly and efficiently instead of just using the scroll bars and scroll arrows.*

# Topic 1 – Word processors

## Arranging blocks and tables

**IT 33**

Foundation/Intermediate/Advanced
Element **1.2,2.2,3.2**
Performance criteria **2**
Range **Software; Edit**

You will often find that you need to arrange some blocks of text in a special way. You may have to include columns of figures, tables and other material that you want to set apart from the main body of your text. This sheet explains how to

- indent blocks of text (set them in from the margins)
- arrange figures in columns and tables.

## Indenting text

Usually, your text will be spaced between the margins set up for your page. However, you may sometimes want to make some blocks of text stand out by giving them a different position. You may want to indent quotations, for example:

> This paragraph has been indented. It doesn't extend to the same left or right margins as the rest of the text on this sheet. You can immediately see that there is something different about this bit of text.

Different word processors have different ways of letting you set indents; most use some form of ruler – a device to let you specify where you want text to start and end and where to put tab positions (see below). You can probably set positions for

- where the first line in a paragraph will start
- where all the other lines in a paragraph will start
- where text will end at the right of the page.

You may want to use any of the following combinations of indents:

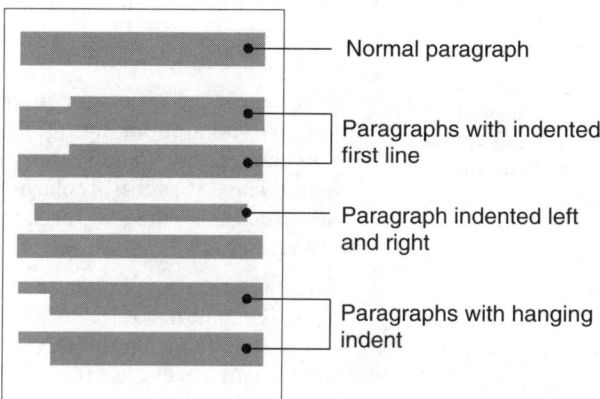

- Normal paragraph
- Paragraphs with indented first line
- Paragraph indented left and right
- Paragraphs with hanging indent

- indent the first line of each paragraph: this gives the layout familiar from traditionally designed books, with the first line of each paragraph starting further in from the edge of the page than the other lines
- indent all lines to the left and right to give an indented block like that shown above
- indent all except the first line of a paragraph. This is called a hanging indent. If you set a tab at the same position as the start of the following lines, you can align lists like this one. There is more about tabs below.

### Activity

Find out how to indent the first line of a paragraph, and how to create a paragraph indented from the left and right, and how to create a hanging indent. Make notes for yourself on what you had to do.

## Columns and tables

Your word processor will let you set tab positions to help you line up columns of text and figures and create tables. A tab position is a marker for aligning text. When you press the Tab key, the caret will move to the next tab position and line up your text with it. You should use tabs and not spaces to line up text in columns. Most word processors offer these types of tab:

- a left tab lines up the start of the text at the tab position
- a centre tab centres the text around the tab position
- a right tab lines up the end of the text with the tab position
- a decimal tab lines up the decimal point (.) in a number at the tab position (or the end of the text if there is no point).

### Activity

Using your word processor copy the following table, which illustrates the different types of tab.

| Left tab | Centre tab | Right tab | Decimal tab. |
|---|---|---|---|
| Red | Red | Red | 45.67 |
| Orange | Orange | Orange | 123456.00 |
| Blue | Blue | Blue | 1.23 |

### Key points to remember

- You can indent text to alter its position between the margins.
- Use tabs to line up text in tables or with a hanging indent to arrange lists – don't use spaces.

### Putting it into practice

*Using tabs to line up the text, create a timetable of your activities for a typical week.*

# Topic 1 – Word processors

## Finding and replacing text

**IT 34**

Foundation/Intermediate/
Advanced
Element **1.2,2.2,3.2**
Performance criteria **1,2,4,6**
Range **Find; Software; Edit; Reorganise; Information; Combine**

Imagine you have just typed a long report about a visit to a local employer. When you have finished, you suddenly realise you have spelled the name of the company wrongly. How can you correct it? You could read through the whole document looking for the name and changing it each time you spot it, but this would take a long time and you might miss some. Your word processor has a special Find or Search option to help you find bits of text in your document and change them if you want to.

## Finding text

You might need to find bits of text for several reasons. For example:

- You want to find out about a particular person's contribution to a project. You can use Find to move from one mention of the person's name to another.
- You want to check the prices in a document. You can use Find to look for anything that begins with the character £.
- You want to remove cross-references in brackets in the text and put them as numbered notes at the end of the document. You can use Find to look for all uses of the character [.

> **Hint**
> A case-sensitive search for 'Times' finds only 'Times'. A case-insensitive search also finds 'times', 'timeS', 'tiMeS', and any other combination.

You can search for anything from a single letter to several words. You can probably use an option to make the search case sensitive. This means the text will be found only if it uses the same mix of upper- and lower-case letters as you have typed in the Find dialog box. Find and Replace may be listed as separate options in the menu, or there may be a single option. If your program has a single option, there will be two spaces in the dialog box: one for you to type the text you want to look for, and one for the text you want to replace it with. If you want just to find text and not change it, type the same text in both spaces. This prevents you accidentally replacing your found text with nothing and so deleting it.

### Activity

Load a document you have already typed. Use the Find option to search for the word 'and'. When the text is found, you will probably be offered some options, including 'Find the next use of the text' and 'Cancel the search'. If your program has only one option for Find and Replace, there will also be options to replace the text; ignore these for now. Experiment with the Find options until you are sure you know what your program can do.

## Replacing text

Sometimes you may want to change the text you are searching for; in the situation mentioned at the start of this sheet you would need to replace the misspelled name with the correct spelling. You can do this using a Replace option. This time, you will need to type the text you want to search for and the text you want to replace it with. For example, if you had typed Glasman Corporation in place of Glassman Corporation, you could search for Glasman and change it to Glassman.

You can probably specify that the text matches the case used in the document (so if the found text starts with a capital, so will its replacement).

> **Hint**
> If you use a Match case option to replace glasman with glassman, 'Glasman' is replaced with 'Glassman' and 'GLASMAN' with 'GLASSMAN'.

### Activity

Using your document again, choose the Replace option to search for 'and' and change it to '&'. Look at the options offered on the Replace dialog box. You can probably choose to replace all instances of the text, but leave this for now. When the text has been found, you can probably choose to replace it, leave it and move on to the next instance, cancel the search or replace all instances of the found text without further warning. Experiment, but don't use a 'Replace all' option at the moment. Close your document without saving it.

### Key points to remember

- You can find text and make no change to it, or find text and replace it with different text.
- When the word processor finds the text you are looking for, you can replace it and search again, leave it as it is, replace all instances of the text, or stop searching.
- You can make a search case sensitive, and make replacements match the mix of upper- and lower-case used in the text you have found.

### Putting it into practice

*You will probably find opportunities to use the Find and Replace options as you work on existing documents. Remember that you can use Find or Replace to help you check your work, move around documents and make changes.*

# Topic 1 – Word processors

## More about finding and replacing text

**IT 35**

Foundation/Intermediate/Advanced
Element **2.1,2.2,3.2**
Performance criteria **1,2,4,6**
Range **Find; Software; Edit; Reorganise; Information; Combine information**

Many word processors offer quite sophisticated find-and-replace facilities. If you know how to use these, you can often save yourself time and effort, working more efficiently and effectively. This sheet helps you to find out how to

- use an option to replace all instances of a piece of text without making mistakes
- restrict a search to part of your document.

## Being careful

You have probably already discovered that your word processor offers an option to replace all instances of a piece of text without asking you to confirm each change. It may be called 'Replace all'. This is a global replace operation. Although it can save time, you should use it with care.

> 'I had typed a report for my supervisor and when she checked it she decided that she didn't want the new product referred to as AS2 (its original code name), but as PT2, which would be its commercial name. I did a global replace of 'as' to 'pt', telling the word processor to match the case. Of course, it changed 'as' to 'pt', 'has' to 'hpt' and every other word with 'as' in it to have 'pt' in it! I panicked, and did another global replace of 'pt' to 'as', but then all the words that should have 'pt' in them changed to have 'as' as well – like 'astion' for 'option'. So I was no better off. It took me ages to fix it.'
>
> Kevin, Quality assurance officer

### Activity

Load a document you already have into your word processor. Use 'Replace all' to change 'he' to 'she' without checking each change. What has happened to your document? Close it without saving it.

■■ *You will find that all instances of the characters 'he' in your document have been changed to 'she', making nonsense of the text by changing 'the' to 'tshe', for example. It is very difficult to restore your document to its proper state. To avoid making a mess of your documents like this, be very careful when using a global replace option. Make sure the sequence of characters you are searching for will appear only in the context in which you want to change them. For example, if you change 'man' to 'woman' you will also change 'demand' to 'dewomand'.* ■■

You can

- put spaces either side of the word you want to change, if it is a whole word (e.g., find ' man ') you will miss instances of the word that are followed by a punctuation mark and will have to look for these separately
- make the search case sensitive if the word you want to change always starts with or includes any upper-case letters. A case-sensitive search will only find instances of the text that match the combination of upper- and lower-case letters you have used in the dialog box – so a case-sensitive search for 'May' won't find 'may'
- use an option to match whole words only, if your word processor offers this
- check each change rather than using a 'Replace all' option.

You should always replace the first few instances of text you are searching for individually and check them before using a global replace option, unless you can be very sure that the search won't pick up text you don't want to change.

Even if you search carefully, you will still need to check your work thoroughly afterwards. Your find-and-replace operation will miss words that have a different form (a search for 'man' won't find 'men', for example) and there may be text that you also need to alter around the changed words; you will need to change 'he' to 'she', 'his' to 'hers' and so on if you change 'man' to 'woman'.

## Speeding up a search for text

If you search through a long document, it may take some time. You may be able to restrict a search to speed it up if you know that you want to find or replace text in only one part of the document.

### Activity

Which of the following options does your word processor offer to let you restrict a find-and-replace operation?

- Set a page range (e.g., search pages 20–35).
- Search only forwards from the position of the caret.
- Search only backwards from the position of the caret.
- Stop searching at the end of the document (if your word processor otherwise continues the search from the start of the document).

# Topic 1 – Word processors

## More about finding and replacing text (continued)

### Key points to remember

- You need to be very careful when using a global replace option that you don't change bits of text you didn't intend to change – it may be very hard to reverse.
- You may be able to restrict a search to a page range or in some other way to speed it up.

### *Putting it into practice*

*Next time you have to make changes to a document, see if you can use any of the more advanced find-and-replace techniques described in this sheet to help you.*

# Topic 2 – Spreadsheets

## Changing cell contents

**IT 38**

Foundation/Intermediate/Advanced
Element **1.2,2.2,3.2**
Performance criteria **1,2,3,5**
Range **Find information; Software; Edit; Make calculations; Appropriate intervals**

Before making any changes to the contents of a cell you must first find it. In a small spreadsheet this is easy, you can move around a spreadsheet using the arrow keys until you reach the cell you want. With a large spreadsheet, moving around one cell at a time can take too long. To solve this problem each spreadsheet program lets you to go straight to any cell in the sheet.

### Activity

Find out how to go directly to any cell using your spreadsheet program. Load the program and use this shortcut to move the cursor straight to cell Z99. Move the cursor back to cell A1.

■■ *If you had any problems with this activity spend a bit more time using the Go To shortcut to move around the spreadsheet.* ■■

Before you make changes to a spreadsheet you should always check that:

1. You are working on the right sheet – if you are working on a spreadsheet that is filled in every week, each sheet will look alike and it is easy to make changes to the wrong one. Always check that you are in the correct sheet before you make any changes.

2. You are changing the right cell – use the row and column headings to help you to check that you are making the change to the proper cell.

Once you have moved to the cell you want to change, you can

- enter completely new contents by typing what you want and pressing the Return key; you should do this if you want to completely replace one item with another
- **blank** the contents of the cell altogether; you would do this if you have placed an entry in the wrong cell but do not want to replace it with anything else.

### Glossary
**blank** – when you blank a cell in a spreadsheet you take away the contents of that cell. Most spreadsheets have a special command to let you do this.

### Activity

This is a set of figures that look at the spending budget of a small business. Enter the details into a spreadsheet (make sure you use a formula to calculate the totals).

|   | A | B | C | D | E | F |
|---|---|---|---|---|---|---|
| 1 | BUDGET | | | | | |
| 2 | | Jan | Feb | Mar | Apr | Totals |
| 3 | | £ | £ | £ | £ | £ |
| 4 | Phone | | | 70 | | 70 |
| 5 | Electric | | 50 | | | 50 |
| 6 | Rent | 200 | 200 | 200 | 200 | 800 |
| 7 | Postage | 30 | 30 | 30 | 30 | 120 |
| 8 | Sundries | 15 | 15 | 15 | 15 | 60 |
| 9 | Totals | 245 | 295 | 315 | 245 | |
| 10 | **Overall total** | **1100** | | | | |

Make the following changes:

1. The figure for electric has been wrongly entered and should be changed to 40.
2. The phone bill is due in April, not March, and should be moved.
3. Only £10 per month is to be spent on sundries.
4. A mail-out is to be done in March and the postage figure will be increased to 60 for that month.

■■ *Your spreadsheet should now look like this:*

|   | A | B | C | D | E | F |
|---|---|---|---|---|---|---|
| 1 | BUDGET | | | | | |
| 2 | | Jan | Feb | Mar | Apr | Totals |
| 3 | | £ | £ | £ | £ | £ |
| 4 | Phone | | | | 70 | 70 |
| 5 | Electric | | 40 | | | 40 |
| 6 | Rent | 200 | 200 | 200 | 200 | 800 |
| 7 | Postage | 30 | 30 | 60 | 30 | 150 |
| 8 | Sundries | 10 | 10 | 10 | 10 | 40 |
| 9 | Totals | 240 | 280 | 270 | 310 | |
| 10 | **Overall total** | **1100** | | | | |

# Topic 2 – Spreadsheets

## Changing cell contents (continued)

▮▮ *Items 1, 3 and 4 meant making changes to entries. Item 2 was slightly trickier as the entry in cell D4 had to be blanked and re-entered into E4. Notice that although a number of changes have been made to the file, the overall total has stayed the same.* ▮▮

Because figures in spreadsheets are easy to change and the updating of totals is automatic, they are often used to look at what would happen if things changed in the future. Before you start to experiment with figures in a spreadsheet you should make a back-up copy of the file.

### Activity

Using the spreadsheet you created in the previous activity, answer the following questions.

1. If the rent increased to £205 a month from March onwards and the telephone bill was likely to be £80 instead of £70, what totals would be affected, and by how much would the overall total increase?

2. If the changes above are made, by what amount would spending on postage need to be brought down so that the overall total stays at £1100?

3. Working on the original figures (by re-loading the back-up copy of the file), what totals will be affected if £30 less is spent on postage in March and this amount is spent instead on sundries in April?

▮▮

1. *The increase of £205 in the rent would affect the monthly totals for March and April, increasing both by £5. The total for rent would be increased by £10. The telephone bill increase would also affect the March total, increasing it by a further £10, while the total of the Phone row would also increase by £10. The overall total would increase by £20 to £1120 as a result of these changes.*

2. *If the reduction in spending on postage is spread over all four months, the amount per month needs to go down by £5 to make sure that the overall amount spent does not exceed £1100.*

3. *This change will affect both the March and April totals. It will also affect the totals of the amounts spent on both postage and sundries. The overall total, however, will stay the same.* ▮▮

### Key points to remember

- Spreadsheets let you to move straight to any cell in the sheet.
- Contents of cells can be changed or blanked altogether.
- Spreadsheets can be used to experiment with figures and find out what will happen if things change in the future.

### *Putting it into practice*

- Using a back-up copy of your personal budget spreadsheet file, see what effect changes in your spending will make to your personal finances.
- What would happen if your travel costs doubled?

# Topic 2 – Spreadsheets

## Adding and deleting rows and columns

**IT 39**

Foundation/Intermediate/
Advanced
Element **1.2,2.2,3.2**
Performance criteria **2,3,4**
Range **Software; Edit;
Make calculations;
Reorganise; Information**

As spreadsheets grow and change you may find that you need to add or delete rows or columns. You may also need to create space for new items or **delete** old ones that may no longer be needed. All spreadsheet programs allow you to add or delete rows or columns. However, like all big changes, these additions and deletions should be done with care. Always make a back-up copy of the file before you start making changes.

> **Glossary**
> **delete** – when you delete a row or column it is removed from the spreadsheet altogether and the other rows or columns move up or across to close the gap.

Below is part of a spreadsheet that has been set up to store details of a petty cash system. As **petty cash vouchers** are returned, the money is paid and the voucher details entered in the spreadsheet. As vouchers can contain more than one item, there is a column that calculates the total of each voucher. There is also a row containing the totals of each item of expenditure.

> **Glossary**
> **petty cash voucher** – these are numbered pieces of paper that allow people to buy items for a business. They are used for things that are regularly needed such as stamps, stationery, petrol and cleaning materials.

| Month: | January | | | | | | |
|---|---|---|---|---|---|---|---|
| Voucher | Date | Stationery | Petrol | Postage | Cleaning | Refresh. | Totals |
| 0451 | 1 | 2.68 | | 3.45 | | | 6.13 |
| 0453 | 1 | | 10.75 | | | | 10.75 |
| 0454 | 4 | | | | | 6.87 | 6.87 |
| 0455 | 5 | | | 2.97 | | | 2.97 |
| 0456 | 5 | | | | 1.99 | | 1.99 |
| Totals | | 2.68 | 10.75 | 6.42 | 1.99 | 6.87 | |

### Activity

Can you think of a time when you might want to

1. add a new row to this spreadsheet
2. add a new column to this spreadsheet?

■■

1. As details of each new voucher are entered, a new row will need to be added to hold them.
2. If an extra item of expenditure is added to the sheet, a new column will have to be created. ■■

When you add rows or columns, you should check to make sure that any formulae affected are changed if necessary. Because rows are added above the cursor, when you want to add a row, you should place the cursor in the row beneath the one you want to

### Activity

Set up the spreadsheet above and then add a new row between the last voucher number and the totals so that you can enter this information:

Voucher No. – 0457,
Date – 6,
Stationery – 5.93.

Enter the formula to calculate the total for that voucher number.

Will you need to make any other changes if you add this row?

■■ As the new row falls outside the original range used in the formulae to total each category of expenditure (such as stationery and petrol), it is not taken into account when these are calculated. Each of these formulae will have to be changed to take the new row into account.

If the row had been added in the middle of a range of cells (for example between vouchers 0451 and 0453) the formula would have been automatically adjusted to take account of it and no changes to formulae would have been necessary. ■■

Columns are added to the left of the cursor, so when adding a new column you should position your cursor to the right of the column you want to insert.

### Activity

Add a new column between Refresh. and Totals to hold entries for Sundries. Enter the formula to calculate the total for that category.

Does this affect any other cells?

■■ This column falls outside the original range of the formula used to calculate each voucher number. Each voucher number formula will have to be re-entered to take the new row into account. ■■

When you make changes to spreadsheets, the master spreadsheet should also be changed if necessary. A new petty cash sheet will be used each month, so permanent changes, such as the adding of a new column, should also be made to the master sheet so that they are there for the following month and do not have to be done again.

# Topic 2 – Spreadsheets

## Adding and deleting rows and columns (continued)

### Activity

When might you want to
1. delete a row in the petty cash spreadsheet
2. delete a column in the petty cash spreadsheet?

▋▋

*1 If details of a voucher are entered twice by mistake one of the rows will have to be deleted.*

*2 If an item of expenditure is no longer to be paid from petty cash the column with this item will have to be deleted.* ▋▋

When entries are blanked, the contents of the cell are deleted but the cell itself remains. When a row or column is deleted, however, it disappears completely from the spreadsheet. In the case of a row, the entries below it are moved up and renumbered. With a column, entries to the right of it are moved left and given new letters. It will be as if the row or column had never existed.

### Activity

As the company has now decided to get an account with a local garage and pay petrol bills monthly by cheque, the petrol column is no longer needed and should be deleted. What steps should you take before you delete this column from the spreadsheet?

*Before you delete any data you should*

- *make sure you have a back-up copy of the file in case of mistakes*
- *check that you are not deleting any data that may be of use later.*

*In this case the column would be deleted only from the master spreadsheet after the date on which petrol payments stopped being paid through petty cash. The change would not be made to any files that had entries in the petrol column.* ▋▋

### Activity

In the petty cash spreadsheet the entry for voucher number 0451 was wrong. It should have been entered into the previous month's sheet. Delete this row from the spreadsheet. Will you have to make changes to any formulae?

▋▋ *As this row has cells referred to in a formula, some spreadsheet programs will show an error message when it is deleted. To solve this problem you will need to re-enter each formula that has been affected by the deletion.* ▋▋

### Key points to remember

- You can add rows and columns to a spreadsheet and delete them.
- You should always check to see if any formulae need to be changed.
- Master spreadsheets should also be changed if permanent changes are made.

### *Putting it into practice*

- In the petty cash spreadsheet, if you deleted columns C and D, in what column would postage now be?
- If you were to go on to add a new column C, in what column would postage be then?

• 272 •

# Topic 3 – Databases

## Making changes

**IT 42**

Foundation/Intermediate/Advanced
Element **1.2, 2.2, 3.2**
Performance criteria **1, 2, 4, 5**
Range **Find information; Software; Edit; Reorganise; Appropriate intervals**

Once you have typed records into a database you then need to keep them up to date.

### Activity

Think of three times when you need to change a database that stores employees' details.

■ *You could have chosen any of the following:*

- *if employees move, their addresses would need to be changed*
- *if an employee's rate of pay changes, their record would need to be brought up to date*
- *when mistakes have been made they need to be corrected*
- *when a new employee is hired, a new record will need to be added to the database*
- *when an old employee leaves, their record will have to be taken off the database.* ■

Every database has a different way of making these changes. The information below should help when you come to make changes to a file in the database program you are using.

You should make sure that:

- *You have found the right record.* Before you make any changes to a record you should double check to make sure you have the right one. If you put some goods sold in the account of the wrong customer, that customer would get very angry when they receive a bill for the wrong amount.
- *The changes you make match the rest of the file.* If you have not used the database before, you should look at other records to make sure that you know how that field has been entered before (whether to use all capitals or a mixture of capitals and small letters). If you are using the information from the database to make up a report it will look much better if all the information is printed out in the same style.
- *You have a way of working out which changes have been made and which have not.* If many changes are to be made, or more than one person is working with the same database, it is important that each person should know which changes have already been done so that none are missed out or done twice. If, for example, you have been asked to change an employee's address and the change is not made that person might not get their wages.
- *Make sure that no-one sees private information who is not supposed to.* Don't walk away from the computer and leave it so that anyone can look at your work. You could get into a lot of trouble with your employer if someone's personal information gets into the wrong hands.

### Activity

You have been given a lot of changes to make to a database you have never used before, more than can be done at one time. How would you make sure that your work matches the rest of the file and how would you keep track of the changes you have made?

■ *Before making any alterations to the file you should look at how the other records have been entered. Notice which fields are entered all in capitals and which in a mixture of capitals and small letters.*

*To keep track of the changes you have made to a file, sheets containing information that has already been typed should be marked in some way and kept apart. You should try to avoid stopping typing in the middle of a sheet but if you have to, make a clear mark showing where you should start next time.* ■

Before you make changes to a database file, you should always make a back-up copy of it on another disk. If the worst happens and you lose the file, you will always have a recent copy to fall back on.

### Key points to remember

- When making changes to a database you should be careful to note which changes you have made to avoid missing them out or doing them twice.
- You should make a copy of your file every time you alter it.

### Putting it into practice

- *Practise making changes on a database file you are using.*
- *Keep a log of your work, writing down the date, how many records you altered and whether you made a back-up copy of the file.*

## Topic 3 – Databases

### Finding a record

Foundation/Intermediate/Advanced
Element **1.2,2.2,3.2**
Performance criteria **1**
Range **Find; Information**

Before you can begin to **edit** a record in a database you need to find it. You can find a record either by knowing its record number or by knowing what is in one of its fields.

*Glossary*
**to edit** – to make changes

#### Finding a record by record number

When you put records into a database, the computer gives each one a record number. The first record you enter is given the record number 1, the second 2 and so on. If you know the record number, a database program will let you go straight to any record in the file.

**Activity**

Can you think of an advantage and a disadvantage of finding records by record number?

▌▌ *An advantage of using a record number is that you will always find the record you want as long as you've got the right number. No two records have the same record number.*

*A disadvantage is that you won't always know the record number of the record you are looking for. If, for example, you want to find an item of* **stock** *in a file that has 100 records, you are much more likely to know the name of the item than you are to know the record number.* ▌▌

*Glossary*
**stock** – goods that a business holds in store

#### Finding a record by what is in one of the fields

You can find a record in a database if you know what is in one of the fields. Every database program will do this differently, but they will all ask for the name of the field that is to be searched and what you are looking for in that field. For example, if you wanted to find someone with the surname Jones in a database file of customers, you would search the SURNAME field for the name 'Jones'.

**Activity**

Can you think of a problem with this way of finding a record?

▌▌ *The problem with this way of finding a record is that it is not as exact as searching by record number. It is possible for two or more entries to be the same. You must be sure, before you make any changes, that you have the right record.* ▌▌

Sometimes it is easier to find the entry you want if you sort the file in order of the field that you are searching. If, for example, you wanted to search a file for someone with the surname Jones, you would sort the file in order of the SURNAME field. It is easy then to look through any matching names and pick out the record you want.

### Key points to remember

- When searching for a record you can use either the record number or the contents of one of the fields.
- It is important to check that the correct record has been found before alterations are made.

### Putting it into practice

- Practise finding records in a database you are using.
- Time how long it takes you to find each one and check to see if you are getting any quicker.

# Topic 3 – Databases

## Sorting the database

**IT 44**

Foundation/Intermediate/Advanced
Element **1.2,2.2,3.2**
Performance criteria **4**
Range **Reorganise; Information**

*Glossary*
**sorted** – rearranged in order

Many jobs done with databases are made easier if the data is **sorted** in order. Data is sorted in three main ways.

## 1 Sorting alphabetically on a character field

This can be in ascending order (starting with A and ending with Z) or descending order (starting at Z and ending with A). An alphabetic sort will be used to sort any character field, even if the characters are not letters (for example, a telephone number that is made up of numbers, brackets and spaces).

### Activity

Write down the order in which you think these code numbers would be put by an ascending alphabetic sort.

a  4546W
b  99T
c  1239X
d  242X

▇ *The order you should have chosen is c, d, a, b. An alphabetic sort does not look at how big a number is. It will look at the left hand number first. If these are the same it will go on to look at the number to the right and so on. This means that 1239X comes before 242X because the left-hand number is lower.* ▇

To sort the codes above in order with the lowest numbers first, they should have been entered with extra zeros. This means that 99X becomes 0099X, 242X becomes 0242X and 1239X remains the same.

## 2 Sorting by number on a numeric field

Numbers can also be sorted in ascending order (starting with the lowest number and going up) or descending order (starting with the highest number and going down).

### Activity

In the following lists, to put the best first, would you use an ascending or descending numeric sort?

1  Salesmen in order of the value of goods they have sold.
2  Students in order of the position they gained in an exam.
3  Employees' hourly rates of pay.

▇ *In number 1 and number 3, best is biggest so these should be sorted in descending order. In number 2, the position of the student who did best is 1 and the rest follow in ascending order.* ▇

## 3 Sorting by date on a date field

Dates can be sorted in ascending order with the oldest date first and the most recent last or descending order with the most recent date first and the oldest last.

### Hint

A date sort will work only if dates have been put into a proper date field. If they have been put into a character field they will be sorted alphabetically.

Sometimes you need to sort a file on more than one field. When you do this, the first sort is done before the second. For example, if you were to sort a file on town and then surname, the town name would be sorted first and for each town, surnames would then be put into order. For example

This list would be rearranged

| MANCHESTER | BROWN    |
| BIRMINGHAM | JOHNSTON |
| BIRMINGHAM | ADAMS    |
| MANCHESTER | THOMPSON |
| MANCHESTER | PETERS   |
| BIRMINGHAM | CARSON   |

like this

| BIRMINGHAM | ADAMS    |
| BIRMINGHAM | CARSON   |
| BIRMINGHAM | JOHNSTON |
| MACHESTER  | BROWN    |
| MANCHESTER | PETERS   |
| MANCHESTER | THOMPSON |

### Activity

Imagine that you are working with a database that holds the details of the stock held by a business. One of the fields in the file holds the name of the item of stock and another holds the size of the item. Why would you want to sort the file on both these fields?

▇ *It would be useful to have a list of all the stock items in alphabetical order. Within this list it would also be useful to have the size of each item, in order. To do this you would need to sort the file on the field which stores the name of the item of stock, followed by the field that stores its size.* ▇

# Topic 3 – Databases

## Sorting the database (continued)

### Activity

This information has been put into a database:

| No. | Author | Title | Publisher | Year |
|---|---|---|---|---|
| 1. | Rodgers P | The New Lectures | Target | 1993 |
| 2. | Myers, R | More Conundrums | Target | 1986 |
| 3. | Arbroath, K | Travelling About | Signature | 1974 |
| 4. | Singh, V | Indian Ragas | Arrow | 1992 |
| 5. | Rodgers, P | Strung Along | Target | 1988 |
| 6. | Pike, L | Tramlines | Signature | 1981 |
| 7. | Soames, T | Devil's Advocate | Arrow | 1989 |
| 8. | Rodgers, P | Lectures | Arrow | 1973 |
| 9. | Young, F | Stable Arrangements | Quicksilver | 1993 |
| 10. | Ali, A | Time and Tide | Signature | 1991 |
| 11. | Rodgers, P | Songs for String | Target | 1984 |
| 12. | Hill, S | Smart Training | Quicksilver | 1994 |

Write down the new order that these records would be put if they were sorted on:

**1** Ascending order of Publisher and then Year.
**2** Ascending order of Publisher and then Author.
**3** Ascending order of Publisher, Author and then Year.
**4** Ascending order of Author and then Descending order of year.

■ *Your answers should look like these:*

*1.* 8, 7, 4, 9, 12, 3, 6, 10, 11, 2, 5, 1
*2.* 8, 4, 7, 12, 9, 10, 3, 6, 2, 1, 5, 11
*3.* 8, 4, 7, 12, 9, 10, 3, 6, 2, 11, 5, 1
*4.* 10, 3, 12, 2, 6, 1, 5, 11, 8, 4, 7, 9
■

### Hint

When a database sorts two things that are the same (like two books by the same author with the same publisher) the lowest record number will usually be put first.

### Key points to remember

- Data can be sorted alphabetically, by number or by date, depending on the type of field being sorted.
- Records can be sorted into ascending or descending order.
- Databases can be used to sort information on two or more fields.

### Putting it into practice

- Take a printout of a big database file and ask someone to find a piece of information in it. Time them doing this.
- Sort the file in order of the item being looked for and reprint it. Ask the same person to find the same piece of information and time them again.

## Topic 4 – Graphics

### Making simple changes to a drawing

**IT 48**

Foundation/Intermediate/Advanced
Element **1.2,2.2,3.2**
Performance criteria **2,4**
Range **Software; Edit; Reorganise**

Designing a drawing is often a process of trial and error. If you draw something and realise that it is wrong, don't immediately delete it and start again. There are plenty of changes you can make to it. For example, you can

- change its size, shape and position
- change its line style, line colour and fill colour or pattern
- reverse what you have done with an Undo option.

You can also copy an object you need to use in several places on a drawing, and delete objects you don't want.

## Moving objects

Sometimes, it is easier to build up a drawing if you create the parts separately, especially if there is lots of detail in a small area.

### Activity

Find out how to move things with your drawing program; you may be able to drag them with the mouse. Draw the first arrangement, and then move the circle to get the second arrangement.

## Changing the size and shape of objects

You can probably change both the size and shape of an item at the same time, or change just its size keeping the same shape.

### Activity

Draw the first rectangle on the right, select it and change it so that it looks like the rectangle in the middle. Now make it smaller but keep the same shape – like the rectangle on the far right.

## Copying objects

If you are going to need several identical or similar objects on a drawing, it is quicker to create one and then make copies of it. You can make changes to the copies if you need to.

### Activity

Imagine you want to create a sequence of drawings showing someone how to build a bridge from children's building bricks. You could copy the first stage, add to it, copy it again and add more. Using the Copy option, create this sequence.

Shade the bits in each stage of the diagram which you can copy from the previous stage.

# Topic 4 – Graphics

## Making simple changes to a drawing (continued)

### Undoing your changes

If you do something to your drawing and then change your mind, you can usually undo it. Most drawing programs have an Undo option which changes back the last thing you did. There may be a Redo option to do it again if you decide you really did want it after all. You can probably use Undo several times to step back through a whole series of actions.

If you decide you don't want one of your objects, you can delete it. Select it and choose a Delete, Cut or Remove option. If your graphics program shows a Paste option, you may be able to stick the object back in if you used Cut to remove it.

### Activity

Draw a rectangle, then cut it and then use Undo. Try undoing a sequence of actions.

### Key points to remember

- You can move parts of your drawing around.
- You can change the size and shape of things in your drawing.
- You can make copies of parts of the drawing and alter them if you need similar bits.
- You can reverse your changes with Undo and Redo them again if you need to.

### Putting it into practice

*Design a badge for students following your course and make several copies of it showing different students' names.*

## Topic 4 – Graphics

### Making simple changes to a painting

**IT 49**

Foundation/Intermediate/Advanced
Element **1.2,2.2,3.2**
Performance criteria **2,4**
Range **Software; Edit; Reorganise**

Because a painting is just a collection of coloured dots, changing the picture involves changing the colours of the dots. You do this by painting over areas of the picture. You can use any of the painting tools you use to create a painting. Remember that, unlike a drawing, a painting has only one 'layer'; anything you paint on top of something else replaces what was there before, it isn't just put in front of it.

This sheet helps you to find out how to

- copy and move areas of a painting
- use the floodfill tool to replace the colour used in an area of the painting
- make detailed changes.

It is easy to make a mistake while changing a painting. Save your work every few minutes, especially if your program does not have an Undo option to let you reverse your last action.

## Copying and moving areas of a painting

Your painting program probably has a tool to let you cut out an area of the painting and move it to a different position. You can do this if you decide you have put something in the wrong place, or decide you need space for something else.

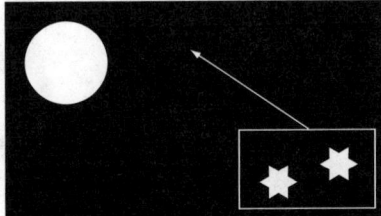

You can probably also copy an area of the painting and stick it back in. It is a good way to make a repeating pattern.

### Activity

Paint a flower, like that shown below, then copy it several times to make a pattern.

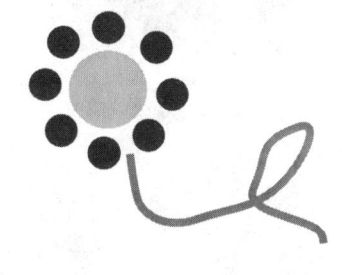

## Changing the colour of an area

If the only change you want to make to an area of your painting is to change its colour, you may be able to use a floodfill tool to do it, rather than recreating the area in a different colour. For example, you may have created a design in red and blue but find when you print it that you get two similar shades of grey. You could use floodfill to change red areas to yellow or white.

A floodfill tool fills an enclosed area with the colour you are currently using. It will change all adjacent pixels of the same colour. When it meets a pixel of another colour, it treats this as the boundary of the enclosed area.

Make sure the shape you want to fill is an enclosed area before using this tool; if there are breaks in its outline which lead to another area of the same colour, that area will also be filled.

### Activity

Using a coloured pen, find out what floodfill would do to the white areas in these pictures.

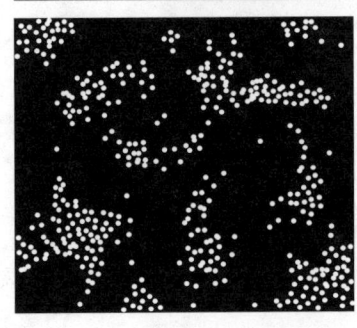

■■ *In the first picture, you would need to use floodfill three times to fill all the areas. In the second, you would need to use it only once. In the last picture floodfill would change only a few pixels at a time as the dots are mostly separate.* ■■

You may be able to choose a 'global' option with floodfill. This means that all areas the same colour as that you click on using the tool will be filled with the new colour – it swaps one colour used in your painting for another.

# Topic 4 – Graphics

## Making simple changes to a painting  (continued)

### Working in detail

Your painting program probably lets you look at areas of your painting in close-up. With your picture magnified sufficiently, you can see the individual pixels that make it up. You can use the pencil tool to change the colour of individual pixels to add fine detail.

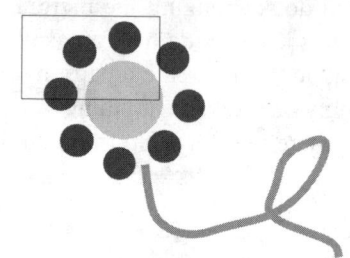

### Key points to remember

- You can move and copy areas of a painting around.
- A floodfill tool lets you change the colour of an enclosed area easily.
- Zoom in on areas of your picture to work in detail.

### Putting it into practice

*Display a picture you have designed in colour and change it to black and white and shades of grey using the floodfill tool so that you can see what it will look like when printed in black and white.*

# Topic 4 – Graphics

## Moving graphics between pictures

**IT 50**

Foundation/Intermediate/
Advanced
Element **1.2, 2.2, 3.2**
Performance criteria **2, 4, 6**
Range **Software; Edit;
Reorganise; Combine**

You may sometimes want to use part of one drawing or painting in a new picture. If you commonly use the same parts in plans or diagrams, you can save time by copying material from one drawing to another rather than redrawing it each time. If you use a painting program, you may be able to cut out or copy an area of a painting and put it into another painting. This sheet helps you find out how to move bits of your picture between drawings or paintings.

## Moving graphics between drawings

Imagine you are working in an architect's office. You have drawn up a plan for a bathroom, and now you have been asked to plan a toilet block for a public building. You have already drawn a toilet in your bathroom drawing. Rather than redraw it from scratch, you can copy it from one drawing to another to save yourself time and effort.

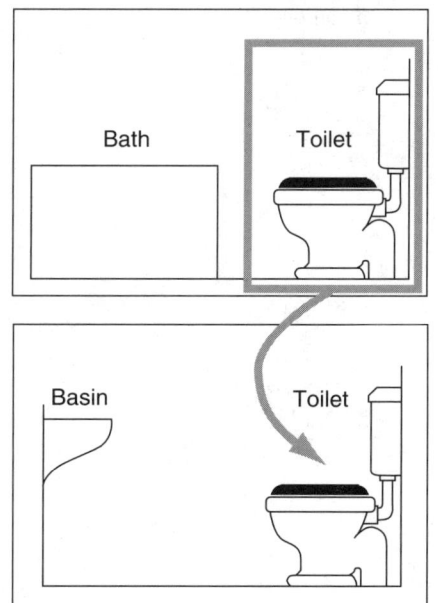

Most drawing programs let you move or copy objects between drawings. Many let you do this using a 'clipboard' – you can store an object or group of objects on the clipboard temporarily and then 'paste' them back into the same or a different drawing. This is called cut and paste. Alternatively, you may be able to open two drawings side by side and drag selected objects from one to another. When you release the mouse button, the objects are dropped into their new place. You will need to find out what your drawing program lets you do.

### Activity

Start a new drawing and add some simple shapes (squares, circles, lines). Open a second drawing and move the objects, singly and in groups, from one drawing to the other.

*If you can move objects between drawings, you can build up a 'library' of parts or objects that you need to use frequently. You can then just copy them from your library drawing into your new drawing each time you need them. It can save you a lot of effort redrawing material you have already created before.*

*If you want to create a drawing which uses a great deal of material from a drawing you already have, the easiest way to do it may be to make a copy of the whole drawing and then delete the bits you don't want and add the new bits you need. This may be quicker than copying a lot of material from one drawing to another.*

## Moving graphics between paintings

If you are using a painting program, you won't have objects that you can select to copy or move. However, you may be able to choose an area of the painting to copy, move or save on its own as a new painting. The Copy and Move options are often restricted to moving and copying an area within the same painting, but they may let you save the selected area as a new picture on its own. You might then be able to copy it into another painting, or begin a new painting with the area you have copied, perhaps make it larger and add more to it.

Suppose you have created a poster to advertise a play. You have used a painting to illustrate the poster, and you want to reproduce part of the picture on the tickets. You can copy a part of the picture and use it in a new painting which you will use for the tickets.

# Topic 4 – Graphics

## Moving graphics between pictures (continued)

Which of these can you do with your painting program?

- Copy an area of the painting and save it out or add it to a different painting.
- Cut out an area of the painting and save it out or add it to a different painting.
- Open a painting made from a cut or copied area and add more blank space around it to start a new painting.

Again, it may sometimes be quicker to make a copy of the whole painting and then remove bits you don't want and add any new material you need.

### Activity

Open a painting you have created and copy part of it out to begin a new painting. Make notes for yourself on what you had to do.

### Key points to remember

- You can save time and effort by copying graphics between drawings and paintings rather than recreating them.
- You may need to use cut and paste or drag and drop to move between drawings.
- You may have to save out an area of a painting if you want to use it again.

### *Putting it into practice*

*If there are components or elements you use in several drawings or plans, copy each of them into a new drawing and save this as a 'library' drawing of components you can use when you need them.*

## Topic 4 – Graphics

### Using colour and pattern

**IT 52**

Foundation/Intermediate/Advanced
Element **1.2,2.2,3.2**
Performance criteria **2,5**
Range **Software; Edit; Appropriate intervals**

You need to choose colours carefully to make sure they work well together and your document is clear and legible. You may be able to use ready-made patterns or design your own patterns to fill areas of your drawing or painting. This sheet helps you to think about choosing colours and patterns, and to find out how to choose or mix colours and patterns.

## Choosing colours

Whether you are using a drawing or painting program, you probably choose the colour you want to use from a display on screen. You may be able to mix your own colours, too.

If you are using a drawing program, you may be able to choose a different colour for the outline of a shape and its fill colour. You may be able to fill shapes with a pattern. You can probably select objects you have already created and choose a new line or fill colour for them. If you are using a painting program, you can use floodfill to change the colour of an area.

### Activity

Copy the following shapes using your drawing program. Use any colours or patterns you like in place of grey and black.

When you are picking colours to use in your drawing or painting, there are several issues to think about. Make sure that

- the colours will reproduce well when printed; if you can only print in black, grey and white, make sure you will be able to tell the different shades of grey apart

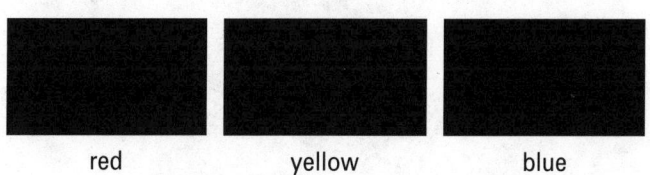

red          yellow          blue

- the colours go well together; don't choose colours that clash
- your work will be clear and legible; for example, yellow text on a white background won't show up well
- you use the right colours if you have to use any corporate colours or fit your work into a standard style.

If you don't have a colour printer, you may find it easier to work just in black, white and shades of grey – you will get a better idea of how your work will look when it is printed.

## Using pattern

Many painting programs let you design a pattern and then use it to fill areas of the painting. Drawing programs often have a selection of ready-made patterns you can use to fill areas. This can save time and give your work a professional look. For example, you may be able to use a pattern of paving and bricks to show areas with different surfaces, or use different types of shading, or show textures.

### Activity

Look at the patterns offered by your program. Can you think of any times when you may want to use them? Can you design your own patterns? Find out how to do it and practise.

▌▌ *If you are combining colours, make sure there is enough contrast between the colours to make the pattern clear.*

*How well a pattern prints out will depend on the type of printer you are using. Many patterns have been designed to look best when printed with a 300 dpi laser printer.* ▌▌

### Key points to remember

- You may be able to mix your own colours.
- If you don't have a colour printer, it is best to work in shades of grey.
- Pick colours that work well together.
- You may be able to fill areas of your drawing or painting with a pattern.

### *Putting it into practice*

*Design any patterns you may need to use for your work, and save them for later use if you can. Some programs let you save and reload patterns. Look in the manual or on-line help for information.*

# IT – Present information — Element 3

## Topic 1 – Word processors

IT56  Checking your spelling and grammar
IT58  Checking the layout of a document before printing
IT59  Printing a text document

## Topic 2 – Spreadsheets

IT61  Printing a spreadsheet
IT62  Printing selected parts of a spreadsheet

## Topic 3 – Databases

IT66  Introducing reports
IT68  Printing selected records

## Topic 4 – Graphics

IT71  Checking a picture before printing
IT73  Printing a picture
IT74  Displaying pictures on screen

## Topic 1 – Word processors

### Checking your spelling and grammar

**IT 56**

Foundation
Element **1.3**
Performance criteria **1,2**
Range **Information;**
**Software; Requirements**

Most word processors have spelling checkers to help you avoid typing and spelling mistakes. Some also have grammar checkers, but this is less common. If your word processor offers these, you should get into the habit of using them on every document you create. This sheet explains how to

- find out about and try out the spelling checker
- find out about and try out the grammar checker.

> **Hint**
> Don't neglect the spelling checker because you can spell well – it is a useful way of finding any typing mistakes or missed spaces.

## Checking your spelling

A spelling checker may let you check your spelling as you type, check individual words, or check your whole text once you have finished typing.

A spelling checker does not look at words in their context, but compares each word with its own dictionary. It won't spot:

- a word used in the wrong context (e.g., 'he combed his hare')
- a word that is wrongly spelled, but coincidentally is the correct spelling of another word (e.g., 'she east dinner')
- grammatical errors (e.g., 'the dog ate it's dinner') – you may be able to use a grammar checker as well.

On the other hand, it will flag as mistakes some words that are correct. These are words that are not in the spelling checker dictionary and include foreign words, proper names, unusual words and specialist terms. Many word processors allow you to build up extra dictionaries of words you use but which aren't in the main dictionary.

### Activity

Look at the following piece of text and underline all the mistakes. Using two different colour highlighter pens, mark (a) all the mistakes which a spelling checker would spot and (b) all the things that are right but that a spelling checker may flag as mistakes.

> I wanted to apply for acommodation in Sheffield so I write to my Aunt Mary because she lives their. I asked her to buy the local news paper and sent it too me.

■ *The spelling checker would pick up the mistake 'acommodation' for 'accommodation'; it would miss 'write' for 'wrote', 'their' for 'there', 'news paper' for 'newspaper', 'sent' for 'send' and 'too' for 'to'. It would probably flag 'Sheffield' and 'Mary' as wrong.* ■

## Checking your grammar

A grammar checker checks your writing against a set of grammatical rules. It will pick up some of the mistakes missed by the spelling checker in the first exercise on this sheet, where a word is correctly spelled but used in the wrong context. For instance, if you write that it is 'to hot to go out', a grammar checker will tell you that it should be 'too hot to go out'.

You may be able to choose a set of rules to suit the type of document you are writing – informal or business writing, for example. The checker will identify any errors and probably suggest corrections. It may also offer explanations of the rules it has applied, and give you the option of ignoring some rules. Even if your grammar is generally good, using a grammar checker is a useful safeguard against silly errors.

Although spelling and grammar checkers are useful, you must also check your work carefully yourself.

### Activity

Start a new document and type some text with deliberate grammatical errors, then run your grammar checker to try to correct it. This will help you to find out how they work and what they can and cannot spot.

### Key points to remember

- Make sure you know how to use the spelling checker for your word processor, and that you know its limitations.
- Make sure you know how to use the grammar checker for your word processor.
- It is important to check the text carefully yourself as well as running the spelling and grammar checkers.

### *Putting it into practice*

*Check the spelling and grammar in a document you have created recently. You may find that your spelling and grammar improve as you check your work and learn which type of mistakes you make most often.*

# Topic 1 – Word processors

## Checking the layout of a document before printing

**IT 58**

Foundation/Intermediate/Advanced
Element **1.3,2.3,3.3**
Performance criteria **3,5**
Range **Software; Information**

It is important to check your finished document carefully before you print it. It can save you time and money if your document is right the first time – printing it again costs extra in effort, paper and printer toner. This sheet explains how to

- look at your document on screen using a Print preview option
- look for errors that could mean you would have to print the document again.

## Previewing your document before you print it

Many word processor programs have a Print preview option. This allows you to look at your document on screen before printing it. The preview mode may show:

- your document at a reduced scale, so that you can check the position of blocks of text and where page breaks occur
- headers and footers, and any other text or graphics that is not normally shown when you are creating or editing a document
- page numbers.

You may be able to make changes to the document when you are previewing it, or you may have to return to some other way of displaying it before you can change anything.

If your document doesn't have a preview option, you can still look at your document at a reduced scale to check page breaks and major features of the layout. You can check page breaks by scrolling through your document at its normal size, but it is often easier to spot mistakes if you can see a whole page at once.

### Activity

Find out whether your word processor offers a Print preview option. If so, try it out. If not, experiment with viewing a document at different scales until you find a scale suitable for checking the appearance of whole pages.

## What to look for

You need to know what to look for when previewing your document. If you are looking at your document at reduced scale, you won't be able to check small details, such as spelling. Instead, look at the layout of the document. Here are some things you might check for.

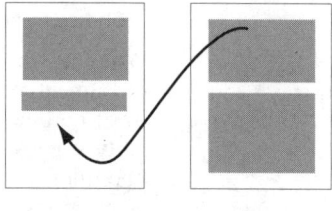

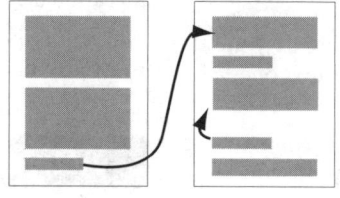

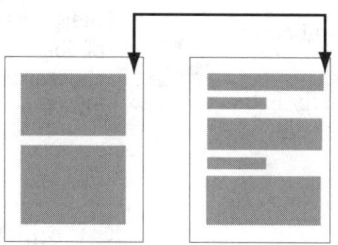

- Page breaks come at sensible points. Make sure there are no pages only half filled with text (except where you want or need this), and that sections don't end with just one or two lines on an otherwise empty page.
- Spacing between blocks of text, and between text and headings, is consistent and correct.
- Headers and footers appear in the right positions.
- You don't have single lines of text at the bottom or top of a page, with the rest of the paragraph on the next or previous page.
- The text is in the right position on the page.
- The margins and indents are consistent.
- Any graphics, tables, charts or other added materials appear in the right places.

### Activity

Make up a checklist for yourself of things you could look at when previewing a document. Make it relevant to the type of documents you personally work on. Print out copies of your checklist and use it when you are preparing to print other documents. You may be able to add to it or improve it as you use it.

### Key points to remember

- Previewing your document before you print it can save time and money.
- Use a print preview option, if your word processor has one, to check whole pages and details such as header and footer text.
- Check the layout and the flow of text from page to page before printing your document.

### Putting it into practice

Next time you have a document ready to print, check it carefully before printing using the procedure you have learned about on this sheet and using your checklist.

## Topic 1 – Word processors

### Printing a text document

**IT 59**

Foundation/Intermediate/Advanced
Element **1.3, 2.3, 3.3**
Performance criteria **3, 4**
Range **Software**

Sooner or later you will want to print your document – you will rarely create a document you never need to send or show to someone else, or file away. You should check your document before you print it and make sure that you know how to use the printer. This sheet helps you to find out about the printing options your word processor offers, including

- how many copies to print
- which pages to print
- whether to print pages upright (portrait) or sideways (landscape).

There are two common ways of using a page: portrait or landscape.

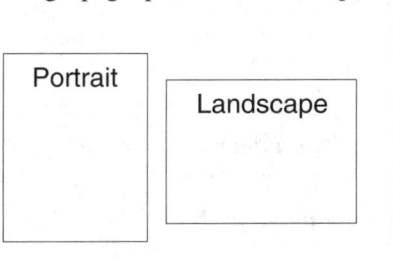

- whether to print the pages in reverse order or their normal order
- printing a draft copy.

You should also find out how to stop the printer if you notice that something is wrong.

## Looking at the options

Your word processor will offer an option Print, or Print document, which you will need to use. It will probably display a dialog box for you to make settings before printing the document.

### Activity

Choose the Print option from your word processor and look at the dialog box. In the list below, tick the boxes beside the options it offers. List any other options.

Number of copies: how many copies of the document to print. ☐

Page range: you can probably choose to print all the document, a range of pages (From...To) or just the current page. ☐

Portrait or landscape: whether to print on the paper upright (portrait) or sideways (landscape). ☐

Reverse order: print the pages from the end of the document to the beginning – you may want to do this if your printer stacks printed pages face down; this way, your document will be in the right order when you pick it up. ☐

Scale: print the document larger (more than 100%) or smaller (less than 100%) than its normal size. ☐

Draft print: print a quick but reduced-quality copy of the document. ☐

NLQ: print a near-letter-quality copy of the document (a high-quality printout from a dot-matrix printer). ☐

Using a coloured highlighter pen, highlight all the options you can already use.

■■ *If there are any options you don't know how to use, look in the manual or on-line help system to find out what they are for.* ■■

## Starting and stopping the printer

The Print dialog box will have a button labelled OK or Print to begin printing. There will probably be some kind of report on screen that the document is printing and how far it has got. If you notice that your document is wrong, you will need to stop the printer.

### Activity

How do you stop the document printing if you notice something is wrong?

■■ *You may be able to press Escape or click on a button shown on screen. You might have to turn the printer off-line or, if you are printing over a network, remove the print job from a queue.*

*After making corrections, you may need to print just some of the pages in the document; don't reprint pages you don't need.* ■■

### Key points to remember

- Make sure you know what all the settings offered on the Print dialog box are for and how to make the settings you need.
- You need to be able to stop the printer in case you notice something wrong with a long document that means your printout would be wasted.

### *Putting it into practice*

*Load a document of several pages and, in a single operation, print three copies of pages 2 and 3 at 80% scale (if your word processor lets you set the scale for the printout).*

# Topic 2 – Spreadsheets

## Printing a spreadsheet

**IT 61**

Foundation/Intermediate/
Advanced
Element **1.3,2.3,3.3**
Performance criteria **1,2,3,4**
Range **Prepare;
Information;
Requirements; Software**

You will often need to have a copy of a spreadsheet for business reports and bank presentations. The main way of showing spreadsheet information is to print it out.

### Activity

Why is it helpful to have a printout of a spreadsheet?

■ *You could have had any of the following reasons:*
- *A printout lets you see more of the spreadsheet than can be seen on a computer screen, giving you a better overall picture of the data.*
- *It is often easier to spot errors on a printout of a spreadsheet than it is on the screen.*
- *If more than one person at a time needs to look at the same spreadsheet the right number of copies of the spreadsheet can be printed out.*
- *A printout can be looked at away from the computer, which means that the computer can be used for other jobs.* ■

This spreadsheet has been used to work out the income of a business over a three-month period.

|   | A | B | C | D | E |
|---|---|---|---|---|---|
| 1 | Income | January | February | March | Total |
| 2 | Product 1 | 1235 | 2134 | 1298 | 4667 |
| 3 | Product 2 | 2564 | 3439 | 2986 | 8989 |
| 4 | Product 3 | 987 | 995 | 1024 | 3006 |
| 5 | Total | 4786 | 6568 | 5308 | |

### Activity

Set up this spreadsheet in your spreadsheet program, using formulae to calculate the totals. What steps would you take before printing this out to make sure that the printer is ready?

■ *Before printing out you should check that the printer is*
- *switched on*
- *properly connected to the computer*
- *loaded with enough paper for the print-out.* ■

### Hint

**Take care that you do not connect any cables between the printer and the computer while either machine is switched on.**

All spreadsheet programs have a command that lets you print out your spreadsheet.

### Activity

Make sure that the printer is ready and enter the command to print the spreadsheet that you have just entered.
- Be sure you save the spreadsheet before you print. If anything goes wrong while you are printing you will not lose any of your data.
- You can save paper when doing test printouts by using the back of other used sheets, using good paper only for final versions.

■ *If you had any difficulty printing out your sheet you will need to check*
1. *that the printer is working properly*
2. *that you have followed the correct instructions in the spreadsheet program.* ■

### Key point to remember

- The main way of displaying spreadsheet information is to print it out.

### Putting it into practice

*Print out a copy of a spreadsheet you are using in school, college or at your work placement.*

# Topic 2 – Spreadsheets

## Printing selected parts of a spreadsheet

**IT 62**

Foundation/Intermediate/
Advanced
Element **1.3,2.3,3.3**
Performance criteria **1,2,3,4**
Range **Prepare;
Information;
Requirements; Software**

Spreadsheet programs give you the choice of printing out only part of any one spreadsheet.

### Activity

When might you want to print out only part of a spreadsheet?

■■ *You could have said any of the following:*

- *If a spreadsheet is in two separate parts, like income and expenditure, you may only want to print one or the other.*
- *For a display or presentation, you might need to print only a part of a large spreadsheet.*
- *You may want to show one person's figures only, or one item of expenditure.* ■■

The spreadsheet below has been set up to store details of the income and expenditure on three holiday cottages over a four-month period.

|    | A                 | B    | C      | D         | E       | F     |
|----|-------------------|------|--------|-----------|---------|-------|
| 1  | **Income**        | July | August | September | October | Total |
| 2  | Property 1        | 350  | 700    | 500       | 350     | 1900  |
| 3  | Property 2        | 280  | 360    | 360       | 280     | 1280  |
| 4  | Property 3        | 400  | 800    | 400       | 100     | 1700  |
| 5  | Total Income      | 1030 | 1860   | 1260      | 730     | 4880  |
| 6  |                   |      |        |           |         |       |
| 7  | **Expenditure**   | July | August | September | October | Total |
| 8  | Mortgage          | 250  | 250    | 250       | 250     | 1000  |
| 9  | Council Tax       | 120  | 120    | 120       | 120     | 480   |
| 10 | Water Rates       | 50   | 50     | 50        | 50      | 200   |
| 11 | Repairs & Renewals|      |        |           | 225     | 225   |
| 12 | Total Expenditure | 420  | 420    | 420       | 685     | 1905  |
| 13 |                   |      |        |           |         |       |
| 14 |                   | July | August | September | October | Total |
| 15 | **Profit**        | 610  | 1440   | 840       | 45      | 2935  |
| 16 |                   |      |        |           |         |       |

### Activity

Why have the monthly headings in this spreadsheet been entered three times?

■■ *If the three sections of the spreadsheet, Income, Expenditure, and Profit are printed out separately, each one will need the month headings shown over the figures. If they are not labelled like this it would be impossible to tell what months the figures refer to.* ■■

Spreadsheets ask you what cells you want to print out. The cells that you want are labelled by their cell reference. The range of cells that you might wish to print is shown by the upper left cell reference and the lower right cell reference.

### Activity

What range of cells would you need if you wanted to print out only

1. income
2. expenditure
3. profit?

■■ *You would print out from*

1. *A1 to F5.*
2. *A7 to F12.*
3. *A14 to F15.* ■■

### Key points to remember

- If you want to display certain parts of spreadsheets, you can specify a range of cells to print out.
- You should take care to label the parts of a spreadsheet when they are printed out separately.

### Putting it into practice

- Find a spreadsheet that you are using that could be printed out in two parts.
- Print out both parts separately.

## Topic 3 – Databases

### Introducing reports

**IT 66**

Foundation/Intermediate/
Advanced
Element **1.3, 2.3, 3.3**
Performance criteria **1, 2, 3, 4**
Range **Prepare;
Information; Requirements**

One of the most important uses of a database is to give information in the form of printouts. To be easily understood, this information should be clearly presented and properly labelled.

#### Activity

Can you spot two problems in the following printout?

| Sname | Fname | Sex | Add1 | Add2 | Add3 |
|---|---|---|---|---|---|
| | Postcode | | Area | | |
| JONES | PETER T | M | Rose Cottage | 7 Fore Street | NEWTOWN |
| | NT45 3CD | | North | | |
| THOMPSON | EMILY | F | 2 Sea View Terrace | Bayside Close | WATERTOWN |
| | WT65 3ND | | South | | |
| WASIM | ALI | M | 37 Bridge Street | | HOMETOWN |
| | HT32 7PQ | | North East | | |

■ *You could have said*
- *the printout is confusing because it does not fit neatly across the page*
- *the headings used don't tell us much about the information*
- *there is no overall heading to explain what the printout is about.* ■

To overcome problems like this, 'reports' are designed that let you show printed information clearly. Reports are set up in advance and stored with the database. Different reports can be set up to display different types of information. In the case of the printout above, the use of a report could improve the presentation by

- adding a main heading
- changing the column headings to describe what is in them
- print out only the fields you really want.

This sample report comes from the same information but it is much easier to read. The main heading states clearly what the printout is about, the column headings describe what is in them and the information fits easily across the page. Only the fields that are really wanted are printed out.

**List of Representatives and the Areas they Cover**

| Surname | Forename(s) | Area Covered |
|---|---|---|
| JONES | PETER T | North |
| THOMPSON | EMILY | South |
| WASIM | ALI | North East |

To print out information in a report you should make sure that you have loaded the correct database file. Each report is given a name when it is stored. Your next step should be to find out the name of the report that will give you the printout you want.

#### Activity

What steps should you take to check that the printer is ready for you to print your report?

■ *Before printing out your report you should check that the printer is*
- *switched on*
- *connected properly to the computer*
- *loaded with enough paper to complete the printout.* ■

**Hint**
If you are testing to see if a particular report looks good, you can save paper by printing on the backs of sheets which have already been used and are no longer needed.

#### Key points to remember

- Printed information taken from a database should be presented clearly.
- Reports are used to add headings and print out selected fields.

#### Putting it into practice

- Find a report that will make your database file look better when it is printed out.
- Use this report to obtain a printout.

# Topic 3 – Databases

## Printing selected records

**IT 68**

Foundation/Intermediate/
**Advanced**
Element **1.3,2.3,3.3**
Performance criteria **1,2,3,4**
Range **Information;
Requirements; Software**

When you are printing out a report, often you want to show only some of the records. To do this you have to search through the whole file, looking for records that match what you want. You need to know

- the name of the field you want to search
- what you are looking for in that field.

A database has been set up by an estate agent to keep the details of everyone who is looking for a house. These are some of its fields:

| Field Name | Data Type | Description |
|---|---|---|
| NAME | Character | The surname of the customer followed by their initials |
| BEDROOMS | Numeric | The number of bedrooms they want in their house |
| REGDATE | Date | The date they registered with you |
| PRICE | Numeric | The most that they will pay for the house |
| AREA | Character | The area in which the customer wants the house |

- With date fields, you will need to check whether to type them as a full date, like 1st January 1994, or in a shortened form, like 01/01/94.

Once you have decided what field you are going to search, and what you are looking for, you will need to find out how to print out only part of the file in the database program you are using. Every program will do this differently but they will all compare the contents of the field with what you are looking for using the following symbols:

| Symbol/ Means | Provides a list of those items that are |
|---|---|
| = equal to | an exact match |
| < less than | below what you're looking for (not including the thing itself) |
| ≤ less than/ equal to | below what you're looking for (including the thing itself) |
| > greater than | above what you're looking for (not including the thing itself) |
| ≥ greater than or equal to | above what you're looking for (including the thing itself) |
| ≠ not equal to | not the same as what you're looking for |

### Activity

Tick the box to show what field you would need to search to print out only these records:

|   | NAME | BEDROOMS | REGDATE | PRICE | AREA |
|---|---|---|---|---|---|
| 1 the customers who want 4-bedroom houses | ☐ | ☐ | ☐ | ☐ | ☐ |
| 2 the customers who will pay more than £50,000 for a house | ☐ | ☐ | ☐ | ☐ | ☐ |
| 3 the customers who registered before 1st January 1995 | ☐ | ☐ | ☐ | ☐ | ☐ |
| 4 the customers who want to buy a house in Newtown. | ☐ | ☐ | ☐ | ☐ | ☐ |

1 You should have ticked the BEDROOMS field.
2 You would find this in the PRICE field.
3 The REGDATE field would tell you this.
4 You would find this in the AREA field.

Before you begin to print out the records you want, you need to work out what it is you are looking for in the field you are searching. In example **4** above, to find people interested in houses in Newtown, you would be searching in the AREA field for the name Newtown.

You need to be careful when you type what you are looking for.

- Make sure you type it in the same way that it was typed into the file. For example, if you type Newtown as the area with a capital N and the rest of word in small letters, some database programs records that have been entered with the area as NEWTOWN, in all capital letters, will not show up on the list.
- When you are looking for something in a number field just type the number. Do not type any extra characters like £ signs, or commas.

# Topic 3 – Databases

## Printing selected records (continued)

You would use these symbols to get a list of the following customers from the estate agent's database:

|  | Field | Symbol | What you're looking for |
|---|---|---|---|
| Those who want a house in Newtown | AREA | = | Newtown |
| Those who want a house with 4 bedrooms or more | BEDROOMS | ≥ | 4 |
| Customers who want a house for 50,000 or less | PRICE | ≤ | 50000 |

### Key points to remember

- It is possible to print out only the records you want from a database.
- To do this you need to make up a search condition using:
  - the field name,
  - a symbol like, =, <, >, ≥, ≤ or ≠
  - the thing you are looking for.

### Activity

Fill in the gaps in the table below to show what you would need to do to get a list of all those customers who:

|  |  | Field | Symbol | What you're looking for |
|---|---|---|---|---|
| 1 | do not want a house in the Oldtown area | AREA | | |
| 2 | registered on or before 01/01/94 | | | 01/01/94 |
| 3 | registered after 01/01/94 | | > | |
| 4 | want a house with fewer than 3 bedrooms | BEDROOMS | | |
| 5 | want a house that costs 120,000 or more | | | 120000 |
| 6 | want a house that costs 80,000 or less | PRICE | | |

### Putting it into practice

- Decide on a search condition you want to make for a database file you are using.
- Look at a printout of the database and mark the records that you think should be printed out when the search condition is used.
- Print out a report using the search condition and see if it picks out the records you thought it would.
- If you have any problems, go back and look at your search condition again to make sure you typed it correctly.

▌▌
1. For those who don't want a house in Oldtown you would look for AREA ≠ Oldtown.
2. To find those who registered on or before 01/01/94 you would look for REGDATE ≤ 01/01/94.
3. Those who registered after 01/01/94 are listed by REGDATE > 01/01/94.
4. To list those who want a house with less than 3 bedrooms use BEDROOMS < 3.
5. To find those who want a house that costs 120,000 or more you should look for PRICE ≥ 120000.
6. Those who want a house that costs 80,000 or less are listed by PRICE ≤ 80000. ▌▌

These three things together, the fieldname, a symbol for comparing it and the thing you're looking for, make up what is called a search condition. All three parts of the search condition must be right before you get a list of the records you want.

## Topic 4 – Graphics

### Checking a picture before printing

**IT 71**

Foundation/Intermediate/Advanced
Element **1.3,2.3,3.3**
Performance criteria **1,2,3,4**
Range **Information; Requirements; Software**

It is important to check your finished drawing or painting carefully before you print it. It can save you time and money if your picture is right the first time – printing it again costs extra in effort, paper and printer toner. This sheet explains how to

- look at your drawing or painting on screen using a Print preview option
- look for errors that could mean you would have to print the document again.

## Previewing your picture before you print it

Many drawing programs let you choose how much detail is displayed on screen while you are working. It is often easy to work with relatively little detail shown – working with just outlines (sometimes called wire-frame mode), or without colours, for example. The screen redraws more quickly if you don't display all the detail in your drawing. Your program may only allow you to add to or change your drawing when you are looking at the drawing with reduced detail shown.

> **Glossary**
> **WYSIWYG** – what you see is what you get; a full WYSIWYG view shows on screen exactly what will be printed.

Before you print your drawing or painting, display it in full. Although it may take a long time to display a complex drawing on screen in full detail, it is worth doing so in order to check that it is correct.

If your drawing or painting contains a lot of fine detail, it is a good idea to zoom in on or magnify areas of the document to check the detail. You probably won't be able to see the whole document on screen at once when you are doing this, so you will have to move around it to look at different areas.

### Activity

Find out about the options your graphics program offers to help you check a picture before printing it. If there is a Print preview mode, what does it show? Can you make changes while previewing?

## What to look for

You need to know what to look for when previewing your picture. You will probably need to check the whole picture at once, and smaller areas in detail. If you worked from source materials, check that you have copied them accurately.

### Activity

Make up a checklist for yourself of things you could check when preparing to print a picture. Divide it into things to check when looking at the whole picture and things to check when looking at details. Make it relevant to the type of pictures you personally work on. Use your checklist for a while, and make any improvements that occur to you as you get more practice at printing and checking pictures.

■ *When checking the whole page, you might look at*

- *the position of the picture and its parts on the page, and whether there are any ugly gaps*
- *how well the colours, patterns, line styles and text work together.*

*When checking details, you might look at*

- *whether you have used line styles, colours and so on consistently*
- *that all parts of a drawing line up as they should, lines join where they should, and so on*
- *that any text is accurately typed*
- *that the picture is clear and legible*
- *that the picture matches the original requirements.* ■

### Activity

Look at the description of a picture here and then at the picture the artist has produced. Mark all the things that you think should be changed before the picture is printed and make a list of the things that are wrong with the picture and how they should be corrected.

> Tracy
>
> Please produce an OHP for my presentation showing the plans for the new garden area at the front of the building. It doesn't need to be very detailed, but please mark the main dimensions so that everyone can see how much of the space it will use up.
>
> Thanks

# Topic 4 – Graphics

## Checking a picture before printing (continued)

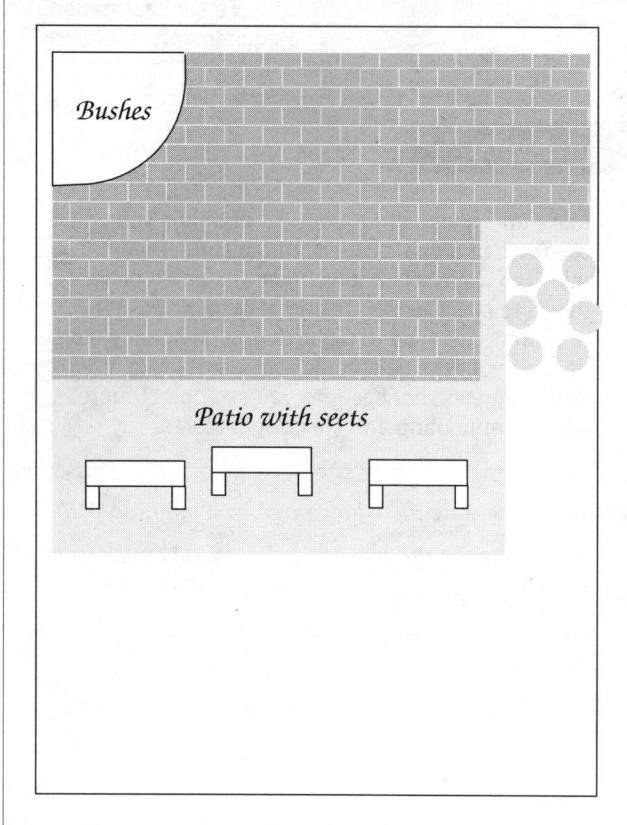

■ *There are several things wrong with the plan. You should have spotted:*

- *Tracy has not followed the instructions properly – she hasn't labelled the plan with dimensions even though she was asked to do so.*
- *The choice of colours for the pattern is poor as the pattern doesn't stand out very well.*
- *Although the area for bushes is labelled, it isn't clear what the area with circles on the right is for.*
- *It's not clear whether the white space to the right of the benches is part of the garden area or not.*
- *The benches aren't lined up properly and aren't evenly spaced.*
- *The choice of font is not appropriate.*
- *'Seats' is spelled wrongly.*
- *The picture is right at the top of the page, which will look odd when the illustration is used as an OHP – the full A4 page will be visible, but only part of it is used.*
- *There is too little white space around the picture – it needs bigger margins.*
- *It's not clear what type of ground the benches are standing on, since the paving is in a separate area.* ■

### Activity

Look at the revised version of the picture below.

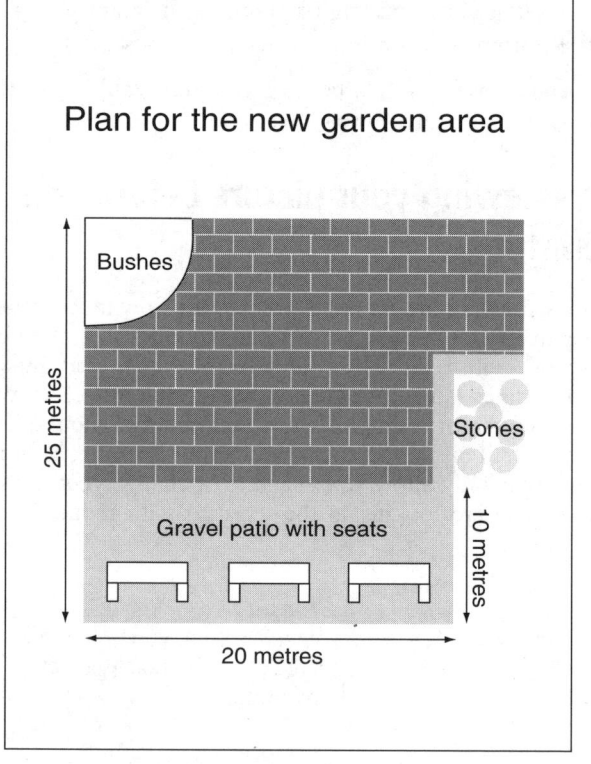

This is clearer, and it fulfils the requirements set out in the note. Can you think of any further improvements?

### Key points to remember

- Previewing your picture before you print it can save time and money.
- Check the whole picture and look at areas in detail.
- Check for consistency, accuracy, an attractive arrangement on the page and that your work is clear and legible.

### Putting it into practice

*Next time you have a picture ready to print, check it carefully before printing using the procedure you have learned about on this sheet and using your checklist. Revise your checklist if you need to.*

## Topic 4 – Graphics

### Printing a picture

IT 73

Foundation/Intermediate/Advanced
Element **1.3, 2.3, 3.3**
Performance criteria **1, 2, 3, 4**
Range **Information; Requirements; Software**

Unless your picture is intended just for display on the screen, you will want to print it out. You should check your document before you print it and make sure that you know how to operate the printer. This sheet helps you to find out about the printing options your drawing or painting program offers, including

- how many copies to print
- whether to print pages upright (portrait) or sideways (landscape).

There are two common ways of using a page: portrait or landscape.

| Portrait | Landscape |

- how large or small to print your picture
- printing a draft copy.

It also encourages you to find out how to stop the printer if you notice that something is wrong.

## Looking at the options

Your drawing or painting program will offer a Print option which you will need to use. It will probably display a dialog box for you to make settings before printing the document. It is important to learn how to make the right settings as it can save you having to print out your work again if you make the wrong settings.

### Activity

Choose the Print option and look at the dialog box. In the list below, tick the boxes beside the options it offers. List any other options not mentioned here.

Number of copies: how many copies of the document to print. It is often quicker to print several copies of a picture at once than to print it several times separately.

Portrait or landscape: whether to print on the paper upright (portrait) or sideways (landscape). Choose the right direction for your picture; a landscape picture won't all fit on a portrait page (and vice versa) at full size.

Scale: print the picture larger (more than 100%) or smaller (less than 100%) than its normal size.

Resolution: the fineness or coarseness of the printed image. This is measured in dpi, dots per inch. It refers to the number of dots used to make up each inch of the printed picture. If you print at a high resolution, your picture will be able to show fine detail well. It will probably print more slowly than if you print at a lower resolution. You may want to print at a low resolution for your drafts, and at high resolution when you have finished your work.

High resolution print-out

Low resolution print-out

Draft print: print a quick, but reduced-quality copy of the document.

Whether to print in colour, in shades of grey (greyscale) or just black and white.

Position: where on the page you want the picture to appear, if it doesn't take up a whole page.

Using a coloured highlighter pen, highlight all the options you can already use.

■■ *If there are any options you don't know how to use and which are not suggested on this sheet, you will need to use the manual or on-line help system to find out what they do.* ■■

### Activity

Experiment with printing at different resolutions. Choose a resolution to use for drafts.

## Starting and stopping the printer

The Print dialog box will have a button labelled 'OK' or 'Print' to begin the print run. There may be some kind of report on screen that the document is printing and how it is progressing. If you notice that your document is wrong, you may want to stop the printer. If your document is only one page long, it is not worth stopping it unless it is taking a long time to print.

# Topic 4 – Graphics

## Printing a picture (continued)

### Activity

How do you stop the document printing if you notice something is wrong?

▌▌ *You may be able to press 'Escape' or click on a button shown on screen. You might have to turn the printer off-line or, if you are printing over a network, remove the print job from a queue.* ▌▌

### Key points to remember

- Make sure you know what all the settings offered on the Print dialog box are for and how to make the settings you need.
- You need to be able to stop the printer in case you notice something wrong.

### Putting it into practice

*Print three copies of a picture you have created already at 80% scale, with the picture centred on the page. Make notes on what you had to do.*

## Topic 4 – Graphics

### Displaying pictures on screen

**IT 74**

Foundation
Element **1.3**
Performance criteria **1,2**
Range **Prepare;**
**Information;**
**Requirements; Software**

You may not always want to print out your pictures. Indeed, if you don't have a colour printer, you may not be able to show your pictures at their best by printing them. Sometimes, you may want to present your pictures by showing them on screen – if you use your picture in a multimedia presentation, for example. This sheet helps you to prepare for displaying your work on screen so that it looks as good as possible. It includes

- choosing colours that work well on screen
- choosing fonts (text styles) for display on screen
- clearing up the screen display
- making choices about screen display.

### Colours and the computer screen

It is easier to choose colours that look good on screen than for printing because you see them on screen when you choose them.

Don't use large expanses of bright colour unless you are sure this is suitable. Lots of very bright colours are hard to look at for long. Although you need contrast, it should make your work clear rather than detract from it. For example, dark green on light green is easier on the eye than red on light green.

> **Activity**
>
> Make sure your monitor is adjusted properly. Check the contrast, brightness, horizontal and vertical alignment, and colour balance to make sure your picture is seen at its best.

### Fonts and the computer screen

Fonts (type styles) with a simple design are usually the clearest and most legible in a screen display. Small text is hard to read; try to use at least 12pt for the smallest text.

> **Activity**
>
> Experiment with different fonts and sizes for text in your graphics program. Display your picture at full size, or the size at which you would show it in your presentation, and choose sizes and styles for text which work well. Make notes so that you can draw on your findings later when you need to work with text in screen displays.

### Clearing up the screen display

You can show your pictures at their best if you clear up everything else on the screen that you don't need. If your picture is large enough, you will probably display it at a size that takes up the whole screen.

> **Activity**
>
> Which of these can you do to make the display of your picture more effective?
>
> - Close down other windows.
> - Remove icons and desktop accessories such as a clock or calculator that may detract from your picture.
> - Remove displays of tools, panels of colours and other items used to create and edit your picture.

### Setting choices for screen display

There are probably several settings you can make to control the screen display and how fast your pictures are drawn.

> **Activity**
>
> Find out about setting the number of colours used in the screen display and improving the display of text on the screen.

> **Key points to remember**
>
> - Choose colours that work well together and aren't distracting.
> - Choose simple fonts in large point sizes for the best display.
> - Remove unnecessary windows, icons, tools and accessories from the display.
> - Choose a suitable number of colours for the screen display.

> *Putting it into practice*
>
> *Display a picture you have created and experiment with different settings. You may decide to alter the fonts or colours you have used. Try tidying up the screen to see your picture at its best.*

# IT – Evaluate the use of information technology — Element 4

## Topic 1 – Understanding the computer

- IT79 Naming the parts
- IT80 Computer equipment and computer programs
- IT81 Starting to use the computer
- IT83 Why you need to work accurately with the computer
- IT84 Avoiding mistakes
- IT85 Naming and organising your document
- IT86 Saving money by using the computer
- IT87 What can a computer do?
- IT89 Using your time on the computer efficiently
- IT92 Finding out about applications
- IT96 Protecting your work during your session
- IT98 Keeping copies of your work – back-ups

## Topic 2 – Solving problems

- IT99 Printers: simple problems
- IT101 Switching the computer on: hardware failure
- IT102 Floppy disks
- IT104 Mouse problems
- IT106 Keyboards
- IT107 Software crashes and general protection faults
- IT108 Opening files
- IT109 Running programs
- IT110 Undoing mistakes
- IT112 Viruses
- IT113 Finding files

## Topic 3 – Health & Safety

- IT114 Repetitive strain injury
- IT115 Back pain
- IT116 Eye strain
- IT117 Monitor radiation
- IT119 Electrical equipment
- IT120 Protecting equipment

# Topic 1 – Understanding the computer

## Naming the parts

**IT 79**

Foundation/Intermediate/
Advanced
Element **1.4, 2.4, 3.4**
Performance criteria **1**
Range **Methods**

This sheet will help you to familiarise yourself with the computer you are going to use, finding out what the parts are called and what they are for.

## The main bits

Your computer will have at least

- a main box which holds the computer itself. This is called the CPU or central processing unit. You may hear it referred to as the system box. It is probably a rectangular box with at least one slot for you to put a floppy disk into.
- a monitor, or VDU. This is like a television screen.
- a keyboard, with keys like typewriter keys.

You may also have a mouse. This is a small hand-held box with one, two or three buttons.

### Activity

Look at these possible arrangements of computer equipment and circle the one closest to your own. Label the parts.

a     b     c

d     e

■ *If you have*

a  *the monitor and the main part of the computer (CPU) are in the same box; the keyboard is separate (an old style).*

b  *the monitor, CPU and keyboard are in separate boxes.*

c  *the monitor, CPU and keyboard are in separate boxes and the CPU stands on end. This is called a tower system.*

d  *the keyboard, CPU and monitor are all in the same, small box. The monitor screen is in a fold-up lid. This is a lap-top or portable computer.*

e  *only the monitor and keyboard are on your desk and are connected to a computer stored elsewhere. This is a called a terminal; the computer may be used by several people at once, each with their own terminal.* ■

### Activity

How many buttons does your mouse have?

■ *Typically, a mouse with one button is used with a Macintosh or terminal, a mouse with two buttons is used with a PC and a mouse with three buttons is used with a RISC OS computer.* ■

## Disks and disk drives

Information used by or created with a computer is stored on disks. Your computer probably has a floppy disk drive. This is a slot into which you can push a floppy disk. The floppy disk will be either a rigid plastic 3½ inch disk, or a bendy 5¼ disk (but don't bend it!). Your computer probably also has a hard disk drive. You can't see this, as it is stored inside the computer.

### Activity

Which of these does your computer have?

- 3½ inch floppy disk drive ☐
- 5¼ inch floppy disk drive ☐
- hard disk drive ☐

### Key points to remember

- A computer usually has a CPU, monitor, keyboard and mouse.
- There are several common arrangements of computer equipment.
- Your computer probably has at least one slot for you to put in floppy disks.
- Floppy disks come in two sizes: 3½ inch and 5¼ inch.

### Putting it into practice

*Look at your computer and make sure you can name the parts. Look at a floppy disk you can use with your computer. Ask someone to show you how to put it in the floppy disk drive.*

# Topic 1 – Understanding the computer

## Computer equipment and computer programs

**IT 80**

Foundation/Intermediate/
Advanced
Element **1.4,2.4,3.4**
Performance criteria **1,2**
Range **Methods**

There is an important distinction between computer equipment – called hardware – and computer programs – called software. This sheet will help you to identify the hardware and software you use and to understand what you can legally do with the computer programs available to you.

## Looking at hardware

The bits of equipment that you use with the computer are the hardware. Typically, you will use this hardware:

- a CPU – the main part of the computer that does all the work
- a monitor, screen or VDU to display your work and let you see what the computer is doing
- a keyboard to type instructions and your work
- a mouse to help you choose things shown on the screen, move things around and help with drawing
- a printer so that you can make a copy of your work on paper
- various cables to connect bits of your computer equipment together.

You can't harm the computer hardware by anything you type or do with the mouse. Even if things seem to go wrong, you will not have caused any physical damage and the situation can be corrected by someone who knows about the computer.

## Computer software

Computer software is the programs you use with the computer. A program is a set of instructions written in a form which the computer can understand. These may be very complex instructions that allow for a lot of choices you may make about your work. They are logically structured and cover all the things you might reasonably want to do. Software is stored on disks but is not itself a bit of equipment.

The software you will use falls into two broad groups. The software that lets you use the computer and tells the computer how to behave is called the operating system. Using this, you can set up the computer as you want it, make directories or folders to keep your work in, make copies of your work and move it around, and look at what you have stored on your disks. The operating system also tells the computer how to behave – how to interpret anything you type at the keyboard, what to display on the screen, and so on.

The software that you use most of the time will be applications software – programs that you work with, such as a word-processing program, drawing program, spreadsheet or game. These programs have been designed for a particular type of task.

### Activity

Find out which applications program you are going to use and for which tasks.

## Using software legally

Software is protected by copyright law. This means that you can't freely make copies of it to use on different computers or to give or lend to other people. Your school or college may have a special licence to use many copies of an application, but it is illegal for you to copy a program and run it on a computer at home or anywhere else. You and your school/college can be prosecuted if you copy software illegally.

### Key points to remember

- Hardware is the computer equipment you use; software is computer programs.
- You can't damage computer hardware by making mistakes as you work.
- Computer programs are instructions the computer can follow.
- You must not make copies of computer programs.

### *Putting it into practice*

*Think about the type of task you want to perform with the computer and find out which programs are available for you to use. You may need to ask someone's advice if you can choose between several.*

# Topic 1 – Understanding the computer

## Starting to use the computer

Foundation/Intermediate/
Advanced
Element **1.4,2.4,3.4**
Performance criteria **2,3**
Range **Methods**

If you have not used the computer before, there will be quite a lot to get used to. Even so, some things are the same from one application to another. This sheet will help you to learn about

- what different parts of the screen display are for and what they are called
- how to do simple operations with the computer.

## Looking at the screen

These days, most computers use a system of windows, menus, icons and a pointer controlled with a mouse.

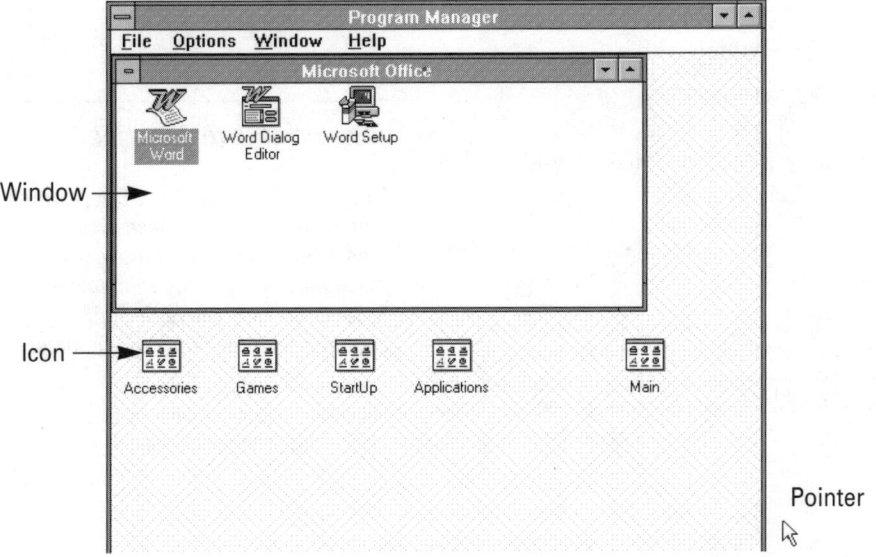

An icon is a little picture which represents something – for example, a disk or disk drive, a program or a piece of work you have done, a printer or some other equipment you use with the computer.

You may see icons like these:

A window is an area of the screen dedicated to a particular task or function. You can move it around, change its size and put it behind or in front of other windows so that you can see the material you are working on.

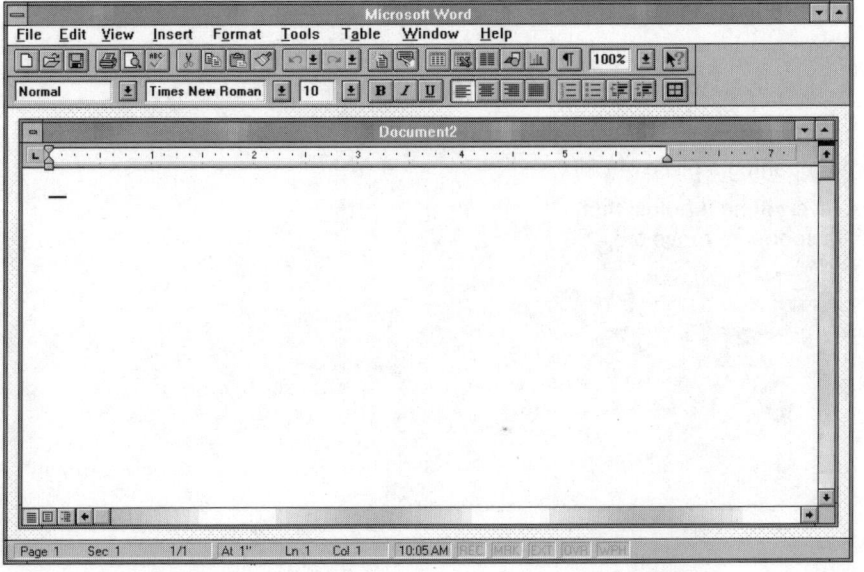

A computer uses menus, too. A menu is a list of options from which you can choose what you want to do.

You give instructions to the computer by using a mouse to point to and click on parts of windows, parts of your work, and on menu options, tools and other icons shown on the screen. You might use

- Windows, with PC-compatible computers
- System 7, with Macintosh computers
- RISC OS, with Acorn RISC OS computers
- Motif, with Unix-based workstations.

If your computer doesn't use a system of windows, you will instead see a screen with text, but no icons or windows. You will need to give instructions to the computer by typing commands, and perhaps by choosing from a menu when you are using a program. If you use a PC and it does not come up running Windows, you may need to start Windows by typing Win and pressing Enter.

• 305 •

# Topic 1 – Understanding the computer

## Starting to use the computer (continued)

### Doing things with the screen display

A mouse is used to move a pointer around the screen. You use the pointer to point, choose and move items in the display. If you can use a mouse with your computer, you will need to master three techniques:

- clicking on an option or icon – press and quickly release a mouse button
- double-clicking on an option or icon – press and quickly release the mouse button twice in quick succession
- dragging an icon – hold down a mouse button while the pointer is over an icon, move the mouse, then release the mouse button.

These techniques form the basis of how you will tell the computer what to do. For example, you may need to

- click on something to select it before you can do anything with it
- double-click on an icon representing an application or piece of work that you want to start using
- drag an icon representing a piece of work to copy it from one disk or folder (directory) to another.

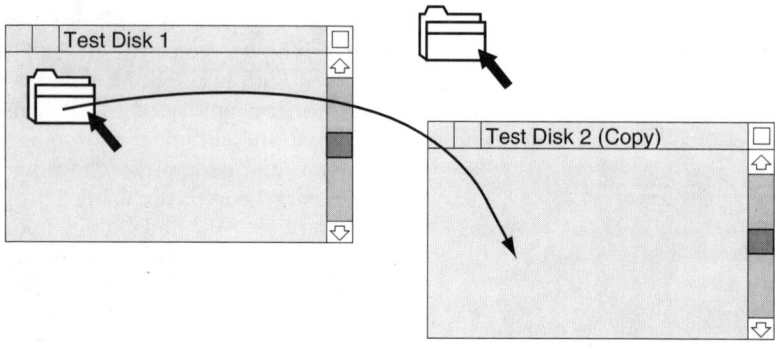

### Activity

Look in the manual or ask someone to help you, and find out how to do these things. You will need to use the mouse techniques described above. Tick the boxes when you can do the tasks.

Change the size of a window. ☐
Choose a tool. ☐
Move a window. ☐
Choose a menu option. ☐
Close a window. ☐
Open a new window, starting an application or opening a piece of work. ☐
Make a window smaller so that you can't see everything it holds, then drag a scroll bar at the edge or bottom of the window to move the contents through the window. ☐

### Key points to remember

- Most modern computers use a system of windows, icons and menus. You give instructions to the computer by choosing options and working with icons.
- You will need to use the mouse to use a computer with windows, icons and menus.
- Different types of computer use the mouse in similar ways.

### Putting it into practice

*Find out how to start up an application you want to use and practise using different parts of the window(s) – make the window bigger or smaller, for example and move through the contents of the window by scrolling.*

## Topic 1 – Understanding the computer

### Why you need to work accurately with the computer

**IT 83**

Foundation
Element **1.4**
Performance criteria **4**
Range **Problems**

Using a computer can save you a lot of time and trouble, but you do have to be careful that your work is accurate. A mistake you make when working on the computer can easily lead to more mistakes. It can also be hard to spot if you don't check your work carefully. This sheet is about why you need to be careful when working with the computer. It will help you to think about

- how mistakes can multiply if you don't spot them
- how mistakes might affect the work you personally do on the computer.

## One mistake can lead to more mistakes

Jamie has used a spreadsheet to calculate his budget for a brochure he has to produce. He has collected quotations for printing 200 copies, 500 copies and 1000 copies of the brochure and typed these into the spreadsheet. He has found out the price for having the text and pictures for his brochure prepared. This is a fixed price and it doesn't matter how many he prints. He wants to use the spreadsheet to calculate how much each brochure will cost if he prints 200, 500 or 1000 copies. These are the prices he should have typed in:

200 copies £400

500 copies £550

1000 copies £700

Preparing material £800

Instead, he types £890 for preparing the materials.

| No. of copies | Price | Preparation | Price per brochure |
|---|---|---|---|
| 200 | £400 | £890 | £6.45 |
| 500 | £550 | SAME | £2.88 |
| 1000 | £700 | SAME | £1.59 |

### Activity

What effect will this mistake have? If you can, highlight the rectangles in the spreadsheet which will hold the wrong value.

None of the prices per brochure will be right. One typing mistake will mean that all the results in the spreadsheet are wrong. The numbers in the last two columns, Preparation and Price per brochure will all be wrong.

One of the benefits of using a computer is that it can do a lot of your work for you. Another is that you should have to provide each bit of information only once. This means that you have to be very certain that you have given the computer the right information, otherwise it will base all the work on the wrong material and you will find that there are mistakes in lots of places.

## Looking out for mistakes in your work

### Activity

Think about the type of work you plan to do on the computer. Can you see how mistakes might multiply? See if you can make up another example from your own work of how one mistake can lead to more.

*You might include copying bits of text or pictures between different bits of work and so continuing a mistake, leaving information out of a calculation or database, and typing in the wrong information in the first place.*

### Key points to remember

- You need to be particularly careful when working with the computer because the way it saves you time also means that a single mistake can have many effects.
- A single mistake in a spreadsheet or database can keep surfacing in your calculations and results.

### *Putting it into practice*

*Ask some of your colleagues in your work placement whether they have ever made a mistake in the type of work you are going to be doing and what effects it had. Explain why you want to know, as they may not want to talk about it.*

# Topic 1 – Understanding the computer

## Avoiding mistakes

Foundation/Intermediate/Advanced
Element **1.4, 2.4, 3.4**
Performance criteria **4, 5**
Range **Problems**

This sheet will help you find ways of working that reduce the chances of you making mistakes and leaving them uncorrected. It covers

- checking your typing or drawing as you work
- looking out for areas you have left blank in a spreadsheet or database
- making rough checks
- checking any corrections you make.

## Checking as you work

If you are working from some source materials or rough notes, it is easy to type in the text and figures you want without taking much notice.

### Activity

Have you ever made any of these mistakes?
- spelling mistakes
- typed in figures the wrong way round – typing 32 instead of 23, for instance
- typed in the wrong information – you might have mixed up two items, perhaps giving someone the wrong address, for example
- missed out information – it is easy to let your eye skip a line, especially if the lines look similar
- copied the same bit twice – again, this is especially easy if much of the material is similar
- typed in something which is wrong in your sources or draft, without noticing the mistake.

▌▌ To avoid mistakes like those:

- *Pay attention as you type. Check on screen rather than just looking at the paper copy you are working from, especially when you are typing in numbers.*
- *Think about what you are typing: does it make sense? Does it seem right to you?*
- *If you suspect something is wrong, check immediately. Ask someone else if you need to – you may forget later.*
- *Every few lines or so, check quickly on the screen to make sure your work looks right. You will probably be able to spot gaps and anything you have copied twice.*
- *If you are working with a spreadsheet or database, check quickly that there are no cells or fields left blank before you move on to a different record or different area.*
- *When you are copying in columns of figures, it is easier to keep track of where you have got to if you lay a ruler or another piece of paper across the columns and move it down a line at a time as you go.* ▌▌

## Making rough checks

No one would expect you to check all the values in a spreadsheet by doing the calculations yourself, but you should do a few spot checks to make sure the values are about right. For example, if you have compiled a list of prices and one price is very much more or less than the others, you should check that one.

### Activity

Imagine you work for an insurance company and you have used a spreadsheet to calculate the proportion of houses with burglar alarms in different areas. This is your list. Which figures would you check?

12%, 21%, 8%, 98%, 0.1%, 9%, 11%, 56%, 17%, 15%, 20%

▌▌ *Although you would expect variations in different areas, the figure 0.1%, 98% and 56% are so different from the others that you would probably want to check these.* ▌▌

If you are working with a word processor, check that the text is about as long as you expected it to be. Your word processor probably reports how many pages are in the document.

### Key points to remember

- Check the information you enter into the computer as you type it. Look out for errors in your source materials as well as copying information wrongly.
- Check there are no gaps or blank spaces and that your work is about as long as you expect.
- Make rough spot checks on a few calculations.

### *Putting it into practice*

*Make up a list of the checks you can do on the type of information you enter into the computer. When you next have to use the computer, check carefully to see if you can spot any mistakes as you work.*

# Topic 1 – Understanding the computer

## Naming and organising your document

Foundation
Element **1.4**
Performance criteria **2,5**
Range **Compare;**
**Methods; Working safely**

One of the advantages of using the computer for your work is that you can keep different versions of it and return to an older version if you regret changes you have made. This is important for keeping your work safe, but you have to take care that you don't use an old version of a document when you didn't mean to. You need to organise your work so that you

- always use the most recent versions of a document unless you decide to return to an earlier version
- keep your back-up copies of documents up to date in case you need to use them.

This sheet will help you to plan a system for keeping your versions of a document in order.

## Old and new versions

It is a good idea to keep some of the previous versions of a document, at least until you are sure you won't want to go back to an older version. However, if you have old versions of a document around, you have to be particularly careful that you don't open and begin work on an old version rather than your more recent version.

'While I was on holiday, my boss got a temp to do my job. When I came back, I opened what I thought was the latest version of the database and spent the day entering new information. Later, I found out that the temp had made lots of changes to the database and saved it in a different directory. I hadn't used the most up-to-date version at all. It was impossible to copy all the changes and I just had to do my day's work again.'

Elifcan, PA

### Activity

Can you think of any ways of organising your work to prevent this?

■ *You may have thought of putting old versions of your document into a special directory or folder on the computer. Perhaps you thought of giving your documents names that tell you how old they are. If you decide to put old versions in a folder or directory, make sure you still give them names that help you to tell them apart in case you do want to go back to an older version. You also need to make sure that when you copy a document into the folder it doesn't replace another document that is already there and has the same name.* ■

### Activity

Imagine you have created a document called Rept. You have made changes to it three times. How could you name the three versions so that you could tell them apart?

■ *You may have suggested a numbering system such as Rept1, Rept2, Rept3. This certainly makes it easy to see the order in which you worked on the different versions. Make sure you know the number you have got up to, though. It is easy to open a directory or folder and use the document with the highest number, but there may be a more recent version stored somewhere else. As long as you organise your files properly, this shouldn't be a problem.*

*You may have suggested a system like ReptMon, ReptTue, ReptWed. The day of the week shows you quickly the order of the documents and the most recent, but if your work runs over more than a week there may be confusion. You could use the date instead: Rept2Jan, Rept3Jan, Rept4Jan.*

*Your computer probably has an option to show you the date and time a document was last altered. You can use this to double-check that you have the right version of a document before you begin work on it.* ■

### Activity

Find out how to display the date and time a document was last changed and try it out. You can show these and other details for all your documents when you look in a directory or folder.

## Organising back-up copies

You should always keep back-ups – copies of your work – in case something goes wrong and you lose or spoil the document you are working on. The back-ups will be useful only if you can find the version you want, though. Use the same system for naming the back-up copies as you do for naming your working copies of your documents. It will then be easy to find the right back-up copy if you need one.

### Key points to remember

- Use a sensible system of naming and store your documents in an organised manner to avoid using an old version of a document by mistake.
- Look at the computer's report of the last time a document was changed or saved to help you check that you are using the most recent version.

### *Putting it into practice*

*Work out a system for naming versions of the documents you create and work on. Try out your system for a couple of weeks, and make any improvements you think are needed.*

# Topic 1 – Understanding the computer

## Saving money by using the computer

**IT 86**

Foundation
Element **1.4**
Performance criteria **1,2**
Range **Compare;
Methods**

If you use the computer efficiently, it can save money as well as time and effort. However, if you are careless about how you use the computer, you can end up wasting a lot of money. People waste most money on unnecessary printing. This sheet will help you to think about printing wisely to save money.

## Printing wisely

You can save a lot of money by being careful and thoughtful about when and how much of your work you print out. Printing more than you need to wastes time, paper, printer toner and electricity. It is so easy to print out work, that often people do it when they don't really need to. Check your work on screen, and print it only when you have made any corrections needed. There will probably be a few mistakes you don't spot until your work is printed, but you can reduce these by checking carefully on screen first.

Only print one copy of a document first and check this. If you print several copies of a document and then find that there is a mistake in it, you will have wasted a lot of paper and printer supplies.

### Activity

Devise a list of guidelines to help you avoid unnecessary printing. Think about whether you really need to print anything, and if so whether you need to print all of it or just part of it, and how many copies you really need. Black-and-white printing is cheaper than colour printing. Draft quality printing is often cheaper than top quality printing.

It is very easy when working with a computer to generate far more paper than the same work done without a computer. If you are careful, though, you should be able to cut down on the paper you use by using the computer.

### Activity

Look at this case study and work out how Sadia could be more economical.

- At 10am, Sadia typed a letter to a client and printed out two copies, one to send and one to file. She spotted a mistake, so she corrected it and printed another two copies.
- At 11am, Sadia printed out the electronic mail she had received to read while sitting in the coffee room for her break.
- At noon, Sadia printed her CV so that she could mark up changes to it and apply for a job.
- At 2pm, Sadia's supervisor had lost page 3 of a report she had printed for him. She printed the report again.
- At 4pm, Sadia printed 20 copies of a memo because she didn't know how many people she had to send it to and she wanted to be sure she had enough copies.
- At 5pm, Sadia typed in and printed out her shopping list so that she could go shopping on the way home.

▌▌ *Sadia has done a lot of printing that she didn't really need to do. She should have*

- *checked her letter on screen and corrected it before printing it. If she only printed one copy first, she could have checked this and then printed the second copy when she was sure the document was correct.*
- *read her electronic mail on screen – that's what it's intended for.*
- *checked and corrected her CV on screen and printed it only when she thought it was finished.*
- *printed just page 3 of the report.*
- *found out how many copies of the memo she needed and printed just the right number, or printed one and photocopied it when she knew how many she needed.*
- *written her shopping list by hand on the back of a piece of scrap paper – such as one of her wasted printouts.* ▌▌

Remember that printing doesn't only use paper, it also uses toner and electricity; if you can write something by hand, it may save money to do so.

### Key points to remember

- It is possible to cut down on the office resources you use if you use the computer carefully.
- A major source of waste when using the computer is unnecessary printing. It is usually possible to cut down the amount of printing you do quite considerably.

### *Putting it into practice*

*Keep all the work you print out during a day in a pile until the end of the day. Look through the pile and see how much of it you really needed to print. Could you economise on printing?*

# Topic 1 – Understanding the computer

## What can a computer do?

Foundation
Element 1.4
Performance criteria 1,2
Range **Methods**

Whether or not you have used a computer before, you will have seen many images of computers – in newspapers, magazines, etc., – and probably have some ideas about what a computer can do. This sheet will help you to check your ideas, and separate fantasy from facts. It will also help you to decide which tasks a computer can do to help save you time and effort.

## The computer as a brain

The computer can work things out as you do with your brain. It can make connections between different pieces of information and store information just as you remember information. Some computers are capable of 'learning' and drawing on what they have done in the past to make suggestions or choices but a computer can't think and it can't be independently creative. All the computer can do is follow instructions. These instructions can be very complex, and may enable the computer to do things that would be impossible for a person. What a computer can do is limited by what we can tell it to do; its instructions are only as good as the person who wrote them.

### Activity

A computer can be instructed to play chess and can beat most human opponents. Why do you think the computer wins?

■ *The computer can calculate all the possible moves and their consequences and choose the best. A person will miss some. Chess has a limited set of rules and moves.* ■

Computers are not good at solving cryptic crossword clues because these depend on being able to see links across a huge range of experience and knowledge, pick up on puns and jokes and recognise cues characteristic of particular crossword compilers. A person can make some judgements better than a computer. A computer with a medical diagnosis program can judge from a list of symptoms the type of illness a patient may have. However, a human doctor can also tell whether the person seems very ill or not, whether the person is unhappy, how they are likely to respond to different treatments and whether any particular diagnosis is more likely than another.

## The computer as a tool

A computer is useful only for what it can do. You should only use a computer if it can help you to do your work more quickly, efficiently or accurately or present it better. If there is no advantage to using the computer, don't use it. There is a tendency to feel that something done with a computer is better than something done without one. This is not true. Like any other tool, you should use the computer only for what it is good at. In particular, the computer is good at:

- organising information
- doing calculations
- tasks that involve repetition
- working accurately
- allowing you to try out different arrangements and techniques until you are happy with your work.

## Working out figures and looking for information

A computer can't think for itself, but it can follow instructions very quickly. If you need to perform the same calculations on more than one set of figures, or if you want to try out different numbers in your calculations, using a spreadsheet can save you a lot of time. The computer can re-calculate using different numbers in a fraction of a second and can search for and sort out information in a database very quickly.

### Activity

Imagine you have a card index system for keeping customers' names and addresses. You have organised them alphabetically by customer name. One day, you have to find all the customers in or near Manchester so that they can be invited to a local event. What would you have to do?

■ *You would need to look at each card in turn to find all the clients based in Manchester. If you had the details on a database, the computer could easily look for Manchester in the address, or for an M postcode.* ■

## Re-using materials

Once you have typed some information into the computer once, you should never need to type it in again. You should always try to make the computer re-use information you have given it instead of retyping it. If you do retype anything, there is a possibility that you will introduce a mistake. In addition, if the information changes, you may have to update it in more than one place – it is then easy to let your work become inconsistent.

### Activity

Think about what you use the computer for, or are planning to use it for. Will there be any material which you would have to duplicate if you were working without the computer? For example, if you draw plans, do you have to redraw some components each time? If you type letters, do you have to type the same address again and again? If you keep records, do you have to write the same details on several cards? If you work with figures, do you have to perform the same calculations again and again?

# Topic 1 – Understanding the computer

## What can a computer do? (continued)

▮▮ *The computer can help with all these tasks if you use it efficiently. You can often either copy material from one place to another, or use some method of cross-referencing to get information already stored on the computer and use it in another place.* ▮▮

## Correcting mistakes

Using a computer, you can correct mistakes quickly and easily. You won't usually need to re-do a lot of work.

### Activity

Tick a box beside each of these points that applies to your work. Beneath each point, some of the benefits of using the computer are explained.

☐ If I type with a typewriter, I sometimes have to correct small mistakes with correcting fluid. If there are major mistakes, I have to retype one or more pages.

- The computer lets you correct just the bits that are wrong. It makes any necessary adjustments to how text is arranged on the page. When you print your work, you can't see that corrections have been made.

☐ If I calculate figures and some of them are wrong, I need to work out all or most of the calculations again.

- The computer can automatically update all the calculations when you correct any of the figures; it doesn't make mistakes in arithmetic.

☐ I sometimes need to spend a long time searching for lost or misfiled information in a card index or filing system.

- The computer can search very quickly through a lot of information and sort it into order for you.

☐ If I make a mistake on a drawing, I may have to use correcting fluid, paste over the mistake or redraw all or part of it.

- The computer lets you change just the bits that are wrong. When you print the drawing, you can't see that corrections have been made.

### Key points to remember

- A computer can do many tasks that involve calculations and comparisons better than a person can.
- A computer can't think for itself, make judgements or be creative.
- A computer is a tool; use it for what it is good at.
- You shouldn't need to enter the same information into the computer twice; you should be able to re-use it.
- You may be able to get the computer to do automatically for you some tasks which you have to do yourself at the moment.

### *Putting it into practice*

*Ask around amongst the people you work with or study with to find out how they use the computer to help them with their work. Make a note of any ideas which may help you with your own work.*

# Topic 1 – Understanding the computer

## Using your time on the computer efficiently

**IT 89**

Foundation/Intermediate/
Advanced
Element **1.4, 2.4, 3.4**
Performance criteria **1, 2, 3**
Range **Compare;
Problems; Evaluate;
Systems**

For many people, particularly while they are studying, time to use the computer is limited. Unless you have a computer available to you all the time, you will need to plan your sessions with the computer so that you can get as much done as possible. This involves preparing in advance. This sheet will help you to prepare for a session on the computer by

- checking and correcting any paper copies of your work
- planning what you want to do with your time on the computer
- making sure you have all the work you need with you.

## Working away from the computer

You will always need to check your work on the computer. Sometimes, you may want or be able to check by displaying your work on the computer screen and looking at it, but if you have only limited time with the computer you might decide that it is worth printing out your work to check when you are away from the computer. You will have to balance this against the extra paper and printer resources you will be using to print out the work.

When you are away from the computer, you can

- compare your printed work with any sources or original documents you used
- look for spelling or typing mistakes in your work
- look at the arrangement of the work on the page and for any inconsistencies in the way you have arranged your work
- think about how to do your work, how to arrange it and the styling options you will use
- draw up a rough plan, outline or draft of the work you need to do.

Don't depend on being able to remember what you don't like about the printed copies of your work. Instead, mark them up clearly and boldly with a brightly coloured pen. If you make your corrections in pencil or black ink, you may miss some of them and then have to waste time on the computer later by making corrections to work you thought you had finished.

### Activity

What type of preparation can you do for your work on the computer? Maybe you can mark up corrections on a draft, or sketch out the form of a drawing you are going to do. All your thinking and planning can be done away from the computer.

## Deciding what to do

You should always come to the computer with a clear plan of what you are going to do. This will mean that you need to have an idea of how much you can get done in the time available to you, and what the minimum is that you need to get done. Always do this, or the most important tasks, first. If you will be using any features of the program or computer that you haven't used before, research them first. You can read the computer manual, or talk to someone who can do it already.

### Activity

For a week, keep a log of what you get done on the computer during your sessions. This will help you plan future sessions as you will find out how long tasks take you.

As long as you have planned what you want to do, you should be able to spend all your time at the computer actually working, not wondering how to do something or what to do next.

## Make sure you take everything you need

Spend a little time making up a list of the things you need and checking you have them all. This is likely to include sources, notes, drafts, corrected copies, reference materials, disks and disk labels, back-ups to update, pens and note paper. You don't want to waste time looking for something you have forgotten.

### Key points to remember

- If you don't have much time to spend working on the computer, make the most of it by preparing properly in advance.
- Check printed copies of your work, plan what you are going to do and prepare any drafts before you use the computer.

### *Putting it into practice*

*Make up a plan for your next session on the computer. Decide what work you want to get done, how long it will take, what you need to take with you, and what preparation you can do in advance. After the session, evaluate your plan.*

# Topic 1 – Understanding the computer

## Finding out about applications

**IT 92**

Foundation/Intermediate/Advanced
Element **1.4,2.4,3.4**
Performance criteria **2,3,4**
Range **Compare; Methods; Evaluate; Systems**

Sometimes you may need to find out about applications which may help you with tasks you have not tried on the computer before. You may need to evaluate applications which are already available in the setting where you work with the computer or you might have to find out about applications that you could buy. This sheet helps you to identify and use sources of information about computer applications and think about the type of applications you may need to use.

## Information in the school, college or workplace

You will probably be able to find information about the applications which are already available in your school, college or workplace. If there is a computer systems manager, or someone who works in the computer room, they may be able to

- give you information sheets about the different applications available
- let you look at the manuals for applications that are available
- give you a demonstration of the applications and show you what they can do
- talk to you about your requirements and what you could use.

### Activity

Find out whom you could talk to about the applications available in your setting. You might be able to make an appointment to see them to discuss the work you want to do with the computer.

■■ *Don't forget that your colleagues or fellow students may also be a useful source of information. They may have worked on similar material in the past and have found ways of doing some of the tasks you now need to do. Ask about what they have used, whether it was good and what its shortcomings were.* ■■

## Computer magazines

There is a large range of computer magazines. They are a valuable source of information. They frequently carry reviews of applications, articles on how to tackle different types of work, and comparisons of different applications or equipment. Many of the advertisements also contain valuable information, but remember that they won't tell about the shortcomings of the products they describe.

Some computer magazines are dedicated to a particular type of computer, but others cover different types of computer system – such as PC, Macintosh, Acorn RISC OS and Amiga. It is very important when you read reviews and advertisements to make sure you are reading about the program running on the type of computer you have. You won't get an accurate impression of how well a program will run on your PC if you have read a review of the Macintosh version of the program.

### Activity

Does your school or college get any computer magazines regularly? Spend some time looking through them to become familiar with the format and the type of information you can get from them. You can also look in public libraries and in newsagents.

## Direct mail

When you buy and register an application, your name is placed on a mailing list and you will probably be sent information about new applications and updated versions (upgrades) of applications you have. You may be able to see a file of this marketing information if someone in your organisation keeps it.

You can phone or write for details of applications you have seen advertised or reviewed in magazines; most software companies are happy to send you a detailed description of their products and this should help you decide whether the application can do what you want and run on the computer you have.

## Knowing what you want

When you want to look for an application, you need to be clear about the type of work you want to do. Do you want to work with text, graphics, numbers, information or music, for example? Then begin to narrow down what you want and be as specific as possible. If you want to draw graphs, what type of graphs do you want? If you want to arrange text and graphics, what type of document do you want to produce – a newsletter? A booklet? OHP slides? The more information you can gather about what you need to do, the easier it will be for you to assess applications and for other people to help you with suggestions.

### Activity

If you currently need to find out about an application for a task you want to do, write a brief description of the task. Think about what you will need the application to do. For example, if you want to lay out a newsletter, you will need a program that lets you use more than one column of text and can put pictures alongside your text. Start researching the possibilities. Keep a log of where you look, whom you ask and which sources of information were most valuable.

# Topic 1 – Understanding the computer

## Finding out about applications (continued)

### Key points to remember

- There are probably some sources of information about computer applications in your school, college or workplace. There may be someone you can ask, and a bank of resources to look at.
- Computer magazines carry valuable reviews, evaluations and advertisements that can help you to find out about applications.
- Make sure you know what you want before you start looking at applications – it will make it easier for other people to help you and for you to assess the applications you find.

### Putting it into practice

*Devise a system for keeping track of information you find about computer applications. You may just decide to keep a folder of leaflets and reviews. If such a resource already exists in your setting, find out how to use the information and who can help you find your way through it.*

# Topic 1 – Understanding the computer

## Protecting your work during your session

**IT 96**

Foundation/Intermediate/
Advanced
Element **1.4, 2.4, 3.4**
Performance criteria **4, 5, 6**
Range **Problems;
Working safely**

It is important to save your work at regular intervals during your session on the computer. If you don't do so, and there is a computer failure or you make a serious mistake, you may lose a lot of work. This sheet will help you to

- plan a strategy for saving your work at regular intervals
- find out if there is an option to save your work automatically at intervals
- decide how frequently to make back-up copies of your work.

## Saving your work while working on it

It is easy to get carried away when you are working well and forget to save your work regularly. This is dangerous, though. If you don't save your work, there is no permanent record of it. If the computer is turned off, if there is a power failure, or if the application you are using goes wrong, you may lose all your work and not be able to get it back. You might even make a mistake yourself, and not be able to recover your work.

When you start a new piece of work, don't wait until you have finished your first version before you save it. Save it instead after about 10 minutes. Continue saving it every 10 minutes or so. This way, the most you can lose is ten minutes' work.

### Activity

Exactly how often you want to save your work will depend on several things. Decide how frequently you would want to save your work in each of these situations.

- You are spending most of your time at the computer thinking, and only actually using the computer occasionally.
- You are working on a long and complicated document that takes perhaps a minute or two to save each time.
- You are working on a picture that would be very difficult to re-do.
- You are copy-typing figures or text – it would be annoying but not difficult to re-do it.
- Your time with the computer is limited.

▐▌ *If you aren't actually getting much done in 10 minutes, you will want to save your work less frequently. If your document takes a long time to save, you may decide to save it every 15 or 20 minutes – it will cut down your working time if you save it every 10 minutes. You should save your work more frequently if it is difficult to recreate; you may decide to leave it longer if it is easy to redo. If you have limited time with the computer you will be tempted to skip saving your work so that you can get more done in your session. However, if you do lose your work, it will be more inconvenient for you to have to recreate a lot of it. You will need to find a balance you are happy with.* ▐▌

You will probably also want to take into account how reliable the application is and how used to it you are. If you know that the application is reliable and you are used to using it, you are less likely to make mistakes and less likely to lose work through a failure, so you may feel safe leaving your work a little longer between saves.

Some applications have an option to save your work automatically after you have saved it once. This avoids the risk of you forgetting to do it yourself. If possible, set the computer so that it gives you a warning before saving your work. If you don't, it may replace a good version of your work with a spoiled version.

## Back-ups

A back-up is an extra copy of your work that you keep as a precaution. While you are working, you should make a separate copy of your work every couple of hours or so. This gives you extra protection against losing your work.

### Key points to remember

- It is important to save your work at intervals while you are working on it.
- Your application may be able to save your work automatically for you, which will protect you against forgetting to save it frequently.
- You must make an extra copy of your work every so often.

### Putting it into practice

*Once you have thought about how frequently to save your work, follow your plan for a week and then review it. Do you feel you are saving at the right interval? Are there some pieces of work you should save more frequently?*

# Topic 1 – Understanding the computer

## Keeping copies of your work – back-ups

**IT 98**

Foundation/Intermediate/
Advanced
Element **1.4,2.4,3.4**
Performance criteria **4,5,6**
Range **Problems;
Working safely**

As well as saving your work at regular intervals, you must keep extra copies of your work in case you lose your working copy or it becomes damaged. Even if you store your work on a hard disk, it is important to keep extra copies for security. A copy of your work which you keep in case something goes wrong is called a back-up. This sheet will help you to

- plan when to make back-ups
- organise your back-ups to make your work as safe as possible.

## Making back-ups

You should make a back-up each day when you finish using the computer. Make copies of all the work you have changed during the session. If you work for several hours, make back-ups more frequently than this – every two hours or so is a good idea.

Your back-ups protect you against losing all your work if you damage or destroy the copy you are working on. Even if your work is stored on a hard disk, it is possible to lose it. You might delete accidentally, or make a serious mistake which spoils your work and then save it without realising, replacing the good copy you had on the disk. Hard disks occasionally go wrong. Because a hard disk stores so much work, you can lose a great deal if it goes wrong and you don't have back-ups. Even if you keep your work in an area on the network, you must make back-ups. The network keeps your work on a hard disk the same as the hard disk in any other computer, so it too can go wrong. The network manager will probably also make back-ups of everything on the network, but may not do this frequently – you might still lose a lot of work if something goes wrong.

You can make a back-up copy of your work on floppy disks or another hard disk linked to your computer or the network.

### Activity

How will you make your back-ups – on floppy disks or another hard disk? How often will you or do you make back-ups?

■■ *It is a good idea to have some copies on floppy disk even if you can back up onto a hard disk. You can take floppy disks with you, so you don't need to keep all the copies in the same place. This is a useful precaution against fire and theft.* ■■

## A system for keeping back-ups

In many organisations, the information held on the computer is extremely valuable – many businesses couldn't operate without their computer documents. For this reason they are very careful to keep plenty of up-to-date back-ups of all work.

■■ *The plans on the computer are all the work we do, really. Printed copies are passed on to clients, the council and the builders, but our work is all done on the computer. We are told to save our work every 15 minutes and make our own back-ups onto a different hard disk every two hours. The network manager takes a full back-up every night and puts one copy, on magnetic tape, into the bank vault. Another copy is kept in the building in a fireproof safe. They reuse the tapes once a week, so there is always a full week's back-ups in at least two places.'*

Sadia, architect

Some organisations keep three sets of back-ups, reusing the disks every three days. For instance, on Monday the back-ups are made on disk A; on Tuesday on disk B; on Wednesday on disk C; on Thursday disk A is used again, and so on.

### Activity

Can you think of any advantages of this system?

■■ *This system offers an extra level of protection. If you made a serious mistake one day and didn't realise, you could save the spoiled document as your back-up. If you realised your mistake the next day, you could still recover your work from the back-up for the day before. The set of three back-ups gives you two chances to spoil your back-ups before noticing your mistake and restoring your work.* ■■

You should keep at least two back-ups of your work, and never carry or keep all your copies together. If your work is kept on a network and backed up by the network manager, keep a back-up of your own on floppy disks; you can take it home to keep it safe. Try to keep back-ups of important work in different buildings if you can; you could leave a copy with your parents or at a friend's house. If you keep them in the same building, they could all be damaged or stolen. If you carry them around together, you may lose them all at once. If you have to travel to use the computer, carry your working copy of your work (unless it is on the hard disk) and one back-up to update; leave another back-up at home and take that one in the next day instead.

### Key points to remember

- It is very important to keep up-to-date back-ups in case you lose or damage the working copy of your work.
- Keep more than one set of back-ups and use them in rotation.
- Don't keep or carry all your sets of your work together.

### Putting it into practice

*Work out a plan for keeping back-ups. Follow your plan for a week and then review it. Think about whether your work is safe enough, or whether you need to keep extra back-ups or back up more often.*

# Topic 2 – Solving problems

## Printers: simple problems

> **IT 99**
> Foundation/Intermediate/
> **Advanced**
> Element **1.4,2.4,3.4**
> Performance criteria **3,4,5,6**
> Range **Evaluate; Systems;
> Problems; Working safely**

## Problems with printers

Printers seem to attract gremlins like no other piece of computer equipment. Sometimes they work perfectly and then stop for no apparent reason. Sometimes they will print everything except one particular document (which will print happily on other identical printers). And sometimes they just refuse to print anything at all.

It always seems that it's the printer's fault, but usually the printer is doing its best to carry out an impossible task. For instance, Derek had spent two days preparing a complex presentation document. It was a long document (over 30 pages), with lots of graphs, pictures and fonts, and it looked brilliant on the screen. Derek needed 50 copies, and he had left the printing to the last minute. However, when he tried to print the document, the printer jammed, and his clumsy attempts to unjam the paper broke the printer. He had to spend the afternoon trying to find another printer that was free to print the document, and finally did the photocopying at 8 o'clock that night.

> **Activity**
>
> Think back to the last time you tried to print a document and nothing came out of the printer. What was the problem and how did you solve it?

■ *This is the commonest printing problem. Here is a checklist of what you should do if your printer won't print.*

1. Check that the printer is switched on! Although this sounds obvious, it is easy to forget to switch it on – everyone (including the author) has done it.

2. Check that the printer and the computer are properly connected. Occasionally the printer cable can slip out of its connectors, although most cables today can be secured by clips or screws.

3. Check that the printer is on-line. 'On-line' means that the printer is switched on and ready to receive documents to print. Most printers can be turned off-line so that print jobs can be interrupted to replace paper or toner cartridges, for example. Sometimes the printer goes off-line automatically in these circumstances, but does not go back on-line automatically. To put the computer on-line, press the 'On-line' button on the printer so that the 'On-line' indicator light comes on.

4. Check that there is paper in the printer. Almost all printers will refuse to print if there is no paper – this prevents damage. Modern printers will display a message asking for paper to be inserted.

5. Check that the printer has not run out of ink or toner. Usually, it will display a message asking for a new cartridge to be inserted.

6. Check that the paper has not jammed. Paper can become jammed anywhere on its path through the printer, and usually a jam is obvious from the unpleasant sounds. Paper jams are described in more detail below.

All these problems require you to take some action; they

> **Activity**
>
> If you have a laser printer, try to print a document when there is no paper. Write down the message that the printer displays. Would this have helped you if you didn't know what the problem was?

■ *Messages displayed by the printer are usually helpful, but only if you can decode them. For example, on a Hewlett-Packard LaserJet 4, 'MP LOAD DL' means 'Put a DL-sized envelope in the multi-purpose paper tray' and 'PC LOAD A4' means 'Put some A4-sized paper in the paper cassette'. Unfortunately, the printer's display is very small and can show only very short messages. If you get such a message, you may need to consult your printer manual.*

*You may also get help from the program itself, with a message such as 'Printer not responding' appearing on your monitor. Usually it means that the printer is switched off, not connected or off-line.* ■

> Never try to unscrew or dismantle any part of your printer, even if it is switched off. Printers are pieces of electrical equipment, and you could electrocute yourself. Printers are designed so that you can solve most problems without taking them apart. If you think that it is faulty, call a technician.

## Paper jams

Paper jams are one of the commonest causes of printing problems, and you have almost certainly experienced one.

> **Activity**
>
> Describe what happens when the paper jams in your printer. How do you solve the problem? If you are not sure, read the section in your printer's manual about clearing paper jams. If the jam occurs in the middle of a print job, how do you complete the job?

# Topic 2 – Solving problems

## Printers: simple problems (continued)

■■ *Paper jams are often quite alarming – the paper bunches up inside the printer and makes crumpling and clicking noises. If allowed to continue this can damage the printer but most printers are designed to cope with the occasional jam. When the paper jams, take the following steps. Remember to take care not to touch exposed metal within the printer. Very high temperatures are used in many printers, and it is easy to burn yourself.*

1. *To stop the printer from continuing to try to print, take it off-line by pressing the 'On-line' button so that the indicator light goes out. Some printers do this automatically when a jam occurs. If the printer continues to try to print, switch it off.*

2. *Next, find out where the jammed paper is. On a dot matrix printer this is usually easy to see, it will be somewhere within the paper-feeding mechanism (either the roller itself or the toothed cogs that feed the paper through). On a laser printer, the path that the paper takes is much longer than on a dot matrix printer and there may be several places at which a jam can occur. Finding the paper may involve opening various flaps around the printer's case; see your printer's manual for details if you can't find these flaps.*

3. *Remove the jammed paper completely from the laser printer. This is usually easy, provided the paper has not been torn. When you find it, take hold of one end with both hands and pull gently but firmly, so that it rolls out in one piece. Then close any flaps that you have opened on the printer.*

   *Removing paper from dot matrix printers can be much trickier. First, tear off any pages that have already been printed and then tear off any un-fed sheets. This leaves only the jammed sheets to deal with. Then try to turn the roller by hand so that the paper is fed out backwards – this avoids making the jam worse. If you're lucky, the paper will come out in one piece, but more often than not some bits of paper get torn off and lodge themselves within the printer. Sometimes you can get these out by continuing to turn the roller, but usually you will need to use a pair of tweezers to pull them out.*

4. *If you were printing sticky labels, check that none has come off the backing sheet and stuck itself inside the printer. Such labels can quickly destroy the printer. If a label does get stuck in the printer, call your supervisor or a technician to deal with the problem. Do not attempt to use the printer.*

5. *Finally, reload the paper and finish your printing. Laser printers will usually pick up where they left off (provided they have not been switched off, all you need to do is put them back on-line). You may need to reprint the pages affected by the jam.*

*If you have switched your printer off, you will need to check which pages still need to be printed and tell the software to print the unprinted pages.* ■■

## Faint printing

Sometimes the text that appears on your paper is very faint.

### Activity

Think back to the last time that your printer started to print faintly. How did you deal with the problem?

■■ *Dot matrix printers work by banging small pins against an inked ribbon so that the ribbon hits the paper and leaves ink on it. When the ink inside the ribbon's cartridge runs out, the ribbon is unable to re-ink itself and the image gets gradually fainter. To solve the problem, take out the old ribbon and fit a new one.*

*Faint printing on a laser printer is usually caused by the toner cartridge running low, and happens quite suddenly. The solution is to replace the old cartridge with a new one. Sometimes, gently rocking the old cartridge from side to side will redistribute the toner left inside it so that you can print a few more good pages. This is a trick worth trying if you don't immediately have a new cartridge to hand.*

### Key points to remember

- Many printing problems have simple solutions, usually requiring a simple action by the user.
- Paper jams need to be cleared with care.
- The messages given by computers and printers are frequently unhelpful; always consult the manual to find out what they mean.

### *Putting it into practice*

*Keep a log of the printing problems that you encounter and how you solved them. Use this to help solve other problems in the future. Make a poster containing useful advice for dealing with problems on your printer and stick it to the wall by the printer.*

# Topic 2 – Solving problems

**IT 101**

Foundation/Intermediate/Advanced
Element **1.4, 2.4, 3.4**
Performance criteria **3, 4, 5, 6**
Range **Problems; Working safely; Evaluate; Systems**

## Switching the computer on: hardware failure

The last thing you expect when you switch your computer on is for it to fail to start properly. Fortunately, complete disasters are rare, and there are several things you can do before declaring your computer 'dead'.

### Activity

Write down the sequence of actions you go through when you switch your computer on. What indications do you have that the computer is working normally?

■ *Various things happen when you switch the computer on. Most significantly, the light beside the power switch should come on. Your monitor will probably switch itself on as well, and there should be various noises from within the computer as it starts up its hard disk, checks its floppy disk drives and starts its cooling fan. Your screen then displays various messages before presenting you with your normal start-up screen (possibly Windows, the Macintosh desktop, a menu or the command prompt).*

*You can tell that something has gone wrong when one of the above fails to happen. Your computer may display a message when certain problems occur.* ■

### Activity

Suppose you switch on your computer and the power light fails to come on. What might be wrong?

■ *If the power light is off, take the following steps:*

1. *Check that the computer is plugged into the mains and that the mains switch is on. It is not unknown (especially in offices) for computers to be unplugged so that vacuum cleaners can be used.*

2. *If the computer is plugged in at the mains, unplug it. Check that the power cable is connected properly and then plug the computer back into the mains and try again.*

3. *If the computer still doesn't work, unplug it again and replace the fuse in the plug. Reconnect the computer and try again.*

*If all of these steps fail, then something is wrong with your computer. You will need to call an expert to deal with the problem.* ■

### Activity

You switch your computer on and it makes all the usual noises, but the monitor stays blank. What might cause this?

■ *Since the computer itself seems to be working, the problem must lie with the monitor. You can carry out the following checks.*

1. *If the monitor has its own on/off switch, check that it is on. There is usually a light on the front of the monitor to indicate this.*

2. *Switch the computer off and check that the monitor is properly connected to the computer.*

3. *Check whether the monitor takes its power supply from the computer or directly from the mains. If the monitor needs to be plugged into the mains, check that it is properly connected, as described above.*

*If these steps fail your monitor may be faulty and you should call in an expert.* ■

If the computer starts correctly, but the usual messages fail to appear, you could have a serious problem.

### How a computer starts up

Switching on a computer ('booting' in computer jargon) starts a whole series of processes, all of which need to be completed successfully if the computer is to work properly. The following description is based on that for an IBM-compatible PC; other computers carry out something similar.

When you switch the computer on, a program stored in a chip in the computer starts to run. This program controls the start-up procedure. Most PCs begin by checking how much memory they have and that it is all working properly. They then check for floppy disk drives; first the A drive and then the B drive if there is one; you'll hear a noise and see the drive lights flicker.

If there is a floppy disk in drive A, the computer tries to use that for the rest of the start-up sequence. If not, it uses the hard disk (C drive). In either case the disk that is used is called the 'boot disk'.

On the boot disk there are (or should be) two files: CONFIG.SYS and AUTOEXEC.BAT. The PC first looks at CONFIG.SYS, which contains information about such things as the mouse, keyboard or other devices attached to the computer. This enables the computer to 'see' these devices. Then the computer looks at AUTOEXEC.BAT, which contains a list of programs that should be run by the computer when it starts. Most of the messages you see when the computer starts come from information displayed when the computer is processing CONFIG.SYS and AUTOEXEC.BAT.

# Topic 2 – Solving problems

## Switching the computer on: hardware failure (continued)

### Activity

The two most likely causes of a computer appearing to start correctly, but not displaying the messages you expect are:

- a non-bootable floppy disk has been left in the disk drive
- the hard disk has stopped working.

Which of these causes is serious and which is not?

*Damage to the hard disk can be very serious, usually leading to the loss of all the data and programs stored on the hard disk. Some hard disk problems can be fixed using disk repair software (on a floppy disk) but don't experiment with these if you don't know how to use them, you could make the problem worse. If you suspect that your hard disk is damaged, call your technical support staff for help.*

*If you have simply left a floppy disk in the drive, take it out and restart the computer. This is something that everyone does from time to time, and it causes no damage to either the disk or the computer.*

## Other problems

If your computer is part of a network, the problem may not lie with your computer at all, it might be a network problem. Call your network supervisor for assistance.

In vary rare and extreme cases, switching on the computer could short-circuit part of its electronics, possibly causing a fire. Follow the safety procedures advised in your college to deal with this.

Sometimes, computers fail to start properly for no apparent reason. Try switching the computer off for a couple of minutes and then switching it on again. If this kind of problem becomes frequent it could be an indication that something more serious is about to go wrong, so you should call in an expert.

### Key points to remember

- Most problems when starting a computer concern the power supply.
- Disk repair software can solve many hard disk problems.
- Serious failures can cause fires.

### *Putting it into practice*

*Draw up a check-list for your colleagues detailing what they should do if their computer fails to start properly. You will need to consult the resource sheet 'Switching the computer on: software failure' to complete this.*

# Topic 2 – Solving problems

## Floppy disks

**IT 102**

Foundation/Intermediate/Advanced
Element **1.4,2.4,3.4**
Performance criteria **3,4,5,6**
Range **Problems; Working safely; Evaluate; Systems**

### Keeping disks safe

Floppy disks rarely suffer problems, but they need to be handled carefully to avoid accidental damage.

Laura worked in an office with a lot of computers. Although she had storage boxes to keep her disks in, she found it convenient to keep the disks that she used often lying on the desk, so that she could get to them quickly. On her birthday, some of her colleagues bought her a magnetic paper clip holder, which she also put on the desk. But when she went to use her floppy disks she found that her computer could not read the data on them, and nor could any of the other computers. The support technician quickly identified the problem: the magnetic paper clip holder had affected the magnetic coating on the disk, destroying the data. Laura took the paper clip holder home and kept all her disks in a box from then on.

#### Types of floppy disk

The main kind of floppy disk in use today is the 3½" disk. This is used by most computers, including IBM-compatible PCs and Apple Macintoshes. Some computers can also use 5¼" disks, while a few (such as the Amstrad PCW) use 3" disks. In the past, 8" disks were also used.

To be useful, a disk must be formatted. This involves placing a magnetic 'grid map' on the disk so that the computer knows where to place data and where to get the data from. Different computers use different formats, so, even if the disk is the right size for the drive, it is unlikely that data stored on a disk by one computer can be retrieved from that disk by another type of computer.

#### Activity

Floppy disks can be damaged by dust and dirt, liquid, magnetism, heat and bending/cutting. In each of the following situations, say why the disk was damaged.

1. A 5¼" disk posted to a client was stapled to the accompanying letter.
2. A 3½" disk was used as coffee mat.
3. A disk was left on a desk while shelves were being screwed to a plastered wall.

■ In 1, the damage was most probably caused by a staple going through the disk itself. Even if the staple missed the disk, magnetism in either the staple or the stapler could destroy the data. If you need to send a disk to somebody else, use a special padded or stiffened envelope and avoid staples and paper clips. Make absolutely certain that you keep a backup of the data.

*Situation 2 leaves the disk vulnerable to both heat and liquid. If liquid gets inside the case it will damage the disk, while if the drink is hot it will destroy the disk's magnetisation, and the data with it.*

*In situation 3, there is likely to be a lot of dust in the air, which could get inside the disk's casing. As the disk spins in the disk drive, the drive head (a small metal probe that reads and writes the disk's data) comes into contact with the magnetic surface of the disk. If there is dust on the disk, it can catch on the drive head and scratch the disk, causing loss of data. In extreme cases, it can destroy all the data on the disk.* ■

#### Activity

Find a disk that you are certain has no data on it and dismantle it. If your chosen disk is a 3½" or 3" disk you may need to lever the case open with a sharp tool, so be careful not to injure yourself. A 5¼" disk can be cut open with strong scissors. Describe the components of the disk. (Don't try to reassemble the disk; taking it apart destroys it.)

■ *If nothing else, you will now know why floppy disks are so-called. Within the case, you will find two sheets of a soft, fibrous cleaning paper, which help to keep the disk's surface clean. Between them is a thin circular sheet of plastic, coated with a magnetic oxide on both sides. This is the floppy disk, everything else is just protection for the disk.* ■

Now you can see why disks are fragile and why they have protective cases. The case of a 3½" disk actually does a very good job under normal circumstances, to the extent that some people are prepared to throw them around the office when they need to give someone a disk. Don't be tempted!

#### Activity

Write down a plan for keeping your disks safe from damage. You need to protect them from all the possible sources of damage listed earlier.

■ *The best way to protect floppy disks is always to keep them in a proper disk box, with a lid. This helps to keep dust off the disks. Five-and-a-quarter-inch disks should always be returned to their paper sleeves after use. Don't leave disks lying around on your desk; they are vulnerable to dust, spills and being knocked to the floor. Keep your disks well away from any likely sources of magnetism or heat; a shelf, away from a radiator, is a good place.* ■

# Topic 2 – Solving problems

## Floppy disks (continued)

## Problems with disks

Assuming that your disks are properly stored, there are still other problems that can arise when using them.

### Activity

Make a list of the problems that you have encountered when using floppy disks. For each problem say whether or not you were able to solve it.

■ *The most common problem with floppy disks is being unable to save a file on the disk. This is usually accompanied by a message from the computer saying something like 'Access denied' or 'Disk full'. The second of these messages is reasonably clear; the file you are trying to save is larger than the available space on the disk. You can either delete unwanted files from the disk to make enough room or use another disk.* ■

### Write-protected disks

When you want to make sure that you don't accidentally erase the data on a disk, you can write-protect the disk (i.e. prevent the disk drive from making any changes to the disk). Three-and-a-half-inch disks have a hole in the top right-hand corner of the case, with a small slider that can cover the hole. If it is covered, you can write data to the disk; if the hole is open the disk is write-protected.

Five-and-a-quarter-inch disks use a small notch cut into the side of the case. To write-protect the disk, cover the notch with a sticky label.

Notice that the hole must be uncovered to write-protect a 3½" disk, but the 5¼" disk requires the notch to be covered.

'Access denied' and other such messages are less helpful. Check that the disk is not write-protected. If it is, there may be a good reason, so check what is on the disk before making any changes. If the disk is not write-protected it may either be unformatted or have the wrong format. You can make the disk usable by formatting it (although if it was a disk of the wrong format you will destroy any data on it, which another type of computer might have been able to use).

If your computer refuses to format a disk, either the disk is write-protected or the disk is faulty.

### Key points to remember

- Floppy disks are easily damaged.
- Floppy disks should be stored in closed boxes, away from heat and magnets.
- Most problems with floppy disks are due to using write-protected disks.

### *Putting it into practice*

*Check through your floppy disks to see which of them are write-protected and which are not. If you find any disks on which you do not want to change the data (such as original program disks or disks that you are keeping as a record of what you have done) write-protect them.*

# Topic 2 – Solving problems

## Mouse problems

**IT 104**

Foundation/Intermediate/
Advanced
Element **1.4,2.4,3.4**
Performance criteria **5,6**
Range **Problems;
Working safely**

Most computers now require a mouse in order to operate them effectively. Because mice are partly mechanical devices, over time things can go wrong with them.

## How a mouse works

There are several types of mouse, and only the most common is described here. When you move the mouse, the ball within rolls, turning two rollers set at right-angles to each other. Each roller turns a wheel, with slots in it. On one side of each wheel is a light, and on the other side is a light detector. As the wheel turns, the light is alternately let through by the slots and blocked by the wheel. The circuitry in the mouse detects this and uses the signal from the light beam to calculate how far the mouse has moved. This is then translated into information that the computer can understand.

### Activity

Turn your mouse upside down and remove the cover that keeps the ball in place (You should be able to do this by hand; if you need to use a screwdriver, or if the ball cover is permanently fixed, don't attempt this activity.) Remove the ball and describe what you can see. Then replace the ball and its cover.

■ You should see two small rollers at right-angles to each other, together with a third spring-loaded roller. This roller keeps the ball firmly pressed against the other two rollers. You might also have seen part of the mouse's circuitry. Do not touch this. ■

### Activity

Here are some other problems with mice. Try to match each one with a likely cause.

1 The mouse pointer does not appear on the screen.
2 The mouse pointer appears but does not move when you move the mouse.
3 The mouse pointer moves erratically in bright sunlight.
4 The pointer moves properly, but clicking the mouse button has no effect.

A The computer recognises the mouse but the program you are using does not.
B The mouse buttons are worn out.
C The computer does not recognise that you have a mouse attached.
D The mouse's light-sensing circuitry is being swamped by light coming through gaps around the mouse buttons.

■ The answer to *1* is **C**. Check that the mouse is properly attached to the computer; if it is, check your mouse's manual to find out how to solve the problem or ask for help.

The most common reason for situation *2* is **A**. You should consult the program's manual and your mouse's manual to find a solution. This problem can also be caused by the mouse being accidentally disconnected from the computer (check the cable) or by the ball being removed from the mouse. This practical joke has led some colleges to seal the ball cover – which means that you can't clean the ball or the rollers.

Situation *3* only happens with some mice and is caused by **D**. Bright desk lamps can have a similar effect. The cure is to take the mouse away from the light or to use a blind.

Finally, situation *4* is usually caused by **B**. If you have trouble with single clicks or with dragging the mouse pointer, then it's likely that the mouse button has worn out. There is no cure, you'll need to buy a new mouse. However, if you have trouble with making a double click but no problems with single clicking, check your software to see whether you can alter the time interval between clicks to make double clicking easier. ■

### Key points to remember

- The mechanical parts of a mouse can break down quite easily.
- If you have checked for mechanical problems, the problem may lie with your software or the mouse's software.
- Broken mouse buttons cannot be mended.

### Putting it into practice

*Write a mouse maintenance sheet for your colleagues. If they are using the same type of mouse, include information about any problems you have encountered and solved.*

# Topic 2 – Solving problems

## Keyboards

**IT 106**

Foundation/Intermediate/Advanced
Element **1.4, 2.4, 3.4**
Performance criteria **3, 4, 5, 6**
Range **Problems; Working safely; Evaluate; Systems**

Keyboard problems can be split into three categories: hardware problems, setup problems and user problems (i.e., incorrect use of the keyboard).

### Hardware problems

Like mice, keyboards are partly mechanical devices, and can therefore be broken quite easily.

#### Activity

Here are some ways in which keyboards can get damaged. Which of them can happen to a new keyboard and which to an old keyboard?

1. liquid spills over the keyboard, causing a short circuit in the keyboard's electronics
2. dust and dirt gather under the keys, preventing a proper connection from being made when you press the key
3. one or two keys fail to work properly

▐▐ *Situation 1 can happen to any keyboard, old or new. Liquids damage keyboards very easily, and some people use thin, transparent keyboard covers to protect the keyboard from accidental spills. These covers can interfere with your typing, so they are not popular.*

*Situation 2 affects older keyboards, although not all will be affected. When it happens, you might find that you have to press very hard or sharply to make a key work properly, which can rapidly wear out the key. To deal with the problem, use a vacuum cleaner every so often to remove the dust. (Check that the tops of the keys won't be sucked into the vacuum cleaner!)*

*Situation 3, surprisingly, affects very new and very old keyboards. Keys sometimes fail to work because of faulty manufacturing; if this is the case, your supplier should provide you with a replacement. On very old keyboards the keys and their connections can simply wear out. This nearly always means buying a new keyboard.* ▐▐

### Set-up problems

These involve your keyboard's connection to the computer and the software your computer needs to tell it what type of keyboard you have.

#### Keyboards and languages

Although the basic elements of any keyboard are the same from country to country, different languages require different keyboard layouts to cope with such things as accented characters or different characters. In the UK, for example, our keyboards all have a '£' symbol, which is missing from US keyboards. Since most computers are of US origin, unless you tell your computer that you have a UK keyboard the computer will assume that you have a US one and give you a $ character whenever you press £.

#### Activity

Here are two possible keyboard set-up problems and three possible causes. Match each problem to the right cause (the other cause is a red herring).

1. When you turn your computer on it stops and displays the message

    ```
    Keyboard error
    Press <F1> to resume
    ```

2. the wrong characters appear when you press certain keys.

- **A** Your keyboard is not connected to the computer.
- **B** You are using a keyboard made in a foreign country.
- **C** Your computer is set up to expect a keyboard with a different language or key layout.

▐▐ *Problem 1 is famous in the computer world. After all, if the keyboard isn't working, what good will pressing F1 do? The answer is A, because what the message really means is 'Plug the keyboard into the computer and then press F1'.*

*If you answered B to problem 2, you've been fooled by the red herring. Most keyboards are made overseas, with different versions being supplied to different countries. Your keyboard may have been made in Taiwan, for example, but it is still a UK keyboard. What matters is the computer's setup C, as described in the box.* ▐▐

### User problems

Keyboards have a number of keys that are unfamiliar to typewriter users, as well as others that can be pressed accidentally, giving the wrong results.

# Topic 2 – Solving problems

## Keyboards (continued)

### Activity

Some or all of the following keys may be present on your keyboard. For each one, if it appears on your keyboard, describe what it does and what problems might occur if you accidentally press it.

- Caps Lock
- Print Screen (or PrtSc)
- Num Lock

▌▌ *The effects vary from situation to situation, but here's what you can expect. Caps Lock will make every letter you type a capital letter. This is fine if you want capitals otherwise you could end up having to retype everything. Print Screen attempts to send the current screen display to the printer (on IBM PCs). If your printer is not turned on, this may appear to cause the computer to crash, because the computer will wait patiently for the printer and will not allow you to do anything else. (If you are running Windows, Print Screen copies the screen display to the Clipboard, causing no problems.) Num Lock affects the numeric keypad on the right-hand side of your keyboard. When Num Lock is on, numbered keys display numbers on the screen; when Num lock is off, the keypad acts as a set of cursor keys.* ▌▌

Other keys can also cause problems, depending on the type of computer. Consult your computer's manual to find out what any keys that you don't recognise do.

### Key points to remember

- Keyboards are mechanical devices, subject to wear and tear.
- Computers usually need to be told what keyboard layout/language the keyboard uses.
- Pressing certain keys can have undesirable effects.

### *Putting it into practice*

Write a 'Keyboard troubleshooting' guide for your colleagues. Include any problems that you have had and the solutions that you found.

# Topic 2 – Solving problems

**IT 107**

## Software crashes and general protection faults

Foundation/Intermediate/
Advanced
Element **1.4, 2.4, 3.4**
Performance criteria **3, 4, 5, 6**
Range **Problems; Working safely; Evaluate; Systems**

## What is a crash?

A crash occurs whenever a program unexpectedly stops running properly. Crashes are caused by mistakes (or 'bugs') in programs, and there is usually very little you can do to stop them happening; a crash is not your fault.

Crashes are always undesirable, and their effects can range from being a nuisance to endangering life and limb. They tend to happen most often in new software or when you are pushing a program to its limits (such as creating a complex page with tables and graphics in a word processor).

### The causes of crashes

A crash occurs when the program tries to do something impossible. For instance, if the document that you are trying to save is bigger than the available space on the disk, then the program might crash (unless the programmer has guarded against this and told the program what to do instead).

Another possibility is that a calculation might result in a number that a computer cannot understand. All computers have limits on the range of numbers they can use, and the programmer can't be certain that some combination of values won't cause a problem. The most common crash of this kind occurs when a program attempts to divide a number by zero, giving the result infinity, which computers can't handle.

In a more complex situation, two programs running at the same time might interfere with each other by trying to use the same piece of memory. Eventually, one or other program will try to use that part of memory and will be unable to find what it expects, leading, normally, to a crash.

### Activity

For each of the following situations, say whether the most likely effect of a crash would be: time-wasting, but no damage done; loss of data and work done; financial loss; dangerous to human life.

1. word processing program crashes when trying to save a file
2. word processing program crashes when trying to open a file
3. nuclear reactor control program crashes
4. a database crashes, losing all of the names and addresses of a company's clients.

■■ *1 would lead to data loss; 2 would probably be just time-wasting; 3 could easily endanger human life; and 4 would probably lead to financial loss. However, all of these depend on the situation in which they occur, for example, if the database crash involved a hospital's patients' details there could be a danger to life.* ■■

### Identifying a crash

Sometimes a crash is obvious. At other times, the program might appear to be doing something but taking a very long time over it.

Deciding whether a program has crashed or is simply taking a long time to complete a task is not always easy, and to some extent is a matter of experience. You'll get used to the normal amount of time that the computer takes for common tasks, and if it takes more than three or four times as long as usual then you may have a crash.

If you are using a different computer from the one you normally use, and that computer is slower than yours, then everything will seem slower than usual. You need to make allowances for this when deciding whether the computer has crashed or not. If the computer shows no sign of completing its task you should first check to see whether the hard disk activity light on the front of the computer's case is flashing. If it is, then the computer is using the hard disk and all is probably well.

Next, check the screen: you may find a message somewhere on it saying '27% complete', or there may be a coloured 'progress bar' that increases in length. If the message or the progress bar gets updated every few seconds then the program has not crashed.

If there are no signs of activity, try pressing one or two cursor keys. If the cursor on the screen moves, then the program is still running.

### Dealing with a crash

First of all, don't panic. Don't press lots of keys to try to make something happen, and don't immediately switch the computer off. You may be able to close down just the crashed program. If you don't know how to do this, find someone who does. Then close down any other programs, saving your work. When you have safely closed down all of your programs (including Windows, if appropriate), then is the time to restart your computer.

### Activity

Why should you not switch the computer off immediately when a crash occurs?

■■ *Your main aim is to avoid losing your data. If other programs are still running, you could lose the data in those programs by switching your computer off. Report crashes to your technical support staff.* ■■

# Topic 2 – Solving problems

## Software crashes and general protection faults (continued)

### General protection faults

This kind of crash happens when running Windows 3.1 on an IBM-compatible PC. A general protection fault (or GPF) occurs when a program tries to use memory that Windows is protecting for use by another program. The program trying to use that memory is then unable to so and has no alternative course of action.

When a GPF occurs you'll see a dialog box like:

---

**TEXTART**

An error has occurred in your application.
If you choose Ignore, you should save your work in a new file.
If you choose Close, your application will terminate.

[Close]    [Ignore]

---

You can try choosing Ignore, but it usually results in the same dialog box reappearing. When you choose Close, you will see another dialog box:

---

**Application Error**

TEXTART caused a General Protection Fault in module TEXTART.EXE at 0006:0541

[Close]

---

This information is of use only to the original programmer. If the same GPF occurs repeatedly, it is a good idea to write down this information so that you can give it to the software company's technical support staff when reporting the problem. Otherwise, just choose Close.

Choosing Close should close down the application that crashed but leave the rest of Windows running as normal. As a rule, you should be able to restart the crashed program and start work again, but sometimes the GPF is sufficiently serious not to allow this. The only solution then is to close all the programs that are running, exit Windows and then restart Windows from MS-DOS.

In Windows 3.0, GPFs are called 'unrecoverable application errors' or UAEs. These always cause the program to crash and always require you to exit and restart Windows.

### Protecting yourself from crashes

There is only one way to protect yourself from the effects of a crash, and that is to save your work often and back up your data regularly. If you do that, then the worst that can happen is that you lose work you did between the time of your last save and the time of the crash. For more information about backing up data, see the Resource sheet 'Hard disks'.

---

**Key points to remember**

- Crashes are unavoidable.
- Crashes can have serious effects.
- Try to minimise the loss of data when a crash occurs.

*Putting it into practice*

*Keep a written record of crashes that happen to you and how you dealt with them. This might also help you to avoid the situations that led to those crashes. Also, find out whether there is a procedure in your organisation for reporting and dealing with crashes.*

# Topic 2 – Solving problems

## Opening files

**IT 108**

Foundation/Intermediate/Advanced
Element **1.4, 2.4, 3.4**
Performance criteria **3, 4, 5**
Range **Evaluate; Systems; Problems**

Files (such as word processor documents, spreadsheets and databases) have to be opened before they can be used. Usually this is not a problem; provided you store your files in sensible places on your hard disk you will always be able to find and open them. However, you may occasionally encounter problems.

## Case study

Paul worked as an accounts assistant in a small company, and regularly used several spreadsheet files in his work. However, on one occasion, the spreadsheet program crashed as he tried to open a file. He restarted the program and tried again, but the same thing happened. Then he tried to open another file, but this time there were no problems. A third attempt to open the problem file again caused the program to crash.

Fortunately, he had a back-up copy of the file on a floppy disk. The program had no difficulty in opening the back-up file, so Paul deleted the problem file and copied the back-up version to his hard disk. He concluded that the file that caused the problem had been damaged in some way.

### Activity

When a file is damaged (possibly by accidentally switching the computer off while the program was still running), trying to open the damaged file has several potential consequences. Which of the following is not likely to happen when you try to open the file?

1. The program loads only a part of the file.
2. The program crashes.
3. The program repairs the damage and restores the data in the file.

■ *Situation 1 is a little unusual, but sometimes happens. If you notice that only part of a file seems to have been loaded, save it immediately using a new name and then compare the file with your most recent back-up. You should be able to avoid losing all of your data in this way. If 2 happens (which is most likely), you will have to go back to your most recent back-up. Programs are available that try to repair damaged files, but they require a high level of technical skill to use, and are only worth using for very large files. Situation 3 is pure fantasy; it isn't possible for a program to know that data has been lost from a file.*

*It is very important to keep back-up files to protect yourself from the worst consequences of a damaged file.* ■

A damaged file is not the only reason that you might have difficulty opening a file. Several more are listed below.

- Wrong program

  A file created by one program might not be in a format that another program (even of the same type) can use. There may be an option to 'Import' files from other programs (including other types of program, so that, for example, a spreadsheet might be able to open a database file). Depending on what computer you are using, identifying the correct program to use can be easy (for example on a Macintosh, where the name of the program used can be displayed on the screen) or almost impossible (for example on an IBM PC). In the latter case, the filename extension may be your only clue. For instance, .DOC should indicate a word processor file, .TXT an ASCII file, .DBF a database file, .WKS a spreadsheet file and .PCX a graphics file.

- Wrong version of a program

  Although newer versions of a program will be able to open files created by older versions of the same program, the reverse is not true. A file created by, say WordPerfect 6.0, cannot be opened by WordPerfect 4.0. Identifying which version of a program created a document is possible only by trial and error on some computers.

- Wrong type of computer

  A file created by one type of computer cannot usually be opened on a different type of computer.

- Insufficient rights

  If you are working on a network, you will almost certainly find that there are some files that you are not allowed to open.

- Wrong filename

  Sometimes, all that is wrong is that you have typed the filename incorrectly. It can be quite hard to spot your mistake.

- Insufficient memory

  Large files may need more memory than your computer has available after loading the program. This is particularly true of large graphics files, which can occupy several megabytes of RAM.

# Topic 2 – Solving problems

## Opening files (continued)

### File formats

In order for a program to be able to make sense of the data in a file it must record the data in such a way that it can reconstruct the appearance of the file exactly when it is next opened. For example, in a word processor file the word processor must store all the information about font changes (bold and italic), location of pictures, margins, headers, footers and so on, as well as simply storing the text. Each program does this in a different way, which is why Microsoft Word, for example, cannot always open files created with WordPerfect. Fortunately, most software companies provide facilities for opening files from other programs, although some of the layout information frequently changes.

### Key points to remember

- Different programs use different file formats.
- Filename extensions can be used as a guide to which program should be used to open a file.
- Always keep back-up files of your work.

### *Putting it into practice*

*Make a list of the main programs on your system. Add to the list the filename extension(s) that each program normally uses and the version number of the program that you are using. If a program has an 'Import' option, include in the list the types of file that the program can open in this way.*

### Activity

For each of the following situations, say what you think the source of the problem is.

1. Your word processor fails to open a file called CUSTOMER.DBF
2. Your spreadsheet program gives the message 'Unable to open file' when you try to open a file on another computer in the network.
3. On an IBM-compatible PC, you ask your word processor to open the file SALES.DOV and you receive the message 'No such file'.

■ *In 1, the filename extension DBF should suggest to you that you are trying to open a database file, not a word processor file. Some word processors can do this, but not many. Situation 2 is typical of networks. In this case, the network allows you to see what files exist on the other computer but not to open them. If you really need to open the file you will have to ask the network administrator to give you the necessary rights. In 3, you should suspect a mistyped filename, particularly if your word processor always uses DOC as its filename extension. The correct filename is probably SALES.DOC* ■

# Topic 2 – Solving problems

## Running programs

**IT 109**

Foundation/Intermediate/
Advanced
Element **1.4,2.4,3.4**
Performance criteria **3,4,5**
Range **Evaluate; Systems; Problems**

Most of the time when you are using a computer you use the same programs and run them in the same way. Sometimes, though, a program refuses to run.

There are three main reasons for a program not running: lack of memory, a damaged file or inadequate hardware.

### Activity

A computer that has always run your favourite program with no problems suddenly refuses to run that program. In all other respects the computer appears to be working normally. Which of the three reasons given above is most likely to have stopped your program from running?

■ *Because you know that the program worked properly in the past, you know that you have enough memory and sufficiently powerful hardware. By elimination, that leaves only a damaged file as the likely culprit. Tracking down the exact file is sometimes possible, but the cure usually involves reinstalling the program from the original disks that it was supplied on. Consult an expert before you attempt to do this, as the problem may be more involved than just reinstalling the software.*

*Lack of memory usually only causes a problem when you buy a new program some time after you bought the computer. For example, suppose your computer has 4 Mbyte of RAM and your software's manual says that the program requires 6 Mbyte to run. (This figure usually assumes that no other programs are running at the same time.) Clearly, the program will not be able to run in this situation. You will usually receive a message such as 'Insufficient memory to run program' when this happens.* ■

### Activity

Your computer has 8 Mbyte of RAM and your favourite word processor (which requires 4 Mbyte of RAM) is running. You try to run your database program (which requires 6 Mbyte of RAM) at the same time, but you receive a message saying that you have insufficient memory. Why is this?

■ *After running your word processor, you have only 4 Mbyte free for other programs. It is this figure, not the total amount of memory in your computer, that you have to take into account when working out whether you can run another program.*

*You will be able to run your database if you close your word processor first. If you absolutely have to have both programs running at once, the only cure is to buy more memory and fit it to your computer. You should consult an expert to do this.* ■

Lack of memory can also be caused without you realising that other programs are even running. However, when you start your computer several programs are run, and these all take up small amounts of memory, which can add up to a large enough total to prevent some programs running. If you add a new piece of equipment to your computer, such as a scanner, the extra memory used by the program that controls the scanner might be just enough to stop another program, which used to run quite happily. Solving this problem requires detailed knowledge of how your computer is set up, and should only be attempted by an expert.

The third reason for a program to fail to run is because one or more components of your computer system is not up to the task. For example, a program might require a colour screen in order to run, or a particular microprocessor.

### Activity

Your computer has a black and white screen, but you want to use a colour graphics program. Which of the following is likely to be occur?

1. The program will allow you to create colour graphics in spite of your black and white screen.
2. The program will refuse to run.
3. The program will run, but only in black and white.

■ *1 is highly unlikely. The ability to display colours is inherent in the computer, and no amount of clever software will allow you to work in colour on a black and white screen. The most likely outcome is 2, but it is just possible that 3 will occur (provided the program has been written to cope with a black and white screen).* ■

The golden rule is never to buy software unless your computer meets all of the requirements of that software. Ideally, your computer should exceed the minimum requirements, since software manufacturers tend to be over-optimistic about how usable the program will be on a computer that just meets the minimum requirements.

# Topic 2 – Solving problems

## Running programs (continued)

### Key points to remember

- Programs will run only if the computer matches certain minimum requirements.
- The main reasons for failure to run are insufficient memory, inadequate hardware and damaged files.
- Other programs can reduce the amount of memory available to run other programs.

### Putting it into practice

*Check your software manuals for details of the minimum requirements for each program to run. Then check your computer to see that it matches those requirements. Keep a record of your computer's specification so that you can compare any new software against it.*

# Topic 2 – Solving problems

## Undoing mistakes

**IT 110**

Foundation/Intermediate/Advanced
Element **1.4, 2.4, 3.4**
Performance criteria **3,4,5,6**
Range **Problems; Working safely; Evaluate; Systems**

## Making mistakes

Everybody makes mistakes. While writing this resource sheet, the author made several typing mistakes, all of which (by the time you read this) should have been corrected. The important thing to remember is that software usually contains features that help you to correct your mistakes.

Most of your mistakes would be simple typing errors If you spot these as you type you can correct them by editing your text, but you should use your word processor's spell checker as a safety net when you have finished your document and are ready to print it. Spelling mistakes can wreck a job application or an advertisement, so make use of the tools available to correct them.

Other mistakes may occur when editing the text. Suppose you decide to copy a sentence, but accidentally delete it instead. You should be able to choose an 'Undo' or 'Undelete' option to restore the text. Some programs use such options in different ways, so it is worth getting to know exactly how they work in the program you are using.

### Activity

Open a document and practise deleting and undeleting text. Where does your word processor put the text when you undelete it?

■ *You may find that your text is always put back in the position from which you deleted it. In other programs, it will be put back at the current cursor position.* ■

Programs other than word processors may also contain undo facilities, but they tend to use them in a different way, depending on the type of program.

### Activity

Open a graphics program, if you have one (e.g., MacPaint, Windows Paintbrush). Experiment with the undo option. What does it do?

■ *Graphics programs sometimes appear to use the undo facility in a very strange way. For example, if you draw several straight lines and then choose 'Undo', you might find that just the last line that you drew is deleted, or you might find that all of the lines were deleted. It all depends on what the program considers to be a single action. In some programs you may be able to use several levels of undo, so that choosing it once deletes the most recently drawn line, choosing it again deletes the next most recent, and so on. In yet other programs, choosing 'Undo' twice in succession leaves you back where you started, i.e., the second 'Undo' undoes the first 'Undo'.*

*All this means that you can't take 'Undo' for granted; you have to learn how to use it.*

*As a rule, 'Undo' works only on data in memory. If you save a file you can't undo the save and get the previous version of the file back. 'Undo' will also not undo changes to a file that has been saved, closed and reopened. Printing operations cannot be undone either, although if you are quick you can cancel a print job before it is sent from the computer to the printer.* ■

### Activity

For each of the following actions, say whether you can or cannot undo it.

1. deleting a word from your word processor document
2. deleting a page from your word processor document
3. saving a file
4. drawing a red circle in a graphics program.

■ *Unless you are very unlucky, only 3 cannot be undone. A few programs will also keep the previously saved version of the file on the disk, using a slightly different name, but it is comparatively unusual.* ■

### Key points to remember

- Spell checkers are easy to use and provide a safety net to correct errors.
- Most programs have an 'Undo' or 'Undelete' option.
- 'Undo' works differently in different programs.

### Putting it into practice

*Make a list of how the 'Undo' or 'Undelete' options in each of your programs operate. Include any special features, such as multiple levels of undo.*

# Topic 2 – Solving problems

## Viruses

**IT 112**

Foundation/Intermediate/Advanced
Element 1.4, 2.4, 3.4
Performance criteria 3, 4, 5, 6
Range **Problems; Working safely; Evaluate; Systems**

### What is a virus?

Nothing in computing is more misunderstood than the subject of viruses. If you are careful, you need never lose data to a virus. The first step is to understand what a virus is. The precise definition of a computer virus varies from person to person, but a simple definition is that a computer virus is a computer program, written by a human programmer, that is designed to copy itself from disk to disk and disrupt the way that the computer works or damage the data stored on the computer. Notice that nowhere in this definition is there any suggestion that computer viruses have any connection with the viruses that cause disease in humans. You cannot catch a disease from a computer virus, and a computer cannot catch a virus from you!

### Activity

Which of the following statements about computer viruses are true and which are false?

1. Viruses are mutated programs.
2. Viruses can copy themselves from one computer to another.
3. Computer viruses are a special form of biological virus.
4. Viruses can cause loss of data.

▌▌ *Statement 1 is not true. No normal program can suddenly turn itself into a virus. Statement 2 is true; by copying themselves from disk to disk they can be transmitted from one computer to another. They hide themselves on floppy disks, and when an 'infected' disk is placed in another computer the virus copies itself to the new computer's hard disk. As new disks are inserted into the infected computer, the virus makes more copies of itself on those disks, which can then be passed to other computers, affecting them as well. Viruses can also be transmitted around networks. 3 is a common myth, based on the way that both types of virus behave. Statement 4 is true of many viruses. Nobody is really sure why some programmers write viruses. It is a crime in many countries to do so.*

*Virus attacks are rare, but can have serious consequences. The effects of viruses can range from displaying silly messages on your screen to deleting all of the data on your hard disk (which could cause loss of life if it happens on a hospital's computer). A virus can wait on your computer for quite a lengthy period before it does anything; some spring to life only when certain programs run or on certain dates.* ▌▌

### Activity

Here are some viruses and their effects. Which one is the most dangerous?

- Ping Pong – displays a ping pong ball that bounces around your screen and stops you from working.
- Michelangelo – deletes all the data on your hard disk but only if you start the computer on 6 March (the anniversary of Michelangelo's birth).
- Pathogen – deletes data, but only at certain times of the week. Displays the message 'Smoke me a kipper, I'll be back for breakfast – But some of your data won't!'.

▌▌ *Ping Pong doesn't affect your hard disk, but might lose you some unsaved work. Pathogen and Michelangelo are more dangerous, but Pathogen is more easily triggered. Of course, this means that Pathogen is more quickly detected and won't infect as many disks, so you could argue that Michelangelo, which could lie low for a year or more, infecting hundreds of disks, is more dangerous.* ▌▌

### Protecting your computer from viruses

A virus can only get onto your computer if you let it. This means that it must be given a chance to run (remember that it is a computer program, and just as you can't use your spreadsheet program without running it, a virus can't copy itself without first running). Viruses are very good at hiding themselves and you need special software to find them before they can run.

### Activity

Which of the following will stop a virus getting onto your computer?

1. never using floppy disks
2. checking the list of files on a disk before you use it
3. using a special program to check for viruses.

▌▌ *1 will certainly work, but you'll find it hard to get any software onto your computer and you won't be able to do any back-ups, so it's not a sensible option. 2 won't work because viruses make a point of hiding themselves; simply looking at a directory of files on the disk won't help to find a virus. 3 is the best approach. An 'anti-virus' program, if used properly, will do three things. First, it will check your computer's hard disk and memory for any viruses that may be present. Second, it will provide a means to remove any viruses from your computer. You should read your anti-*

# Topic 2 – Solving problems

## Viruses (continued)

virus software's manual to find out how to do this. Third, if you use it to check every floppy disk that you put into your computer, it will prevent viruses from gaining access.

If your computer is on a network your network supervisor should provide additional anti-virus measures to prevent viruses from being transmitted around the network.

### Key points to remember

- Viruses are self-copying, data-damaging programs.
- Viruses can be kept off your computer by using anti-virus software.
- Virus attacks are rare but potentially disastrous.

### Putting it into practice

Find out the procedures in your organisation for checking for viruses and make sure that you abide by them. If there is no such procedure, try to have one set up.

# Topic 2 – Solving problems

## Finding files

**IT 113**

Foundation/Intermediate/
Advanced
Element **1.4,2.4,3.4**
Performance criteria **3,4,5,6**
Range **Problems; Working safely; Evaluate; Range**

### Case study

Alan had prepared a set of documents for his boss that were needed for an important meeting. Just before his boss left for the meeting, she said, 'Oh – can I have a copy of those files on disk please?' But Alan couldn't remember where they all were, and by the time he had tracked them down and copied them to a floppy disk, his boss was ten minutes late for the meeting.

Everybody wants to avoid this situation, but it's easy to forget where your files are.

### Activity

Which of the following might be a reason for not being able to find a file?

1. You have saved the file in a different folder from usual.
2. Your computer has deleted the file without telling you.
3. You have forgotten the name of the file.

■ *1 is an easy mistake to make, especially if you work for more than one person or on lots of different projects. 2 is almost impossible and definitely not a good excuse if you can't find a file. Computers don't delete files unless you tell them to. 3 is very common. Some computers make life harder than others in this respect. If you use an IBM-compatible PC, which allows only very short filenames, you often find yourself using hard-to-remember filenames like JNSLS95.WKS (a spreadsheet file containing sales information for January 1995). The name may seem easy to remember at the time, but a year later you won't remember whether the name means 'January sales', 'June sales' or even 'Jane's list'.* ■

### Activity

One way to make it easier to remember where you put files is to use sensibly named folders (or directories). What do you think each of the following documents contains?

1. JANUARY.WKS, stored in C:\SPREAD\SALES\1995
2. JUNE.DOC, stored in C:\WORDPRO\BOARD\MEETING\MINUTES
3. FERRARI.PCX, stored C:\GRAPHICS\CARS

■ *These should be much clearer. 1 is a spreadsheet of sales for January 1995, 2 is a document containing the minutes of the company's June board meeting, and 3 is a picture of a Ferrari. Notice how 1 is much clearer than trying to put all the information into one filename (JNSLS95.WKS). Whenever you create a new document, think carefully about which folder to put it in. Once you have developed a good system, stick to it. It will speed up the finding of files and help you to decide, at a later date, which ones can be safely deleted.* ■

### Activity

Despite setting up a good system for storing your files, you have accidentally put one of them in the wrong place, and now you can't find it. Which of the following ideas would be the best way to try to find it?

1. Look through every folder (or directory) on your hard disk, checking to see whether your missing file is there.
2. Get the computer to search for the file.
3. Give up and recreate the file from a printout.

■ *1 would eventually work, but you would have to check through dozens of folders and possibly hundreds or thousands of files. Even then you might miss what you were looking for. 2 is definitely the best idea. Computers are much faster at this kind of task. The method you use will depend on your computer but most computers have some way of finding files provided you know the filename (or part of it). For example, Windows users can use the 'Search...' option from File Manager's File menu. The task is not as easy in MS-DOS; change to the root directory by typing CD\ and then type DIR /S followed by the name of the file you have lost. MS-DOS will then tell you where the file is. (This method will not work on older versions of MS-DOS.) 3 smacks of desperation. If the file definitely exists, it will always be quicker to search for it than to try to recreate it. Nobody gets paid to do work twice!* ■

If you have searched for the file but can't find it, you may have stored the file on a different disk drive. This happens all too often if you have more than one hard disk or are using a network. The only way to find the file (unless you have a separate program that can search more than one disk) is to search each disk individually.

If searching other hard disks also doesn't work, it might be that you were searching for the wrong filename. Suppose you saved the file as JSMITH.LET. If you search for JSMITH.DOC, you won't be able to find the file. In this case you could try using wildcards in your search: try JSMITH.* instead of JSMITH.DOC.

It is also possible that you saved the file on a floppy disk instead of a hard disk. To find the file will mean searching all the likely floppy disks.

If all this fails, but you are sure the file exists, some programs (especially word processors) will allow you to search for files containing certain words. Consult your software's manual to see if this option is available.

# Topic 2 – Solving problems

## Finding files (continued)

### Key points to remember

- Files can be lost either because you don't know the name or because they have been stored in the wrong place.
- Use folders (directories) to save files in easily locatable places.
- You can use facilities provided by your computer to locate missing files provided you know at least part of the filename.

### *Putting it into practice*

*Look at the folders on your hard disk and see whether your files are stored in a sensible set of folders. If not, create the necessary folders and move and rename files so that they are more easily found.*

## Topic 3 – Health and Safety

### Repetitive strain injury

**IT 114**

Foundation/Intermediate/
Advanced
Element **1.4, 2.4, 3.4**
Performance criteria **5, 6**
Range **Problems;
Working safely**

Repetitive strain injury (RSI) has received a lot of publicity recently, due mainly to the growth in the use of computers in offices. This resource sheet will concentrate on the prevention of RSI, rather than its treatment.

If you feel any pain in your hands, arms or shoulders after long periods of work with a computer, see your doctor immediately. A delay of even a couple of days can turn an easily treatable problem into a lifelong illness.

### What is RSI?

RSI is not an illness in itself, but a term that describes several disorders. The main one affecting computer users is carpal tunnel syndrome. The carpal tunnel, formed by the bones in the wrist, is the passage through which tendons, nerves and blood vessels pass. If the tendons become swollen through misuse they can pinch the blood vessels and nerves increasing pain in the wrist and arm and numbness in the fingers. Once the tendons become swollen, it is easier for further irritation to occur, leading to more swelling and more irritation – a vicious circle. Permanent damage can result if the condition is not treated quickly.

RSI is not new; similar conditions have affected manual workers on production lines for many years.

### Activity

Do some typing yourself and indicate which of the following joints you move a lot while typing and which tend to remain fixed:

|  | Move | Fixed |
|---|---|---|
| Fingers | ☐ | ☐ |
| Wrist | ☐ | ☐ |
| Elbow | ☐ | ☐ |
| Shoulder | ☐ | ☐ |

■ *You probably found that for most of the time your wrists and elbows stay fixed in one position and that you move your finger joints to press the keys and use your shoulders to move your hands around the keyboard. If your wrists are bent (and stuck in one position) the constant*
*finger movements can cause irritation in the carpal tunnel.*

### Case study

A short while after she started work as a data inputter (using a computer keyboard), Jane noticed that she was getting shooting pains in her arms towards the end of a day's work. The pains vanished on the way home, but returned late the following day.

After a couple of days of this pain, Jane found that the pain did not go away in the evening. Her arms hurt when lifting a saucepan or just turning a door handle. The following morning she went to see her doctor.

Jane's doctor told her not to go to work and to rest her wrists and arms as completely as possible. He also suggested that she put ice-packs on her wrists to relieve the swelling.

### Activity

The doctor also gave Jane some advice on how to prevent carpal tunnel syndrome from recurring. Some of the things she was told to do would need help from her employer, while others she could take care of herself. For each piece of advice, tick the box according to whether Jane, her employer or both together need to take action.

1. Improve your typing technique. Jane's doctor pointed out that her wrists should be kept straight, bent neither upwards nor downwards. Jane tended to rest her wrists on the desktop as she typed, which forced her hands to bend upwards.

   Action by: Jane ☐ Employer ☐ Both ☐

2. Use a wrist rest. A wrist rest in front of the keyboard can help to keep the wrists straight.

   Action by: Jane ☐ Employer ☐ Both ☐

3. Adjust the height of your chair. Most typists sit in comparatively high chairs so that their hands and wrists naturally fall into the right position.

   Action by: Jane ☐ Employer ☐ Both ☐

4. Sit correctly. Jane should sit well back in her chair so that her back is properly supported. Her feet should be flat on the floor (or on a footrest), and her calves should be perpendicular to the floor. She should not rest her arms on the arms of the chair.

   Action by: Jane ☐ Employer ☐ Both ☐

# Topic 3 – Health and Safety

## Repetitive strain injury (continued)

5. Take regular breaks. Jane should avoid typing for long periods. She should pause every 10 minutes or so and every 30 minutes leave the keyboard and do something else. When not typing, Jane should avoid resting her hands on the desk; she should rest them in her lap or do something different with them

    Action by:   Jane ☐   Employer ☐   Both ☐

6. Use an ergonomic keyboard. There are special keyboards available with the keys arranged in a way that helps to keep the wrists straight.

    Action by:   Jane ☐   Employer ☐   Both ☐

7. Change your mouse. Using a mouse can also cause carpal tunnel syndrome. Changing to a better-quality mouse can reduce the strain on the wrist.

    Action by:   Jane ☐   Employer ☐   Both ☐

8. Avoid other repetitive activities that flex the wrists. Jane's job might also involve other tasks that use the wrists a lot, such as using a stapler.

    Action by:   Jane ☐   Employer ☐   Both ☐

❚❚ *Jane's employer has a responsibility to provide equipment such as an adjustable chair, an efficient mouse, wrist rest and (if other things don't help) an ergonomic keyboard. The employer should also provide adequate breaks. Jane must take responsibility for using the equipment, for her own technique and her activities outside work. They should both discuss issues, such as the other tasks she has to perform, which might help to alleviate Jane's condition.* ❚❚

### Glossary
**ergonomic** – describes equipment designed to fit the user

### Further information about RSI
Your local office of the Health and Safety Executive will be able to supply you with free leaflets about prevention of RSI. The European Commission's guidelines for working with computers are contained in Directive 90/270. All employers must comply with this directive.

### Key points to remember
- The group of illnesses known as RSI are potentially crippling.
- RSI can be prevented by good working conditions and typing technique.
- Consult your doctor immediately if you feel any pain at all in your upper limbs after working with a computer.

### Putting it into practice
*Draw up a list of things that you can do to avoid RSI in your own particular situation.*

# Topic 3 – Health and Safety

## Back pain

**IT 115**

Foundation/Intermediate/
Advanced
Element **1.4,2.4,3.4**
Performance criteria **5,6**
Range **Problems;
Working safely**

Back pain is one of the biggest causes of lost working days in Britain. Although computers are not commonly associated with back pain, there are situations in which they can cause problems.

### Activity

One of the causes of back pain is a bad sitting position. Next time you use a computer check which of the following things you do when you sit down.

|  | No | Yes |
|---|---|---|
| Sit with back upright | ☐ | ☐ |
| Feet flat on floor | ☐ | ☐ |
| Sit well back in chair | ☐ | ☐ |
| Sit in an adjustable chair | ☐ | ☐ |
| Look slightly down towards computer screen | ☐ | ☐ |

▌▌ *The way you sit at a computer can lead to back pain. One of the problems with computers is that it is very easy to sit in a fixed position for long periods. If your position is not good, then you may place unnecessary strain on your lower back muscles. Ideally, you should have ticked 'Yes' for all the items. The chair's height should be adjustable so that your typing position is comfortable. Your eyes should be about 70 cm (28 ins) from the screen and you should be looking slightly down towards it.*

*Every so often, change your position very slightly. Stand up every half hour and bend backwards.* ▌▌

Back pain can also be caused by trying to lift a computer. Computers (and monitors and printers) are heavy objects. If you have to move a computer to a new position, it is easy to forget this and try to lift too heavy a weight or to lift it awkwardly. Computers cause particular problems in this respect, since they are often placed in positions that make it difficult to lift them using a proper lifting technique.

Important points to remember when living heavy objects are:

- Don't try to lift too much. Monitors cause the most problems; they are very heavy for their size, and they are awkward to hold.
- Keep your back straight. The spine is at its strongest when it is upright and there are no sideways forces on it.
- Bend your knees. If your back is straight you will need to bend your knees to lift a heavy object. This makes the lift easier, because your leg muscles are stronger than your back muscles.

### Activity

The following diagrams show people making mistakes when lifting computers. For each one, say what the person is doing wrongly.

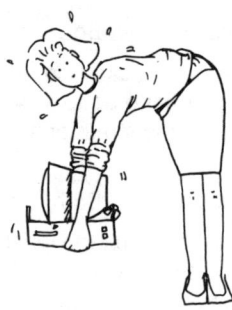 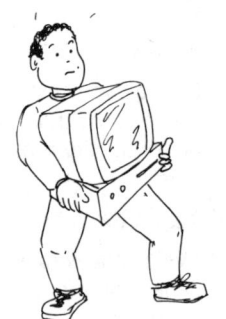

▌▌ *In the first diagram, the woman is bending over to pick up the computer, when she should be crouching to keep her back straight. In the second diagram, the man is trying to lift too much, with the result that he is placing too much stress on his back. (He is also unable to see where he's going – a recipe for disaster!)* ▌▌

If an object is very heavy, or is in a position where it is not easy to use the proper lifting technique, get help. Two people can make a safe lift where one person cannot. If no one is available to help you, wait until there is.

If the object is placed at the back of a desk, don't reach over the desk to lift it. Instead, slide the object towards you.

If you find that you are suffering from persistent back pain, consult your doctor, as well as taking the steps described above to prevent it. Your doctor may be able to offer additional treatment.

### Key points to remember

- Back pain can be caused by a poor seating position or by poor lifting technique.
- Your monitor should be correctly positioned.
- Consult your doctor if you experience back pain.

### *Putting it into practice*

*Monitor your own sitting position for a few days to see whether you are sitting properly. Adjust your seat if necessary.*

# Topic 3 – Health and Safety

## Eye strain

**IT 116**

Foundation/Intermediate/
Advanced
Element 1.4, 2.4, 3.4
Performance criteria 5, 6
Range **Problems;
Working safely**

Working with computers can force you to stare at the computer's monitor for long periods. Your eyesight itself may not be adversely affected but there are several problems that can be caused if your eyes are strained.

### Activity

Have you noticed any of these things while working at a computer?

| | Yes | No |
|---|---|---|
| Leaning forward to read the screen | ☐ | ☐ |
| Headaches | ☐ | ☐ |
| Dry eyes | ☐ | ☐ |

▮▮ *If you have to lean forward (perhaps because the text is too small or there is reflected glare on the screen) you will be forced into a bad sitting position that can lead to problems with your back and wrists. You could also find yourself having to move your eyes a lot to read the text, which can cause headaches.*

*Another cause of headaches is placing your monitor above eye level, which tends to cause you to move your eyes between the desk and the monitor. Wearers of bifocal spectacles have particular problems because they have to tip their head even further back than normal.*

*People tend not to blink very often when staring at a computer screen. If you don't blink often enough, your eyes can start to feel dry and painful. This may be enough to stop you from using the computer for a short while.*
▮▮

### Key points to remember

- Eye strain can be caused by a large number of factors.
- Eye strain can lead to other problems, for example, with your back.
- You can change the magnification of your screen display to improve readability.

### Activity

The following factors can affect your eyes. For each one, check that your working position is correct.

- Your eyes should be about 70 cm (28 ins) from the screen. If you are too far away, you may find it difficult to read the screen, while if you are too close you will have to move your eyes a lot to read the text, which will tire the eye muscles.

- Apart from being at the correct distance from your eyes, the monitor should also be at the correct height. You should be looking slightly downwards at the monitor, with your eyes roughly level with the top of the monitor. The monitor should not be placed on a shelf so that you have to look up at it.

- Your screen should be large enough for the work you are doing. A large screen can display more text than a small screen, or the same amount of text at a larger size. Alternatively, you can sometimes 'zoom in' to increase the size of the text on a small screen.

- The display should be neither too bright nor too dark, and its contrast level should allow you to read text comfortably. Most monitors allow you to adjust brightness and contrast.

- Light reflected from the screen can obscure part of the display if the monitor is wrongly positioned.

### Activity

Eye strain is comparatively easy to prevent. What would you do to deal with the following situations?

1. At certain times, the sun reflects strongly from the screen into David's eyes. He has to lean forward and sideways to see the screen clearly.
2. The text on Judith's screen is very small, which she finds hard to read.
3. Ali finds that the bright white background hurts his eyes.

▮▮
*1 David's problem could be dealt with either by repositioning his desk or by fitting a roller blind over the window.*

*2 For Judith, you could try using a bigger monitor. Alternatively, check whether her program has a 'Zoom' option which could magnify the text.*

*3 Ali's problem could be solved by adjusting the brightness and contrast controls on his monitor. It might also be possible to change the screen colours; green or pale blue text on a black background works well for many people.* ▮▮

As with all matters related to health, you should consult your doctor if you suffer from persistent problems related to eye strain.

### Putting it into practice

*Modify the way that your computer is set up so as to minimise the risk of eye strain. Use the list in the second activity to help you.*

# Topic 3 – Health and Safety

## Monitor radiation

**IT 117**

Foundation/Intermediate/
Advanced
Element **1.4,2.4,3.4**
Performance criteria **5,6**
Range **Problems;
Working safely**

The topic of monitors (or VDUs) and the radiation that they emit is highly controversial. The main reason for this is a suggested link between working at VDUs and miscarriages among pregnant women. If you are concerned about this, the best thing to do is to talk to your doctor and find out as much about the subject as possible. This resource sheet will help you to understand what radiation is emitted by monitors and what the potential effects on health are.

### Electromagnetic radiation

Electromagnetic radiation is the term used in physics to describe a wide range of phenomena, some of which are definitely harmful and some of which are precisely the opposite. Ordinary visible light is one kind of electromagnetic radiation, as are radio waves, microwaves, ultraviolet light, infrared light, X-rays and gamma-rays. Of these, high levels of microwaves, ultraviolet light, X-rays and gamma-rays

### Activity

A VDU is almost identical in design to a television set, and both emit the same kind of electromagnetic radiation. The potentially dangerous radiation is strongest at the back and sides of the television or VDU. Nobody is worried about watching television for long periods, but they are worried about working with VDUs. What differences are there between the ways in which televisions and computers are used which might increase the risks from VDUs?

■■ *The biggest difference is that you sit much closer to the screen when working at a computer than you do when watching television. This puts you much closer to any potentially harmful radiation. Some people also have to work at the computer all day, every day, whereas you don't often watch television for so long. In some offices, you might also have to sit close to the rear and sides of other people's VDUs, where the radiation levels are highest.* ■■

### Activity

Although the risks from VDUs are unproven, it is wise to be cautious and to minimise any possible risk, especially when this can be done at no cost. Which of the following does your set-up have:

- low-radiation monitor
- radiation screen over the display
- Seating position at least 1.2 m (4 ft) from the sides or back of other people's monitors
- LCD screen.

■■ *If your computer is reasonably new (only a year or two old) it should already have a low-radiation monitor. A radiation screen over the display can help to protect you, but not all of them work very effectively and none of them help with radiation from the back and sides of the monitor. Sitting well away from the back of other monitors is a simple solution if the workplace can be easily rearranged. Finally, if you are using a portable computer it probably has an LCD screen, which does not emit potentially harmful radiation.* ■■

### Key points to remember

- All monitors produce radiation of various kinds.
- It is possible that there is a link between VDUs and miscarriages.
- You can minimise the level of radiation by using radiation screens and low-radiation monitors.

### *Putting it into practice*

*Contact your local office of the Health and Safety Executive and obtain further information about radiation from monitors. Make your own judgement about the risks.*

### VDUs and miscarriages

During the 1980s, research was published that suggested a link between working with VDUs and having a miscarriage, which caused understandable alarm. Further research at first seemed to confirm the risk, but later work has shown no connection at all. This kind of research is difficult to carry out, and you should be cautious when interpreting the results. If there is a problem, it might be due to the stressful working conditions sometimes experienced by young women working at VDUs rather than electromagnetic fields.

Nevertheless, the manufacturers of VDUs have responded by producing low-radiation monitors. These are now required by law under the European Commission Directive 90/270.

# Topic 3 – Health and Safety

## Electrical equipment

**IT 119**

Foundation/Intermediate/
Advanced
Element 1.4, 2.4, 3.4
Performance criteria 5, 6
Range **Problems;
Working safely**

Computers (and monitors and printers) are electrical equipment, and as such should be treated with the same care as any device powered by electricity.

### Activity

What are the risks associated with electrical equipment?

*There are two risks: fire and electric shock. Fires can be caused by faulty connections that lead to overheating, which subsequently ignites inflammable material. Dust has a tendency to collect inside computers, so it is advisable for a qualified person to remove the computer's cover every six months or so and carefully remove the dust.*

*You can get an electric shock if the computer is faulty or if you touch the internal circuitry while the computer is plugged in. You should never open the case of a computer unless you are qualified to do so.*

### Fire extinguishers

Fire extinguishers are colour-coded to identify their type.

Water extinguishers are red and work by smothering the fire and cooling the surrounding area so that fire cannot restart. They should never be used on electrical fires because water conducts electricity and could electrocute anyone who comes into contact with it.

Carbon dioxide ($CO_2$) extinguishers are black. They work by depriving the fire of oxygen and are suitable for small fires. However, they are not good at preventing the fire from restarting because they don't cool the area around the fire very much.

Powder extinguishers are blue. They smother the fire, cutting off the supply of oxygen, but don't cool the area as much as foam or water extinguishers.

Foam extinguishers are green. They work in the same way as powder extinguishers, but the foam is more effective at cooling the surrounding area. Unlike water, the foam does not conduct electricity.

### Activity

Suppose that a fire broke out inside or near a computer in your office and you are the first person to notice it. What would you do first?
- grab a fire extinguisher and put the fire out
- raise the alarm, giving everyone the chance to evacuate the building safely
- call the fire brigade.

*A fire in a computer should be treated in the same way as any electrical fire. Raise the alarm first. Only then should you attempt to put the fire out using a suitable extinguisher. Somebody else should call the fire brigade.*

### Activity

You have raised the alarm and people are leaving the building, according to the fire drill. The fire brigade has been called, and the fire is still very small. All four types of fire extinguisher are close at hand. List the three appropriate types of fire extinguisher in order of their suitability.

*The best order is foam, powder and carbon dioxide. Foam has most of the benefits of water without the risks, and while powder and carbon dioxide are not as good at putting out the fire, they don't carry the risk of electrocution. You shouldn't use a water extinguisher at all, even if it's the only kind available; you'll only put yourself and others at greater risk.*

Once a computer or printer catches fire it is ruined, so don't hold back with the fire extinguisher in the hope of saving the computer.

When the fire is out, turn off the power to the computer by unplugging it from the mains. This will prevent sparks from causing another fire and reduce the risk of electric shock.

Like any piece of electrical equipment, computers and printers can, if faulty, give you an electric shock.

### Activity

When might you get an electric shock from a computer?

*Unless the computer has been badly constructed, you won't get a shock from it unless you remove the case. If simply touching the case gives you a shock, turn the computer off, unplug it and make sure that no one else uses it. Contact the supplier to get the computer repaired.*

Unless you have been specifically trained to repair computers you should never remove the case. You need a qualified technician to repair and service it and if you want to add internal equipment (such as more memory or a new hard disk) your IT department will be able to do the job far more quickly and safely than you can.

# Topic 3 – Health and Safety

## Electrical equipment (continued)

**Key points to remember**

- Computers are electrical devices and can cause fire or electric shocks.
- Electrical fires are best extinguished by foam extinguishers.
- Always get a qualified person to carry out any work inside the computer.

*Putting it into practice*

*Check the locations of fire extinguishers so that you know where they are. If they are not close enough or are of the wrong type, consult your Health and Safety Officer.*

# Topic 3 – Health and Safety

**IT 120**

Foundation/Intermediate/
Advanced
Element **1.4,2.4,3.4**
Performance criteria **5,6**
Range **Problems;
Working safely**

## Protecting equipment

It is easy to cause physical damage to a computer so you should try to prevent accidents wherever you can. This resource sheet provides an overview of some common problems; you will almost certainly be able to think of other dangers and ways to avoid them.

### Activity

The following parts of a computer are easily damaged. For each part, list one way of causing accidental damage in an office.

- monitor
- system unit
- keyboard
- mouse
- floppy disk drive

■ *Spilt drinks are the biggest problem and they can damage any part of the computer. For instance, tea, soft drinks and even water can damage the keyboard by interfering with the keyboard's electrical contacts. The consequences of a spill can be far more serious for the system unit or the monitor, either of which could be completely destroyed by short circuits caused by liquid. One cup of coffee could destroy a £2000 computer and thousands of pounds worth of valuable data – or even start a fire that wrecks a whole building!*

*Any part of the computer can be damaged by dropping it, even from a small height. Hard disks are particularly sensitive to such knocks.*

*Floppy disk drives are vulnerable to things being put inside them. Small items can get in accidentally when you insert floppy disks; for instance, a 'PostIt' note on the disk can get stuck inside. You should also avoid poking anything inside.* ■

### Activity

You are working at a computer and have just made a cup of coffee. In which of the following places would it be unsafe to put it?

1. on the desk, between you and the keyboard
2. on the mouse mat
3. on the desk, behind the keyboard and beside the system unit
4. on top of the monitor
5. on the printer.

■ *You can't assume that you'll never spill a drink, so you need to make sure that the consequences are minimal. For this reason, 1 is a bad choice, since if you reach for the cup and knock it over it will almost certainly fall on the keyboard. 2 is better (it's away from the keyboard), but even small spills could make the mouse mat sticky and affect the operation of the mouse, if not damage it. 3 is practical and safe; a spill should cause minimal damage. 4 and 5 are asking for trouble; in each case the cup will probably be balanced in an unsafe place and would almost certainly cause damage to the equipment if spilt.* ■

### Activity

It's not just the computer itself that can be damaged. For each of the following items, read the description of the likely risks and suggest one way of avoiding damage.

1. Floppy disks can be damaged by folding, touching the surface, spilling liquid on them or placing them near magnets.

   Safety suggestion _____

2. Printers contain delicate mechanisms which can be damaged by paper clips and staples. A scratch on the printing drum can cause streaks on every piece of paper printed.

   Safety suggestion _____

3. Scanners are as delicate as printers and are even more vulnerable; it is much easier to send a staple through the scanner by accident.

   Safety suggestion _____

4. CD-ROM drives usually use a motorised loading tray and this can cause accidents. It might knock over a cup or, if left open for any reason, could be accidentally struck and damaged. This is particularly true of CD-ROM drives in floor-standing computers.

   Safety suggestion _____

# Topic 3 – Health and Safety

## Protecting equipment (continued)

1. *The best way to protect floppy disks is to keep them in a closed box. Keep them well away from telephones, printers and other objects that contain magnets.*

2. *Try to make sure that nothing is fed into the printer with the paper. This shouldn't be a problem if you only ever print on new paper, rather than trying to re-use old paper, which might have hidden staples or paper clips.*

3. *Check every sheet of paper for staples and paper clips before you put it through the scanner. This is the only way to be safe.*

4. *Don't put your cup in front of the CD-ROM drive, put your cup at the side of the system unit, not the front. If you have a floor-standing computer, place the computer away from where you or others might walk by and hit the open tray.*

### Key points to remember

- Most parts of a computer are vulnerable to physical damage.
- Spilt liquid can damage almost any part of a computer.
- Other devices also need protection.

### Putting it into practice

*Rearrange your computer's setup and your desk to minimise the risk of accidents. Stick a label to the printer warning people of the risks.*